The Self-Healing Mind

The Self-Healing Mind

*Harnessing the Active Ingredients
of Psychotherapy*

Brian J. McVeigh

OXFORD
UNIVERSITY PRESS

OXFORD
UNIVERSITY PRESS

Oxford University Press is a department of the University of Oxford. It furthers
the University's objective of excellence in research, scholarship, and education
by publishing worldwide. Oxford is a registered trade mark of Oxford University
Press in the UK and certain other countries.

Published in the United States of America by Oxford University Press
198 Madison Avenue, New York, NY 10016, United States of America.

© Oxford University Press 2022

Library of Congress Control Number: 2022939237

ISBN 978–0–19–764786–8

DOI: 10.1093/med-psych/9780197647868.001.0001

1 3 5 7 9 8 6 4 2

Printed by Integrated Books International, United States of America

Contents

Preface

Helplessly watching my brother lose control during epileptic fits or explode into violent psychomotor seizures when I was young stimulated within me an interest in anomalous psychological behavior and the enigma of volition. I was fascinated by how one mind could produce what seemed to be different selves. I also sensed that the mind, after a perturbation, resets and cycles through to stabilize itself. Time, I concluded, was a key variable for understanding mental processes. I also wondered how the subjective experiences of my brother, who was diagnosed with autism, differed from my own, and what purpose the colorful tapestry of introspectable consciousness served. "Thinking," "cognition," and "consciousness" failed to capture the nuances, textures, and fine distinctions of experience.

I suspected that historical changes in psyche offered clues. I came across Julian Jaynes's theory that increasing social complexity, marked by the civilizational chaos of the Late Bronze Age Collapse, culturally upgraded mentality. I elaborated on Jaynes's ideas by identifying "features of conscious interiority" (FOCI) as vital components of psychological adaptation (McVeigh, 2016a, 2016b, 2017, 2020). The mutable and ever-changing nature of the psyche began to steer my research interests. I decided to pursue a career in anthropology whose very definition is the exploration of diversity, variability, and long- as well as short-term social transformation of the human species. Such ruminations on neurocultural plasticity shaped my choice of a PhD dissertation topic: "spirit possession" in a Japanese religious movement. I witnessed how the "possessed" articulated their distress and reformulated their problems through ritualized exorcisms (McVeigh, 1997a). Working part-time in my family's funeral business also impressed upon me the need for the bereaved to process searing grief by passing through a step-by-step period of mourning.

Teaching in Japanese universities for many years was another formative intellectual experience. I saw firsthand how the relentless educational pressures impacted the developmental experiences of students. This taught me how self and larger political forces interconnect. Constantly proving their self-worth via overly scripted behavior and too many standardized tests spawned unhealthy self-dramatization (McVeigh, 2000). I learned how managing self-presentation for the wrong reasons traps one in a sociopsychological dynamic that breeds self-deception, apathy, and estrangement from healthy social relations (McVeigh, 1997b, 2002, 2006a; see also relevant chapters in McVeigh, 2014). But I also observed how the strains of exam preparation, as well as other stresses from living in a hyper-competitive society, were alleviated by comforting ceremonies, reassuring formalities, and fulfilling one's social-role expectations (McVeigh, 1998). Routinized, controlled chains of behavior decelerate one's fervid struggles and restore self-regulation and mental health.

Fieldwork experiences and reconstructing ancient mentalities, then, converged in an appreciation of how the psyche's historical malleability and its therapeutic self-mending properties are cut from the same cloth. Whether understood as an individual's lifetime or in terms of centuries, time can radically restitch our mental fabric (McVeigh, 2015, 2016c, 2016d).

Intrigued by the mind's properties of self-repair, I began work at an addiction and recovery facility and became a licensed mental health counselor. My experiences confirmed for me the mind's ability to reformat itself by exploiting the features/functions of conscious interiority (FOCI, e.g., guided imagery, self-narratization, self-autonomy, excerption). These features operate as resources and materials. Woven by history, they intricately pattern our mental life and can be rewoven for therapeutic effect. In the event of a major disorder, FOCI, crucial facets of the mind's capability to self-heal, facilitate recovery by restructuring and mitigating maladaptive tendencies. My agenda, then, is to describe how FOCI inform the psychological processes underlying the effectiveness of psychotherapeutic techniques and interventions.

Acknowledgments

Books are products of collaboration. Without the edifying experiences of the many patients I have met and worked with, this book would not have been possible. I am impressed by their courage, respect their resiliency, and value their candor.

A good supervisor should provide not only guidance and encouragement but also inspiration. I have been fortunate to have benefited from dedicated supervisors whose knowledge has found its way into this book: Grace Smythe-Young, Steve Lape, Mike Loiselle, and Neil Cervera. A special thanks to Neil Cervera, who has also been an invaluable and patient mentor, advisor, and consultant on matters of therapy. Numerous colleagues, with whom I have had the pleasure to work and have enriched my edification, deserve mention and appreciation: Alison Miller, Choyo Daniel-Wilson, Christina Glenn, Donna Askew, James Jeffreys, John Harris, Joyce Williams, Kenny Glover, Phyllis Fusco, Rainier Perkins, Sean McLean, Shakira Hall, Vicky Lewis, Victor LaRegina, and Wayne Griffith.

I would like to thank the professors who introduced me to and trained me in mental health counseling: Ellen Cole, Gayle Morse, Emily Martin, Donald Graves, Alicia Harlow, Patricia O'Connor, Jerome Farrell, Marisa Beeble, Susan Cloninger, and Andrea Barrocas Gottlieb. I would also like to express my gratitude to Sarah Harrington and the editors at Oxford University Press, as well as a number of anonymous reviewers, whose useful comments, constructive criticisms, and helpful suggestions were indispensable for strengthening my arguments.

I owe a debt of gratitude to Marty Seligman, whose penetrating intellect and inspiring curiosity in no small measure made this book possible. The astute observations of Marcel Kuijsten have as always given me much food for thought. The insightful commentary of William Rowe has also greatly strengthened my arguments. Others whose commentary and advice have been invaluable include Frank Young, Laurence Sugarman, Charles Rap, Albert Pfadt, Bill Woodward, John Hainly, Ken Gross, Mark Landau, Scott Greer, and Stephen Shigematsu-Murphy.

Finally, and as always, my wife, Lana, and family have afforded me support and a safe place to mediate, research, and write. For this I am profoundly grateful.

Abbreviations

Abbreviations for systems of psychotherapy that appear in the text indicate primary associations and therapeutic traditions that were originally associated with particular interventions or techniques.

ACT	Acceptance and commitment therapy
ADT	Adlerian psychotherapy (or individual psychology)
APS	Adaptive phasic structures
BFT	Brief therapy
BT	Behavior therapy
CBT	Cognitive behavior therapy
CCT	Client-centered therapy
CF	Common factor
CNT	Contemplative psychotherapy
COW	Conditions of worth
DBT	Dialectical behavior therapy
EFT	Emotionally focused therapy
EMDRT	Eye movement desensitization and reprocessing therapy
EXT	Existential therapy
FET	Feminist therapy
FOCI	Features/functions of conscious interiority
FT	Family therapy
GST	General systems theory
GT	Gestalt therapy
INT	Integrative therapy
IPT	Interpersonal therapy
JT	Jungian therapy (or analytic psychology)
MCT	Multicultural therapy
MI	Motivational interviewing
NT	Narrative therapy
PAT	Psychoanalytic psychotherapy
PD	Psychodrama
PDT	Psychodynamic psychotherapy
PPT	Positive psychotherapy
PT	Play therapy
RCT	Randomized controlled trial
REBT	Rational emotive behavior therapy
RSP	Role-self perspective
RT	Reality Therapy
SIT	Stress inoculation training
SOLT	Solution focused therapy
TA	Transactional analysis

Notes to the Reader

During a graduate seminar an anthropology professor stated, "I don't like the word 'culture.'" This surprised me, coming from an eminent scholar in a cultural anthropology department. Later I understood her objection: like many key concepts, it is overused, ill-defined, or not defined at all. "Consciousness" is like culture. The word is everywhere; it has been fetishized. It permeates books, academic journals, scholarly discussions, and news articles alike. Rarely is it defined. Consciousness is to psychology what "vitalism" or the "life principle" was to biology. No one seems to know what it is, but everyone presumably knows what it means. Like vitalism, it is chased down with scientific zeal, but it often carries metaphysical or even mystical connotations; it obscures more than it reveals. One is tempted to discard it altogether.

In this book, my use of "consciousness" corresponds with the older nineteenth-century sense of subjective introspectable self-awareness, i.e., not the vague, generic meaning of perception, cognition, or thinking. I carefully define what I mean by it and use it interchangeability with "conscious interiority." To be even more explanatory, I also use "FOCI": a package of interrelated "features/functions of conscious interiority." Given the centrality of FOCI for my arguments, I want to alert the reader that my usage is more precise than what is common in the literature.

Another problematic usage concerns "client" versus "patient" in psychotherapy and counseling. Many prefer "client" as it indicates personal autonomy and thus rescues the seeker of help from the indignities of the medico-bureaucratic industry, restoring a sense of self-control and personhood. Others use "patient," meaning an individual in need of help who receives expert treatment. Both sides of the debate have merit. But for the sake of convenience I use "patient." However, in a few sections where a healing system has explicitly challenged the assumptions of the medico-psychiatric establishment, I use "client."

A central argument of this book is that common factors, shared by all systems of psychotherapy, account for why the mind is able to self-heal. In order to remind the reader of such commonalities underlying different psychotherapies, throughout this book I employ abbreviations that refer to the well-known systems of treatment. This convention is intended to add coherency and to interlink my arguments.

The dream of any writer is to appeal to as many audiences as possible. The conventions of different genres make this challenging, to say the least, and definitions of "readability" vary. In order to satisfy the interests of researchers, scholars of different disciplines, and graduate students while sparing practitioners, undergraduates, and the general public from more detailed material, I use a number of appendices to supplement chapter content.

Prologue: Searching for the Active Ingredients of the Self-Healing Mind

The Power of Self-Healing

Physicians, medicines, pills, surgeries, casts, and bandages do not fix what is broken. They only create the circumstances in which the human organism is able to mend itself. Indeed, the body possesses an impressive array of natural self-healing mechanisms that fight infections, repair cells, and can even destroy cancer cells. As just one example, consider the immune system. We are exposed on a daily basis to all types of pollutants, toxins, invasive organisms (viruses, bacteria, parasites), and other environmental stressors. But the body possesses a sophisticated two-part defense system: the general (nonspecific) and adaptive (specific) immune system. The first consists of "cell-eating" or phagocytic cells (a type of white blood cell) that devour the body's invaders. Besides the bloodstream, various kinds of phagocytes are garrisoned in different regions of the body (e.g., macrophages in the lungs). Another sort of white blood cell, "natural killer cells," zero in on cellular bodies hijacked by viruses, while cells invaded by viruses manufacture interferons that set off alarm bells, thereby arming killer cells. During an infection, the human organism also produces proteins which encase any invader, making the search-and-destroy mission of the phagocytes easier. When injured or infected, the body uses inflammation to defend itself. Swollen tissues alert the immune system to the location of the attack by boosting the blood supply to the battle site, creating a surge in the ranks of phagocytes, and increasing the permeability of small blood vessels so that large molecules can leave the bloodstream and raid the infected area.

If phagocytes cannot identify invading entities, the immune system calls up the adaptive division that specializes in producing specific antibodies: white blood cells called B lymphocytes. These have receptors and markers. The former attach the antibody to a foreign entity in order to tag the invader, while markers fit themselves to phagocytes which recognize and destroy the invaders. B lymphocytes come in thousands of varieties and are designed to identify certain antigens (or specific markers) of the invaders. Once a B lymphocyte binds itself to an antigen, B lymphocytes are given the order to quickly reproduce themselves of the same kind. Some B lymphocytes become "memory cells" that, after the invasion has been defeated, remain in the body ready to attack if the same invader returns. Another type of cell, T lymphocytes (helpers, killers, suppressors, memory, and others), specialize in confronting viral antigens outside infected cells. Helper T lymphocytes coordinate the chemical signaling system that orders the B lymphocytes to attack and trigger the production of killer T lymphocytes.

If physicians come across a medicine that enhances the body's own defenses, the logical next step is to investigate its constituents, i.e., its active ingredients. Such an approach applies equally to psychotherapy.

The Potentiality of the Self-Healing Psyche

In the case of psychological healing, what are the "active ingredients"? What are the innate active principles that confer a curative effect that individuals themselves bring to a clinical setting? I submit that the mental processes that help us get through the day are the same ones that can heal our psyches. People, after all, are inherently rational (positively self-constructive) as well as irrational (when burdened with self-defeating thought processes, abnormal or maladaptive behaviors can develop in the same way as normal or adaptive behaviors do). When applied in a therapeutic context, the active ingredients are in a more concentrated form. These ingredients can be distinguished, identified, and itemized. In this book I focus on the psycho-repair processes that can be explained by FOCI (consciousness).

PART I

THE ADAPTIVE MIND, CONSCIOUSNESS, AND IMPLICATIONS FOR THERAPY

1
Purposes and Premises

The Therapeutic Properties of Subjectivity

Chanting, praying, testimonials, interrogating "possessing spirits," monthly pilgrimages to a sacred headquarters—these were routine activities of the True Light Supra-Religion (Sūkyō Mahikari), a Japanese spiritual organization. Curious about what trancing might tell us about consciousness, I spent two years with members of Mahikari. A central practice of Mahikari was exorcism—a ritualistically evoked "spirit" would speak through the possessed. What interested me was how, in order to induce possession, a hypnoidal state (trancing) could so easily suspend consciousness (McVeigh, 1997a). This fieldwork experience is a good place to begin because, reflecting back on it, I now realize that Mahikari members were practicing a type of spiritualized psychotherapy[1] which has inspired the approaches of this book. The purpose of this chapter is to introduce the reader to the three interrelated perspectives: (1) positive psychology and, more specifically, positive psychotherapy; (2) the "common factors" of therapeutic effectiveness; and (3) a Jaynesian therapeutic paradigm. Before continuing, I want to clearly state that this work does not offer new therapeutic techniques or recommend certain therapies over others. Also, it is not a survey or overview of the many systems of therapy, though of course it relies on their insights to illustrate relevant points.[2]

Positive Psychology: First Approach

What impressed me most about many Mahikari members was how even when their prayers were not answered (e.g., a wife losing her husband to cancer), many continued to diligently attend services, make generous donations, and remain steadfastly committed to the organization. It was clear that they had undergone a values-based inner transformation. Regardless of my own unbelief in possessing spirits, my time with Mahikari members—who were friendly, welcoming, and "rational" despite beliefs that were not mainstream—later in my career made me appreciate the findings of positive psychotherapy (PPT) (Appendix A).

Positive psychology is a corrective reaction to earlier, more traditional psychotherapeutic approaches, such as psychoanalysis, behaviorism, and other systems that primarily target mental illnesses for intervention. PPT practitioners are less interested in the "disease model" and dysfunction and more concerned with promoting mental health and well-being. Rather than focusing on negative symptoms and maladaptive behaviors, PPT is the scientific study of positive human functioning and "flourishing" on different levels—biological, personal, relational, institutional, cultural, and global (Seligman & Csikszentmihalyi, 2000). The PPT approach involves three basic "positives": (1) emotions—content with one's past, happy in the present, hopeful for one's future; (2) individual traits—personal strengths and virtues; and (3) institutions—behaviors that strengthen communities (Seligman & Csikszentmihalyi, 2000).

Mahikari writings, meetings, and testimonials were peppered through and through with the word "grateful" (*kansha*). During exorcism a spirit would speak through the possessed, revealing why an individual was burdened with illnesses, emotional distress, economic difficulties, family issues, or other sundry problems. The possessed might be accused, admonished, or reprimanded by the "attaching spirit." The target of such dressing-down would then be expected to apologize for some transgression, and quite often the possessed confessed their need to be more thankful for the boons granted by one's ancestors or family. While positive emotions speak to the very sociality of human nature, gratitude in particular connects us deeply with others since we must consider what they have given us. Gratitude, then, is about cultivating a connectivity that binds us to others (Watkins, Van Gelder, & Frias, 2009).

In Mahikari one should be thankful for being on the receiving end of another's empathy (*omoiyari*). This is related to the positive emotion of compassion, which means identifying with and relieving the pain and suffering of others (obviously central to the practice of medicine, counseling, and other helping professions) (Cassell, 2009). Another key positive value is "humility of the heart" (*kokoro no geza*) (cf. Batson, Ahmad, & Lishner, 2009; Tangney, 2009). Forgiveness, another prized norm of Mahikari, has also been a topic of PPT investigations (McCullough et al., 2009).

Something else that impressed me about Mahikari members was how, without seeing trained mental healthcare providers, not a few were able to overcome traumatic events and experiences. It was as if some hidden ingredient was at work in their psychic healing. Participant observation among members offered me the opportunity to witness their remarkable courage, or the virtue of voluntarily confronting challenging and personal risks to pursue worthy goals, a topic investigated by Pury and Lopez (2009). Their tenacity (*konjō*) and endurance (*gaman*) resonated with toughness. This capacity for arousal and energy when called upon promotes adaptive coping strategies and improves emotional stability (Dienstbier & Pytlik Zillig, 2009). Despite great personal suffering, many members went through post-traumatic growth and made sense of their loss; they were able to develop personally, renegotiate objectives and priorities, and discern new meanings (Davis & Nolen-Hoeksema, 2009). In the face of adversity, they came to appreciate "benefit finding and growth," acquiring an appreciation of their own strengths, increasing their self-reliance, and discovering untapped resilience (cf. Lechner, Tennen, & Affleck, 2009). Other targets of PPT research that resonate with Mahikari's teachings are undying hope and cheerful optimism (Rand & Cheapens, 2009; Carver et al., 2009; Peterson & Steen, 2009).

A vital tenet of PPT is that we are endowed with the innate resources that can overcome psychopathological distress and heal our own minds (Seligman, 2002). Different candidates have been suggested to explain our inner strengths. Here I submit that consciousness itself—or to be more precise, "features or functions of conscious interiority" (FOCI)—constitute common factors (CFs). The latter describe elements that underlie the effectiveness of all therapies. The search for CFs, which is part of the integrative psychotherapeutic perspective (INT) (Norcross & Goldfried, 2005), advocates the idea that therapies are successful because they share the same self-mending processes (Appendix B). Numerous lists have been drawn up detailing what these factors might be, but for my purpose I focus on those that are hidden in plain sight: FOCI. The CF perspective is the second approach adopted in this book, while the operation of FOCI as reparative processes is the signature component of the third approach: a Jaynesian therapeutic paradigm (as explained below). My argument is that if the different elements of consciousness are therapeutically focused, self-healing is more likely to occur.

Common Factors as the Grammar of Therapy: Second Approach

A set of underlying mechanisms explains treatment success more than the unique features of different therapies. Indeed, researchers commonly refer to the "dodo bird effect," i.e., all major therapies produce comparable measures of success.[3] The goal is to discern and then apply core ingredients that different therapies offer.[4] This book highlights the nature of certain pivotal mechanisms of self-healing, i.e., FOCI.

It is among what are termed "nonspecific factors" of therapy that CFs are to be found. Nonspecific means what is general, all-purpose, and noncharacteristic. It designates universal CFs that all therapies share and "refers to theoretically unspecified agents of change, the effects of which are not limited to particular problems or disorders" (Jørgensen, 2004, p. 520). Such factors are not specific to a certain therapeutic system; rather, they are common to most or all therapies and are "effective in treating different kinds of problems, although to different degrees, depending on especially pathological severity" (Jørgensen, 2004, p. 520). Nonspecific factors are analogous to grammar—all languages operate by way of nouns, verbs, adjectives, etc. CFs, then, which FOCI operate as while in their healing mode, are like the fundamental rules of human language.

"Specific," which is analogous to a language's vocabulary and idiomatic expressions, indicates more precise interventions.[5] In the same way that the subtle nuances of each word add precision to one's communication, specified techniques afford specialized and more focused treatment procedures. Specific indicates what is unique and characteristic; it means those practices that are realized by applying individualized therapeutic approaches and refers to methods that have an "empirically supported effect in the treatment of problems or disorders" (Jørgensen, 2004, p. 520).

Table 1.1 Linguistic Analogy of Specific and Nonspecific Techniques and Treatments

Linguistic Analogy	Techniques and Treatments	Appropriate to What Level of Severity
Vocabulary and idioms	Specific: particular interventions	High
Grammar and syntax	Nonspecific: common factors	Low to moderate

Specific, then, designates procedures that are particularly valuable in treating certain kinds of problems (Garfield, 1995, p. 138) (Table 1.1).

Bohart (2000) contended that all therapies work well because they share one easily overlooked ingredient—the patients themselves and their own, inherent restorative potential. They are the "main characters, the heroes and heroines of the therapeutic stage, and they are the most potent contributor to psychotherapeutic change" (Duncan, 2002a, p. 38; see also Bohart & Tallman, 1999; Duncan & Miller, 2000). But I want to go one step further and ask: What is it, specifically, in the patient that facilitates positive change? My answer is FOCI. For my present purposes, then, the CFs in question are "within" the individual. My goal is to survey the key techniques of psychotherapeutic traditions and illustrate how FOCI are actually marshalled by mental healthcare providers in their healing endeavors.

Simply stated, treatments possess efficacy because of: (1) specific therapeutic interventions; (2) nonspecific factors that all therapies share; or (3) a combination of the two (Cuijpers et al., 2019). Common sense tells us that number 3 is the best answer, but given how FOCI are taken for granted as agents of therapeutic change, this book stresses number 2.

A Jaynesian Therapeutic Paradigm: Third Approach

The work of the maverick psychologist Julian Jaynes (1920-1997) informs the third approach. He controversially claimed that consciousness is not biologically innate but was culturally learned by about 1000 BCE (1976).[6] He framed his theories in an array of interlocking arguments that are difficult to neatly summarize, but some of his ideas possess therapeutic merit and can be elaborated upon as a paradigm. One does not have to accept all of Jaynes's ideas, and I encourage the doubting Thomases to skip portions concerning the historical origins of FOCI if these parts offend one's intellectual sensibilities. I hope that the sections on understanding the therapeutic benefits of FOCI should, at least, have some value to the reader. I have included the Jaynesian account of the origins of FOCI because it is absolutely essential to comprehend how something unfolded through time in order to study it. Moreover, a historical perspective highlights our remarkable neurocultural plasticity (Appendix C).

Jaynes himself never developed in any full-fledged manner the therapeutic value of what he understood to be conscious interiority. However, a few tantalizing quotes of his strongly suggest that he had an optimistic opinion of the power of the mind to improve itself and for people to positively change themselves. "We all know the concept of psychosomatic disease; well let's reverse that to psychosomatic health" (Jaynes, 2012b, p. 288). He hoped people could cultivate consciousness so as to enhance self-control (e.g., "those of us who want to give up smoking can just make a decision to do so, and that's all there is to it"). The idea is to train conscious interiority so that we become more suggestible to ourselves (Jaynes, 2012c, p. 345). Learning how to become more suggestible allows enhanced control over behavior than is possible with ordinary, everyday consciousness.

Jaynes noted that if the nature of consciousness were better theorized, the therapeutic mechanisms of cognitive behavioral therapies could be understood. Jaynes provided a "strong theoretical framework" for guided imagery, paradoxical therapy, visualizing practices, and other cognition-changing, reframing, and restructuring interventions. He specifically believed that narratization and excerption can be retrained in healthy ways. The type of therapy does not matter as long as the patient believes it can provide relief and "redirects behavior into more adaptive modes" (Jaynes, 2012a, p. 319).

Next I present the six aspects of a Jaynesian therapeutic paradigm. Appreciating nonconsciousness as well as atypical cognition (e.g., hypnosis) is especially essential, as both evidence a historically earlier substrate of preconscious mentality.

First Aspect: Nonconscious Mentation

The history of psychology needs to be rewritten. It is not about an emerging recognition through the centuries of the submerged parts of the psyche—the so-called discovery of the unconscious in the 1800s.[7] The real mystery is why, before the first millennium BCE, the historical record offers no evidence of what we call conscious subjective mentality (McVeigh, 2010). This comes as a shock to those of us who assume that conscious self-awareness is an innate, indispensable, and essential human trait. The point is that rather than introspectable conscious awareness, nonconsciousness is our basic form of cognition.

If most cognition transpires without awareness, we are forced us to ask what the difference is between conscious and unconscious mentation. We assume that the former is the mind's default mode, when in fact nonconsciousness is primary. In other words, consciousness, especially since it often interferes in our everyday activities (try being conscious of every key when one types), is the real mystery. If most of our mentation is indeed nonconscious—the proverbial iceberg in which most of the floating mountain of ice is submerged—what is the purpose of consciousness?

Some researchers contend that people are robotic conscious automata (Huxley, 1896, p. 244), i.e., consciousness has no real purpose; it is a mere epiphenomenon that, like steam billowing from and trailing behind a train, cannot change the direction of the tracks. Or consciousness is like the colorful pattern of a mosaic, which is held in place by its stones, not the colors (Hodgson, 1870, p. 416; see also James, 1890). Though he vehemently disagreed with the conscious automata theory, Jaynes captures this idea when he describes this agency-denying perspective: consciousness is the "melody that floats from the harp and cannot pluck its strings," the "foam struck raging from the river that cannot change its course," the "shadow that loyally walks step for step beside the pedestrian, but is quite unable to influence his journey" (Jaynes, 1976, p. 11). An individual can actually accomplish many task nonconsciously. Nevertheless, conscious interiority does have a purpose. As explained in Chapters 2 and 3, it accelerates, facilitates, and makes cognition more effective.

Second Aspect: Hidden in Plain Sight—the Inherent Self-Healing Potential of FOCI

The sentence "colorless green ideas sleep furiously" is obviously semantically nonsensical. Nevertheless, we intuitively appreciate its grammaticality.[8] This is true of FOCI. In the same way grammar automatically slots words into understandable structures,[9] thereby allowing sentences to effortlessly roll off our lips, conscious subjective experiences bubble up out of nowhere and wash across our psychoscape, like water from a flowing but hidden spring. When needed, the mind calls upon FOCI to function as corrective and reparative catalysts. But the spontaneous, apparent naturalness of conscious interiority has fooled us into believing that it must be an evolved, inbuilt feature of mind. In fact, its recent historical trajectory can be traced (Jaynes, 1976).

By the late second millennium BCE the highly routinized, rigid codes of behavior, strict hierarchical relations, and supernatural voices and visions that governed societies were no match for growing social complexity. As the gods retreated into the heavens, mentality underwent a transformation that saw an upgraded, supererogatory form of cognition emerge, i.e., FOCI. Carefully excavating the remnants and relics of ages past reveals that our supposedly inborn consciousness developed only recently on the basis of metaphors. The expansion of our introspectable abilities over time, then, is the issue that needs addressing. History itself stands witness to a continual conscious interiorization; i.e., over the centuries more and more weight has been given to the "inner stuff" of the person relative to the external world.

FOCI are activated when habitual, automatic nonconscious operations reach their limits of routine problem-solving (Chapter 2). We take these aspects of mentation for granted, but they can be fundamental for therapeutic interventions. In some instances they are mobilized as mechanisms that the mind utilizes to heal itself. However, under certain circumstances, e.g., if life experiences or innate vulnerabilities overwhelm a person, these inbuilt tools of corrective cognition can lead to runaway consciousness. Consequently, FOCI end up hindering mental health and mutate into psychological processes in need of modification themselves (Chapter 4). And yet FOCI themselves, which can be theoretically tied together (Chapter 3), can be deployed as therapeutic techniques to correct distorted cognition and hyper-interiorization.

My agenda is to illustrate how assumptions, important concepts, methods, and counseling traditions that many professional helpers employ on a daily basis possess a coherency afforded by conscious interiority. I do this by viewing techniques from a range of psychotherapies through a Jaynesian therapeutic lens in order to better illuminate their effectiveness (Chapters 6, 9, 10, and 11). Readers, especially seasoned clinicians, will already be familiar with most of these interventions. My hope is that they see anew what they take for granted—the features of conscious interiority—and reframe them from a treatment perspective. Chapter 5 is intended to historically contextualize the relation between conscious interiorization and the emergence of psychotherapy.

Table 1.2 summarizes how FOCI enhance cognition, but it also provides other expressions (right column) that are more or less synonymous with FOCI (left column).

Third Aspect: Mental Imagery as an Artifact of Adaptive Hallucinations

Most assume that the hallucinations that plague the minds of those diagnosed with serious mental disorders are inherently psychopathological. However, many individuals experience benign hallucinations. Though these unwelcome verbal and visual intrusions in themselves may not be pathological, they can be psychologically distressing. What, then, are the therapeutic implications of acknowledging that hallucinations in and of themselves are not pathological?

Lacking an introspectable inner self-directing behavior, preconscious individuals were governed by hallucinatory divine voices and visions. The idea that in archaic times hallucinations were an integral part of "normal" mental functioning admittedly raises not a few eyebrows. But consider something we utilize every day and that is often pressed into therapeutic service: mental imagery. These quasi-perceptions are descendants of hallucinations, now watered down in vividness and under voluntary control, but still utilized in cognition. Jaynes stated that his ideas on hallucinations might relieve much of the distress of being labeled "crazy" by having patients understand that hallucinations are a relapse to an older mentality that was perfectly normal at one time but is now obsolete (Jaynes, 2012a, p. 319; see also Kuijsten, 2012a). Other researchers who have contended that hallucinations can be potentially positive include Beavan (2011); Chin, Hayward, and Drinna (2008); Hayward et al. (2008); and Pérez-Álvarez et al. (2008).

Table 1.2 Summary of How FOCI Enhance Sociocognitive Processes

Features/Functions of Conscious Interiority	How Features/Functions of Conscious Interiority Enhance Cognition
Spatialization of psyche	Introspectable stage for manipulating mental imagery Mental space to visualize in order to imagine different selves, to "picture" problems to be solved from different angles; mind–space unfolds temporally, so that past, present, and future are more clearly delineated; retrospection and prospection are bolstered
Introception	Quasi-perceptual innerverse Experiencing qualia recreates virtual world based on actual physical reality; using semi-hallucinatory mental imagery to "see" different perspectives
Observing self: "I"	Monitoring self Interiorizing one's person and viewing selfhood from perspective of active subject (agent), thereby increasing self-role diversity; enhances subjective perspective-taking, allowing one to imagine different versions of one's self
Observed self: "me"	Monitored self Adopting more roles and increasing self-flexibility; viewing selfhood from perspective of passive object (patient), thereby reinforcing acceptance of other-role diversity; enhances objective perspective-taking, allowing one to adopt the position of others
Self-narratization	Narratizing a personal timeline Mental space offers a place to linearize a personalized timeline, thereby intensifying capabilities of retrospection and prospection; "time-traveling" to contrast and compare different incarnations of selves, thereby allowing improved versions of selves
Excerption	Editing mental contents Selecting out mental representations from one's stream of thought, thereby boosting powers of abstraction, generalization; bolsters vetoing of impulses and decisional capabilities; meta-framing above morass of detailed, concrete, specific precepts that interfere with imaginative, hypothetical, speculative, and conjectural mentation
Consilience	Fitting conceptions together more effectively Bringing mental objects together (just as narratization brings episodes together in a story), thereby allowing more rapid assimilation of concepts; ambiguous perceived objects are made to conform to previously learned ideas, thereby constructing schemas more efficiently; improved abstractive and generalizing abilities lead to higher-order conceptualization
Concentration	Focusing one's mental efforts Peripheralizing irrelevant, unrelated mental material allows for quicker abstraction and generalization
Suppression	Censoring distressing thoughts Deleting and controlling mentation, thereby storing away distracting, distressing thoughts

Table 1.2 *Continued*

Features/Functions of Conscious Interiority	How Features/Functions of Conscious Interiority Enhance Cognition
Self-authorization	Self-legitimizing one's behavior Enhancing control over one's person and decisions; volitional, intentional, and deliberative behavior
Self-autonomy	Sense of agency Feelings of control over one's destiny, self-determination, self-direction, and self-trajectory, thereby fortifying resilience and self-confidence
Self-individuation	Highlighting personal strengths and uniqueness Enhanced ability to self-disclose, thereby more clearly delineating individual traits and uniqueness of self-identity that may benefit others
Self-reflexivity	Cultivating insight A sharpened sense of selfness; increasing self-distancing between "I" and "me," thereby supporting self-objectivity and self-corrective abilities

Fourth Aspect: Lessons from Altered Cognition

Hypnosis has wandered "in and out of laboratories and carnivals and clinics and village halls like an unwanted anomaly" (Jaynes, 1976, p. 379). It is the "black sheep" on a list of unanswered questions that psychology has struggled to answer. Jaynes's comments about hypnosis apply to other eruptions of altered cognition, such as "spirit possession" and, though not as exotic these days and better understood, meditation.

Fortunately, anomalous psychological states have recently "emerged from under a shroud of misconceptions at the fringes of academia" (Lifshitz, 2016, p. 4). Such phenomena can tell us much about more typical cognition, such as FOCI. Any comprehensive accounting of human psychology cannot afford to sweep hypnosis under the theoretical rug. Hypnosis and meditation are distinct types of mentality. However, they appear to overlap in phenomenology, cognitive mechanisms, neural substrates, and significantly for our purposes, potential therapeutic benefits. Achieving control over maladaptive patterns of behavior and unwelcome thought patterns is often the aim of hypnosis and meditation (Lifshitz & Raz, 2012, p. 6).[10]

Taken together, the various manifestations of mentality—conscious interiority, hypnosis, meditation—are like a colorful tapestry with different patterns but woven together from the same threads. The challenge is disentangling and isolating the threads so as to understand the psychological processes behind these phenomena (Chapter 13).

Hypnosis: The Therapeutic Benefits of Turning Consciousness Off

Why does hypnosis provide an "extraordinary enabling" that allows people to do things they cannot ordinarily do except with great difficulty? (Jaynes, 1976, p. 402). Answer: it allows an "extra enabling" because its temporary erosion of FOCI permits a return to an earlier mentality in which verbal commands—whether from hallucinated gods or one's social superiors—authorized behavior. Hypnosis is the inhibition of a historically newer layer of mentality that was culturally acquired (i.e., FOCI).

Regrettably, a number of myths and misunderstandings still surround hypnosis.[11] However, appreciating hypnosis is of great import because it points to our inherent neurocultural plasticity and, by extension, possesses potential for helping us come to terms with FOCI. What is remarkable about hypnosis is that its very existence seems to deny our most cherished assumptions about conscious self-control and scientific idea about personality (Jaynes, 1976, p. 379). That crucial elements of our psychoscape can be so easily and readily arrested demonstrates the wavering and malleable nature of FOCI, meaning that these elements are learned (rather than biologically innate). And if they are learned, then they must have arisen during a certain historical period.

Two commonly cited "threads" of hypnosis—selective concentration and suggestibility—are not unique to hypnosis; indeed, they are evident to varying degrees in different expressions of mentality that can be placed on a continuum. On the left side is hypnotic trance (focused selective concentration and high suggestibility), while on the right side is conscious interiority (selective concentration and low suggestibility). In the middle are hypnoidal states, products of moderate selective concentration and suggestibility (Figure 1.1). Concentration, though a FOCI, can force a shutdown of ordinary consciousness if highly focused.

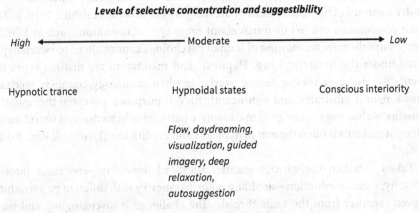

Levels of selective concentration and suggestibility

High ◄—————————— Moderate ——————————► Low

Hypnotic trance   Hypnoidal states   Conscious interiority

Flow, daydreaming, visualization, guided imagery, deep relaxation, autosuggestion

Figure 1.1. Continuum of concentration and suggestibility.

Fifth Aspect: Metaphors as an Example of Meta-framing

A patient, acknowledging his debilitating mental illness, stated, "my brain is like an engine. It needs new parts." "Don't put my problems on the front page!" demanded another patient (i.e., keep what you hear in group confidential). Another patient, describing his predilection to run from the police, told me, "I have bunny feet." Complaining about an incessant smoker, a patient said, "He smokes so much he smells like a human ashtray." Commenting on what he thought was an individual's balderdash, a patient exclaimed, "That's Saranwrap; I can see right through it!" In group a patient warned a wary member about rushing into a new relationship by advising him, "Don't be an astronaut if you're afraid of heights." These examples illustrate how effective colorful language is in getting one's message across. Metaphors, of course, are used not just among patients, but among all of us in everyday settings.

Metaphors play a pivotal role in the creative use of words. Their deployment can be described as our capability to "step back" from the natural and social environment and search out its familiar features and employ these to explain the unfamiliar and generate "as if" knowledge forms. Introspectable, subjective self-awareness is itself the result of how metaphors, psyche's basic building blocks, have expanded our psychological toolkit in response to social complexity (i.e., FOCI themselves are grounded in culturally learned metaphors; they are not innate mental features).

Metaphors are instances of the essential psychological mechanism driving adaptation: meta-framing or scaling new heights to survey matters from a different, better-informed perspective. This defines the mind—always moving forward, striding across stepping stones, one foot on the past and the other about to land on suppositious possibilities. Specific operations of this climb-and-overlook process are abstracting and analogizing.

Some view metaphors as clever tricks of the mind. But they are embodied conceptualizations that help us process experiences. For example, Mahikari is held together by a complex array of beliefs. Despite its unscientific nature, the persuasiveness of Mahikari's worldview is generated by a certain cohesiveness based on tropes about cosmic energies and a divine light that heals a person's body, psyche, and spirit. Moreover, one's personal problems and tragedies are metaphorically articulated into a moralistic narrative about salvation and the beneficence of the Godhead. Mahikari provides many examples; the point is, regardless of place or period, metaphors are widely used by everyone not just in religious settings, but in all domains of life.

Conscious Interiority as Turbocharged As-if-ness

Describing consciousness is challenging because we are fooled into believing it is integral to most perceptual, conceptual, and behavioral processes. Pinning it down is like building sandcastles near lapping waves. But one property that characterizes its features is as-if-ness. The more sophisticated mentation becomes, in all its problem-solving, reasoning, hypothesis-testing magnificence, the more pronounced are its as-if capabilities. The import of this mental maneuver was recognized by the philosopher

Hans Vaihinger (1852-1933), who characterized as-if-ness as "fictionalism": an "idea whose theoretical untruth or incorrectness, and therewith its falsity, is admitted, is not for that reason practically valueless and useless; for such an idea, in spite of its theoretical nullity may have great practical importance" (1935, p. viii). The as-if perspective is related to how we accept a provisional proposition for the sake of achieving some goal. It accounts for meta-framing, metaphors, role-playing, dramatization, hypnosis, and our ability to temporally project ourselves into an imaginary future, as well as a "willing suspension of disbelief" necessary to enjoy the arts. Vaihinger's theory of useful fictions, pragmatic contrivances deployed for navigating reality that are discarded as soon as they lose their utility, greatly influenced Alfred Adler's "fictional final goal," which guides and dictates most of an individual's actions. George Kelly (1905-1967) also based his "personal construct psychology" on Vaihinger's premise that our thinking is better understood as useful hypotheses rather than representations of objective reality.

At its simplest, therapy is about persuading a person that they can momentarily "pretend" and participate in the power of as-if reality, a temporary space in which better habits of thought can be cultivated. Psychotherapies and their interventions and techniques can be understood as meta-framing and reframing. The goal is a second order of awareness—"awareness of one's awareness process" (GT)—or interiorizing one's interiority (a form of heightened self-reflexivity). Arguably, then, despite their differences, all therapies have one basic aim in common: encouraging individuals to step back and take a more objective, detached view of their thoughts, emotions, and behaviors. Such a reframing of our circumstances, a specific instance of meta-framing, permits us to assess our innate strengths, recruit hidden resources, press into service more adaptive life strategies, and gain insight.

Sixth Aspect: Emotions as Interiorized Affects

Over the centuries, as interpersonal relations became more convoluted due to social changes, our repertoire of sentiments expanded so that we now experience more feelings about feelings. This interiorization of more basic affects is an example of meta-framing. To go one step further, "emotionalizing emotions" describes Jaynes's two-tiered theory of emotions, i.e., a layer of feelings culturally constructed over basic affects inherited from mammalian evolution (Chapter 12). This conscious interiorization of basic affects has both advantages and disadvantages. Meta-emotions grant us the benefit of having a bigger menu of more precise, nuanced feelings that enhance interpersonal communication. But the drawback is that such an extensive list of choices can complicate our reactions by obscuring the original affect. Moreover, meta-framed emotions become more intense and prolonged since our narratizing selves project them into the past or futurize them, turning them into never-dying ghosts with sentiments and old resentments that haunt our psychoscape.

In order to look at affects from a clinical perspective, Chapter 12 examines emotionally focused therapy (EFT), which aims to expand and reorganize emotional reactions; strengthen the bond between individuals (partners if in the context of family therapy, or FT); and encourage patients to reframe their emotional assumptions and establish healthier interrelations. Chapter 12 also explores the role of emotions from a positive psychological perspective. Watson and Naragon (2009) note that positive affectivity is a trait (moderately heritable) associated with cheerfulness, enthusiasm, and energy. It possesses elements of joviality, self-assurance, and attentiveness. Not surprisingly, low levels of positive affectivity are linked to depression.

A final example of Jaynesian therapeutics that might be mentioned: understanding the nature of consciousness helps us see the complex interplay between what Jaynes called "sensory pain" and "conscious pain" and why, for example, some amputees still feel sensation in missing limbs (2012d). Here is not the place to address this issue, but I note it as an example of the potential of a Jaynesian therapeutics.

Other Themes, Topics, and Applications

A number of topics thread their way throughout this work that contextualize the three main approaches (PPT, CFs, and FOCI). Some are theoretically informed and empirically supported, others preferential perspectives shaped by personal experiences, while some are admittedly more speculative.

Temporality and the Adaptive Psyche

The word "change" appears quite often in much of the psychotherapeutic literature; such ubiquity results in the term sounding insipid and anodyne. However, change should be viewed as possessing active, goal-oriented connotations. The mind is incessantly adjusting, accommodating, and adopting resources from outside itself to renovate and expand its capabilities. Adaptation, then, broadly understood, is a foundational premise (Chapter 8).

Historical Changes in Psyche
Adaptation unfolds across different temporal spans. The several timescales that configure and condition psyche are: (1) bioevolutionary adaptations; (2) developmental stages spread over an individual's life span; (3) the mind's ability to self-correct when navigating day-to-day challenges; (4) the mind's resilient capacity to self-repair and overcome maladaptive behaviors when confronted by a mental disorder. The notion that humans are imbued with innate rhythms of self-healing influences my interest in stages of change. When something overtakes our natural ability for self-healing, the obstacle–transition–restoration arc becomes derailed. So we require someone (such as a counselor) to patiently bring us back on track and jump-start the reparative process.

Researchers tend to overlook another timescale. Indeed, a great failing of mainstream psychology is its neglect of changes in mentality over a few generations or several centuries. This is the fifth timescale—cultural modifications of mentality, historically driven by growing social complexity. Exploring changes spanning this temporal scale is called for because understanding the historical origins of conscious interiority (a theoretical "pure" research project) can help us appreciate more clearly how recuperative mental processes operate (practical, clinical applications) (Chapters 9, 10).

Adaptive Phasic Structures

Adaptation, as it relates to temporality, can be conceived as processual flows expressed in relatively predictable rhythms, rituals, and patterns of transition. Individuals typically accommodate change by passing through tripartite "adaptive phasic structurations" (APSs): (1) destabilizing problem and identification of obstacle; (2) transitioning instability (but a phase pregnant with possibilities); and (3) re-stabilization and psychosocial restoration and resolution.[12] Much of therapeutic theorizing and clinical practices are conceptualized as transpiring through steps that reflect these basic phases of transition.

The Systemized, Serialized, and Dramatized Self

Spirit-possessed members of Mahikari would adopt different personas and roles, such as angry spirits or ancestors. Of course, most of us do not ordinarily self-present as possessing supernatural entities. However, the psyche's abilities to produce dramatic personas (possessing spirits) as well as everyday self-presentation are both explained by as-if psychological operations. The roles we perform are intimately related to our selves. Such a view inspires the "role-self perspective" (RSP) (Chapter 7). As there is no such thing as a completely socially detached role, selves are "roled" within the context of social relations. RSP is grounded in the therapeutic technique of gaining self-objectivity through distancing one's observing "I" from the observed "me"; this can be achieved through acting and role-playing which are grounded in as-if-ness. RSP assumes sociopsychological processes to be inherently dramaturgical, i.e., life is a stage with constantly changing scenes and sets to which we must adapt by working on a repertoire of various personas and interactional modes. The theater is not merely a nifty metaphor for daily life; rather, social existence *is* by its very nature dramaturgical. The enactment of pre-scripted social schemata should not necessarily be considered mere formalities lacking authenticity. Roles determine how individuals fit into society and what function or part they play in relation to others; their execution impacts other people. If done properly and for the right reasons, role performance can be authentic and fulfilling, as it integrates an individual into family systems and wider social networks of friends and acquaintances.

Besides viewing the self as a product of dramatized sociopsychological behavior, two other aspects of self deserve attention. The first is how the self is multifaceted, complex, and culturally contextualized, i.e., its operations demand that we analyze it as part of a system (Chapter 7). This systems theory approach also has relevance for groups and families (Chapter 11). Second, the self's shifting, temporal, and narratizable nature make it best understood as a serialized entity.

Multiculturalism: "Every Person Is a Culture"

An answer to a question on a test I took for counselors about multiculturalism reads: "When you have a client from a different culture than your own, choose options that gather information on how their cultural background could affect their actions and decisions." The implication seems to be that if a client somehow *seems* familiar to a therapist, the need to pursue a multicultural approach, as if individuals fit neatly into predetermined categories, is unnecessary.

A more productive approach is to assume that "every person is a culture," i.e., all counseling is cross-cultural. In the same way anthropologists explore far-off societies from every angle (kinship system, language, political economics, social relations, values and norms, religious beliefs, etc.), a thoughtful therapist makes an attempt to come to terms with the complexity of each and every individual. Each person—being a dynamic, complex constellation of socioeconomic factors; ethnocultural influences; sexual and gendered identities; spiritual sentiments; personal predispositions; familial traditions—possesses her or her own culture. The nature of this "individualized culture" (self-individuation) must be appreciated when treating a patient. Identities are subject to the vagaries of historical change and cultural variation. However, human nature, by its very definition, is inherently adaptable. At the end of the day, it is the individual who—though he or she may require facilitative guidance to gain insight and perspective—brings all the features together and utilizes them, constructing a personalized developmental trajectory (Chapter 14).

Tying the Approaches and Themes Together

This book adopts a Jaynesian paradigm of what is commonly called consciousness. Contrary to received opinion, consciousness is not the outcome of evolution. Rather, it was recently configured by historico-cultural vicissitudes, and in the same way it helped societies adopt, it can aid in therapeutically restoring individual mental health.

Identifying CFs of the psyche's self-reparative potential permits us to focus on what works in therapeutic settings. Such active ingredients are baked into FOCI. Investigating how we as a species adapted psychologically to massive historical changes from which conscious interiority emerged highlights our innate resiliency as a species. Positive psychology highlights our hardiness and irrepressible nature, traits sometimes hidden away in our underground and background psychological processes (nonconsciousness). Incorporating atypical cognition into our analysis, such as hypnosis and meditation, helps us delineate the features and functions of consciousness. Examining the operations of self as an element of FOCI also sheds light on consciousness.

Meta-framing, of which conscious interiority is an example, allows us to rise above and objectively cognize ourselves. It permits us to construct a higher conceptual stage on which we act out hypothetical, as-if scenarios—thus my attention to metaphors, role-playing, the theatricalized facets of sociopsychological functioning, and meta-emotions. Our inherent dramatizing tendencies involve learning scripts; rehearsing for new roles; managing self-presentations; switching personas; and donning new and dropping old masks. Also, the inherent temporality of psyche relates to how we adjust to novel stresses and life's turning points, both major and minor. APSs are the mechanisms that facilitate coping, or more prosaically, rituals and regularized practices of everyday life. Another theme to be examined relates to the implications of FOCI for understanding multiculturalism and human diversity (self-individuation).

Table 1.3 summarizes this book's approaches and the topics addressed.

Table 1.3 Approaches, Themes, Topics, and Applications

Approaches

- 1st: Positive psychology
- 2nd: Common factors
- 3rd: Jaynesian therapeutic paradigm and its six aspects:
  - (a) Nonconsciousness as the primary, default mode of cognition
  - (b) FOCI as supererogatory and corrective cognition
  - (c) Mental imagery as a vestige of the innate ability to hallucinate
  - (d) Altered cognition: hypnosis and meditation
  - (e) Meta-framing and metaphors
  - (f) Emotions as meta-framed affect

Other Themes, Topics, and Applications

- Temporality as a crucial facet of psyche and adaptive mechanisms
- Self: sequential, dramatized, and as part of a system
- Group dynamics
- Therapeutic interventions and skills
- Cultural diversity and self-individuation

Taking Stock

In this chapter, three interrelated theoretical pillars were introduced: (1) positive psychotherapy; (2) the CFs of therapeutic effectiveness; and (3) a Jaynesian therapeutic paradigm informed by a well-defined notion of consciousness. But what does this latter term mean exactly?

In his book about consciousness, one author peppers his work with "awareness without awareness"; "consciousness without awareness"; "awareness of which the organism is unaware" (or "fore-consciousness"); "unconscious awareness"; "cortical consciousness"; "unawareness of unawareness"; "awareness without awareness of awareness—or consciousness of without consciousness of consciousness of." We are told that "awareness can be conscious or can be unconscious." We also learn that we can be conscious but not aware, and a "denial of absent conscious awareness becomes an agnosia for an agnosia, or an absent awareness of an absent awareness—in other words, absent self-consciousness" (Locke, 2007, p. 106).

Such convoluted phraseology illustrates the impoverishment of our modern psychological vocabulary.[13] Indeed, the word "consciousness" is weighted down with such a heavy conceptual burden that it strains to the breaking point any intellectual edifice. Consciousness may mean: (1) the neurophysiological state of not sleeping (wakefulness); (2) the neurophysiological state of not being in a coma; (3) sensation/perception; (4) awareness; (5) self-reflexivity/self-awareness; (6) what one's inner self introspects upon; (7) concepts, cognition, or thinking broadly understood. The problem with consciousness, then, goes beyond its ambiguity and vagueness. Its conceptual promiscuousness and lack of definition rob it of any usefulness. It is pressed into service to describe neurological processes and subjective experiences that are strikingly disparate. Its overuse causes confusion and conflation. In order to understand how and why therapeutically focused consciousness works, it is necessary to carefully define it and disentangle consciousness from other types of cognition. In other words, certain mental processes need to be extricated from the confusing morass of mental operations collectively called mind. It is time to dissect consciousness and view therapeutic processes through its lens. Clearing the theoretical thicket is the purpose of the next chapter.

Notes

1. Though from their perspective they were engaged in a religious endeavor.
2. The interested reader is fortunate to have a number of texts that conveniently review these systems, e.g., Corey (2009); Fall, Holden, and Marquis (2017); Prochaska and Norcross (2013); and Wedding and Corsini (2014).
3. From the dodo bird in *Alice in Wonderland*: "Everybody has won and all must have prizes!" In addition to therapeutic factors (e.g., effects come from the therapist, the therapeutic relationship, specific techniques associated with a particular therapeutic approach),

extratherapeutic influences play a role: environment of the patient; various vulnerabilities and problems of the patient; presence or absence of social support; particular events impacting the course of therapy; patient personality traits and other personal factors; the patient's own resources and resilience; the patient's life experiences.

4. Cuijpers et al. (2019) point out that, when it comes to treating mental disorders, it is one thing to know that a specific treatment is effective, but it is a different matter to understand how a treatment leads to a positive outcome, i.e., we do not necessarily understand the mechanisms of change.

5. Cf. Dow: "If there is a universal structure to symbolic healing, then we can regard it as due to a deep structure. The different cultural forms [or techniques or interventions] of symbolic healing can then be regarded as surface structures manifesting the rules set by the deep structure" (1986, p. 56).

6. I will not offer a detailed recounting of Jaynes's theories. The interested reader is directed to his 1976 book and collections edited by Kuijsten (2006, 2012a, 2016) as well as McVeigh (2013a, 2013b, 2015, 2016a, 2016b, 2016c, 2016d, 2016e, 2017).

7. The title of Ellenberger's (1970) 900-page book that impressively details the emergence of "dynamic psychiatry."

8. Actually, Noam Chomsky (1957) famously composed this sentence to make the point that certain probabilistic models of grammar are inadequate; he used the sentence because it had never been spoken before.

9. *Not* in the sense that these are innate structures with which we are born.

10. Though "contemplative experiences" (CNT) are often associated with hypnosis and meditation, other phenomena can also have therapeutic effects, e.g., induced spirit possession.

11. Yapko summarizes the misconceptions about hypnosis (2012, pp. 30–44).

12. Such three-part transitions are inherent to all levels of nature, e.g., note the stages of a neuron firing: (1) threshold of excitation; (2) peak action potential (depolarization, repolarization, hyperpolarization); and (3) resting potential.

13. From McVeigh's (2008) review of Locke's book (2007).

2
What Is Consciousness?

Clarifying the Stuff of Mind

Cognition versus Consciousness

As a skeptical third grader, I wondered why, if I could speak English so easily and effortlessly, I had to sit through a class in which we laboriously dissected sentences into nouns, pronouns, verbs, adjectives, adverbs, articles, prepositions, conjunctions, and interjections. Surely it was not necessary to study something so instinctive, intuitive, and spontaneous as language use. Eventually I realized that appreciating the parts of speech and how a word is used in a sentence not only demystified advanced reading and writing, but also improved the expression of my own thoughts. Learning grammar also made the studying of foreign tongues a less daunting task, allowing me to see patterns and commonalties across different languages. And of course linguists can list many reasons why studying word classes and syntax is inherently valuable.

In the same way that we routinely use grammatical forms without a clear awareness of their technical workings (not to mention employing the almost infinite shades of meaning each word carries), we regularly rely on an impressive range of psychological terms to convey our thoughts and feelings. Unless we are researchers or poets, we usually do not ponder on how imprecise, loose, and promiscuous this usage may be. Of course there is no shortage of research on psychological processes and how they should be represented. Nevertheless, despite mountains of scholarly works, we still lack a commonly accepted and scientifically standardized terminology for much of our discussions about psychology. Usually this is not a problem, since context provides definitional focus for a long list of "mind words" for perception, conception, cognition, thinking, thought, sentiment, affect, mood, feeling, emotion, etc. Though these words carry nuanced differences (e.g., the distinction between emotions and thinking is usually clear), many assume that they all more or less describe a similar phenomenon, often subsumed under "mind" or "consciousness." This leads to unscientific speculation: "Do animals have minds?"[1] Or "will artificial intelligence advance enough that it becomes conscious?"[2]

So what of the phenomenon we call "mind"? We tirelessly work with a formless mental material that we weave and spin into rich tapestries we take in with our mind's eye. These internalized belongings are more ourselves than any other personal possession. Though unseen by others, the invisible psychic stuff of each individual is a type of personal introcosmos. Into this place of places that is no place, we can readily retreat; it is a nowhere of infinite wherevers that permit long journeys, as well as time travel to settled pasts or hopeful futures of locations not yet. This mysterious space pulls us back with recollections and reminiscences while pushing us forward to aims of burning desire and ambition-laden dreams. It is here we suffer stinging memories, secret shame, and half-forgotten heartaches one day, while the next we savor our fortunes, treasure our successes, and are grateful for everyday pleasures. In this psychocosmos of limitless potentialities, we plan new possibilities while rationalizing away our fears and irrationally creating new ones. As a species we reason into existence with shining clarity entire techno-utopian landscapes, but just as often we make dark and cloudy these same worlds with purposes unclear and nonsensical.

Is it possible to sort out the terms we regularly employ to denote psychologicality in the same manner that we improve our reading and writing skills by familiarizing ourselves with grammar? A strictly standardized and completely consistent terminology is neither desired nor necessary nor even possible. Nevertheless, I contend that at least for clinical purposes, tidying up our linguistic labels will go a long way in helping us discern how various techniques and interventions relate to one another, cohere, and operate. This book, in order to make a modest contribution to cleaning up treatment terminology, proposes that what is vaguely called "consciousness" can be broken down into FOCI. Given that so much of our mental healing transpires on the back of consciousness, it behooves us to get a conceptual grasp on what this term signifies. The purpose of this chapter is to clarify the meaning of conscious interiority.

Many researchers assume that "cognition is cognition," a complicated array of processes to be sure, but something that is more or less the same in all places and periods and has not changed much throughout history. The same can be said about consciousness. Indeed, some use "cognition" and "consciousness" interchangeably; and this is the problem, for "cognition" needs to be unpacked. Modern languages afford us a menu of terms to describe mentation. This fact indicates not merely its complexity, but that cognition differs from what I term "conscious interiority."

What Conscious Interiority Is Not

A more refined set of terms, then, should be utilized to describe psychological phenomena. Because it is rarely defined in the literature (or if it is, it is done so tautologically), the use of consciousness as a concept is at best confusing and at worst unscientific. Consciousness for my purposes is not sensation, perception, concept formation, thinking, reasoning, or deliberation (see Appendix D). Contrary to popular belief, these latter mental processes transpire automatically and nonconsciously. Even learning does not involve conscious interiority. Certainly we are conscious of the behavior of learning something new, but we are not directly conscious of the mental processes involved in learning. Consciousness does not reflect mental contents; rather, it is a product of cognition. The assumption that we are aware of most cognition is an illusory myth. In fact, we are only aware of a small sliver of mentation. Psyche is primarily nonconscious.

Defining Conscious Interiority

By "conscious interiority" I mean an introspectable selfness that is indefinable, elusive, and affords us a keen sense of inwardness that is so powerful we are convinced we can spy an inner landscape with our mind's eye. Conscious interiority is a functionally specific state that describes particular abilities, such as introspection. "Cognition" is an inclusive term, while "consciousness," a moment-to-moment product of cognition, is narrower in definition. In order to disentangle the different strands constituting consciousness, Chapter 3 elaborates on Jaynes's original list[3] and unpacks its constellation of features and functions.[4]

Consciousness operates by way of analogy. This meta-cognition constructs an interiorized parallel "space" with an analog "I" that can observe that metaphorical space and move about within it. It operates on any (perceptual) reactivity, excerpts relevant aspects, narratizes, and stitches them together in a mental space in which meanings can be manipulated like things in ordinary space (Jaynes, 1976, pp. 65–66). Conscious interiority operates on objectively observable things (Jaynes, 1976, pp. 65–66). In other words, it is a reproduction of what is called the real world, and nothing exists in consciousness that was "not an analog of something that was in behavior first" (Jaynes, 1976, p. 65). We typically become conscious when prescripted, habitualized routines cannot meet the challenges of navigating the environment:

> Consciousness creates a hole or gap in the deterministic web of causal relationships that shapes human behavior, so to speak. Under familiar, comfortable circumstances, certain causes lead smoothly to certain behavioral responses. Consciousness can disrupt and alter these connections, thereby disengaging behavior from its usual causes. (Baumeister & Sommer, 1997, p. 79)

Table 2.1 compares conventional assumptions made by mainstream psychology concerning FOCI with a Jaynesian perspective (see Appendix E).

Underground and Background Psychological Processes

What does it mean to say that the human psyche possesses great depth but not much surface area? Or why is that the "least interesting aspect of good conversation is what is actually said?" What is "more interesting is all the deliberations and emotions that take place simultaneously during conversation in the heads and bodies of the conversers. The words are merely references to something not present." Or consider the

Table 2.1 Views on FOCI Compared: Mainstream Psychology versus Jaynesian Psychology

Approach to Understanding FOCI	Origins	FOCI Developed Due to	Neuroanatomical, Neurological Changes over Time That Are Related to FOCI	Role of Genetics in Development of FOCI
Folk beliefs/ assumptions of mainstream psychology	Deep past	Evolution	Neurological, neuroanatomical structures altered	Yes
Jaynesian psychology	Late Bronze Age	Recent sociohistorical changes, linguistic enculturation of mind-words	Neurological, neuroanatomical structures unaltered	No

statement that there "may be an enormous amount of work or thought behind a given message or product. Yet it may be invisible. Making things look easy is hard. Clarity requires depth" (Nørretranders, 1998, pp. 94, 80, 79). In attempting to "grasp all that I am," consider the words of St. Augustine, the Bishop of Hippo (354–430), who wrote that he was "struck dumb with astonishment" by the abyss of his mind. It is "not large enough to contain itself. But where can that uncontained part of it be? Is it outside itself and not inside? In that case, how can it fail to contain itself?" (Augustine, quoted in Warner, 1963, p. 219).

Two words from the aforementioned paragraph demand our attention: "invisible" and "depth." Both are metaphoric expressions—the former concerning visibility and the latter spatiality—and have been used to describe the counterpart of increased interiority in modern times: nonconscious mental activity. More specifically, theoretical work on nonconscious cognition began in the nineteenth century when two counterintuitive and inconvenient facts became clear. First, interiority does not in any simplistic fashion reflect experiences we have of the external world (i.e., consciousness does not correspond with what one's senses perceive). Second, the "I" of our subjective interiorized experience is not the initiator of our actions—the nonconscious portions of our psyche are; or we might say that the self of our interiority "portrays itself as the initiator, but it is not, as events have already started by the time consciousness occurs" (Nørretranders, 1998, pp. 129, 242).

Mental activity below the radar screen of experience has variously been called "unconscious," "subconscious," and "preconscious," but I use "nonconscious." Nonconscious cognition is not unconscious Freudian activity, repressed material driven out of sight of the mind's eye. Rather, it is mental activity that is conscious-less (cf. Dennett, 1987, p. 162). Whatever it is called, the aspects of the mentation that are out of awareness still operate, "spreading activation amongst themselves, and in some cases serving to support the edifice that's made it to consciousness" (Carver, 1997, p. 97). Therefore, much information reduction occurs in the nervous system:

> Most information flow in the brain is . . . unconscious. The soul is not "richer" than the body; on the contrary, most of the processing in our central nervous system is not perceived. The unconscious (which was discovered and elucidated long before Freud) is the most ordinary process in the nervous system. We just look at the results, but we are able to direct the focus of attention. (Kornhuber, 1988, p. 246)

The failure to appreciate the difference between conscious interiority (a small product of cognition) and nonconsciousness (most of cognition) has generated many myths and much confusion. Unfortunately, early researchers equated cognition with conscious cognition. They have been "cleaning up after this misconception ever since" (Bargh, 1997, pp. 50–51). Researchers, incapable of "seeing" mental activity while introspecting, were forced to look "behind" and "below" interiority for invisible mental processes.

An appreciation of nonconsciousness cognition is essential, as its processes produce conscious interiority. Moreover, many of us hardly know ourselves since our lives are lived with only a vague awareness of the vast number of experiences that constitute our psychic being. Consequently we often engage in self-deceiving games that need to be exposed in a constructive, careful, and nonjudgmental manner. Compared to deceiving others, it is how we lie to ourselves that is difficult to discern; that it is not so much the roles we present to others, but rather the roles we perform for ourselves that can be problematic. Since nonconscious processes are largely inaccessible and operate so efficiently, we actually do not know ourselves (at least not necessarily through direct introspection) (Wilson, 2004). Individuals, incessantly making subtle, meaning-laden linkages and associations unawares, need to be attentively listened to in a supportive but gently prodding manner. In this way, insight is hopefully co-constructed in a therapeutic alliance between the patient and the therapist.

Consciousness as a Type of Meta-Framing

From the earliest days of infant development to the last days of one's life, the individual's mind is an unfinished work in progress. It is relentlessly moving forward, adapting and adopting new information. It does this by abstracting (selecting out what is relevant; details can get in the way of expedient analysis), analogizing (searching out the environment's familiar features to explain the unfamiliar and generate "as if" forms of knowledge, i.e., metaphors) (ADT), and scaffolding ("stepping back" from the environment to transcend our circumstances). Taken together, these processes can be referred to as "meta-framing." This describes the fundamental driving principle of mental operations, both at the collective/societal and individual/psychological level.

More specifically, FOCI are specific examples of the general psychological drive to meta-frame. The continuous reframing of our circumstances not only is the basis of our daily navigations through life, but also describes the hypothesizing and theorizing behind our grandest intellectual achievements as a species (McVeigh, 2016c). "Meta-framing" is a general term describing how analysis graduates from a base level to a higher one (e.g., metaphysics, meta-cognition, meta-representation, meta-referentiality, meta-discourses). Wolf Werner's "metaization," which describes how a movement "from a first cognitive, referential, or communicative level to a higher one on which first-level phenomena self-reflexively become objects of reflection, reference and communication in their own right" (Wolf, 2011, pp. v–vi), captures these meanings (Table 2.2).

The discussion of meta-framing is intended to illustrate the significance of appreciating how historico-cultural developments configure psychological processes. A key but specific example of meta-framing concerns how new introspectable faculties have transformed experiences; indeed, history stands witness to an ever-increasing "psychological interiorization" since approximately 1000 BCE. Such conscious interiorization propels forward the conjecture, speculating, and reasoning that result in techno-scientific advances. Analogizing and abstracting have actually altered spatio-visual perceptions, expanding our introspective skills and allowing us to adapt to changing social circumstances. In toto, human knowledge is arguably the result of the never-ending climbing up to higher and higher vantage points that affords us the ability to objectively survey the world (aesthetics has also have followed this trajectory of increasing abstractness; witness developments in late nineteenth-century and early twentieth-century art).

An example of a meta-framing process is self-reflexivity. This results from the distancing between "I" and "me" and allows us to set targets for self-improvement; it permits us to conceive the difference between our self-concept (who I am or am not) and our self-ideal (who I should or should not be).

Metaphors as a Type of Meta-Framing

Inspired, innovative language often deploys metaphors, which are specific instances of meta-framing. Our innate proclivity to imaginatively use metaphors characterizes our worldview and conveys to others our predicament. Much has been written on metaphors, and it is recognized that they constitute a crucial capability of the human mind. They are more than the "preserve of poets, artists, and high priests" (Landau, 2017, p. 8).[5] Indeed, language itself is an organ of conceptualization, so when new social realities of the Late Bronze Age erupted on the historical scene, linguistic metaphors of what we call conscious mind emerged to produce a new psycholexicon (Jaynes, 1976). Metaphors of mind place psychological events within the individual; this is due to the socially pragmatic benefit of centering and positioning personal agency and responsibility in individuals. Metaphors help us adapt to our

Table 2.2 FOCI as Meta-Framing Processes

Features/Functions of Conscious Interiority	As Meta-Framing and Meta-Framed Processes
Spatialization of Psyche	Going beyond real physical space and interiorizing a stage "in" the individual where hypothetical scenarios are envisioned for experimental runs of possible behaviors
Introception	Perceptual physical reality is transformed into a virtual, mentalized world, thereby increasing "realness" of superceptive experiences (qualia); the representativeness of the external environment is transcended and interiorized.
Observing Self: "I"	One's self as meta-framing subject; one transcends one's self ("me's")
Observed Self: "me"	One's self as meta-framed object; one is transcended by one's self ("I")
Self-narratization	Rising above, looking down at, and jumping behind or jumping ahead on one's personal timeline
Excerption	Overlooking one's stream of consciousness and selecting out mental content
Consilience	Standing above and over mental content and arranging and rearranging them
Concentration	Surveying one's mental material and setting aside unneeded mental resources
Suppression	Supervising and storing away unsettling and upsetting thoughts and feelings
Self-authorization	Looking down at one's self and identifying what ("who") motivates one's thoughts and behaviors
Self-autonomy	Surpassing one's accepted level of self-determination and exceeding one's sense of agency
Self-individuation	Gaining perspective on what is singular, special, and unique about one's self; allows one to take stock of one's characteristics which might be mobilized to benefit the group
Self-reflexivity	A honed sentiment of selfness that encourages one to step back and take an inventory of one's traits, strengths, faults, and weaknesses

surroundings, both social and natural, by allowing us to reframe difficult-to-conceive experiences and then communicate them to others. But such a linguistic maneuver is arbitrary; there is little reason why metaphors of mind could not be "over," "above," or "on top of," rather than "within," "internal," or "inner."[6]

Landau makes four core claims about the centrality of metaphors: (1) they are ubiquitous, "woven into our sociocultural environments and daily experiences"; (2) they are basic cognitive mechanisms, not a mere "decorative frill" or a "colorful but essentially useless embellishment to 'normal' or 'proper' language"; (3) they are a universal feature of cognition that interact with the social and cultural context; and (4) metaphors matter since they have real implications for judgment, creativity, political attitudes, compliance with health recommendations, the quality of our relationships, etc. For example, social metaphors that describe other groups can perpetuate stereotypes and dehumanizing and discriminating representations of marginalized groups (Landau, 2017, pp. 7–10).

Mind as Metaphor

Attempts to analyze the mind inevitably entail more metaphors, more sophisticated instruments, and more roundabout methods that ironically increase indirectness, circuitousness, and distance between subject (investigator) and object (psyche). This inadvertently creates a bewildering world of reflections of reflections. For this reason, metaphors should not be regarded as literary ornaments used to prettify hard-to-express thoughts. They are the very fabric from which the mind is woven, and thus crucial for therapeutic interventions. The mind, by its very nature, cannot be completely understood in an absolute sense. Psyche cannot look at itself without using another mirror. This may be frustrating to those who adopt a hard-nosed, reductionistic approach. But to the more intellectually humble and nimble, it does not mean that psychology is doomed from the start or is a vain attempt. The recognition that using tools to see how another tool works does not mean our understanding is severely restricted; it just means that the thing to be examined—the mind—is not what we thought it was.

The Therapeutic Usefulness of Metaphors

The family therapist and hypnotherapist Milton Erickson saw metaphors as providing tools for effective intervention (Kirmayer, 1986). Metaphors possess a powerful potential that can assist patients in treatment for three reasons. First, the meaning they generate comes from the patients themselves; it is their unique creation about their life experiences, granting them a sense of autonomy and ownership over their own treatment. Metaphors personalize meaning, making patients feel invested in their own narrative of recovery and rehabilitation. They also make therapy less jargonistic and therefore, for some, less intimidating. A therapist can, in collaboration with a patient, expand and elaborate metaphors suggested by the patient, thereby turning them into a potent therapeutic force. They can inject therapy with creative playfulness. Patient-originated metaphors are often parts of a larger narrative account that affords an individual self-identity and defines their social roles, sometimes offering them a much-needed perspective at a critical junction in their lives.

The second therapeutic aspect of metaphors is that, as parts of narratives, their colorful and concrete descriptions can be either negative (allowing them to see how their conceptual worldview is limited by an idea) or positive (opening up new vistas of meaning). Finally, as units of meaning in semantic systems, tropes can be built upon or can activate hidden, nonconscious networks of meaning.

Metaphors, then, allow patients to discover new meanings, uncover what is hindering their self-healing, and recover their mental well-being. In a group in which a patient was acting silly, a member instructed him not to "get all Jerry Lewis." One member warned me that he could not predict when he might lose this temper: "There's no warnings on this label." A patient advising another how to prevent his wife from negatively portraying him to child protective services said, "Don't let her paint your picture." Describing his psychological isolation while incarcerated, one individual said, "While in prison I built a wall around myself." Being homeless was often described as "couch surfing." Another individual, suffering the indignities of lacking shelter, said the "street became my family and the concrete my friend." A patient explained why he could not pay for child support: "I can't draw water from an empty well." When I asked a patient why he did not inform me that he could not attend a session, he told me he did not possess a cell phone, which made him feel alone and isolated: "A man without a cell phone is like a man without a country." "I was working like a Hebrew slave," explained an individual when describing his diligent efforts at work. One patient described his treatment plan, of which he was proud, like a substructure for a house: "You need a firm foundation." Expressions about false impressions were common: "He's gold plated but there's rust underneath"; "He's a thug in a three-piece suit." One patient explained that he became suddenly energized because "I put batteries in my own back." To describe his early rapid success in recovery, a patient stated, "I was moving like a freight train" (see Appendix F).

The Creative Potential of Language to Construct Cognition

Some patients, not privileged with a good education, nevertheless employ colorful, poetic language, and rhyming: "If it doesn't apply, let it fly"; "Being broke is no joke"; "When I use [substances] I lose"; "We need to be 'actual factual'" when confronting life's challenges; "He was a public pretender not a public defender" (describing a substandard legal defense); "What's the name of the game? 'Cops and robbers'" (recounting one's relationship to the judicial system); "They enter with gratitude, leave with attitude" (a resident of a substance use facility criticizing other residents who did not appreciate their time in recovery). Some patients would repeat a word or use half rhyme or homonyms: "Give time time" (take one day at a time since recovery can be overwhelming); "Better to be smart than hard"; "If I lose what would I lose?" (i.e., if relapse occurs, what will it cost personally?); "I thought I was beating the system but it was beating me" (a patient describing his cycle of arrests and rearrests); "Poor me, pour me another drink." Speaking of others in a therapeutic community who he believed were jealous of his recovery, one patient told me, "those haters are my motivators." When I once asked a patient a question on a topic she was just about to bring up, she lit up with "my thoughts must be written on my forehead—how did you know I was thinking that?" Another patient, discussing support from other residents while struggling with substance use, said, "Drugs do not have the power of the full House" [community residence]. Enthused by his early success in recovery, a patient told me, "Like a heavy locomotive, once it [therapy] gets going it's hard to stop."[7]

From "Mind–Body" to "Mind–Body–Interiority" Paradigm

After an explicit recognition of interiority in the seventeenth century, it would take several centuries of mystified thinking until we realized that the introspectable space we call conscious interiority was not the mind in its entirety, but only a small chamber of a much larger edifice. Invisibility and a spatiality of depth characterize this grand structure, with its unknown palatial halls, concealed quarters, and hidden rooms connected by secret passages that lead to even deeper unexplored caverns. It is in these spaces that the sociopsychological foundations of the human condition stand. And yet strangely, despite all the evidence for nonconscious cognition, researchers have been "made to jump through methodological hoops to establish nonconsciousness beyond any reasonable doubt." Psychology might progress if it adopted the same level of skepticism for theories that include a role for consciousness (Bargh, 1997, pp. 4–5). The stubbornness of research psychology illustrates the sway of folk psychology over those who should know better. In any case, we have come to accept without any qualms a host of claims to the effect that information processing (sophisticated hypothesis-testing, memory-searching inference) transpires even though it is entirely inaccessible to subjective introspectable self-awareness (Dennett, 1987, p. 162).

In order to make the centrality of nonconscious mental processes clearer, I suggest that we discard Cartesian mind–body duality and replace it with a more fruitful triality of: (1) conscious interiority; (2) nonconscious mind; and (3) body. Concomitant with this, we should discard the dualistic spatial metaphor of inner and outer, and employ the visual trope of: (1) introspectable mental processes (an introcosmos witnessed by the mind's eye); (2) invisible mental processes (nonconscious cognition); and (3) the physically visible world (body and environment). Recent work in cognitive science demonstrates that most thinking is done nonconsciously, and most cognition is invisible to our introscape. By recognizing a third element (invisible mental processes), an entire world of encyclopedic knowledge and complex processes is acknowledged that accounts for the tremendous amount of labor going on within our minds. These invisible processes also account for the apparent automaticity, spontaneity, and unthinkingness of much of our actions. The delegation of habitualized, routine processes to the nonconscious

frees up processing capacity for the novel, creative work that only conscious processing can provide—the chess master who can look far ahead because the calculations that burden his or her opponent's attentional capacity are made for him or her nonconsciously, the tennis champion for whom the decisions as to where to run and which type of shot the opponent will attempt are made preconsciously, freeing him or her to surprise and perplex the opponent with a novel bit of strategy. (Bargh, 1997, p. 10)

Three Types of Nonconscious Processes

I summarize the key differences between consciousness and nonconsciousness. The latter is characterized as fast, implicit, and automatic, while the former is slow, explicit, and involved in deliberative decision-making. Conscious interiority contains any thought, memory, or feeling that we introceive at any given moment (or to use a theatrical metaphor, "downstage" cognition). Three types of nonconscious processes can be proposed. The first is underground mentation, or the inaccessible architecture of mind ("offstage"). The second is the quarantined nonconscious of dissociated content. Traditionally this describes the Freudian unconscious, often linked to the past and childhood events and experiences. A boiling cauldron of unacceptable or unpleasant memories, untoward urges, or unresolved conflict, this "backstage" of cognition is only accessed with great difficulty. The third type of nonconsciousness is much more accessible. The "preconscious" (another Freudian term) is a sort of mental waiting room and consists of anything that could potentially be brought into the conscious mind ("upstage"). These are unrepressed memories that we extract for a specific purpose and constitute "background" cognition (Table 2.3) (see Appendix G).

Taking Stock

This chapter has explored the importance of distinguishing between cognition (something inclusive) from consciousness, a moment-to-moment product of cognition that is much narrower in operation. Consciousness was defined as an upgraded

Table 2.3 Types of Nonconscious and Conscious Cognition

Type of Process	Accessibility	Freudian Terminology	Comments
Nonconscious	Inaccessible architecture of cognition ("offstage")	N/A	Only indirectly apprehended
Quarantined nonconscious	Difficult to access content ("backstage")	Unconscious	Repressed, dissociated material
Preconscious	Accessible content ("upstage")	Preconscious/ subconscious	"Mental waiting room"
Conscious interiority	Accessed content ("downstage")	Conscious mind	Introception

form of mentation that allows us to "shortcut behavioral processes and arrive at more adequate decisions. Like mathematics, it is an operator rather than a thing or repository. And it is intimately bound up with volition and decision" (self-authorization) (Jaynes, 1976, p. 55). Investigating the function of "underground" and "background" psychological processes (nonconsciousness), as well as metaphors, assists us in understanding consciousness.

The next step in coming to terms with the nature of conscious interiority is to break it down into its components (FOCI). This is the purpose of the next chapter. Such an analysis illuminates how FOCI specifically facilitate psychic self-repair.

Notes

1. Of course they do. However, they are so qualitatively different from human minds that apples and oranges are being compared.
2. The belief is that an extra line of code or sophisticated algorithm is all that is needed, as if the sprinkling of technological fairy dust will magically transform a machine into a sentient being, is premised on some breathtakingly simplistic notions about the nature of mind. Note that the expressions "artificial consciousness," "artificial emotions," "artificial feelings," or "artificial sentiments" somehow sound less feasible, indicating how the words we use shape our assumptions about what is possible.
3. (1) Spatialization of psyche; (2) excerption; (3) analog "I"; (4) metaphor "me"; (5) narratization; (6) conciliation (Jaynes, 1976, pp. 59–66). In an Afterword to his 1976 book, Jaynes added "concentration" and "suppression," but also wrote that his list is incomplete (Jaynes, 1991, p. 451).
4. This expanded list has been informed by my explorations in historical psychology and archaeopsychology. See McVeigh (2016a, 2016b, 2016c, 2016d, 2016e, 2017, 2020).
5. The literature on metaphors is too immense for a review. But the reader is directed to Gibbs (1994, 1999, 2003); Gibbs and Steen (1999); Kövecses (2000, 2002, 2003, 2004, 2005).
6. Note "understand," from "under" plus "stand."
7. For their part, mental health counselors are fond of nifty acronyms (e.g., PAIN: "Pay Attention to your Inner-self Now") and alliteration (the 4 S's needed to be a good parent: Sacrifice, Suffering, Submission, Surrender; the 5 P's: "Proper Preparation Prevents Poor Performance).

PART II

THE BENEFITS AND COSTS
OF CONSCIOUS INTERIORITY

3
The Advantages of Conscious Interiority

A professor of French advised a class I attended not to stress over memorizing vocabulary lists. "What's important is the grammatical framework. You can always look words up in a dictionary, but if you don't know how to put them into the language's machinery and produce grammatically correct sentences, knowing individual words won't help." Earlier I introduced the idea that a language's grammar and its vocabulary are analogous to nonspecific factors and specific techniques, respectively. The former refers to the common ingredients that all people share; our psyche mobilizes FOCI as reparative catalysts when it needs to heal itself. Particular factors are the interventions that characterize and divide the different psychotherapeutic traditions. It is time to examine the nonspecific factor of conscious interiority as a collection of features.

Conscious interiority is a mentally spatialized analog of the physical world, and mental acts are analogs of bodily acts. When broken down into its constituent aspects or FOCI, it can be categorized into three groupings: (1) a "place" cluster that relates to an imaginary space in which we can use the mind's eye to test and rehearse behaviors, spread out temporality into a linearized past, present, and future, and thereby narratize our plans more clearly; (2) a "positioning" cluster that enhances our abilities to arrange, rearrange, and coordinate mental contents more effectively; and (3) a "person" cluster that involves psychosocial relations and interactions between oneself and others (kin, social groups, and collectivities) as well as between one's "I" and "me" (interself relations). This chapter explores the features and functions of conscious interiority by categorizing them into these three clusters—place, positioning, and person—and explains their relation to corrective cognition.

"Place" Cluster: Testing and Rehearsing Behaviors in Mental Space

Many of the most powerful metaphors we use to conceptualize the mind are based on spatiality, e.g., we are enculturated to believe that psychological processes occur "within us." This is the most primitive and fundamental feature/function of conscious interiority upon which other FOCI are elaborated.

Mind-Space: An Introspectable Stage for Manipulating Mental Imagery

Common sense tells us that psychological processes transpire "in" our heads (or sometimes our hearts). Of course this is not true, any more than "three-ness" can be found in three apples. And yet the entire field of neuroscience sometimes seems premised on the putative spatiality of mind. But mind is generated by and grounded in our neurological apparatus; it is not located in the head. Belief in the spatiality of psyche emerged about three thousand years ago, driven by metaphors that, depending on place and period, positioned mind in the heard, heart, stomach, lungs, liver, blood, etc. Modern European linguistic traditions usually place psychological processes in the head. Some patients of mine have creatively built upon this metaphor: "I hate being in my own head"; "My head is like an attic—full of junk"; "My head contains corrupted files"; "My head is a bad neighborhood that you don't want to go to alone." "Better stay out of this neighborhood," one patient said while tapping his forehead. Another stated that "therapy is like someone from the outside looking in at me," as if his inner essence was somehow inside him.

Metaphors of place linguistically cavitate the body (e.g., "in my head," "in my heart"), hollowing out a psychoscape "visible" only to the mind's eye of the individual. Spatialization is the cornerstone of our ability to adopt an imaginary, conjectural, and subjunctive mentality; it is a place to more clearly formulate goals and objectives. It affords one a secret, simulated stage on which one can rehearse behaviors that require practice or are too risky if carried out in the physical world. Mental space also affords a place to visualize different selves and grants a virtual location for "loosening techniques" so that alternative possibilities, fantasy, imagination, and mental experimentation with opposite behaviors of what we would usually do (e.g., trying something new, leaving one's comfort zone) can be performed (Gestalt therapy, or GT).

Introception: Exploiting Quasi-Perceptions and Semi-Hallucinations

From the spatial trope is generated a visual metaphor: the mind's eye existing in our head that can visualize mental contents. The spatialization of psyche generates an introcosmos modeled after the real perceptual physical world. Amazingly, it is in this private innerverse of surplus reality that perceptions are somehow transmuted into superceptions—perceptions that go beyond what our senses can ordinarily deliver to us. Such interiorized experiences are semi-hallucinatory, with the most prominent being visual. Also common are auditory and musical (replaying voices or tunes in one's head). More rare are imaging quasi-perceptual olfactory, haptic (touch), and taste experiences. Consciousness has different modes: verbal (imaginary conversations, perhaps with oneself); perceptual (imagining scenes); behavioral (imagining ourselves doing something); physiological (monitoring our fatigue, discomfort, or appetite); and musical (imagining music). These seem all quite distinct, with their own properties. Such modes undoubtedly possess different neural substrates, indicating the complexity of the neurology of consciousness (Jaynes, 1991, p. 452).

FOCI, or interiorized cognitive processes, are a form of covert mental behavior. This type of cognitive behavior is "visible" in a special way, i.e., it is introspectable so that our behaviors can be witnessed by the mind's eye in a private subjective space. Such interiorized behaviors are not perceptions of the external world, but rather introceptions; these are not a bio-evolutionary adaptation, but rather were shaped by linguo-conceptual metaphors. Introception developed historically for the same reason writing or mathematics did: as civilizations became increasingly complicated, more sophisticated and adaptive sociopsychological forms were demanded. Metaphoric expressions allow us to analogize external behaviors, so that what is observable, objective, and perceptual becomes unobservable, subjective, and introceptual. The resulting introceptions form a key feature/function of conscious interiority. These inner quasi-perceptions add a powerful capability to our arsenal of adaptation. Semi-hallucinations provide us with the power to instantaneously time travel (to imagine oneself in the past or future), teleport ourselves (to virtually "go to" other places), and to enact actions without having to actually carry out plans that might be time consuming, costly, or dangerous. Such subjectively simulated or "consciousized" behavior permits an effective way of envisioning new possibilities, circumstances, and inventions.

Mental Imagery as the Descendant of Hallucinations

Some patients have difficulty evoking mental imagery. But a patient once commented on how for him, mental imagery was vivid, and described it as being like watching a "replay of a movie." The lesson here is that individuals have differing introceptual skills. Sometimes vivid imagery may call up more intense negative emotions. Indeed, picturing an event with less intense imagery might make a past traumatic episode seem less threatening. In any case, these watered-down hallucinations still perform an adaptive role in everyday life. The qualia of introspectable mental imagery are the descendants of hallucinatory voice and visions that governed preconscious societies. However, the vividness of mental imagery and our acceptance of their reality-representing nature has diminished, and they have over time evolved into semi-hallucinatory mental imagery.

Mental imagery can be better appreciated if we divide mentation into several types of "ceptions" (Table 3.1). The first type are perceptions (more specifically, exteroceptive, interoceptive, proprioceptive, equilibrioceptive, etc.). The second are conceptions or nonconscious mental representations, while the third are superceptions: how our psyche superimposes or projects a layer of experience over ordinary perception.[1] Superceptions subsume three subtypes: (1) introceptions: semi-hallucinatory mental imagery, visualizations, or inner quasi-perceptions; (2) extraceptions: audiovisual hallucinations interpreted as divine

Table 3.1 Consciousness, Superceptions, and Authorization

	Preconscious Individuals	Conscious Individuals
Superceptions	Extraceptions: audiovisual hallucinations	Introceptions: semi-hallucinatory mental imagery
Authorization from	Supernatural entities: gods, ancestors	Self: "I" governs "me"

voices and visitations in ancient times and experienced as transpiring outside but near the individual (peripersonal); and (3) vestigial extraceptions: anomalous behaviors, e.g., hallucinations experienced by modern-day schizophrenics and some neurotypicals (voice-hearers) (McVeigh, 2013a).[2]

Romme and Escher (1996) submit that hearing voices has a functional role in aiding people to cope with their struggles. They noticed key differences between "good copers" and "bad copers." They found no connection between the characteristics of hearing voices and specific psychiatric illnesses, indicating that voice-hearing is not the result only of psychopathology. Romme et al. (1992) sent questionnaires to 460 people with chronic hallucinations who responded to a request on a television show. They received 254 replies, of which 186 could be used for analysis (it was determined 13 were probably not experiencing hallucinations). They found that 115 reported an inability to cope with voices, 97 were in psychiatric care, and copers were significantly less often in psychiatric care (24%) than non-copers (49%). Romme et al. (1992) discovered that successful copers used certain strategies for dealing with hallucinations.[3] Corstens, Longden, and May (2012) introduced a therapeutic approach called "Talking with Voices" that is derived from the theory and practice of Voice Dialogue (Stone & Stone, 1989). The Stones postulated that selves are composed of "sub-personalities" that require reintegration. Corstens, Longden, and May (2012) explain how the therapist can raise awareness of the origin and meaning of voices and help voice-hearers engage with their different selves (e.g., primary or dominant selves that push away "disowned selves") in order to raise awareness of the meaning and origin of voices. Jones and Coffey (2012), in their thematic analysis of the personal meanings behind hallucinations, contend that a biologically based psychiatry with its medico-physical explanations is inadequate for acknowledging the actual experiences of voice-hearers.

"Positioning" Cluster: Arranging and Coordinating Mental Contents More Effectively

Resting upon the belief that within the individual exists an imaginary mental space is the idea that in this mind-space "things" can exist. The logic is not complicated: a "place" is where objects can be deposited, moved about, compared, and inventoried. The functional point of having a psychoscape in which we can vicariously experience the world is to have a location within which interiorized entities can be positioned, repositioned, and stored. Some of these mentalized objects are not directly introspectable, that is, they lack quasi-perceptual, imagistic qualities (e.g., abstract notions). However, the very belief that some psychological stuff effectively dwells in our minds somewhere is all that matters.

Observing Self: "I"—Interiorizing One's Person

Spatialization affords a pretend place where our physical persons can be reincarnated as two types of virtual avatars of selfhood: "I" and "me." The former is the self-as-subject or the subject of awareness. This active aspect of selfhood is imbued with a sense of control, agency, and action; it does things. The "I," an interiorized representation of one's physical person, can move about in the introcosmos and experience inner quasi-sensory experiences. The "I" may have a behavioral (imagining oneself carrying out an action) or a physiological mode (monitoring one's appetite, fatigue, or physical discomfort). The observing self allows us to imagine ourselves doing something in order to assess if our planned action is effective, thereby avoiding the risks and hazards of an actual behavior.

The "I" Engaged and Transcendent

The "I" is not a fixed structural entity. It has two aspects. The first is its existence in a definitional relationship to other mental material (the engaged "I"). Like a point in geometry, the "I" is an elemental notion upon which our conscious landscapes our built. In other words, as a point is defined by properties (axioms), the "I" comes into existence in reference to one's "me's." The "I" can only become something definable when it emerges from "me's" (as we look back on our older selves as we move forward through time). This happens continuously.

The "I" can also be an absolute point of reference, unmoved by the flow and commotion of mental churning, as in meditation (the transcendent "I"); this is its second aspect.[4] As a geometric point lacks length, area, or volume, this above-and-beyond "I" does not have any easily defined attributes. Because it is constantly meta-framing without end, it is the observer that cannot be observed, the perceiver that cannot be perceived. It is always one step ahead of what we think we are thinking or doing. The operation of the transcendent "I" might be viewed as a heightened meta-framing of one's subject-self above and beyond whatever is occurring to us or in us. Conscious interiority can be described as a transcognitive process, i.e., stepping above one's swirl of thoughts and roiling ocean of emotions to gain perspective. What the engaged "I" and transcendent "I" share in common is their incessant recreation.

Observed Self: "Me"—Increasing Role-Diversity and Self-Flexibility

The counterpart of the "I" is the "me," i.e., the self-as-object or the object of awareness. This controlled, passive aspect of selfhood is acted upon and monitored by the "I." Different "me's" can be conceived as various roles we perform for others as well as for ourselves. A sense of the self's passive aspect is evident in why, according to a patient, he would easily become upset: "I can't help it when I overreact. I'm merely a mirror. All I can do is reflect how others treat me." Another individual once told me that always being observed while in a therapeutic community made him feel he had no self-control—"it robs me of my manhood." Still another patient, characterizing the loss of control while under the restrictions of the judicial system, said, "Parole is like prison minus the bars and walls."

The Interrelationship of Subject-Self and Object-Self

Together the "I" and "me" constitute a unity, an agent-recipient dynamic, interacting and defining each other; like ying and yang, one cannot exist without the other. The many permutations of the "I"-"me" interplay are grounded in and develop from universal psychomotor activities and physiological experiences (a person[5] controlling their body), as well as intrapersonal relations (how person-in-control relates to person-under-control). While "intrapersonal" designates processes occurring within the individual, "interself" means a relationship between the various elements ("I" and "me") constituting an individual's total selfhood. Other relevant societal interactions concern "one's person and one's roles" and "one's persons and false personas" (deception). Developmental and socializing experiences result in individuals internalizing these dynamics, i.e., interpersonal relations become intrapersonal, consciously interiorized experiences. Person is replaced by self, roles by role-selves, and deceiving others are transmuted into self-deception. Linguistics underpins these sociopsychological dynamics: personal pronouns (subject pronouns versus object pronouns); voice (active/agent versus passive/recipient); and syntax (subject versus direct/indirect object). In the theatrical arts, the way in which an actor enacts their role (as well as how a writer creates fictional characters) parallels how subject-self and object-self interrelate. Moreover, the manner in which soul or spirit of age-old religio-philosophical traditions relate to one's earth-bound, materialistic body seems to follow the same pattern (McVeigh, 2006b).

Self-Narratization: Mapping a Personal Timeline to Better Plan One's Goals

Spatialization allows us to spread out time as a succession of events upon which we can imagine ourselves moving, toward the past or toward a future that has not yet even occurred. Once detached from the limitations of physical reality, edited mental sceneries provide the "I" not just with a panorama of previous and current events, but with hypothetical and imaginary "could be's," "maybe's," "should be's," as well as future possibilities. We take self-narratization for granted, but note that while hypnotized, the "beforeness and afterness of spatialized time is missing" (Jaynes, 1976, p. 391). When subjectively self-aware, we use the "spatialized succession of conscious time as a substrate for successions of memories" (Jaynes, 1976, p. 391).

Self-narratization, or linearizing a personal timeline, actually involves a number of other processes (especially excerption and consilience) that are explained below. The need to make sense of events is a fundamental human need, but we often get derailed from perceiving matters clearly or we put up defenses to avoid dealing with painful thoughts. "Insight" occurs when a patient steps back and is able to see things from a new perspective, to have an understanding of why things have progressed the way they have. One patient, wistfully looking back at his life and recognizing how previous experiences shaped his outlook, told me, "The past, that's what built me. Now I want to take the house down and rebuild it."

Based on the notion that storytelling determines the meaning we attribute to our experiences and that the individual is the expert on their own life, narrative therapy (NT) views people as constructing their own worldviews and advocates the idea that we can rewrite our stories. Such stories do not merely mirror life, but shape it (Polkinghorne, 2000). Showing people that the meanings they attach to their life stories play an active role in self-conception allows them to re-author their personal narratives.

The goal of NT is to help individuals recognize what forces have influenced their narratives (e.g., familial dynamics). Specifically, such stories may include feelings of regret, guilt, shame, or self-blame. In order to guide a patient to a point from which they can discern how certain self-interpretations of their narratives can be maladaptive, a number of therapeutic techniques can be used. The first is deconstruction, or "externalizing the problem," i.e., viewing issues as outside oneself, rather than as an integral part of one's identity, so as to afford alternative choices and allow a menu of different stories. Once this is done, reconstruction/reauthoring can occur. The patient should be encouraged to drop self-limiting stories so that they can increase awareness and control over misconceptions. In this way, they can be encouraged to explore new options for problem-solving. Hopefully, a different, more optimistic self-interpretation can be rewritten. This can be done by having an individual separate themselves from maladaptive identities assigned by others (e.g., as a "victim") (Polkinghorne, 2000).

How we regard our personal timeline shapes our motivation and self-autonomy.[6] We cannot travel back in time to undo things. However, what is crucial about self-narratization is that it makes us capable of visualizing and hypothesizing the place we have not traveled to yet, allowing us to introceive new paths and plans. Taking a positive psychological perspective, Boniwell (2009) proposes an "optimally balanced time perspective" in which an individual learns how to objectively view their past, present, and future and then engage these temporal components more flexibly.

Processing our narrated selves is a skill. The past can be problematic for those who have been abused. "The past is something to reflect on, not live in." Another patient stated that he does not "look in the rearview mirror because objects may appear larger than they are." Still another patient summed up his philosophy with "the past is history, the future is a mystery, the present is a gift." People, whether therapists, counselors, or patients, are works in progress, unfolding through time. There is a temporal aspect about being a person that is inherent to our existence, i.e., we have no choice but to advance, to move forward. The hope is that when tomorrow arrives we can help others by revealing their inner strengths and by showing them how to bootstrap their way through the vagaries and vicissitudes of life.

Excerption: Editing Mental Representations for Higher-Level Conceptualization

The "I" edits, or excerpts, from the "collection of possible attentions to a thing which comprises our knowledge of it.... Actually we are never conscious of things in their true nature, only of the excerpts we make of them." Excerption is the "selection that picks and chooses among the many options" that the psyche manufactures (Nørretranders, 1998, p. 243). This ability of conscious interiority permits us to "see" only one aspect of a thing, in the same way we can only devote a limited amount of attention to something in the external world. Excerption is not the same as memory: an "excerpt of a thing is in consciousness the representative of the thing or event to which memories adhere, and by which we can retrieve memories." Reminiscence is a "succession of excerptions" (Jaynes, 1976, pp. 61–62).

Inspired by the psychosexual paradigm of development and informed by the infant/mother studies of Margaret Mahler,[7] object relations theory views early development as greatly shaping later development. Patients can be taught to excerpt certain representations of those who have played a formative role in their upbringing and to gain a healthier perspective on their internal objects relations. Individuals who struggle with early childhood and familial experiences may be educated about internal objects. These are internalized representations that influence the way we perceive others and why we choose certain individuals over others to form relationships.

Consilience: Fitting Concepts Together More Efficiently to Augment Abstraction

A key process of the mind is the assimilation of knowledge. But if assimilation is "conscious-ized" it becomes consilience:[8] a somewhat ambiguous perceived object is made to conform to a previously learned schema. What the conscious psyche does in mind-space is what narratization does in mind-time (metaphorically spatialized time). It brings things together as conscious objects in the same way that narratization stitches episodes together as a story (Jaynes, 1976, pp. 61–62). Excerpts or narratizations are made compatible with each other in the same way new stimuli from external perceptions flooding the mind are made to agree with internal conceptions. Cognition usually automatically and continuously incorporates novel stimuli into previously acquired schema, despite slight differences. This is necessary as we never, from moment to moment, experience things in exactly the same way. "If I ask you to think of a mountain meadow and a tower at the same time, you automatically [resort to consilience] by having the tower rising from the meadow." However, if you think at the same time of the mountain meadow and an ocean, consilience is unlikely to occur and you will probably think of one and then the other; the mind can bring them together only by assimilation (Jaynes, 1976, pp. 64–65). A number of principles govern compatibility; these are learned and are informed by the structure of the world. The surrealism of dreaming is explained by out-of-control consilience: the mind, liberated from the rules of the world and disengaged from reality, does not follow predictable and conventional patterns.

Concentration: Peripheralizing Unrelated Mental Content

The inner analog of sensory perceptual attention is concentration (Jaynes, 1991, p. 451). Focusing one's mental efforts is intimately related to excerption, as well as to other processes in subtle and complicated ways. Maintaining the proper amount of attention and concentration means striking a balance between being unable to focus and excessive focus (hyper-interiorized concentration). When excerption is not working properly, the psyche dysfunctionally attends to environmental and internal stimuli and ends up distracted or unable to change its focus of attention in a proper manner.

Ironically, intense concentration may be one feature of conscious interiority that, somehow shutting other FOCI off by increasing perceptual constancy, leads to trancing. This helps temporarily turn off and suspend FOCI, generating a hypnotic state.

Suppression: Censoring Distressing Thoughts

The opposite of concentration is suppression, or the behavioral analog of repugnance, disgust, or turning away from what we find annoying (Jaynes 1991, p. 451). Suppression means to consciously force unwanted information out of our awareness. It means to intentionally choose to not indulge in what is ordinarily accessible even though we *can* be aware of it—a thought, feeling, or action.

Nonconsciousness: Touring the Machinery of Our Minds

Educating patients on the implications of nonconsciousness helps in demystifying mental operations and cultivating insight. Relevant here is repression which, of course, is key to Freudian and psychodynamic theorizing; it is understood as a defense mechanism in which distressing thoughts are prevented from rising to the level of conscious awareness (psychoanalytic psychotherapy, or PAT). Repression is the disposal of things in the corners of the mind. With repression (and its conceptual cousin, dissociative amnesia), unwanted impulses are forced from awareness and into the unconscious. One is not aware of what the psyche has unintentionally made nonconscious. Unlike suppression, it involves quarantining unpleasant thoughts, feelings, or impulses that do not subjectively register in the conscious regions of the mind. Theoretically, repressed material cannot be made conscious by an act of will, so that what is repressed is accessible only through therapy (while suppressed material can be intentionally recalled).

Getting to know ourselves is as much a challenge as getting to know others because nonconscious cognition is the most salient part of our psyche. The myth of open-book self-objectivity, i.e., that we are transparent to ourselves, is a major hindrance in therapy. But like the nose on our faces, it is not that easy to clearly step back and get to know ourselves. To understand our own issues more clearly demands an incessant self-introspection. The best way to gain such insight is by humbly listening to what others (or a therapist) have to say about oneself.

Acknowledging the role of nonconscious processes helps us recognize aspects of our own background and identity and their impact on others. Coming to terms with one's biases (especially if we like to believe that we do not have any), preferences, likes, and dislikes (which may not be obvious even to ourselves) is actually a daunting challenge (multicultural therapy, or MCT). Becoming familiar with one's set of values, especially if one has never explicitly considered what they are or from where they came, can also be a taxing endeavor. Moreover, to make matters even more complicated, our values evolve in reaction to our changing life circumstances as we mature (acceptance and commitment therapy, or ACT).

"Person" Cluster: The Interrelations of a Social Microcosmos

The search for meaning, purpose, values, and goals is an inherent part of life which resonates with existential therapy. Treatment should not merely alleviate symptoms (existential therapy, or EXT). Rather, it should arm clients with skills to confront their very existence, to guide them on how to be authors of their lives (self-narratization) by finding purpose (with the understanding that "purpose" is something personal, self-individuated). The client must make the decision to change, and as in any clinical situation, the therapist cannot do this for the client. Since the therapist cannot insist upon change, the client should realize that their will is the primary element of self-change. According to one patient, "To attain what I really want, I must change," and before one's self changes, the inter-self process of "I"-changing-"me" must first transpire. "Only I can change the world I have created for myself." The next FOCI possess an existentialist cast, as well as underscoring individual traits, differences, and self-identity.

Self-Authorization: Legitimizing One's Behavior, Volitions, and Intentions

During a tense session in which it felt like no progress was being made, a patient suddenly and angrily declared, "I'm stuck with myself!" I asked the patient to elaborate a bit. He then said in a dismissive tone, "I don't feel comfortable with myself." Often a patient's interpersonal behavior is motivated by the subtext of "I don't like something about you because I don't something like about myself." Attempts to escape from reality is motivated by how we cannot deal with ourselves. But one must like oneself, or at least a part of oneself, in order to recover. The point is that much mental distress is caused by a failure to appreciate how many of our problems originate in how we relate to ourselves, i.e., that many who have difficulty loving others actually suffer from the inability to love themselves.

Related to liking (or disliking) ourselves is self-forgiveness. This is about more than just making a misstep, but concerns serious personal challenges. This is a type of self-compassion. Forgiving another for some transgression can be quite difficult. However, forgiving oneself is much trickier and some might misinterpret what it means (i.e., making excuses for oneself). Self-forgiveness, of course, demands a recognition of one's failing, but it must also mean a genuine acceptance of oneself in a way that is probably not as easy as some might assume, as it requires genuine humility.

Learning to forgive oneself concerns authorization for a mental act. To whom (or where) we attribute control of our behavior, or locus of control, is key to how we conceptualize how we relate to ourselves as well as others (the social structures in which we are embedded; the "who" of agency). Ordinarily we believe that one's inner person ("I"), rather than supernatural entities as in times past, has control over and governs our immediate behavior ("me"). In the words of one patient, "Don't ask what your recovery will do for you but what will you do for your recovery." In other words, put yourself in charge of yourself. "I have no resume except a strong back," a struggling individual once told me, recounting his efforts to find employment. He went on to explain that he realized he could not depend on others to find work; he authorized himself to take the initiative.

Provided that the therapist's therapeutic rationale is valid, coherent, and meaningful, it can offer an authoritative structure for the patient's emerging narrative, with new meanings about the self (Jørgensen, 2004, p. 534). Indeed, the act of sitting through therapy sessions itself often affords patients the authorization to self-heal. For a therapeutic rationale to be effective, patients must accept it, and it must in some way be compatible with their worldview, attitudes, and values. However, it need not be "true" (Jørgensen, 2004, p. 534; see also Wampold, 2001, p. 25).

Self-Autonomy: How a Sense Of Agency Builds One's Resilience and Confidence

I recall, during an internship, my supervisor, while speaking to disappointed staff about a client who had just absconded, reminding us that our role was to be something less ambitious than save-the-world crusaders. Often heard in certain mental healthcare circles is the expression "agent of change," but "facilitators of change" is more apt. She reminded us that for clients, personal choice plays a salient role in therapy and we cannot simply "cure" anybody. A therapist's task is not to second guess or "get into the head" of patients, but to provide a safe space in which, gently guided, they can connect the dots themselves, even if this means letting them wander and meander a bit (or even, assuming that self-harm or hurting others are not issues, take a break from therapy).

Very much related to self-authorization is self-autonomy; i.e., individual narratization leads to a sense of control over one's destiny.[9] "If you place a bottle on a curb, it won't come to you," explained a patient, meaning that he possessed the self-control not to drink alcohol. A person is regarded as an agency-instilled being; intentionality and responsibility are attributed to the "I" rather than external social forces. Self-autonomy concerns meta-framing beyond our present problems and dealing with the latter directly. If properly cultivated, one can override personal predispositions and social determinants. Incidentally, autonomy, or fostering the capabilities to control the direction of one's life, is implicitly or explicitly enshrined as a key principle in codes for healthcare providers (e.g., American Counseling Association Code of Ethics).

Asking a patient point blank, "Are you satisfied with the world you have created?" can put him or her on the spot, leading to a thought-provoking, stimulating session. It does this because personal freedom, responsibility, and decision-making are highlighted. "I just don't know how to live," groused a patient about making decisions himself. The acceptance of freedom ("I can't accept life on life's terms," complained one patient) can be a burden. As one individual explained his predicament to me, "Life itself is my problem." At termination, one patient, with a newfound healthy perspective and an appreciation of life's small joys, told me, "All we need in life is mashed potatoes" (i.e., he can be content with a moderate standard of living; a luxurious lifestyle is not necessary). Living life itself in the present, with all its gifts, disappointments, hope, and terror, is what matters. A patient in recovery from substance use stated that the "only thing I want to experience now is life itself, now that I'm sober."

A number of terms semantically overlap with self-autonomy or the idea that we are authors of our own behavior. An overview by Wehmeyer, Little, and Sergeant (2009) of theories about self-determination provide a sense of this related concept: (1) it involves the three basic needs of competence, autonomy, and relatedness that are either supported or threatened by social contexts; (2) functional self-determination theory—dispositional characteristics are based on the function a behavior serves for an individual; (3) self-regulated problem-solving; (4) causal agency theory—how we learn to distinguish between "self" versus "other"-determined behavior. Self-efficacy—"believing one can"—is another relevant term. It is an individual's belief in their capabilities to produce desired effects by their own actions (Bandura, 1997, p. vii). Maddux (2009a) links it to physical health, psychological adjustment, and psychological problems, as well as therapeutically guided changes and improvements. "Personal control" is another researched concept that relates to self-autonomy. It helps individuals maintain emotional stability, set reasonable goals, discover new avenues for control, and accept difficult-to-change circumstances (Thompson, 2009).

Self-Individuation: The Social Benefits of Highlighting Individual Differences

In the same way that the individual's personal traits are highlighted and privileged within larger collectivities, one's "I" is differentiated and comes to appear unique when set against the backdrop of interiorized excerptions. The need to distinguish ourselves from others is something that is either encouraged or discouraged by place and period. I suggest that such self-individuation promotes not just personal but also the collective good since it highlights an individual's unique talents that can be used to benefit others (Vignoles, 2009). Discovering one's personal traits not only aids the individual, but also is a boon to others who can benefit from one's personal strengths. A related concept to individuation is self-identity (EXT).

Self-individuation, grounded in and nourished by an individual's own introcosmos, resonates with Rosenzweig's "idioverse," a concept meant to supersede "personality." This describes the totality of an individual's experiences and the unique events of each person's life, as well as their endeavors at creativity (Rosenzweig, 1986, 2003). An idioverse is actually part of what Rosenzweig called "idiodynamics" (his version of the ambitiously integrative biopsychosocial approach) that also included psychodynamic factors and the role of creativity in one's search for personal integration (Kaufman, 2007, p. 364).[10]

Being creative implicates novelty, effectiveness, and authenticity, and leads to vitality and making connections. Creativity should be applied to emotional and intellectual endeavors as well as artistic (Averill, 2009). Creativity, or techniques for adaptive originality, is something that needs to be cultivated during childhood (Simonton, 2009). Related to creativity is problem-solving, which allows us to adjust to life in a positive, healthy way (Heppner & Lee, 2009). Arguably, being creative demands a degree of curiosity, a sentiment often neglected and underappreciated. Seeking out the novel should be regarded as a source of strength. It can benefit social relations and enhance positive emotions and well-being (Kashdan & Silvia, 2009).

Self-Reflexivity—Cultivating Insight, Self-Objectivity, and Self-Corrective Abilities

A self cannot exist without others; it emerges from the matrix of individual-and-others interactions. The self, then, is a social construction, and in the same way that there is no self without others, the introceptual landscape cannot have a subject ("I") without an object ("me"). Indeed, the "I"-"me" dyad is an interiorized version of person-other relations constructed through socialization that generates self-reflexivity (which can only arise from some type of system comprised of parts) (ADT, GT).

The ability to excerpt and "see" oneself in an interiorized place without any physical limitations, and to imagine not-yet versions of our future selves, produces an "I" that introspects upon a "me." Self-introspection causes a recursively regressive mirroring effect—self observing self—resulting in a highly individuated sense of selfness that exists in opposition to others. The perceptual experience of having a bodily self that is both an active doer and a passive recipient of action is interiorized into a psychologized self that is both observing ("I") and observed ("me"). This grants each person the capacity for self-awareness (EXT). From this is generated self-reflexivity in which different aspects of self are produced repeatedly: an "I" observes/monitors a "me," this "me" then becomes an "I," which in turn observes/monitors another "me," ad infinitum. This process serializes awareness of awareness of awareness, etc. Narratization, or stringing a series of selves together, aids in reflexivity and a sharpened sense of selfness. This introspectable linearization of temporality explicitly segments our experiences into past, present, and future, generating a mentalized path on which we can visualize our self moving either into the past or into the future (self-narratization).

Taking Stock

This chapter has categorized FOCI into three clusters—place, positioning, and person—and has explained their relation to corrective cognition. But can cognition over-correct? We assume that psychopathologies possess little or no adaptive value; they are viewed as a deficiency or an excess of functioning (Huemer, Hall, & Steiner, 2012, p. 40). But as maladaptive as they may seem to us, disorders are often attempts at adaptation. Indeed, Nesse (2019), in *Good Reasons for Bad Feelings: Insights from the Frontier of Evolutionary Psychiatry*, argues that nature has left us with a fragile mental apparatus. However, from the perspective of evolution, our psyche's failings are its very strengths. For instance, Nesse points out how anxiety alerts us to dangers, but consequently "false alarms" are the price we pay. Low moods preclude us from wasting our efforts in pursuing unreachable and unreasonable goals. Unfortunately, such feelings sometimes mutate into depression. Addiction and anorexia nervosa may result from a mismatch between our human-made, modern environments and genetically evolved tendencies from our prehistorical past. So it seems that mental disorders are often a case of over-adaptation. The theme of the next chapter examines what happens when consciousness over-corrects.

Notes

1. Perceptions might be described as realis, conceptions as irrealis, and superceptions as surrealis.
2. "Ception" is etymologically descended from "taken" or "seized."
3. Distraction; ignoring the voices; selective listening; and setting limits on their influence.
4. In mystical terms, the transcendent "I" is pure, unadulterated awareness.
5. In this context, "person" designates an individual without a consciously interiorized self.
6. A number of inventories measure time perspective: Zimbardo Time Perspective Inventory; Future Anxiety Scale; Consideration of Future Consequences Scale; Sensation-Seeking Scale (that accentuates present-oriented perspective); Time Structure Questionnaire; Time Reference Inventory; Time Attitude Scale; Time Competence Scale; Stanford Time Perspective Inventory (Boniwell, 2009).
7. Psychoanalytic theorist Heinz Kohut (1913–1981) expounded upon Mahler's ideas, arguing that children who do not adequately differentiate themselves from others run the risk of developing narcissistic personality traits.
8. Sometimes referred to as "conciliation" or the more baroque "compatibilization."
9. "Self-control" is a major theme in psychological studies (Shapiro & Astin, 1998); indeed, many other terms and concepts preceded by "self-" fill journals and books on therapy. These "self-" prefixed notions are inherent aspects of the interiorized mind.
10. Self-individuation reminds us of the important difference between the idiographic (what is different and unique about each person) and nomothetic (average behavior), a distinction recognized as early as the late 1800s.

4

Runaway Consciousness

The Price of Scaled-Up Cognition

To what degree do psychopathologies possess an adaptive element? This is difficult to say, but psychopathology is a compromise between "situational demands" and "personal limitations"; it is an "odd mixture" of volitional (top-down) and biological (bottom-up) causal forces (Huemer, Hall, & Steiner, 2012, p. 41). In other words, neurophysiology can be influenced by executive, willful efforts (though we must be wary of the danger of romanticizing mental illness or blaming the convenient abstraction of "dysfunctioning society"). In any event, the need to encourage a positive mindset and healthy lifestyle in order to cultivate a strong sense of subjecthood empowers patients, who can then see the value of more beneficial interventions in spite of distress caused by over-adaptation.

Everyday and Therapeutic Conscious Interiority

This chapter explores how conscious interiority, which ordinarily is a benefit, can go awry. Usually our consciousness operates on autopilot. This describes the "everyday" type of conscious interiority. But when confronted with a particularly difficult situation (i.e., when a plane veers off course from a predetermined flight plan or when sudden turbulence jolts a drowsy crew into concerned attentiveness), we need to engage in the second type of conscious interiority: therapeutic consciousness (in other words, an aviator will shut off the autopilot and take over manually).[1] While in flight the autopilot is usually turned on, but occasionally it might need to be switched off under certain circumstances. Sometimes even the training of an experienced pilot is overtaken by an airborne emergency. This is when the knowledge of a flight engineer is required, who is analogous to a therapist or mental healthcare provider (though in premodern and more traditional societies, shamans and priests would take over this role). Understanding FOCI allows us to conceive them as therapeutic techniques that can be utilized to correct distorted cognition. FOCI can change cognition.

Excessive and Hyper-Interiorized Consciousness

Conscious interiority, a massive reworking of mentality from about three thousand years ago, presents a "good news, bad news" scenario since it provides us with advantages as well disadvantages. As an adaptation, interiorized cognition provided a host of benefits, allowing an individual to adopt a more hypothetical stance toward the environment. Such hypotheticality inserts a question mark into one's engagement with the world and encourages an as-if, propositional attitude; it also kindles healthy skepticism. Through excerption and consilience we can reframe our experiences; come to know ourselves better (recognize our untapped, hidden talents and innate potentialities, as well as our faults); go beyond what we ordinarily believe and expand our perspectives via meta-framing; bootstrap our way out of self-defeating cognitions and behaviors; attain self-actualization; and perhaps even develop a transpersonal self.

However, the capabilities of conscious interiority that allow us to overcome obstacles also have a darker side, as they can drive us to needlessly doubt what is indicated by objective reality. The same processes that permit us to dream of a better future, hypothesize new ideas, and radically improve ourselves also cause us to worry about what might happen, become unnecessarily aggrieved, and hold ourselves back. When stuck in overdrive, FOCI set in motion runaway cognition, providing the fuel for mental disorders. The bad news is that we do not know ourselves as well as we think we do, so that robust self-masking tendencies lead to self-deception; self-damaging habituation; self-sabotaging; self-propagandizing; self-indoctrinating; and other self-destructive behaviors.

Filled with visions of "new and improved" lives, people structure their personal worldview on the basis of an array of should's, ought's, must's, and absolutist thinking. Due to misperceptions, misinterpretations, or dysfunctional views of situations, a "systematic bias" or "cognitive shift" is generated. Certain attitudes contribute to these shifts, making people experience the world through a distorted lens. In this way, cognitive vulnerabilities are created. The human tendency to turn preferences into demands appears to be a particularly modern problem, supercharged by technology delivering instantaneous want-satisfaction. Consequently, individuals engage in "demandingness" that result from wishful thinking and even superstitious and magical thinking. To satisfy our distorted demands, we procrastinate and avoid thinking things through, ending up with illogical deductions. The tangled circuitry of our mind, with its hodge-podge of jury-rigged components, is prone to convoluted, over-communication; it spins into existence entire worlds of florid desires and unachievable fantasies.

Runaway Cognition

Why do mental processes designed for adaptation run awry? Part of the answer can be found in the very nature of interiorized cognition. Much of behavior is determined by instincts or inborn inclinations toward a particular complex behavior. Considerable debate surrounds the usefulness of "instinct" as a scientific idea (and its related concept, "drive").[2] As conventionally understood, an instinct (or a fixed action pattern) at least delineates the course of a behavior: an environmental stimulus triggers a response in the organism, a short- to medium-length sequence of actions unfolds, and a vital need of the organism is met (e.g., hunger satiated, thirst quenched, threat averted, reproductive sex drive satisfied). Many cognitive-plus-environmental interactions, of course, cannot be handled by the tension–response–resolution circuit (TRRC) of instincts, and require much more complex adaptive processes. This is especially true for highly intelligent animals, whose engagement with their environment produces endless variations of the interplay between psychological processes and the external world. If the cognition of *Homo sapiens* goes far beyond the TRRC, conscious interiority, which is unique to humans, is light years ahead of the TRRC in terms of adaptive potential.

One downside to the package of features/functions constituting conscious interiority is that it lacks a defining feature of TRRCs: a built-in mechanism of cessation (Jaynes, 2012d, p. 171). For example, consider what happens to the sex drive when interiorized. A man fantasizing about sex will occasion physiological responses in erectile tissues, which then recruit other physiological responses together with hormonal changes, the "feedback from which keeps cuing the fantasy until it is difficult to turn conscious attention to other things" (Jaynes, 2012d, p. 171). Such recruitment explains how primary affect becomes secondary emotion. Affect is a biologically determined behavior with a specific anatomical expression and a certain biochemistry, and it dissipates with time (Jaynes, 1991, p. 460). In other words, unlike affect, secondary emotions lack a biologically evolved mechanism of stopping. When affect is interiorized, it is transmuted into emotion. Interiorizing past or future affects turns them into emotions; the latter in turn become feelings and sentiments that color our self-narratizations (Jaynes, 1991, p. 460), making us romanticize the past or fear the future.

A good illustration of recruitment that has serious political and economic implications is the hedonic treadmill, i.e., in our hyper-consumerist and capitalist society, marketing socializes us to increasingly take what we have for granted. But as one accumulates more material possessions and accomplishments, one's expectations also rise in a never-ending spiral, forcing us into a hamster-wheel lifestyle. Hyper-consciousness, then, fuels and is fueled by modern political and economic systems and therefore carries ethical implications (e.g., self-individuation and self-reflexivity bolster ideas of individualism).[3]

Hyper-Interiorized Mental Spatialization and Introception

Becoming more cognizant of the power of the mind's eye to initiate self-healing is evident in the uses of guided imagery. Some patients do not readily articulate their problems into serialized verbalization. However, they may have an easier time exploring and expressing their feelings by describing their mental images; in this way a therapist can gather valuable information about their problem.

While mind-space is a safe place to mentally experiment (GT), it is also the "place" where flashbacks occur. These are acute dissociative states[4] during which elements of a past traumatic event are relived as though they were occurring at that moment. These unwelcome intrusions of disturbing thoughts into awareness are also symptomatic of dissociative identity, dissociative amnesia, acute stress, and posttraumatic stress disorder (PTSD). When unnerved by intrusive imagery (hyper-phantasia) in cases of PTSD, certain aspects of the mental scenery can be changed by altering details of what happened.

Hyper-Interiorized Observing-Self and Observed-Self

Within our psychoscape as well as the external world, we are perceiving subjects ("I") as well as perceived objects ("me"). With this stated, it is incumbent on the therapist to be sensitive to the inner world of the patient (from their "I" perspective), as well as how they feel when they are perceived by others ("me"). "Being perceived" here might mean being socially cataloged and categorized into identity groups (racial, ethno-cultural, sexual, gender, generational, political affiliation, etc.) (MCT). Moreover, if the observing self ("I") becomes too intrusive about what an individual is up to, self-doubt emerges and we become hyper-subjective, suspicious of our own actions, and constantly posing too many queries and self-interrogations.[5]

Hyper-Interiorized Self-Narratization

Narratizing one's own life story affords the individual a certain sense of freedom in the way it offers a choice of direction when one reflects upon one's future. At the same time, this fork-in-the-road perspective comes with a price, since if one is offered a plethora of choices, then doubts, uncertainty, and reservations can plague the mind. So much of our lives are spent being "somewhere else"—bygone "should've done's" or worrying about what might eventually happen later on—rather than living in the here and now. The grand expanse of mind-time, generated by the spatialization of psyche, sets in motion the neuroticisms of yesterdays and tomorrows. Individuals tell themselves stories that interpret their life for them. But due to past negative experiences, these stories may be maladaptive. Individuals might be perceiving themselves as victims with unfinished business. It is possible that their sentiments and lived experiences are not fully encompassed by the appropriate narratives. Indeed, they may even engage in self-surveillance or may see themselves through the filter of the perceptions of others.

If viewed from another angle, time itself can be a particularly useful resource in self-healing. For instance, the place called the future can be exploited, reframed as a place for positing new possibilities and potentialities from which to choose. Patients can be encouraged to "time travel" to improved versions of their selves, or to revisit old selves and "converse" with them about past incidents, mistakes, or regrets. They can be advised to avoid "time disturbances," i.e., rather than "futurizing" (worrying about what might happen) or just recounting the past, they can focus on the here and now by bringing old experiences directly into their present experiences (GT). NT,[6] which sees our realities as ongoing constructions, organized and maintained by the stories we tell ourselves—one's "I" observing one's "me" on all its peregrinations, expeditions, and passages through life—is appropriate as an intervention in this context.

Hyper-Interiorized Excerption and Consilience

Excerption, though usually adaptive, can cause problems. A patient once stated, "When I would think back to that time [of using substances], I would only play the good part of the tape." In other words, he would only excerpt parts of the "tape" that fit into his positive reminiscences. In this case, a patient should be asked to re-excerpt his past, bringing up negative experiences about his past substance use as well. While excerption provides the individual with a powerful mental editing device, this tool can be overused, resulting in excessive excerption. Too much editing, compelled by nonconscious fears or biases, leads to the avoidance of contraindicative facts so that irrational conclusions are drawn even in the face of contradictory evidence. Information that might be useful becomes lost in a fog of half-truths.

Examples of the hijacking of the editing of mental representations include dichotomous or binary thinking: categorizing experiences in extremes or with a rigid either/or logic, e.g., "I am a complete success or a total failure." The ability to so readily and easily rearrange objects of the mind can lead to viewing something as far more significant or less significant than it actually is—magnification or minimalization. Runaway editing also leads to overgeneralization or abstracting a general rule from only one or a few isolated incidents and misapplying it broadly, even to unrelated situations. Selective abstraction is taking a fact out of context and discounting other information so that one's circumstances are misinterpreted. Arbitrary inference is reaching a conclusion without supporting evidence (Beck & Weishaar, 2014, pp. 240-241). Personalization, attributing external events to oneself without supporting evidence, is a consequence of misattributed self-authorization (cognitive behavior therapy, or CBT; rational emotive behavior therapy, or REBT).

Instances of unwarranted consilience (the conscious assimilation of mental representations) is another common example of hyper-interiorization that breeds cognitive distortions. An overly suppositious mind-set leads to too many qualifications, provisos, and conditions—"if only ... then I would be happy." Fox et al. (2016) outline three mechanisms by which we might alter or reduce automatic associations and elaborations of spontaneous thought: (1) reducing the associative chaining of thoughts (arresting consilience); (2) de-automatizing and diversifying the content of thought chains (decreasing thought rigidity and increasing the variety of ideas); and (3) re-automatizing chains of thought along desired paths (forming new, voluntarily selected thinking habits). Hypnosis and meditation can be utilized to de-automatize the chaining of runaway consilience, thereby increasing cognitive-emotional flexibility.

Editing out the maladaptive parts of one's stream of consciousness seems like a commonsensical approach, but learning to first accept faulty parts of ourselves and maladaptive thinking patterns should not be neglected (ACT).

Hyper-Interiorized Concentration and Suppression

Focusing allows us to marshal our mental energies on an immediate problem. But any situation a human organism confronts is experienced as both a figure (focal point) and ground (contextual background). Figure and ground interrelate and adjust to changing needs and circumstances—what was part of the ground can suddenly emerge as a figure, and vice versa. Knowing how to balance one's attention (figure or relevant excerpts) with what can safely be unattended (ground or irrelevant excerpts) is a crucial capability (GT).

Regulating the figure–ground dynamic appropriately avoids distraction as well as hyper-interiorized focusing. Patients with attention deficit hyperactivity disorder (ADHD) have difficulty balancing the figure–ground interplay, i.e., for them distinguishing relevant figures from the ground is difficult. For others, only the figure is attended to while the ground is ignored. Such over-concentration leads to the neglect of the larger context or background information; think of the "absent-minded professor."[7] Learning grounding techniques or cultivating mindfulness (or in the terminology of GT, "contact") can educate patients about proper attentiveness.

Hyper-Interiorized Self-Authorization, Self-Autonomy, and Self-Individuation

If we come to feel that our personal feelings are somehow devalued or we suffer due to the self-neglect of our internal frame of reference, then it is difficult to be a self-determining, self-realizing, and sovereign subject. We put too much weight on the "me"—our passive aspect—of selfhood. One patient, discussing his loss of self-autonomy vis-à-vis his substance use disorder, stated that "the disease was making decisions for me." Given our individuated nature, healing practices need to be crafted to each patient's own self-narrative trajectory. In this sense, the interiorized facets of our humanity are acknowledged. When we view ourselves as an agentive "I" rather than a merely reactive "me," then we can grant more value to our subjective, interiorized world (Zimring, 2000, p. 112). The patient is not merely an inactive receptacle into which therapy can be poured; from a phenomenological perspective, he or she is the center of the world (Adlerian psychotherapy, or ADT).

Sometimes we too conveniently transfer the responsibility of our adversities to others; we are victims of bad parenting, failed marriages, awful supervisors, and systemic racism or sexism. But regardless of any truth to claims about what others have done to us, continually cashing in on victimhood—victim's privilege—can hinder self-improvement, as it depletes our sense of agency and misallocates our mental efforts (EXT).

A hyper-interiorized self can go in another direction. Instead of being too passive, we become overconfident. This can result in inflated self-autonomy in which a sense of ego is ballooned so that we do not accept our limitations, e.g., that we can have it all and obtain every consumerist expectation. Inflated agency can cause a distressing mismatch between our aspirations (ideal self; a better "me") and our abilities (real self; actual "me"). Too much self-individuation leads to the excesses of the "self-esteem" movement in which everyone gets a prize; according to some, this has produced self-absorbed, narcissistic, socially fragile individuals.

The remedy for some when overwhelmed is to de-individuate to a certain degree by subsuming their selves into something larger than themselves. Typically, if a beneficial, positive maneuver, this may mean becoming committed to one's family, the local community, social activism, or a political movement (GT). Or that "larger something" may be the cosmos or religion, leading to a state of self-transcendence or realization of a transpersonal reality (EXT; contemplative psychotherapy, or CNT).

Hyper-Interiorized Self-Reflexivity

Some patients, when confronted with a major life disruption, may need to clarify their expectations and relations with other individuals in their lives, adjust to transitional roles, identify maladaptive communication styles, and find social support to deal with novel roles (IPT, FT). However, in our relentlessly changing, quick-paced, self-centric world, we must learn to ensure that the parts constituting our selfhood also have good relations (interself). Within our interiorized personal universe, our "I's" and "me's" must also adapt to disruptive status changes that demand different responses. We need to mourn the loss of obsolete roles and adopt the appropriate skills to develop new ones. Hyper-interiorized self-reflexivity, then, results from problems between the "I" and "me." These two parts of the self should be regarded as two "persons" who are in a dynamic, dialogical relationship, sometimes consensual and cooperative, but at other times conflictual and confrontational. As among individuals, relations between the "I" and "me" can be ambiguous.

In the Gestaltian tradition, cultivating intersubjectivity (mutual, reciprocal emotional influences between the therapist and client, which implies a search for shared meanings) and dialogue (inclusion and empathetic engagement) are key. However, just as important for self-healing is the eliciting of different "persons" of one's selfhood (i.e., "I" and various "me's") and ensuring they are communicating with each other. The exchange of information should involve not just thoughts, but also deep and intense emotions that have not been adequately acknowledged (EFT). We also need to encourage different components of ourselves to speak emotionally with one another. We should go beyond learning to verbalize and identify our experiences as physiologically registered emotions so as to bridge the deep chasm of the psyche and corporeality (mind-body dualism) (GT). The complex interplay between "I" and "me" is an example of how the mind is a self-regulatory system. Growth oriented, it is inherently self-adjusting and self-correcting (GT).

Self-reflexivity raises difficult existential questions that can only be asked and addressed when we find the courage to stand outside ourselves, i.e., meta-frame ourselves beyond our present circumstances. We often need to distance ourselves from our inner experiences and adopt the stance of the observer ("I") (ACT). The fear of isolation, death, meaninglessness, freedom, and decision-induced panic can be better dealt with when our "I" comes to terms with what our "me" is anxious about (past behaviors, perceived faults and failings, etc.). Emphasizing an interself perspective allows us to become reacquainted with ourselves and learn to like as well as trust ourselves and our decisions (EXT). Instead of controlling or avoiding unwelcome feelings or thoughts (experiential avoidance), we must notice, accept, and perhaps even whole-heartedly embrace disturbing private parts of ourselves (the creative uses of anxiety, depression, and regret) (ADT; dialectical behavior therapy, or DBT). This can be done by surprisingly simple activities such as spending quality "alone time" with ourselves.

Self-Deception: How the "I" Fools the "Me"

Discussing how he had used alcohol and drugs to mitigate his pain, a patient pointed out how he had blocked out attention to what he needed to accomplish on a daily basis. "I brainwashed myself," he told me, anesthetizing himself with the "narcotic of self-deception" (Goleman, 1985, p. 14).[8] Another patient said that self-deception was like "putting a sticker over an engine light that suddenly comes on while you're driving." Self-denial is an analgesia; it is not just a form of self-distraction; it become addictive and habit forming. Another patient mentioned how he "couldn't see myself coming" and "had trouble getting out of my own way," meaning he could not discern how his own deep-rooted, unquestioned assumptions were hindering sound judgment.

Regardless of Freudianism's many failings, its great contribution to psychology was to delineate defense mechanisms that in many ways overlap with the trickery of self-deception (for Harry Sullivan, Freud's defense mechanisms were "security operations"). Goleman lists defense mechanisms that aid in self-deception: (1) reversal, or what is so is not the case; the opposite is true; (2) projection, or what is inside is cast outside; (3) isolation, or to experience events without feelings; (4) rationalization, or making excuses; (5) sublimation, or replacing the threatening with what is safe; (6) selective inattention, e.g., "I don't see what I don't see"; and (7) automatism, e.g., "I don't notice what I do" (Goleman, 1985, pp. 120–123) (see Glossary for more defense mechanisms).

The other great insight of Freudianism is the recognition that we are inherently complicated, conflicted, and inscrutable beings. We all know that with people, "what you see is rarely what you get." This is neither a negative nor positive observation, but a clear-headed recognition of the deep complexity and richness of each individual. We are full of contradictions. This is not surprising. But what is remarkable is how cunning we are at nonconsciously rationalizing away inconvenient truths, denying the evident, and mendaciously fooling ourselves. If the real world cannot be altered by one's actions, then we landscape our introceptual terrain. Those burdened with addiction issues often have great insight into their rationalizations: "I thought I deserved to abuse [substances] because I had been behaving myself for so long"; "I thought I could get high without the lifestyle." "I'm unique" is a common defense mechanism, sometimes heard by those suffering from substance use who did not see the need for treatment.

"Why can't you just admit to something so obvious? Who are you trying to fool?" Such questions we aim at others, often intimates, who deny what to us are objective facts. We all engage in small doses of self-deception; it protects us from uncomfortable truths and the harsh, judgmental demands of self-honesty. However, when relied on too much, self-deception produces psychopathology (delusions) as well as ideological, political, and institutional mendacity. For some of us, our predisposition to self-deception is grounded in our tendency to exaggerate and stretch the truth to such a degree that we often end up fooling ourselves.

Often an individual deceives others because she or he is self-deceiving. When a person consciously and intentionally deceives others, the event (i.e., lying) is usually straightforward. However, the act of self-deception is more insidious; it is not apparent to the person lying to themselves—obviously—and quite often, it is not clear to individuals surrounding the self-deceiver. It is not a matter of "games people play," but rather "games people play with themselves." Deceiving others and deceiving oneself are often entangled, i.e., engaging in one makes committing the other all that easier. If you cannot be honest with yourself, being honest with others soon loses its appeal, and vice versa.

Whether at the interpersonal or interself level, dishonesty frays the lines of communication. In any social interaction, three lines of communication need to be clear of "noise." The first is interpersonal: person A to person B. The second and third lines are intrapersonal (interself): "I"-to-"me" of person A and "I"-to-"me" of person B.

Self-Deception as Part of the Machinery

The mind, I heard more than once from patients, is an "excellent server but a terrible master." According to one individual, the "mind is vicious. It plays tricks on us." Another said the "mind is a dangerous thing," since it is apt to fool us. Self-deception occurs for a number of reasons. The first is due to the very design of the human neuropsychological apparatus itself, which facilitates self-deception. Different parts of our psyche can fool other parts, indicating that an individual's mind is anything but singularly unified. It runs on multiple, parallel tracks. This is the consequence of the expediencies of bioevolution which put together an ad hoc, improvised mechanism. Given the mind's inherent complexity due to the many tasks it must fulfill, multi-tracked processing is its default mode. Minimally, the mind's multifaceted nature might lead to being conflicted about an important life decision. However, this divided nature, if taken to extremes, leads to misinterpretation (cognitive shifts) or even psychotic fragmentation. While most therapeutic approaches acknowledge the mind's parallel processing, the cognitive therapies (CBT, REBT, ACT, DBT) explicitly recognize that the same mental complexity that allows us to adapt can lead to maladaptive responses.

The second reason, related to the first, is how psychological complexity makes us mysteries to ourselves. We hardly know ourselves since most of our lives are lived with only a vague awareness of the vast number of socializations and re-socializations that constitute our oceanic, nonconscious storehouse of knowledge. Consciousness does not automatically shine a light on the darker corners of our mind; that is not its primary purpose. FOCI must be explicitly engaged and, if in a clinical setting, more clearly directed to therapeutic effect. After all, we expend great effort in building ramparts and fortifications on the contested terrain of our minds to guard against painful and distressing assaults. The role of a therapist is to question whether the battlements and barricades are always such useful expedients; a therapist must allow everyone their say and work on cautiously discerning what they actually might mean.

The third reason concerns how the mind works hard to short-circuit apprehension, shame, guilt, and sundry stresses. Anxiety generates noise and static that hinder the rational and healthy reappraisal of situations. But self-deception promotes a trade-off between anxiety and attention. It "compromises full, unflinching attention" (Goleman, 1985, p. 54).

The fourth reason involves the rearranging of the "good-me," "bad-me," and the "not-me" to our liking (Goleman, 1985, p. 104). Any information that threatens cherished self-definitions or does not confirm our preferred narratizations that afford us meaning are shoved aside, perhaps even suppressed. This is why events and past experiences are selectively remembered, reinterpreted, and excerpted. If perception is the filtering of the tremendous amount of incoming information that our sensorium unloads on us, cognition is the sifting of this flood of data. However, our cognitive systems are not neutral, impartial systems, but are shaped by personal, social, and political forces.

How Individual Self-Deception and Institutional Mendacity Interlock

Living for one year in China as an exchange student not too many years after it had emerged from the horrors of the Cultural Revolution (1966-1976) demonstrated to me the human predilection to accept dubious truths spun by authorities. I was struck by how individuals would deny what seemed to be blindingly obvious. Officially sanctioned falsehoods and half-truths have a way of feeding self-deception at the individual level. This explains how social structures, whether in other places or in our own culture, can be maintained.[9] The bending of reality by the power elite and authoritative figures is the fifth reason self-deception occurs. It is so much easier to let others do our thinking for us.

Self-deception, then, operates simultaneously at the level of the individual and in the collective awareness of the group. Moreover, group membership establishes a tacit agreement neither to notice personal feelings of uneasiness or misgivings nor to question anything that challenges the authorization of the group (Goleman, 1985, p. 13). The "we" is as vulnerable as the self to deceptions. The "conglomerate mind" has properties of the individual mind. Groups, whether small-scale (e.g., families) or large-scale (organizations), operate like a consensual mind; they gather information, interpret it, and then distribute instructions, directives, or policies (Goleman, 1985, p. 166). Members, imbued with "we-feeling," mutually self-justify and persuade each other of the official narratives. An arrogance emerges, as do ethical blinders and "unstated belief" in the rightness and morality of a consensual decision (Goleman, 1985, p. 188). Group coziness results in unanimous decisions, and suppressed personal doubt transmutes into self-imposed censorship. Group members take it upon themselves to sanitize information so that it conforms to the collective view. Members are put under pressure to avoid expressing dissenting views.

Shared illusions arise for the same reason individual ones do—to minimize anxiety. Consequently, a two-tiered communication system operates: (1) an overt one dealing with the ostensible mission of the group; and (2) a covert one, "bearing on the unspoken—though commonly understood—anxieties of the group" (Goleman, 1985, p. 163). The dark side of socioaffiliation is seen in how loyalty to the group overrides prudent decision-making. What does not fit in with the collective mind-set is deemed unacceptable. Once a decision is reached, it becomes the group's choice, conveniently allowing individuals to disavow personal responsibility. This often leads to "groupthink" when leaders make what are in retrospect irrational, misinformed, and costly decisions. Critical thinking is sacrificed on the altar of group cohesiveness.

"Honor the Resistance"

Whatever one may think of psychodynamically inspired theories, resistance—as an (often) nonconsciously motivated defense mechanism—is a notion all therapists at some time encounter. We should expect it and should be aware of the various manifestations it might take. Rather than dismissing resistance, which is a type of self-deception, therapists should recognize it as a behavior that if properly handled, can lead to productive outcomes. Resistance, or anything that hinders fixing our problems due to (often nonconscious) motivations, should be regarded as a natural reaction.

Obviously, not participating in one's own recovery is a clear sign of resistance, but as a "bodyguard of the ego," dragging one's feet can express itself in a variety of subtle ways: sarcasm, insensitive jokes, and run-of-the-mill rudeness and incivility are often motivated by resistance. Resistance includes arguing and expressing hostility; inappropriate humor; reticence and being overly reserved; being late; being emotionally absent; overreacting to minor slights; forgetting; talking too much and stealing the spotlight; attempting to control the direction of discussion; changing the topic; responding with superficial answers; challenging the group leader; omitting possibly relevant information; shifting attention/deflection; providing overly abstract, intellectualized answers; prefacing statements with qualifiers ("I agree but ..."); and body language (where one sits in the room or if one's words are incongruent with one's gestures and demeanor).

When confronted with resistance, a therapist needs to adopt a position of calm impartiality, neutrality, and objectivity. No matter what form it takes, resistance should be expected. According to Corey, in a group setting, resistance is a "healthy sign of a group's movement toward autonomy" (Corey, 2012, p. 465). If it is suspected that an individual is self-deceiving, a therapist might ask, "It seems to me that perhaps you're not thinking deeply about why you might have said what you said. Could I suggest to you a reason why I think you feel the way you do?" A therapist might ask if other members would like to comment on what a particular member stated, gently recommending that perhaps they could consider ways in which a member might not be revealing all aspects of a situation.

Taking Stock

This chapter has investigated how conscious interiority, which ordinarily possesses an adaptive benefit, can go awry and require corrective measures. This point can be better appreciated if we look at the modern history of psychotherapy since the latter was an attempt to alleviate psychic disturbances. The next chapter, in order to better appreciate the advantages of FOCI, traces how the development of psychotherapies can be understood as the increasing conscious interiorization of various treatments.

Notes

1. But note that even during "turbulence," the lower levels of routine-maintenance mental activities still operate behind the scenes nonconsciously. They are never "switched off." In other words, "pilot cognition" is built upon neurocultural scaffolding—it does not replace reactive cognition but complements it (here "pilot" does not mean "executive operations" and does not refer to a supervising self, ego-in-chief, or elf ensconced in the head working the controls).

2. But see Jaynes's discussion of "aptic structures" (1976). These innate, evolved organizations of the brain are "meant to replace such problematic words as instincts." Aptic structures "make the organism apt to behave in a certain way under certain conditions" (Jaynes, 1976, p. 31). Such structures are activated during a critical period during the developmental course when an organism is susceptible to specific environmental triggers. Human language is probably a constellation of aptic structures.

3. Though often associated with Anglo-American political economic thought, broadly understood individualism can be thought of as a historical feature of modernization.

4. A dissociative state is characterized by a loss of continuity in subjective experience (disturbance in self-narratization).

5. See McVeigh (2006b) for a detailed treatment of the theoretical implications of the "I" and "me."

6. Originally developed within the context of FT.

7. Interestingly, some people with ADHD complain of hyper-focusing, or becoming so absorbed in an activity that it interferes with daily activities (though currently hyper-focusing is not accepted by all as a bona fide symptom of ADHD).

8. Self-deception and its more severe clinical cousin, self-delusion, have been dealt with recently in Ariely (2012); Baghramian and Nicholson (2013); Bayne and Fernandez (2008); Bortolotti and Mameli (2012); Egan (2008); Fernandez and Bayne (2008); Gerrans (2013); Lazar (1999); Levy (2008); Lynch (2013); McKay and Dennett (2009); Mele (2006, 2007); Michel and Newen (2010); Nobuhara (2014); Pacherie, Green, and Bayne (2006); Trivers (2011); Van Leeuwen (2007, 2013); Wolpert (2008). For reviews of early works and how self-deception and institutional mendacity interlock and reinforce each other, see McVeigh (2002, 2006a).

9. Working for many years in Japan's higher educational system also taught me how dysfunctional institutions encourage a strange self-deception among those who work in them (McVeigh, 2002).

5

A Brief History of the Interiorization of Psychotherapy

The history of consciousness began approximately three thousand years ago. Though a baseline of FOCI has been in play ever since, the particulars of place and period have seen the strength of certain features vary somewhat throughout the centuries. But by the late eighteenth century the scientific advances of the European Enlightenment had eroded the older religious certainties. In reaction to this cold and methodical dissection of nature and the human body arose Romanticism. This development reminded thinkers of older spiritual traditions that imbued the person with latent, mysterious powers. But now, empowered with a sense of unbridled freedom, these potentialities became forces waiting to be let loose from within the individual. Meanwhile the more communal ethos of older social arrangements decayed, assaulted by the politico-economic revolutionary fervor of the late 1700s and early 1800s. This strengthened self-individuation; indeed, the inner contents of the individual increasingly have become the focus of intellectual attention. How all this relates to the development of the systems of psychotherapy is the topic of this chapter.

The Predecessors to Psychoanalytic Theory

The vague boundaries of the mysterious introcosmos, originally and deeply associated with age-old religiosity, began to be investigated and delineated systematically in the 1800s. Renamed the "psychological," this new spatiality became the testing ground for attempts to heal what used to be called the soul but now is referred to as the mind. In addition to the natural-science-based psychiatry and the work of alienists and neurologists, a less medically intrusive but nevertheless revolutionary endeavor of healing the mind—psychotherapy—began to survey the psyche. The "talking cure," a descendant of the older confessional "cure of the soul," offered a map to the labyrinthine and rough mental terrain of the distressed. Psychotherapy's explosive trajectory illustrates how, beginning in the late 1800s, more and more attention has been paid to the interior, invisible, and introspectable dimension of the human condition. Over the decades, psychotherapy itself has become more and more interiorized.

By the late nineteenth and early twentieth centuries, stunning technoscientific breakthroughs and bewildering social complexity began to stretch the capabilities of the human psyche. And the noisy disruption caused by industrialization and the ultra-efficient communications of the information-saturated postindustrial age—dominated by social media that infects the world with an unsettling hyper-reality—continue to burden our cognitive apparatus. The response to all this commotion was an intensification of FOCI as people scrambled to keep up with the dizzying changes. The advances of the psychosciences evidence this.

The Psychoanalytic Discovery of the "Psychological"

Sigmund Freud (1856-1939) is arguably credited with much more than he deserves. In any case, since we take for granted the idea that each individual possesses a hidden introcosmos that deserves investigation on its own terms, Freud's crucial contributions are easy to overlook. Well trained in neurology, he realized that mental problems are not necessarily organic in origin. He appreciated that disturbances in the "psychological" realm—the interiorized dimension of human existence that in Freud's time was not as explicitly recognized as it is today—require subtle interpretive methods, rather than just blunt medico-psychiatric approaches.

Though arguably Freud was a brilliant synthesizer and effective purveyor of ideas, like all great thinkers he adopted and adapted to the prevailing developments of the late 1700s and 1800s. For example, a bedrock notion for psychoanalytic thought is that a cauldron of boiling primitive forces, unknown to us, lurks deep within the psyche and is waiting to burst forth. Resonating with this are the "drives" (*Triebe*) of the psychiatrist Heinrich Wilhelm Neumann (1814-1884). These animalistic impulses wreak havoc if disturbed, as do the passions of the psychiatrist Karl Wilhelm Ideler (1795-1860). Such disruptive sentiments need to be provoked to rebalance mental imbalances. The physician Johann Christian Reil (1759-1813), who coined "psychiatry" (*Psychiatrie* in German), recognized psychic healing as a branch of therapy in its own right. Johann Christian August Heinroth (1773-1843) was arguably the first psychotherapeutically inclined psychiatrist. He divided the personality into the ego (mind, emotions, will), *Fleish* (basic drives, which include our sinful nature), and *Über-uns* ("above us," which means reason or a path to God). He thought of *Gewissen* (conscience) as a "stranger within our ego." Romanticist philosophers such as Friedrich Wilhelm von Schelling (1775-1854) were attracted to hidden but motivating powers below conscious awareness. The physiologist Carl Gustave Carus (1789-1869), who viewed human life as incessant self-destruction and self-construction, was probably the first to pioneer a comprehensive theory of unconscious psychological processes. It was not so much that the unconscious, a cavern dark and deep, was being discovered during the nineteenth century; rather, as the torch of conscious interiority grew brighter, a place to consign all those mysterious forms to which the light of awareness could not penetrate was required. Of relevance here is the philosopher Eduard Von Hartmann (1842-1906), who penned the highly influential *Philosophy of the Unconscious* (1884).

Also of significance during this period was the great interest in the shadowy world of dreams. The physician Ignaz Paul Vital Troxler (1780-1866) conceived dreaming as a deeper level of mentation that occurs even while we are conscious. The physician Gotthilf Heinrich von Schubert (1780-1860) also devoted considerable attention to the symbolism of dreams.

The "classical" Freudian tradition (or psychoanalytic psychotherapy, PAT) assumes significant childhood events and experiences lead to unresolved conflicts that can endure over a lifetime. Tensions are symbolically articulated in fantasies, wishes, and dreams. That the formation of the mind is intimately linked to past experience and that our actions are shaped by our early years may seem commonsensical. While the notion that "the child is the father of the man" was certainly appreciated in the past, for some it may only have been more of an intuition and it was not as explicitly acknowledged as it is today. Understanding repressed experiences is therefore key to evaluating present functioning.

Freud postulated that the personality has three aspects. The first is the id, or the instinctive, primitive part of the psyche. It contains biologically inherited components of personality, including the life instinct (Eros, which contains the sex drive or libido) and the death instinct (Thanatos, which can manifest itself through aggression or compulsion). The superego functions as the self-critical conscience in that it reflects social standards and norms learned from parents, teachers, and other authority figures. Standing between the impulsive, unrealistic id and the moralizing, idealistic superego is the ego, which attempts to mediate between the desires of the id and the aspirations of the superego. It adheres to the reality principle, making meta-framed decisions that satisfy the id's childish impulses and the superego's officious admonishments, sometimes compromising or delaying gratification to avoid the sanctions of society. In Jaynesian terms, the ego is the conscious, self-reflexive facet of selfhood that monitors our behavior, while the superego is the aspirational "I" that inspires us to self-improvement. The id is what is often suppressed.

Despite its flawed concepts—psychosexual stages, penis envy, Oedipus and Electra complexes, etc.—PAT has played an immensely influential role. Many later developments in psychotherapy were elaborations, modifications, corrections of, or reactions to, PAT. For example, Carl Jung's (1874-1961) "analytic psychology" dispensed with the questionable aspects of Freudianism and regarded the libido as a positive life energy that aided individuals in their journey of (self-) individuation. Though some of his ideas about the "collective unconscious" and "archetypes" were infused with mysticism, Jung's system is imbued with a positive orientation. Alfred Adler's (1870-1937) "individual psychology" explored the social dynamics behind personality formation, recognizing that people are primarily socioaffiliative beings. Rather than focusing on what has happened to a person, Adler believed that individuals are motivated more by their expectations about their future than by their past.

PAT, then, has played a central role in the history of psychotherapy. Its many derivations, which for the sake of convenience can be called "psychodynamic psychotherapies" (PDT), lack some of the stricter parameters of PAT (long-term, more intensive treatment, opened-ended or no set termination date). Though cognitive, behavioral, and humanistic approaches have made very significant contributions, it is worth remembering that major notions of psychoanalytic thinking still undergird key concepts in psychotherapy. Many present-day therapists may not be interested in Sigmund Freud or psychoanalytic theories given their serious theoretical flaws. Nevertheless, they most likely have utilized basic psychoanalytic concepts (Corey, 2012, p. 126). To some degree, then, psychoanalytic assumptions guide the practice of many clinicians, though they may not necessarily explicitly employ Freud's notions.

It is Freud's view of the individual psyche as inherently complex, many faceted, multilayered, and messy that needs to be embraced. The psychoanalytic tradition demands that we adopt a hermeneutical method, since people are symbol manufacturing, meaning making, and open to change. PAT's contribution can be distilled down into: (1) resistance; (2) the impact of our past experiences; (3) (counter)transference; and (4) the unconscious. Though Freud himself did not "discover" the unconscious, he did innovatively work it into a therapeutic framework. The unconscious became more salient during Freud's lifetime not because he "discovered" it. Rather its shining counterpart, conscious interiority, started to draw more attention among the psychologically minded in the late nineteenth century. In any event, PAT, since it views people as confused, inscrutable beings, still has something to offer. Consider dream analysis. Though many are skeptical (rightfully so) about this technique, it is not necessarily the contents and their meaning that matter. Rather, it is the emotional tone of dreams that might afford clues to the therapist about what is occurring in a patient's life, as it is widely believed that dreams express wishes, hopes, or fears.

Neo-Psychoanalytic Thinkers

A long list of thinkers maintained core elements of classical psychoanalysis. To the extent that it had become widely accepted that interiorized entities played a role in individual behavior, it is worth mentioning other key contributors to the basic psychoanalytic endeavor. These include Ernest Jones (1879-1958), the biographer of Freud. Abraham Arden Brill (1874-1948) was a prolific writer who helped spread Freud's ideas in America. Hans Sachs (1881-1947) was interested in links among aesthetics, literature, and psychology. Helene Deutsch (1884-1982) was notable for her work on the psychology of women and schizoid and borderline personalities. Theodor Reik (1888-1969) was a loyal advocate for psychoanalysis in America. Sandor Rado (1890-1972) questioned some of Freud's ideas and saw the latter's approach as too formal and caught up in past experiences. He viewed his own "adaptational psychology" as an elaboration of the id concept. Franz Alexander (1891-1964) held the first university chair in psychoanalysis at the University of Chicago. He utilized "corrective emotional experiences" by having patients relive past events. Karl Menninger (1893-1990) recognized the emotional aspects of medical diseases within a Freudian framework. Otto Fenichel (1898-1946), an extremely prolific writer, attempted to clarify Freud's core concepts. Frieda Fromm-Reichmann (1899-1957) advanced our understanding of countertransference.

The "neo-Freudian social theorists" minimized instinctual deficiencies and gave less attention to the past. Their important contribution was to analyze the role of interpersonal relations in the organization of personality and mental disorders (Millon, 2004). Karen Horney (1885-1952) downplayed biological determinants and pursued studies in character analysis (e.g., narcissistic, perfectionism, vindictive sadism). Erich Fromm (1900-1980) focused on the role of societal influences on mental disorders and posed challenging questions by looking at psychological health from a social philosophical perspective.

The "neo-Freudian ego-analytic theorists," while maintaining the role of inborn sexual instincts, proposed the existence of constructive ego instincts that enable an individual to develop and mature. These theorists adopted a more positive approach than classical psychoanalysis. Mental disorders are not due to instinctual conflicts, but arise because adaptive ego capacities fail to develop properly (Millon, 2004). Anna Freud (1895-1982), working with children and adolescents, focused on issues of the maturation of drives and ego functions, adaptation to the environment, and the organization and integration of conflicts and troubling experiences (Freud broke his own rules and had Anna become his analysand). Heinz Hartmann (1894-1970) stressed how autonomous inborn capacities develop in parallel to the primitive drives of the id. Ernest Kris (1900-1957) further developed psychoanalytic ego theory, and David Rapaport (1911-1960) was concerned with the autonomy of the ego (self-autonomy). Erik Erikson (1902-1994) investigated his own self-identity (self-individuation) and came to recognize the inherent, positive, and enabling capacities of individuals ("ego strength"). He developed a more sophisticated sequence of development than Freud's emphasis on psychosexual stages.

Other thinkers of the psychoanalytic approach include Donald Winnicott (1896-1971). He worked in pediatrics and formulated what he called the "false self" to describe the detached and emotionally distant personality ("I" alienated from "me"). Margaret Mahler (1897-1985) explained how psychotic children fail to individualize their identities (thwarted self-individuation and self-autonomy). Michael Balint (1896-1970) and John Bowlby (1907-1990) both worked with children and made contributions to developmental models. Balint examined what he termed the "basic fault," i.e., having missed a crucial socializing experience during the first year of life (1948). John Bowlby (1907-1990), in his work on "attachment learning," stressed the importance of having healthy and stable early relationships. Heinz Kohut's (1913-1981) is notable for many influential contributions on self-psychology. He advocated the value of empathetic "vicarious introspection," i.e., viewing matters from the patient's perspective. He saw the importance of intersubjectivity and sensing the interiorized consciousness of others.

Object Relations Theory

Melanie Klein (1882-1960), a child psychoanalyst, developed "object relations theory": inner templates organize personality and shape perceptions and reactions to future interpersonal dynamics. Such unconscious images and assumptions can be reactivated later in life. Object relations theory is premised on the idea that, rather than instinctive, libidinal, or aggressive motivation, what drives people is their search for satisfying personal relationships with significant others (usually parents). These become represented by internalized objects (real or imagined). Such representations form during developmental sequences in which a person expands their recognition of others. Individuals pass through stages of symbiosis, separation, (self-)individuation, and integration. The aim of therapy is to identify the internalized objects within the patient and ensure healthy socioaffiliation. William Fairbairn (1889-1964) theorized that individuals do not develop properly if "infantile endopsychic objects" do not unfold in a healthy manner due to dissocialization. These prewired, unlearned, universal, and unconscious representations resonate with Jung's collective unconscious. Edith Jacobson (1897-1978) attempted to integrate object relations and the more classical Freudian notions of instinctual drives. Otto Kernberg (1928-) worked to synthesize the object-relations perspective with classical psychoanalytic drive reduction.

Behaviorism: Discarding Introspection and Conscious Interiority

Defining psychology as the denial of mental processes that motivate observable behaviors seems decidedly unpsychological. But for a number of years during the first part of the twentieth century, not a few researchers delighted in dismissing any talk of "inner" occurrences as misguided mysticism. It was behavior, or the prediction and control of an organism's activities by inventorying environmental stimuli, that mattered.

Behaviorism developed from research in learning by the neurologist Vladimir M. Bekhterev (1857-1927) and the physiologists Ivan M. Sechenov (1829-1905) and Ivan P. Pavlov (1849-1936). But broader intellectual trends of the times, such as hard-nosed materialism, no-nonsense reductionism, and commonsensical practicality, emboldened thinkers to attempt to radically redefine psychology as the study of inputs and outputs, as if the individual were void of any trace of subjectivity or sentiments. It was as if the pendulum of the mind-body debate had swung to the external end (observable bodily behaviors) and became stuck there.

The most vocal proponent of behaviorism was John Watson (1878-1958). He made the conditioned reflex a central concept, discarded introspection, and put the "science" into the science of behavior. As if to underline the point that anything associated with the inner realm—conscious interiority—was rejected, he went so far as to deny a role to physiology. Also of relevance here is Edward Thorndike (1874-1949), who pursued work in learning and educational psychology. Despite Watson's pivotal role in spreading the faith of behaviorism, credit should also go to the "forgotten man" of psychology, Knight Dunlap (1875-1949). Though he was the first to systematically use behavioral and learning theories, Dunlap's contributions were outshone by the irrepressible and controversial Watson (though the latter acknowledged that Dunlap convinced him of the value of behavior as the primary unit of psychology) (Millon, 2004, pp. 333, 358). The radical behaviorist and social philosopher B. F. Skinner (1904-1990), one of the most influential psychologists ever, theorized about operant (or instrumental) conditioning and environmental histories of reinforcement that shape behavior. A denier of free will, he believed that if environmental influences could properly be configured, then all aspects of an individual's behavior could be controlled.

From Objective Behavior to Subjective Experience

A number of therapeutic traditions, inspired by behaviorism, evolved from defining behavior as purely observable to something introspectable and occurring mentally, in a place in which an individual can "conscious-ize" and virtually simulate behaviors. Below I offer a cursory review of this intellectual trajectory.

The Legacy of Behaviorism and Neo-Behaviorism

Despite the powerful sway of behaviorism, some innovatively modified its rigid view that no mental or internal springs triggered or shaped behavior. Some attempted to bridge the gap separating internal, covert mind from external, overt behavior. These attempts would lead to what can loosely be called cognitive behaviorism. The neo-behaviorist Clark Hull (1884-1952) saw an important part for biology. From our physicality are created needs, that in turn lead to drives which activate goal-oriented activities that ensure the survival of the organism. For Edwin Guthrie (1886-1959), all learning was based on a stimulus–response association. Neal Miller (1909-2000), who pursued work in biofeedback, acknowledged the role of cognitive expectancies and self-reinforcing thought patterns. Edward Tolman (1886-1959) did not deny internalized thought processes; he saw a role for intervening variables that bridge external stimuli and overt responses. Our behavior is guided by internalized "maps." Importantly, he acknowledged that our actions are not completely determined by past influences but are goal-directed ("purposive behavior"). John Dollard (1900-1980), along with Neal Miller, attempted to translate classical psychoanalytic concepts into Pavlovian and Hullian learning theory. Jules Masserman (1912-1990) linked psychoanalytic concepts to experimentally conditioned and induced neuroses. Andrew Salter (1914-1970) developed "conditioned reflex therapy." He focused on teaching patients to view assertiveness as a positive goal, and self-expression (self-autonomy, self-individuation) as a way to improve personality traits. Joseph Wolpe (1915-1997) developed systematic desensitization to treat what was known as "war neurosis" (PTSD). Hans Eysenck (1916-1997) believed that some anxieties and neuroses are biologically based. Adopting an anti-psychoanalytic agenda, he viewed neurotic symptoms as simple learned habits. Julian Rotter (1916-2014) worked on social learning theory and "locus of control," i.e., the degree to which individuals believe that they, as opposed to uncontrollable external forces, possess control over the outcome of events in their lives (self-autonomy). Albert Bandura (1925-), regarded as one of the most influential psychologists, made pioneering contributions to social learning theory (or social cognitive theory), imitative modeling, self-efficacy, and "vicarious conditioning." Arthur Staats (1924-) integrated Gestalt cognitive principles into social behaviorist theory.

Behaviorism certainly made important contributions, such as tightening up methodology and forcing researchers to carefully define and refine their theoretical constructs. These positives live on in mainstream psychological research. However, having incorporated the advances of cognitive behaviorism, the "cognitive revolution" of the late 1950s and early 1960s centered the pendulum somewhere between the extremes of invisible mental processes and observable bodily behavior.

The history of behavior therapy (BT) can be viewed as developing in three waves. Each one has seen BT become more sophisticated, as it has conceptualized cognition as behavior that is interiorized. The first wave attempted to stay true to behaviorism's founding principles that inner experience, so difficult to measure, was not amenable to serious scientific investigation. First-wave BT was about modifying observable behaviors rather than internal, private events (some accepted the idea of "act or behave in a certain way first, then motivation or inner change will follow"). Second-wave BT sought to replace self-defeating thought patterns with self-enhancing thinking and is illustrated by cognitive therapy and cognitive behavior therapy (CBT).[1] Albert Ellis's rational emotive behavior therapy (REBT) and Aaron Beck's cognitive therapy are examples of the second wave, as is Donald Meichenbaum's (1977) stress inoculation training (SIT). Given the many commonalities found among the second-wave therapies, I subsume them under a "general cognitive therapeutic paradigm." Third-wave therapies grounded in BT became even more interiorized, with their focus on mindfulness, acceptance, and self-awareness (ACT, DBT).

The First Wave of Behavior Therapy

Grounded in behaviorism, BT has offered therapists powerful interventions that are scientific, measurable, and effective. It is difficult to deny BT's practical success and impact on later developments (e.g., it inspired cognitive behavior therapy, though the latter, unlike classical behaviorism, acknowledges internal mental processes and mediating events). BT has become more sophisticated over the years, defining behavior more broadly as anything that helps the organism adapt to changing circumstances, e.g., motor activity, physiological responses, emotions, and cognitions (Antony, 2014, p. 193). Whether visible or invisible, behavior is how we meet the demands of survival. Behavior can be defined as something an organism does to adapt to a challenging, problematic, and dynamic environment; traditionally it connoted something observable and concrete. But most of our behavior is not apparent or easily quantifiable since it is covert and interiorized, i.e., mentalized behaviors or only what can be witnessed by the mind's eye.

The Second Wave of BT: Cognitive Behavior and Rational Emotive Behavior Therapies

The key insight of the general cognitive therapeutic paradigm is that the true cause of an individual's problems is viewed as adherence to dogmatic and irrational beliefs, often resulting from runaway FOCI (Chapter 4). Cognition, emotion, and behavior are intrinsically integrated so that thought distortions, affective disturbances, and maladaptive actions interact and reinforce each other. Other important insights are: (1) adversities often contribute to consequences, but then so do our beliefs; (2) although distorted, maladaptive outlooks sometimes can be traced to childhood and adolescence, and the focus should be on how irrational beliefs continue to maintain distortions; (3) modifying dysfunctional thoughts requires work and practice. The aim is not just about feeling better, but getting better in a more profound manner.

The general cognitive therapeutic paradigm is shaped by what might be called postmodern thinking, but in fact resonates with increasing conscious interiorization: (1) challenged by so many interiorized realities (due to self-individuation), it is difficult to be confident about any absolute certainty; (2) our views about good and bad, right and wrong, are socially *and* subjectively constructed; and (3) given that we are confronted with so many opinions solidified by interiority, we have no absolute way of knowing which goals and purposes are better or worse (again due to self-individuation).

CBT and REBT have strong empirical support. They are pragmatic, focused, and see little need to use valuable session time having patients meander down irrelevant paths or encouraging them to unnecessarily ruminate and stew in their own negative emotions. In this regard, they differ from earlier forms of PAT or PDT. Employing various methods to help clients achieve basic cognitive changes, CBT and REBT aim to alter an individual's belief system and values. They eclectically rely on numerous techniques from many sources.

Compared to psychoanalysis, person-centered, and more humanistic therapies, the general cognitive therapeutic paradigm is less interested in past events. It focuses on what thoughts, emotional reactions, or activities reinforce or maintain current dysfunctional thinking and behaviors.[2] And unlike some other talk therapies, the general cognitive therapeutic paradigm is less concerned with unconscious motivations. While the psychoanalytic approach assumes that the patient can only indirectly access unconscious patterns of thought, the general cognitive therapeutic paradigm operates with the premise that the unconscious can often be readily and directly accessed.

Third-Wave BT: Acceptance and Commitment and Dialectical Behavior Therapies

Third-wave BT carried interiorization even further, partially inspired by Asian religio-philosophical traditions (especially Buddhism) that put much stock in mindfulness and self-awareness. Marsha Linehan's (1943-) dialectical behavior therapy (DBT), originally developed to treat borderline personality (1993), balances the need to change with acceptance of the way things are. Steven Hayes's acceptance and commitment therapy (ACT)[3] shares key philosophical premises with DBT. People readily engage in cognitive fusion, i.e., they become entangled with their thoughts and assume that how they feel is inevitable and that their actions are dictated by their mind. Making efforts to control thoughts and emotions actually makes psychopathological tendencies worse. Patients need to learn to be comfortable with being uncomfortable. Rather than attempting to somehow shun or dismiss unwanted thoughts or feelings (experiential avoidance), patients are taught to accept rather than judge. "Acceptance" does not mean being resigned to one's fate, and "commitment" is about discovering and enacting one's values (self-reflexivity). Looking at things as neither good nor bad and recognizing the downside of automatically meta-framing (thought processes about thought processes) can lead to insight. In other words, patients are asked to take note of or even embrace disturbing sentiments; they adopt the viewpoint of an impartial observer ("I"), watching the noisy, and often disturbing, parade of thoughts march through one's mind. Patients are encouraged to allow their concerns to inform one's thinking and to "embrace one's fears." As one patient put it, "I embraced my depression and it became my friend."

Simply stated, while CBT attempts to teach patients how irrational or dysfunctional their cognitions can be, third-wave therapies show clients how avoidance of negative feelings can lead to other problems. An acceptance of distress itself can lead to change. Symptom relief is an incidental, happy by-product of such accommodation of emotions. Indeed, according to ACT, many psychotherapies, in their attempt to alleviate suffering, actually end up exacerbating symptoms.

The Humanistic Tradition

Behavioral, cognitive, and psychoanalytic theories (and the latter's various derivative psychodynamic systems[4]) dominated the early days of psychotherapy. But another tradition, the humanistic, emerged and challenged their very premises of a pathological view of the patient. This tradition is hopeful, present-focused, and resonates deeply with PPT. It is inspired by the assumption that all people have the capacity to be self-determining (self-autonomy) and for our purposes subsumes client-centered (or person-centered), existential, and Gestalt therapies. Such approaches share a respect for the client's subjective experience—the curative power of conscious interiority—and a trust in the client's capacity to make positive and constructive choices. They emphasize a vocabulary of freedom, choices, values, personal responsibility, purpose, and meaning. The humanistic tradition is a loose confederation of approaches, and significant differences divide Gestalt, existential, and client-centered therapies. For example, while existential therapy takes the position that humans are faced with the anxiety of creating a never-secure identity in a world that lacks intrinsic meaning, client-centered counselors stress self-actualization (self-individuation).

Client-Centered Therapy

A "lost soul is still a soul." This captures the spirit of client-centered therapy (CCT), which, though subsumed under humanistic psychology, is called the "third force" that challenged the premises and prevalence of psychoanalysis and behaviorism. The client-centered counseling of Carl Rogers (1902–1987) is grounded in the goal of self-actualization, which is the innate predisposition to develop all of one's capacities for the maintenance and growth of personality. At the heart of CCT is the belief that the patient is not passive but active, motivated by an organismic valuing process that moves toward wholeness and integration (Rogers, 1957).

CCT, as a part of the humanistic perspective, is very much a "self" approach that, rightly or wrongly, puts much stock in the inner life of the individual and makes phenomenological experience the epicenter of therapeutic focus. Indeed, for client-centered therapists, "reality" is understood as the interiorized private world of the individual. The individual client, rather than the therapist, is positioned center stage. It is the client, as a self-regulating, self-righting, self-healing agent who, possessing an actualizing predisposition (motivation), is in an important sense responsible for their own treatment.

Arguably neglected sometimes in the more strident forms of psychoanalysis and behaviorism, the multidimensional "person" is positioned front and center as a complex, self-determining, and self-realizing agent (self-autonomy). Such person-ness is often hidden behind guarded defenses, reactive resistance, and maladaptive coping maneuvers. Resonating with this client-centered orientation is positive psychology; e.g., self-conscious awareness can override maladaptive thinking and negative as well as external social influences (an understanding that demands an appreciation of multicultural factors, MCT). The idea is to afford the client a sense of dignity, understood here not as a respect for others in the legalistic, pro forma sense, but rather in the spirit of a more direct, individualized, and empathetic connection with others. Client-centered therapists are wary of treatment metaphors inspired by the medical model that reduce the person to a diagnosis or disease (hence in this section on client-centered therapy my use of "client" rather than "patient").

Stating that each individual is a unique constellation of traits and experiences sounds clichéd and commonplace. Nevertheless, given the accelerating techno-bureaucratization of postmodern life and the ever-growing weight of government pa-perwork and the profit-driven insurance industry, the general principle of regarding the client as possessing self-authorization and self-autonomy is therefore essential to any therapeutic endeavor and increasingly has special relevance. And just like the client, the therapist also possesses reality as a person. The role of the therapist is to be transparent, nonjudgmental, open and honest, direct, and clear, and to sustain an engaged, authentic curiosity. If helpers can accept clients, the latter are more likely to accept themselves.

As the pace of history increases, whether due to rapid technological changes, the erosion of values, disintegration of the traditional family, economic dislocation, or simply a cornucopia of overwhelming choices and an overly convenient lifestyle, the groundlessness of human existence spreads alienation. Perhaps this is why Carl Jung once claimed that more than thirty percent of his patients were in therapy because they lacked personal meaningfulness. If this is the case, the general principles of an existential approach have much to offer. This is the topic of the next section.

Existential Therapy: Confronting the Downside of Conscious Interiorization

All centuries can be characterized as being "long" in that they brought in their train, each in its own way, great changes. But the nineteenth century does seem particu-larly lengthy. Industrialization dislocated and disrupted socioeconomic classes and statuses; technologization shrank time and space; science promised heaven on earth while disenchanting us from the natural world; and politics, in a race to keep up with a new system of machine-driven wealth redistribution, increasingly allocated power based on "individual rights." Meanwhile, the old certainties of collectivist belonging were swept aside. While religious institutions lost members, the masses invested their faith in new forms of salvation revolving around selfhood. The soul was explained away, but it was unclear what was to replace it.

It is not surprising that out of this boiling cauldron of alienation and disaffection arose an aching for the surety of definite and reassuring answers. Our place in the universe was questioned, as was the very definition and meaning of being human, now coldly and clinically dissected like a cadaver on the table of science. An exis-tential worldview was forced to acknowledge our self-responsibility for defining and determining individual destiny and identity (self-autonomy, self-individuation, self-authorization). Epitomized by the likes of the philosopher Søren Kierkegaard (1813-1855), who bravely plumbed the depths of inner experience and explored the significance of our mortality, existentialism dared to pose probing and disturbing questions.

Best considered as an approach to understanding the human-ness of our humanity, EXT takes the consciously interiorized experience of being human seriously. Individuals are centers of subjectivity that need to be interpreted. The basis of this therapy is phenomenology, or the direct study of introceptual experiences. Rather than pathologizing or euphemistically rewording in impersonal clinical terms the human reaction to a world of suffering and our inevitable demise, alienation and loss are considered part of life and are taken to be meaningful in themselves. As a reaction against both psychoanalysis and behaviorism, the existential approach views humans as free and responsible beings. Humans are meaning-generating, subjects of experience and objects of self-reflection. The existentialist perspective adopts a holistic view, taking into account the different dimensions of human existence: personal, physical, social, spiritual. The goal of EXT is for the client to comprehend their own being and to find healing through the discovery of meaning.

An important existentialist thinker was the psychiatrist-philosopher Karl Jaspers (1883-1969). He stressed the "inexhaustibly infinite depth of and uniqueness of any single individual" (Millon, 2004, p. 139). Jaspers is also well-known for his notion of the "Axial Age" *(Achsenzeit)*. This describes the period from approximately 800 BCE to 200 BCE as pivotal since, from Greece, the Middle East, China, to India, strikingly similar proto-scientific and religio-philosophical ideas emerged that revolutionized our thinking as a species and set history on a new path. The Axial Age is significant because it crystallized consciously interiorizing trends—abstract thinking, existential inquiries, temporal linearity, and other developments of a psychologically infused worldview—that grew out of an earlier preconscious mentality.[5]

The "Four Givens" of Existentialism

EXT views inner turmoil and conflicts as resulting from an individual's concerns and confrontations with the "four givens." Morita Shōma's (1874-1938) choice of calligraphy introduces the first of these givens. A psychiatrist and the developer of Zen-inspired, existentialist Morita therapy, Morita hung calligraphy of the Chinese character for "death" in his office to remind himself of the importance of avoiding the unlived life, i.e., that being in the here and now is in itself life-affirming. An awareness of death exists within each person, but many of us go through our daily routines in denial about our ultimate fate. Contemplating our end may signify a slow-motion adaptation to our gradual but inevitable decline. Death may also be interpreted metaphorically, i.e., as experiencing loss or failure as we age, leading to grief over what we have lost, in physical health, family members, or friends.

The second given is "freedom," a word that usually has positive connotations but actually can be a heavy burden as it strongly implies responsibility and difficult decision-making. In recent times it seems many people are talented at making up excuses for their behavior, a tendency encouraged by modern culture with its promise of technological conveniences that tempt us with short-cuts, speedy resolutions, and a consumerist throw-away attitude. Freedom can lead to apprehension and fear, but

EXT accepts these uncomfortable feelings as "normal" anxiety, as a part of the human condition. A healthy level of apprehension has the ability to promote personal growth.

Erich Fromm (1900–1980), a witness to the horrors of war and the near collapse of European civilization in the 1930s and early 1940s, saw three destructive types of "escapes" from the fear of freedom. The first is authoritarianism, or a dangerous and unhealthy willingness to slot oneself into a rigid hierarchy. This shifting from self-authorization to being authorized by others surrenders difficult decisions to charismatic leaders who propose fundamentalist political or religious ideologies. The second route of escape is destructiveness or attacking others, especially "outsiders" perceived as weak (denying their self-individuation, self-autonomy, or self-authorization). The final exit from hard choices is robotic conformity, or allowing others to define one's identity, social roles, and selfhood. Consequently one gives up one's self-autonomy and self-authorization. Fromm also distinguished between the dichotomy of "to have" (possessions, ownership of goods) and the more existentialist "to be"; this means to transcend earthly material limitations and engage meaningfully with others and one's authentic self.

Describing her loss of spirituality, a patient once told me, "I was like a fish gasping for air." This vividly captured her feelings of meaninglessness, or the third given, and it is here that Viktor Frankl's (1905–1997) logotherapy is most relevant. This describes, despite the horrors of existence, the grand import of humankind's search for the "will to meaning" (rather than the more impulsively primitive "will to power"). There is nothing academic or abstract about Frankl's challenge to all of us to find meaning in this world no matter our struggles; he himself survived three years in Nazi concentration camps. Frankl recognized the need to develop an authentic relationship between client and therapist. The therapist's openness is considered the crucial quality in building an effective working relationship. He also helped develop the intervention of paradoxical intention, i.e., the deliberate carrying out of a vexing habit or thought in order to identify and remove it.

Living an active life and getting significance out of "nothingness," which seems to be the response of the universe when we interrogate it in our search for some greater purpose, can challenge the most optimistic among us. Many paths lead to a life steeped in significance (being part of a kinship network, career, vocation, education), but finding meaning in relationships is undoubtedly front and center. People need to be connected to something larger than themselves, and for most of us, this is a recognition that we are grounded in a network of other persons (familial, communal, national, religious) with which we share our lives. Humans are inherently socioaffiliative beings whose neurological apparatus has been evolved to operate within a communal context infused with feelings of solidarity and togetherness. The mind is not just a complicated computer; it is configured by the "social brain," designed and wired by evolution to coexist, cooperate, and interact with others.

The final given is isolation. This may take the form of alienation from others, loneliness, or disaffection from the world at large. Luis Binswanger (1881–1966), arguably the first "true" existential therapist, emphasized the role of self-identity (self-individuation). He postulated three modes of existence. The first is *Mitwelt*, meaning the interpersonal, social contextual realm; it concerns one's relationships with other people. The second is *Umwelt*, or the world as experienced in biological and physical terms; it involves one's relationship with the environment. The third, *Eigenwelt* or "own-world," refers to a person's relationship with himself or herself (self-reflexivity). Of the three worlds, one's own-world can be identified with conscious interiority, describing as it does the individual's inner phenomenological experience.

Other notable existential therapists include Eugene Minkowski (1885-1972), who recognized the value of highlighting an individual's inner experience and subjective processes, and Medard Boss (1903-1991), who recommended that clinicians avoid abstract constructs and directly focus on the interpretation of immediate experience. He attempted to integrate Freudian methods with the philosopher Martin Heidegger's (1889-1976) ideas about Being. Key therapists who have carried on the EXT tradition include Rollo May (1909-1994), who warned clinicians against taking a neutral stance during therapy and advocated for the necessity of adopting clear values. Though considered an existentialist, May adopted a humanistic perspective in how he recognized the destabilizing power of deep-seated drives. He believed that rather than transcending, individuals must engage and confront the "daimonic" (from the ancient Greek, meaning both divine and evil forces), whether articulated as unconscious or conscious motives (Millon, 2004, p. 153). The sensitive and inspiring works of Irving Yalom (1931-) also contain humanistic elements. His discussion of the "core" of therapeutic change (what he originally called "curative factors") highlights interpersonal learning, group cohesiveness, catharsis, and existential factors. These "therapeutic factors" resonate with CFs. Yalom also explained the processes common to all group therapeutic approaches.

Gestalt Therapy: Peeling Back the Layers of Conscious Experience

Gestalt—a perceptual whole or unified configuration of experience—indicates the fundamental premise behind GT: humans (like all entities, animate or inanimate) are parts of systems, nodes in dynamic, interacting networks. This approach points to the significance of being sensitive to context, a holistic perspective, and what it means to be embedded in social relations (hence similar to systems theory in family therapy). GT is inspired by a postmodern process-based perspective premised on an interrelated organism-environment field that is composed of mutually interdependent elements. A concrete example of this is the notion that there is no self without the other, or that others define the self. This self-with-other, person-in-relation approach resonates with the theologian Martin Buber's (1878-1965) "I-Thou relationship" (EXT). The bodily oriented (e.g., deep breathing) approach of GT heralded the transition in psychotherapy's goal from the intellectual endeavor of insight to the sensate-focus of body awareness (Yapko, 2012, p. 516). Though the experiential perspective is at first blush perceptual, I contend that its self-focused subjectivity makes it in many ways introceptual.

In their work with GT, Fritz Perls (1893-1970), Laura Perls (1905-1990), and Paul Goodman (1911-1972) synthesized a variety of intellectual developments of the mid-twentieth century, such as existentialism (themes of meaning of life, death, authenticity, freedom), phenomenology (which assumes that subjective experience—conscious interiority—is central to our nature), and humanism (Perls, Hefferline, & Goodman, 1973). Though in some ways a derivative of psychoanalysis, GT adopts a much more optimistic view of human potential, an appreciation of how relations can heal, and a focus on what role conscious awareness itself can play in therapy (i.e., awareness does not always disguise deeper, dark motivations).

Taking Stock

This chapter historically contextualized the relation between conscious interiorization and the emergence of various treatments and interventions. A problematic aspect of the history of psychotherapy has been how—and when—to diagnose. Some behaviors, though apparently anomalous, may be beneficial to an individual. When I was young, some relatives became deeply involved in a Christian group that practiced "speaking in tongues" (glossolalia).[6] After witnessing the behavior firsthand, I wondered where these lines should be drawn between "normal" (nonpathological) versus "abnormal" (pathological) behavior. This is a problem that any clinician faces. Though clearly some presentations are pathological, many occupy a gray area. Matters become especially complicated if a behavior appears to be benign and functions as part of a culturally acceptable array of beliefs. These issues raise a number of questions, such as when to diagnose and how to classify mental health disorders.

In the next chapter I explore issues of categorization, as well as the value of acknowledging the role of mental well-being in a "complete state model" of psychic health, treatment selection, and how this all relates to FOCI.

Notes

1. The lines are blurry between cognitive therapy and CBT, and for the sake of convenience I will conflate the two.
2. Though CBT does not completely ignore the past, the CBT practitioner, if not careful, may overlook salient experiences. Despite its serious failings, psychoanalysis does have a point, i.e., there are cases when the contents of the unconscious are not necessarily so easily revealed due to the repression of past trauma. There are probably situations when the well-trained therapist should *not* take at face value what the patient is saying, i.e., assume that he or she is using language to conceal the "real" problem. While for many patients, a focus

on the present can be more beneficial, in some cases, the past does significantly impact the present.

3. ACT is inspired by relational frame theory, which understands psychopathology as a consequence of taking language literally, as well as avoiding the experiences of thoughts and feelings that are negatively evaluated.

4. These have diverged from their original ideas to the point where they are no longer unified approaches.

5. See McVeigh on the "Jaynes-Jaspers thesis" (2016a, pp. 125-127, 193).

6. Jaynes offers an explanation of this phenomenon (1976, pp. 357-360).

PART III

THE MEANING OF MENTAL HEALTH AND HOW THE PSYCHE ADJUSTS

6

Treating Mental Illness and Facilitating Mental Well-Being

Diagnosing Mental Illness: Classificatory and Interdisciplinary Challenges

Despite good intentions and years of painstaking research behind the compilation of the state-of-the-art "Bible" in psychiatry, the DSM-5 (American Psychiatric Association, 2013) has its limitations, as does any nosological system.[1] For example, some clinicians view kleptomania as part of the obsessive-compulsive spectrum of disorders, reasoning that many individuals experience the impulse to steal as an alien, unwanted intrusion into their mental state. But other evidence indicates that kleptomania may be related to, or is a variant of, mood disorders, such as depression. Also note that depression, anxiety, eating, and substance use disorders are common in individuals with kleptomania.

Another challenge concerns how a single etiological factor can present very different symptoms. At the same time, different etiologies can manifest themselves in similar symptoms. The linkage between cause and effect is often unclear (A to B or B to A?), and any number of factors, such as individual idiosyncratic reactions to treatment, can confound the complex relationship between origin, pathogenesis, what triggers or exacerbates an illness, and presentation. Comorbidity only adds further confusion, as pointed out by Mittal et al. (2006) and Sar et al. (2006).

Valid and reliable assessments must be utilized before labeling a patient with a diagnosis, and historical patterns of misdiagnosis cannot be overlooked; thus the need for clinicians to seek consultation and to be aware of their own biases that hinder proper diagnosing. Also, the tension between universalistic and particularistic approaches calls into question attempts at classification. Nosology is a nomographic exercise. However, since a mental disorder carries a particular meaning for an individual (configured by sociocultural context, personal experiences, and family dynamics and support or its lack), the value of idiographic approaches also needs to be taken into account.

Despite the aforementioned challenges, nosology is crucial—not just because an agreed-upon system of ordering and organizing mental disorders makes matters convenient for clinicians, practitioners, and insurance companies, but because it affords rigor to theory construction. As in physical illnesses, accurate diagnoses can make all the difference between negative or positive outcomes.

The nature of mental well-being and how it relates to issues of diagnosing, positive psychology, and FOCI will be explored in this chapter.

Mental Disorders in Historical Context

I do not claim that FOCI emerged as a tonic for mental disorders. Instead, I argue that FOCI developed as adaptive capabilities to handle increasing social complexity. And like many adaptations, FOCI are a double-edged sword. Despite their benefits, FOCI can spiral out of control (hyper-consciousness) and end up hindering cognition and even aggravate an already existing mental disorder. Indeed, Jaynes suggested that some mala-daptive behaviors, such as "neurotic" behaviors, are "disorders of consciousness" (Jaynes, 2012a, p. 319).

Since I am treating FOCI as facilitators of mental health, it is worth at least bringing up the issue of the nature of mental disorders in preconscious times (before ca. 1000 BCE). The evidence is sketchy. For example, ancient Mesopotamian and Egyptian texts (e.g., the *Ebers Papyrus* from ca. 1550 BCE) *appear* to mention mental disorders. However, references are so ambiguous and imprecise that it is very difficult to discern which disorders they might correspond to in modern times. If we jump to the conscious Greeks, matters become clearer, with Hippocrates (ca. 460-370 BCE) addressing more recognizable ailments, notably "hysteria" and "melancholia."

It is a fascinating question as to what degree, throughout the centuries, historical context has constructed, modified, or exacerbated mental health disorders. Psychopathological conditions result from a combination of predisposing, precipitating, perpetuating, and protective factors (American Psychiatric Association, 2013, p. 19). How the vagaries of history configure such conditions is exceedingly complex, but arguably for certain mental disorders predisposing factors are transhistorical (genetics, organic diseases), as are precipitating elements (immediate catalysts). The social milieu of particular historical periods can significantly shape definitions and perceptions of mental disorders. For example, consider the labels of what is now termed traumatic brain injury. In World War I it was called "shell shock," while in World War II it became postconcussional syndrome (Jones, Fear, & Wessel, 2007). Though perhaps implicit, these different names possess various associations (e.g., the organic or psychogenic debate) that influence therapy regimens and how veterans are viewed by the public.

Some sociohistorical conditions have no doubt perpetuated mental disorders.[2] This is why

significant societal changes contribute to the development of new forms of psychopathology, symptoms, and syndromes that call for new forms of psychotherapy offering slightly different mechanisms of change. Social constructionists would argue that psychopathology and psychiatric diagnoses are also prone to "fashion" in various historical periods, because social processes contribute to the construction of certain syndromes and prevalent forms of pathology. (Jørgensen, 2004, p. 534)

Note that FOCI themselves can be too much of a good thing, snowballing and exacerbating a mental disorder. At the same time, certain protective factors (strong community support, advances in medicine, institutionalized care) work to ensure mental health. One can debate the reasons behind the proliferation of mental disorders and mental illnesses (e.g., profit-driven pharmacological and insurance industries, over-diagnosing, unhealthy lifestyles), but an increase in conscious interiority may be one factor. In other words, we pay a price for an enhanced subjectivity that is more sensitive, easily perturbed, and requires more self-care.

Here I am only delineating some problems that require further examination, but I conclude this section with two points: First, discussions of mind-body dualism are absent from texts predating the first millennium BCE. This makes sense because nonconscious individuals could not possibly conceive of an abstract, introspectable mind-like entity that is somehow opposed to their physical being (despite very questionable translations of archaic texts using "mind"). It was not until the splitting of the psyche from the soma during the early to mid-centuries of the first millennium BCE that mind-body dualism emerged, and even then a modern, clear-cut, Cartesian version of mind-body dualism was lacking.

The second point also relates to the sundering of psyche from soma. With the mind/soul detached from our corporeality, another related duality developed—the mind/soul itself was divided into what is introspectable (conscious and known) and what is invisible (unconscious and unknown). By the late nineteenth century, what was invisible was linked to our physical and animalistic nature. While antecedents of the introspectable-invisible duality suggest themselves throughout the centuries, it was not until the 1800s, as FOCI became even more sharpened, that the conscious-nonconscious division became well defined.

Therapeutic and Paratherapeutic Interventions

The therapeutic endeavor is grounded in the attitudes and approaches that we ordinarily take vis-à-vis others in more mundane settings. Indeed, we can speak of a continuum of therapeutic, paratherapeutic, non-therapeutic, and anti-therapeutic (anything that threatens the healing endeavor). Therapeutic and anti-therapeutic are easily understood, as is non-therapeutic. The paratherapeutic, however, is notable in how it partakes of both therapeutic and non-therapeutic features. For example, the daily routines, schedules, activities, etc., seen in mental health facilities and therapeutic communities are both therapeutic and paratherapeutic. Self-help groups, such as Alcoholics Anonymous (AA), Narcotics Anonymous (NA), etc., though technically non-therapeutic, are arguably paratherapeutic. In this context we might mention psychoeducation, an adjunct to therapy, that provides patients with information in order to facilitate change. Topics include parenting, obesity, smoking, medication management, and skills training on specific areas.

The key difference between ordinary social communication (everyday behaviors) and therapeutic communication (counseling methods) is that the latter is intended to reach deeper levels of understanding where hopefully insight and profound change can transpire (cognitively, affectively, and behaviorally). Such transformations ideally lead to obtaining certain goals. The key traits needed for effective therapy—being flexible, accommodating, warm, friendly, trustworthy, respectful, honest—are actually everyday attitudes and behaviors welcomed by all of us. However, within a therapeutic context, therapists must be more attentive to them, so that they acquire a more concentrated form. It is crucial to go beyond abstract definitions of these concepts and to regard them as concrete behaviors with practical applications. A whole range of "everyday" activities are in fact key ingredients in therapy. These include attending behavior; conveying interest; paying close attention; giving encouragement; and paraphrasing. These all increase the comfort level of patients and let them know that they are in a safe place. We employ these techniques every day, but in a therapeutic setting, clinicians need to be better at what might ordinarily be regarded as niceties.

The Dimensionality of Mental Disorders

Building upon the dimensionality approach to diagnosis of the DSM-5 (rather than the earlier more categorical system), Buser (2014) proposes "eight primary psychiatric spectrums" of mental illness. He points out that mental illnesses overlap and exist on a continuum and are not an either/or phenomenon (psychopathology is a matter of states, not traits). The question should not necessarily be if an individual has been diagnosed with a certain mental illness, but rather to what degree a disorder manifests itself.

On each spectrum the majority of people fall somewhere in the middle range of "normality" most of the time. At the extremes, matters become problematic and diagnosable (Buser, 2014, p. 27). Buser's approach resonates with positive psychology because an individual displaying too few desirable characteristics of the spectrum may have problems just like the person displaying excessive features (i.e., an individual diagnosed with a mental illness) (Buser, 2014, p. 28). An advantage of this paradigm is that it destigmatizes mental illness because we can all be placed on a continuum (Buser, 2014, p. 27).

In Buser's approach, diagnoses do not necessarily map neatly on to each spectrum. For example, ADHD and obsessive compulsive disorder (OCD) are positioned on the same spectrum, though the DSM-5 categorizes them as belonging to completely different groupings. While anyone may have features associated with the eight primary spectrums of mental illness, this is not true for what he labels "specialty areas": disorders under trauma and stressor-related; neurodevelopmental; neurocognitive; dissociative; somatic; eating; elimination; sleep; sexual; gender; and paraphilia. So although these can be conceptualized along a spectrum in terms of degree,

Buser does not include them among the eight primary spectrums (Buser, 2014, p. 87). Below I summarize Buser's eight spectrums.

(1) Depression: Amount of Sorrow—Major Depressive, Persistent Depressive, Disruptive Mood Dysregulation, Premenstrual Dysphoric Disorders

At the shallow end, individuals will have limited or no introspection (self-reflexivity) and are indifferent. At the other extreme, an "endless brooding sort of introspection" and "ceaseless ruminations and regurgitations of the past" (hyper-interiority) characterize severe depression (Buser, 2014, p. 36) (Figure 6.1). Experiences falling mid-range constitute the "normal" emotions, such as sorrow and sadness, and a "reasonable degree of interiority" (Buser, 2014, p. 37). Such life experiences allow the development of empathy and healthy character formation.

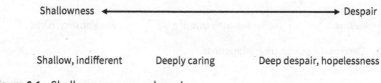

Figure 6.1. Shallowness versus despair.

(2) Mania: Creativity Scale—Bipolar I, Bipolar II, Cyclothymic Disorders

Individuals suffering from full-blown mania obviously require a diagnosis (though many non-hospital-based clinicians rarely see florid mania because it often leads to hospitalization). But at the other end of the spectrum are people whose affect is flat and have low energy, lack creativity, and *joi de vivre*. In-between are individuals who make it a point to enjoy themselves and display their creative side (Buser, 2014, p. 43) (Figure 6.2); they spontaneously engage in meta-framing, reframing, and feel comfortable with hypothetical, as-if experiences.

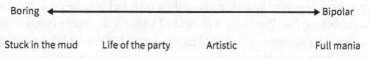

Figure 6.2. Boring versus bipolar.

(3) Anxiety: Amount of Vigilance—Disorders of Generalized Anxiety, Separation Anxiety, Panic, Social Phobia, Specific Phobia, Selective Mutism, Agoraphobia

The diagnosis of anxiety disorder is very common. Confronted with something that triggers apprehension, an individual poorly selects (mis-excerpts) from their train of thoughts those that justify and exaggerate their fear. A vicious cycle is established: anxiety, distorted cognition, and increased anxiety (hyper-interiorization, which might lead to arousal of the autonomic nervous system, i.e., fight, flight, or freeze response). Overcharged emotions affect selectivity of attention so that concentration becomes over-focused. At the other end of the spectrum are individuals who are reckless (Buser, 2014, pp. 48-49) (Figure 6.3). In the middle of the spectrum are those who can enjoy living without being either panicky or imprudent; they have just the right amount of vigilance necessary for daily living.

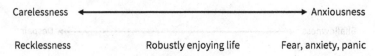

Figure 6.3. Carelessness versus anxiousness.

(4) Psychosis: Intensity of Dreams and Visions— Schizophrenia, Schizophreniform, Schizoaffective, Brief Psychotic, Delusional Disorders

Psychosis is the "hardest one in which to identify a range of normal expression" (Buser, 2014, p. 53). Psychosis relates to what Fonagy et al. have termed "psychic equivalence mode," in which "feelings and fantasies are experienced as reality and not as mental states representing reality" (2002, p. 199). Buser suggests that we change "how psychotic are you?" to "how strong are your dreams and visions?" In this way a spectrum begins to emerge (Buser, 2014, p. 53). At one end are those who lack vision and inspiration; perhaps their "as-if" function operates minimally. At the other end are those who struggle with delineating the line between reality and the less than real. They experience intense and sometimes overwhelming eruptions from hidden parts of the psyche. These may take on a life of their own and may be considered alien to the individual's psyche. Psychosis is associated with extraceptions (such audiovisual hallucinations are instances of vestigial bicamerality).[3] In the middle part of the continuum are experiences that can be personally profound, meaningful, transformative, or even sacred (Buser, 2014, p. 53) (Figure 6.4). Therapists need to be especially

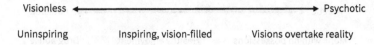

Figure 6.4. Visionless versus psychotic.

sensitive when working with patients who have strong spiritual encounters or have experienced benign hallucinations so as not to impose their own worldview.

(5) Focus: Amount of Focusing Ability—Attention Deficit/Hyperactivity, Obsessive Compulsive Disorders

Sustaining appropriate attention and concentration means striking a balance between not being able to focus (ADHD) and excessive focus (OCD). Whether constantly distracted or lacking the ability to change one's focus of attention (hyper-interiorized concentration),[4] properly attending to environmental and internal stimuli is a case when excerption goes awry (Figure 6.5). Well-regulated concentration and engagement are needed to mitigate boredom, anxiety, and depression, while anhedonia, apathy, boredom, multitasking, and restlessness are largely manifestations of disrupted attention that characterize many mental illnesses (McCormick, Funderburk, Lee, & Hale-Fought, 2005).

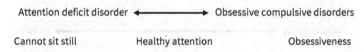

Figure 6.5. Attention deficit disorder versus obsessive compulsive disorders.

(6) Substance Abuse: Amount of Pleasure Seeking/Addictiveness—Substance-Related and Addictive Disorders

A healthy enjoyment of life requires steadying oneself between an abstinent, frugal, and Spartan existence versus a hedonistic, self-indulgent, and debauched lifestyle. The latter depictions fit in with a loss of self-autonomy. One patient, describing how he rediscovered his self-worth through self-control, said, "I realized I was bigger than a can of beer." Many psychologically distressed individuals try to conquer their unhappiness by pursuing more and more pleasure (hyper-hedonia). However, we cannot alter our capability to experience pleasure due to built-in genetic features (Kahneman et al., 2006). Living in moderation means not denying or disavowing psychic elements that need expression (Figure 6.6). We are all familiar with the holier-than-thou

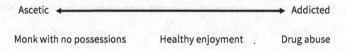

Figure 6.6. Ascetic versus addicted.

television evangelists and self-righteous politicians who publicly rebuke immorality (Buser, 2014, p. 69). These are individuals who have not regulated their desires properly and have been overtaken by them. What is needed is a transcendence of polar opposites, despite their contradictions, until their conjunction emerges and a third, meta-framed element appears (transcendent "I"; cf. JT's "transcendent function").[5]

(7) Autism: Degree of Connectedness to Others

Individuals who are poor at social communication and interpreting social cues (not just of others, but of themselves, i.e., impaired conscious interiority) are diagnosed with autism.[6] Such individuals also have a strong proclivity to engage in overly ritualized behaviors. The opposite of such a description are those who are enmeshed in relations and exercise an overbearing control of others (Figure 6.7). Or they have problems with self-governance (self-autonomy) and become codependent on others. But healthy relations demand holding the middle ground between being too connected (enmeshed) and too unconnected (detached).[7]

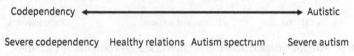

Figure 6.7. Codependency versus autistic.

(8) Personality: Amount of Blame Cast to Others—Antisocial, Avoidant, Borderline, Dependent, Histrionic, Narcissistic, Obsessive Compulsive, Paranoid, Schizoid, Schizotypal Personality Disorders

Individuals with personality disorders cannot see their own role in their problems (lack self-reflexivity) and do not learn from negative experiences.[8] They continue with socially maladaptive behaviors, either blaming others or themselves for their problems. Often, those who come in for treatment are more interested in fixing others (including their therapist) and not themselves. At one end of the "blame" spectrum are individuals who all too readily find fault with others (externalize blame; an overdeveloped sense of self-autonomy). At the opposite end are those who are full of

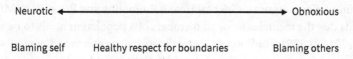

Figure 6.8. Neurotic versus obnoxious.

self-reproach, self-accusation, and excessive and misappropriated guilt (internalize blame; underdeveloped sense of self-autonomy) (Figure 6.8). People diagnosed with a personality disorder have locus of control issues (external or internal). Because their psychoscape is restricted, rigid, and inflexible, they cannot easily hypothesize better solutions to their problems.

The Complete State Model: Well-Being versus Illness

Two approaches are crucial for appreciating health from a comprehensive perspective: the pathogenic, which views health as the absence of disease or disability, and the salutogenic, which acknowledges the presence of positive abilities (Keyes, 2014). In the context of mental well-being, Keyes introduces the "complete state model," consisting of the *presence* of positive states of human capacities and functioning (flourishing) as well as the *absence* of disease or infirmity (psychopathological perspective) (Keyes, 2005, pp. 539; 2014). It is not so much a matter of "health *or* illness" but rather "health *and* illness" (Keyes, 2005, p. 539). Various writers use different terminology, but for my purposes "mental health" is a composite of mental illness (or its lack) plus mental well-being (or its lack).

To specify the elements of the complete state model, Keyes suggests dual continua. The first is mental well-being: high mental well-being versus low mental well-being. The second is mental illness: high mental illness versus low mental illness (Keyes, 2014). Different permutations of what the two dimensions produce when combined can be described. The overriding point is that the "absence of mental illness does not imply the presence of mental health" (Keyes, 2014, p. 182). And to go one step further we can posit that, somewhat counterintuitively, the "presence of mental illness does not imply the absence of mental health" (Keyes, 2014, pp. 182-183; see also Keyes, 2009). This view challenges the "dominant assumptions of the medical model and promotes a dimensional, rather than dichotomous, understanding of mental health and mental illness" (Linley et al., 2009, p. 35).

Because mental illness and mental well-being belong to separate dimensions (though highly correlated), preventing and treating mental illness will not necessarily lead to more mentally healthy individuals (Keyes, 2002, p. 220). Typically, treatment targets persons with mental illness, risk-reduction prevention targets those vulnerable to mental illness, and mental health promotion targets those with good mental health and those with less than optimal mental health (Keyes, 2014, p. 180). With this in mind, Keyes argues for Mental Health Promotion and Protection (MHPP) and contends that the mental state of all members of a population needs to be addressed (Keyes, 2014, p. 179). Traditional mental illness interventions and mental well-being interventions (positive psychology) should both be considered.

Many focus on the importance of preventive medicine for physical health (dieting, nutrition, exercise, avoidance of dangerous substances); we should do the same for mental health. Besides genetic, constitutional, and temperamental predispositions, a number of risk factors (aggravating stressors in the social environment) can trigger or exacerbate mental disorders. For example, childhood abuse and physical neglect have a significant effect on the development of borderline personality disorder, while emotional neglect has a significant effect on the development of dissociative disorders (Sar et al., 2006). The question then becomes how to cultivate protective factors that afford the individual resilience. PPT offers a rich cornucopia of answers and suggestions (Lopez & Snyder, 2009; Compton & Hoffman, 2013). Cultivating FOCI not only aids in the self-repair of mental health, but also can act as a preventive measure. And since FOCI are learned, they are inherently malleable, making them excellent points of entry for the interventions of positive psychology.

Therapeutically Focused FOCI and Complete Mental Health

The effectiveness of utilizing FOCI as an intervention tool to improve mental health (i.e., treating mental illness *and* enhancing mental well-being) probably varies depending on the severity of mental illness, i.e., the more severe, the less effective. If we conceive Figure 6.9 as a "map" of complete mental health, we can speculate on where therapeutically focused FOCI are most associated and how FOCI can be used as interventions to bring about improved mental health. This is admittedly speculative, but the point is that FOCI should be regarded as parts of any treatment. Ranked in order of FOCI's treatment effectiveness, these are: (1) flourishing with no mental health illness; (2) moderate mental health with no mental illness; (3) languishing with no mental illness; (4) languishing with mental illness; (5) moderate mental health with mental illness; and (6) flourishing with mental illness (Keyes, 2014, p. 179; 2007).[9]

Psychotherapy Integration and Systematic Treatment Selection

Psychotherapy integration[10] poses the question: which treatment, and by whom, works for a particular individual who has a certain disorder and under what circumstances? (Norcross & Beutler, 2014, p. 500, emphases in original). Though it sounds

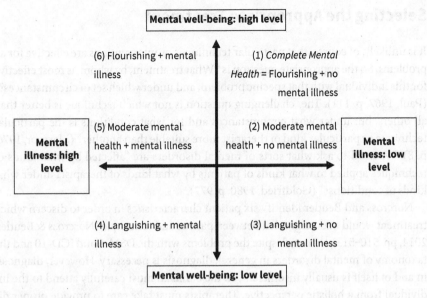

Mental well-being: high level

(6) Flourishing + mental illness

(1) *Complete Mental Health* = Flourishing + no mental illness

Mental illness: high level

(5) Moderate mental health + mental illness

(2) Moderate mental health + no mental illness

Mental illness: low level

(4) Languishing + mental illness

(3) Languishing + no mental illness

Mental well-being: low level

Figure 6.9. Map of mental health.
Adapted from Keyes (2007); modified.

remarkably ambitious, psychotherapy integration is an attempt to tailor therapy to the needs of each patient (Norcross & Beutler, 2014, p. 502).[11]

For their part, Norcross and Beutler combine elements of the four types of integrative approaches (technical eclecticism, theoretical integration, assimilative integration, CFs). They label their approach as systematic eclectic (systematic treatment selection or prescriptive). They attempt to customize treatments and therapeutic relationships to the specific needs of individual patients, as defined by a constellation of diagnostic as well as particular nondiagnostic considerations (Norcross & Beutler, 2014, p. 501). They borrow effective methods from across theoretical schools (eclecticism), match those methods to particular clients using evidence-based principles (treatment selection),[12] and adhere to an explicitly and orderly (systematic) model (Norcross & Beutler, 2014, p. 501). Norcross and Beutler list five principles of their brand of integrative psychotherapy: (1) rather than idiosyncratic theory, integrative therapy is derived from outcome research; (2) all psychotherapies have a place; (3) the patient is more important than their disorder; (4) optimal treatment methods *and* healing relationships (rather than just techniques); and (5) as clients advance through therapy, their progress is tracked and the selection and matching of therapeutic methods evolve accordingly (Norcross & Beutler, 2014, p. 502). Below I describe Norcross and Beutler's systematic eclectic approach because I believe it is built upon the best of traditions of integrative psychotherapy.

Selecting the Appropriate Treatment

It is unlikely, of course, that particular techniques or interventions are effective for all problems. So the appropriate question is "What treatment, by whom, is most effective for this individual with that specific problem, and under which set of circumstances?" (Paul, 1967, p. 111). The "challenging question is not which technique is better than all others, but under what circumstances and for what conditions is the particular technique or particular kind of therapist more suitable than another" (Marmor, 1976, p. 8). We need to ask what sorts of mental disorders are "affected by what kinds of techniques applied to what kinds of patients by what kinds of therapists under what kinds of conditions?" (Goldfried, 1980, p. 977).

Norcross and Beutler identify six patient characteristics in order to discern which treatment would make a good fit between patient and technique (Norcross & Beutler, 2014, pp. 510–513).[13] First, despite the problems with the DSM-5 and ICD-10 and the taxonomy of mental disorders in general, diagnosis is necessary. However, diagnosis in and of itself is usually insufficient, so the clinician must carefully attend to the individual from a holistic perspective. Therapists must take care to provide proper diagnosis of mental disorders, exercising cultural sensitivity, and recognizing historical and social prejudices (some argue that the safety of a patient trumps assigning a diagnosis). Second, a multicultural approach is necessary, as race, ethnocultural background, sexual orientation, gender, disability status, and age may impact coping style, reactance level, and how an individual progresses through stages of change. If a patient is from a culture with which the therapist is unfamiliar, extra attention should be given to diagnosing, and unnecessary pathologizing needs to be avoided. Historical and social prejudices resulting in misdiagnosis of certain cultural groups (especially those from disadvantaged backgrounds) need to be acknowledged (MCT). Culturally "influenced expressions of common mental disorders" (Ancis, 2013, p. 3) need to be recognized, and we cannot assume the criteria of the DSM-5 can be applied to all individuals regardless of culture.

The coping style of patients is the third characteristic. Do they externalize (impulsive, stimulation seeking, extroverted)? Internalize (self-critical, inhibited, introverted)? Do they require symptomatic reduction or what might be called "deeper change"? What is the severity of a mental disorder, and how is it assessed? The number of symptoms? The intensity of symptoms? The impact of symptoms on the quality of life? The likelihood of the illness resulting in permanent disability or death? Moreover, should severity be conceptualized similarly for all illnesses or be disorder specific (Zimmerman, Morgan, & Stanton, 2018)?[14]

A therapist needs to recognize how personal beliefs can affect diagnosis and what in a patient's life exacerbates a disorder. Also, any potential impact a diagnosis may have on a patient needs to be considered. Personal decisions—e.g., to avoid lifestyle choices that lead to stressors—can play a role in controlling mental disorders. From an abstract perspective, we can conceptualize those in need of help as both "subject-patients" (active, agent, self-autonomous) and "object-patients" (passive, victim, controlled by a dysfunction). Certainly cases exist when an individual is clearly the helpless victim of an unforgiving mental disorder. Illnesses happen to people, they are "not willed or induced by motives, attitudes, and the like" (Huemer, Hall, & Steiner, 2012, p. 40).

Fourth, patients with high levels of reactance level need nondirective, self-directed, or paradoxical techniques, whereas those with low levels of reactance work better with more directive techniques. Fifth, a patient's values, personality type, attachment style, and previous experiences in therapy need to be taken into account. Finally, stages of change gauge an individual's readiness to change. This could be understood as a period of time as well as an array of tasks required for making progress to the next stage. Related to discerning what stage a patient is at is the need to determine the degree of insight patients possess vis-à-vis their illness (good, fair, or absent). Such inquiries might be reconceptualized as to what degree is the patient's subject-self ("I") able to monitor their object-self ("me").

Character Strengths and FOCI

Peterson argues that the absence of "character strengths" may be symptomatic of mental disorders, i.e., so why not use the lens of normality to better view abnormality (Peterson, 2006, p. 35)? Relying on Peterson's research, Rashid and Seligman (2014) contend that while the absence of character strengths may not apply to all mental disorders (particularly those such as schizophrenia and bipolar disorder that have clearer genetic markers), a good number of disorders may be understood in terms of underdeveloped strengths as well as the presence of symptoms. For example, "depression can result, in part, because of a lack of hope, optimism and zest, among other variables; likewise, a lack of grit and patience can explain some aspects of anxiety and a lack of fairness, equity and justice might underscore conduct disorders" (Rashid & Seligman, 2014, p. 472).[15]

Certain FOCI resonate with some of Peterson's twenty-four character strengths (which form his classification of "values in actions") (2006). For example, "judgment" (critical thinking or "thinking things through and examining them from all sides") involves selecting out mental representations from one's stream of thought (excerption). This boosts the powers of abstraction and generalization, as well as decisional capabilities, the vetoing of inappropriate impulses, and supporting self-corrective abilities. "Perspective" (wisdom or "being able to provide wise counsel to others; taking the 'big picture' view") demands adopting more roles so as to allow one to adopt the position of others. "Self-regulation" (self-control or "regulating what one feels and does; being disciplined, controlling one's appetites and emotions") overlaps with self-autonomy (self-determination, self-direction, and a sense of control over one's destiny). Self-regulation fortifies one's resilience and self-confidence. "Social intelligence" (or "being aware of the motives and feelings of self and others; knowing what to do to in different social situations; knowing what makes other people tick";

Rashid & Seligman, 2014, p. 471) demands being able to objectively gauge others' behaviors but also one's own, i.e., self-reflexivity and self-distancing between "I" and "me" to enhance self-objectivity.

Limitations of the Therapeutic Applications of FOCI

Here let me stress that hyper-interiorization cannot explain all symptoms, and FOCI may be limited in coping with certain (probably the more severe) mental disorders. And no specific treatment neatly resonates with all the FOCI. Instead, these features of consciousness offer a framework for appreciating how certain mental processes can be helpful. How a practitioner utilizes FOCI will depend on the particular intervention being utilized and the problems being addressed. Of course what the patient brings to the therapeutic encounter also matters.

Ideally, of course, we hope that patients cooperate with their therapists in finding answers and being active participants in their own treatment. Some therapists might want to psychoeducate patients on FOCI. But not all patients are necessarily amenable to being "practical scientists" (CBT's "collaborative empiricism"). Due to life experiences, the local particulars of enculturation, socioeducational background, and personal traits, individuals differ in their awareness and access to their inner subjective world.

In any case, the use of FOCI needs to be tailored to each individual (individual differences in the ability to use mental imagery, self-introspect, excerpt, self-narratize, etc.). Despite the push for manualized treatment, idiographic approaches—each individual possesses a set of idiosyncratic vulnerabilities and sensitivities which should be taken into account when administering treatment—are still optimal (ADT). This means that for purposes of treatment, a patient's coping styles, internalizing or externalizing proclivities, reactance level and resistance, and culture should all be taken into account (PPT). Understandably, some do not want to share everything with their therapists. "The closed mouth doesn't get fed," a patient reminded recalcitrant group members. Indeed, the need to be willing to receive help is vital to recovery.

A therapeutic focus on CFs may be enough for some individuals in the treatment of what might be called "nonspecific" problems of interpersonal relationships. However, such approaches may be insufficient if the nature of the presenting problem is not simply interpersonal or if it is secondary to a severe biological illness (Parloff, 1986, p. 528). As a patient's problems progress in severity, "specific and technical factors become relatively more important" (Jørgensen, 2004, p. 522; see also Crits-Christoph, 1997; Stevens et al., 2000). Nevertheless, even in cases where the diagnosis is critical, nonspecific approaches may provide "relief from the associated symptoms of demoralization and enable the patient to comply with 'specific' psychological or somatic treatment techniques and procedures" (Parloff, 1986, p. 528).

Taking Stock

This chapter looked at the challenges of categorizing and diagnosing mental health disorders and how these relate to FOCI. It also explored the "complete state model" which incorporates well-being as an important construct in positive psychology.

In a group discussion I led at a substance use treatment facility, some preferred to introduce themselves with "I *am* an addict," as it reminded them they have a serious problem; it "kept me on my toes," in the words of one individual. Others found the expression demeaning. They preferred "I *have* an addiction." One member pointed out that he felt he had a repertoire of other roles, such as father, husband, employee, etc., that competed with his role as a substance user. The distinction between the two expressions illustrates the importance of self-labeling and the relation between language and the roles we adopt and how we perform them. It also implicates an important of aspect of mental well-being: the roles we perform, i.e., how the "I" directs the "me." Self-change can be impressive: an individual with a criminal record once told me, "I used to glorify my name in the newspaper when I got arrested. Not anymore. Now I'm ashamed."

The next chapter looks at the nature of self-repair from a dramaturgical perspective while also taking into account the self as something systemized (part of larger systems) and serialized (adapting over time).

Notes

1. Cf. the International Classification of Disease-11 (ICD-11; which mostly aligns with the DSM-5); the Psychodynamic Diagnostic Manual (PDM); the Hierarchical Taxonomy of Psychopathology (HiTOP); Research Domain Criteria (RDoC); and Power Threat Meaning Framework (PTMF).
2. For histories, see Millon (2004); Scull (2015); and Zilboorg and Henry (1941).
3. Extraceptions are a subtype of superception. Psychoses seem to be a disturbance of processes of superception. Perhaps delusional disorder (for individuals who have distorted beliefs but otherwise have preserved functioning) describes some type of abnormal introception.
4. Note that the DMS-5 does not categorize attention deficit hyperactivity disorder and obsessive compulsive disorder together. The former is a type of "neurodevelopmental disorder," while the latter falls under "obsessive compulsive and related disorders" (which also includes excoriation, trichotillomania, body dysmorphic, and hoarding disorders).
5. Note the relevant term "enantiodromia," or a phenomenon whereby any force that manifests in excess inevitably produces its opposite at the unconscious level.
6. A neurodevelopmental disorder.
7. Not "disconnected," as this indicates that an individual was at one time socially connected.
8. "Personality" implies persistent traits that are stable over time.
9. In another version we have: (1) complete mental health (flourishing); (2) incomplete mental health (languishing); (3) complete mental illness (floundering); and (4) incomplete mental illness (struggling) (Slade, 2010; see also Slade, Oades, & Jarden, 2017).

10. Variously called eclecticism, treatment adaptation, responsiveness, prescriptive therapy, and matching.

11. Given the proliferation of techniques and therapies, Marquis (2009) offers suggestions for using an "integral taxonomy of therapeutic interventions" and cautions against the "tyranny of technique."

12. Relevant here are Goldstein and Stein (1976) who published *Prescriptive Psychotherapies*, which argued for applying different treatments for people depending on their particular problem. Arnold Lazarus (1932–2013) advocated eclecticism with his "multimodal therapy" that matched treatment techniques to the patient's problems (1976, 1981).

13. Besides the role of patients, the type of diagnosis also makes a difference. After all, each disorder possesses its own cognitive specificity as well as a cognitive profile.

14. Zimmerman, Morgan, and Stanton contend that because the functional impact of symptom-defined disorders depends on factors extrinsic to those disorders (e.g., self-efficacy, resilience, coping ability, social support, and cultural and social expectations), the severity of disorders should be defined independently from functional impairment (at least for depression and personality disorders) (2018, p. 258).

15. Their argument is summarized in an extensive chart listing twenty mental disorders called "Major Psychology Disorders and Dysregulations of Strengths" (Rashid & Seligman, 2014, pp. 472–476).

7
The Nature of Self
Systemized, Serialized, Dramatized

Some roles are assigned, or at least feel as if they are: "I felt like a mule, a beast of burden," said someone complaining of how he felt that his efforts as a worker to support his family went unappreciated. Attempting to convey his feelings of how institutionalization had shaped his self, another patient told me regretfully that "I have a prison personality." In a group a member listed the various identities he had or that had been assigned to him, as if taking an inventory of scripts: "I've been an addict, dope fiend, recovering addict, substance user, substance abuser, and junkie."

Other roles we adopt. Explicitly expressing a personal role can be liberating: "I'm an eagle, not a pigeon. I like to fly alone"—said by a particularly introverted patient articulating his preference not to associate with others. He claimed he functioned best when allowed to freely move about. "I'm a street warrior!" proudly claimed another when confronted with why he allegedly displayed aggression toward another patient. One individual, on more than one occasion, talked about the roles he played, alternating between being an irresponsible, immature "little boy" and a responsible, mature "grownup man."

Listening carefully to how an individual describes him- or herself, of course, informs us of what scripts they adopt to navigate through life, cope with challenges, and define their selfhood. But what is a self? A role? And how do these concepts, two of the most commonly employed words in the social sciences, relate? In this chapter I examine these issues from three angles: the self as systemized, serialized, and dramatized. But first some commentary on the nature of the self.

The Nature of Selves

Like consciousness, "self" is a word used in a myriad of ways. For the sake of clarification, we need to distinguish between two uses. The first is intrapersonal. The self is not an irreducible "psychological atom" or "executive ego." Rather, the self is a product of one's cognition, projected onto the introspectable stage of conscious interiority. The self does not reflect the mind's contents. Instead, it is manufactured from one's mental material and comes in two basic forms, i.e., subject-selves ("I") and object-selves ("me"), whose interactions constitute interself relations. The second use of self is interpersonal, i.e., understood as observable behaviors presented to others.

The interpersonal self is not a unitary entity, consistent across different situations. Rather, it is manifold, differing in expression according to circumstances, culturally constructed and contextualized, emerging at the intersection of sociological forces.

The intrapersonal and interpersonal selves of the same individual interrelate in highly complex ways. Many terms prefixed by "self-" describe these interrelations. For example, the oft-heard "self-esteem" is connected to acceptance by others, evaluation of one's performance, comparison, and the efficacy of individual action. Hewitt (2009) analyzes this notion as a socially constructed emotion and relates it to personal understandings of where one is in relation to contradictory emphases in American culture: individuality versus community; striving for success versus self-acceptance; the search for happiness versus contentment with one's present situation. Another example is self-verification, something which individuals put great efforts into in order to preserve their self-definitions by seeking to confirm them. This is fundamentally a positive and adaptive process. Intrapersonally, self-verification may foster authenticity; improve physical health; reduce anxiety; and enhance self-esteem. Interpersonally, it fosters trust and intimacy (North & Swann 2009). The protection of one's self-image by excuses was originally related to "reality negotiating." However, Higgins and Gallagher (2009) have investigated how it can be either adaptive or maladaptive, and link it to the positive sociopsychological processes of hope, as well as social support and coping.

Implications of Interself Relations

Usually we relate to ourselves in an ordinarily reflexive manner ("I" and "me" interact). But putting a distance between one's subject-self and one's object-self occurs for different reasons and can be characterized as negative (self-alienation) or positive (gaining self-objectivity). Such distanciation can be conceptualized in person deictic terms (words and phrases that refer to a specific time, place, or person in context). The subject-self is the "speaker," while the object-self is the "addressee" or "other," producing three deictic perspectives. In the first both subject-self and object-self are the first-person; one approaches oneself as "myself." In the second perspective the subject-self is the first-person while the object-self is the second-person; one addresses oneself as a "you" with a curious, probing, interrogative, or censuring attitude. In the third perspective the subject-self is the first-person while the object-self is the third-person ("another"). Conceiving our object-self as "you" is perhaps unusual but, for some of us who think deeply about how interiorization configures interself dynamics, plausible. However, addressing our object-self as "another" is unorthodox, perhaps even perplexing. It might be viewed as inquiring about suppressed knowledge, confronting unprocessed nonconscious material, coming across a surprising facet of our selfhood, or discovering unknown untapped potential. Perhaps the "other" designates a radical acceptance of the here-and-now (DBT). From an existential point of view, encountering our inner "other" might mean that we should not ask (ourselves) what the meaning of our lives is. Rather, we should recognize that we are being "questioned by life" (Frankl, 1992, pp. 113-114). In other words, life, here conceptualized as the unpredictable, unknown, and awe-inspiring "other," deep within us, addresses us. Or the "other" might mean something or someone to which we surrender ourselves (cf. the Greek *kenosis* meaning "emptying"—i.e., "self-emptying"—and becoming fully open to the divine).

Selves as Part of a System

Attempting to understand the self leads to some challenging philosophy of mind questions. Is there a core self whose multifacetedness is displayed during interaction with others? An essential ego? We assume complicated endeavors must have a coordinating, regulating, supervising manager of some type. Nature has many examples of remarkably complex systems and animal behavior that to us simply "must" have an executive, controlling center of some sort (e.g., ant colonies, herd behavior).[1] However, complex behaviors and organisms are always part of systems informed by distributed, consensual, and collective cognition, and are couched in systemic flows of information that produce stunning results. This systems theory approach applies to the psyche and questions of selfhood. Indeed, it is an illusion that a homunculus, dwelling in our heads, is working the levers. No directing supervisor is necessary. The individual psyche is a system or a collection of subsystems that responds differently depending on social situation, a point stressed by Eric Berne (1910-1970) in his "transactional analysis."

A Systems Theory Approach

A system is composed of units that stand in operational relation to each another (like an "I" and a "me"). Once combined, they constitute an entity or whole (the whole is greater than the sum of its parts), so individual units cannot be understood in isolation as elements that function separately. This is the underlying notion behind systems theory. In the older, reductionistic paradigm, the goal was analysis (breaking down), isolating things, and making a list of the components of the organism. However, a more productive approach involves synthesis (building up) and looking for interrelationships within the organism and with its surroundings. Rather than describing living things using a "machine metaphor" (organisms as passive, responding to external stimuli, simple causation), an "organismic metaphor" better captures their nature as complex systems. Delineating interrelationships allows us to view systems as cybernetic, or as a regulatory system that operates by means of feedback loops. Negative feedback loops maintain equilibrium, while positive feedback loops result in further change, accelerating deviation. Human interactions, rather than linear, mechanistic, and one-way, are complex, circular, and reciprocal.

Systems theory was inspired by thinkers such as the biologist Ludwig Von Bertalanffy (1901–1972), who noted the differences between "closed systems" (inert, inorganic matter) and "open systems" (living entities). The latter are systems of "negative entropy" (extracting energy from the environment via their own activity), continuously engaging in reorganization vis-à-vis their environment. Regarding living things as open systems means that they can self-organize and actively participate in their own construction, i.e., they can change themselves so that patterns and order emerge from the interaction of the components of a system without explicit instructions, either from the organism itself or from the environment. Such reorganization allows a dynamic interaction between person and surroundings, as well as random (stochastic) processes that result in rapid and novel adaptations. "Triadic reciprocity," or how behavior, environmental stimuli, and personal factors (cognition, temperament) all determine each other in "complex, mutually influential interactions" is an example of a systems approach. Such "reciprocal determinism" (rather than one-way determinism) examines how the causes behind behavior are shaped by the behavior itself (Whitcomb & Merrell, 2013, p. 6).

Why Psychological Healing Is Different: The Networked Psyche

Different bodily systems are armed with their own self-healing defenses. However, one system in particular—our neurological apparatus—is unique. As an information-processing mechanism, the brain has been intricately designed to be interlinked with, interconnected to, and plugged into the social and natural environment. Consequently, the brain is more than just another bodily part. As a networked entity constantly updated by its surroundings, the brain, working within a cultural matrix, generates a mind requiring self-repair responses infinitely more complicated than other organs. Indeed, arguably more so than physical health, restoring mental health benefits from external assistance, such as a supportive environment, healthy social interaction, and sometimes an attentive listener who offers salubrious counsel and empathy.[2] Since external factors enhance (rather than directly cause) the healing process, we can we view them as "inactive ingredients."[3]

Also note that in the conventional medical model, a person (subject) has a disease (object) that in a sense is detachable, i.e., it can be observed and measured through tests. But when an individual presents with a mental health issue, the sociorelational model seems more apt. This is because the afflicting entity or disorder, while on the one hand an object, also shares something of the person (subject) since it springs from and is identified with the person (emotions, thoughts, sense of selfhood, and other facets of subjectivity). Physical pain is more straightforward, while psychic pain is more difficult to treat, enmeshed as it is with avoidance, ambivalence, resistance, and self-conscious biases (Havens and Walters, 2012, p. 7).

The Sequential Self

The self is a contingent, constitutive entity. No "central meaner" or "owner of record" holds a governing position. "Our tales are spun, but for the most part we don't spin them; they spin us. Our human consciousness, and our narrative selfhood, is their product, not their source" (Dennett, 1991, p. 418). The "I" is not a deeper or more real "executive ego"; like the "me," it is a moment-to-moment creation, manufactured by the mind. Though commonsensical psychology imagines the self as supervisory central-processing mechanism imbued with decision-making powers—like a puppeteer pulling the strings—such a view is a socio-ideological construct.[4] Rather, the self is the product of many decision-making processes that occur unawares. This is not to deny agency to individuals, but to problematize "free will" by arguing that decision-making is intricate, compounded, multiple, and for the most part, invisible. The self is an object of the conscious introspectable mind, metaphorically "seen" by the "mind's eye." As such, it is a product of complex nonconscious cognitive processes (Jaynes, 1976). The self, lacking a single psychological source, is in a sense a fiction, but a very useful one.

Resonating with this view is the Buddhist-inspired "pearl view" elaborated by Strawson (1997).[5] Our selves exist serially and sequentially, one at a time—"me now," "me now," "me now"—like pearls on a necklace. Selves are "Subjects of Experience that are Single Mental Things" (SESMETS). No essential continuity underlies our sense of selfhood, and neither agency nor personality is necessary to account for the self. This is a radically disjunctive view, reinterpreting what feels so intuitively unitary to us as fluctuating and fleeting (Gallagher & Shear, 1999; Strawson, 1997). Our sense of selfhood is selectively created from a stream of thoughts, images, sentiments, and life episodes (excerptions and self-narratizations). The self is a consequence of an interiorized flicker-fusion effect (still photographs projected successively on a movie screen afford the illusion of continuity and movement); it is an illusory construct. A serial view of the self does not mean, however, that selfhood is not real. It does mean that the self does not exist in the way our minds trick us into believing it exists.

As intriguing as SESMETS is, some may find this Buddhist-flavored view of selfhood disturbing, as it suggests that no core, essentialist ultimate identity is to be found. SESMETS raises thorny philosophical questions: Who or what is registering our experiences of transitory, successive selfhood? Who or what is the "audience" that self-reflexively perceives what is being psychologically registered? Incorporating a continuous meta-framing into the equation helps answers these questions. In other words, we have a laddered selfhood produced by an "I" incessantly climbing rungs on a ladder (through time) and looking down at earlier selves (that then become "me's" of one's memories). The ladder stretches upward into the future, so the "I" can imagine not-yet selves on higher rungs without end. Or we might say that the self leapfrogs through time, jumping off from its previous versions.

The Staginess of Sociopsychological Processes

One of the most anxiety-provoking parts of learning about counseling was having to role-play. I remember worrying about putting on a good performance in front of my classmates; I was concerned that I would hyper-introceive what I should be doing, thereby missing the point of the exercise. I found myself thinking of the behaviors to which a therapist needs to attend: posture, appropriate eye contact; countenance; smiling (not too much but not too little); shifting around in the chair; where to place one's hands; minimal encouragers; etc. I could not help but wonder if the patient could see through my over-thought attempts at self-control and self-observation (needless to say, it is just as important to carefully monitor the behaviors of patients, as these obviously provide crucial clues to their state of mind).

The students ("audience") were tasked with noting and commenting on the skills being displayed (or not displayed) by the "therapist" and filling out a peer rating form. They also had to observe the "patient's" underlying emotions, nonverbals, etc., giving them the opportunity to focus on the particulars of how a therapist and patient interact. This sort of training permits students to become more cognizant of the subtleties of social behaviors. Being a member of the "audience" was quite useful since observing how other students played the role of the therapist allowed me to compare notes and consider how I might (or might not) respond to what a patient says. Eventually, the length of the role-playing was extended and audiovisually recorded. This allowed us to observe our own performances as therapists and patients, which unless one is naturally extroverted and has experience on the stage, can be somewhat unnerving. But once a practice session commenced, the role-players would relax. Every now and then, a "therapist" and "patient" would respond to something said with a warm, knowing smiling or break out in hearty laugher, sharing a moment of spontaneous, genuine congruency.

While playing the therapist, fears of forgetting which skill would be appropriate for whatever the patient said self-consciously crowded my psychoscape. Several tracks of thinking played—competed?—in my head: (1) focusing on attending to the patient's general presentation (posture, facial expressions, verbal expressions, tone, etc.); (2) trying to discern what their words meant and preparing to respond to what the patient said; (3) wondering what I should say after the patient paused; and (4) monitoring my own behavior ("I" observing "me") and considering how my self-presentation was impacting the patient. With practice, these tracks eventually became integrated. Soon I became more comfortable having my mind run on parallel tracks while playing the role of the therapist. I learned how to "just go with what the patient is saying," rather than hanging on and analyzing every word. I reminded myself that I should just listen to whatever the patient stated, as their words should, for the most part, drive the agenda of the session.

When I played the patient, I also felt self-conscious as I tried to present a performance inspired by personal experiences but one that was not too revealing. As role-playing sessions became longer, I grew concerned that I was running out of topics that could be narratively stretched out. However, I found playing the patient role was far easier than taking on the therapist part. In the former, I could just ad lib my way through the session and be myself. Eventually it felt natural.[6]

The purpose of such aforementioned staged performances is to train therapists to be self-conscious of their own behaviors and to consider how these might affect the delivery of care. But of course, we all go through mundane social life "acting" to one degree or another; some performances are just more theatrical than others. This is not a point new or novel, but its import lies in how it says something note-worthy about our nature, as explicated in the next section.

The Role-Self Perspective and the Developmental Trajectory

One's life is a series of stage-mountings, entrances, and exits. The role-self perspective (RSP) regards the life trajectory in developmental terms. Therefore personal growth is a matter of being prepared for key turning points. But transitions may be either mundane and minor, or life-changing and major (APSs). Adopting and cultivating the most appropriate role-selves prepare one for life stages and crisis points.

A common task of a therapist is to assist a patient in gaining perspective on their changing life roles. Here the work of researchers such as Donald Super is relevant. He conceptualized an individual's roles as child, student, leisurite, cit-izen, worker, spouse, homemaker, parent, pensioner (Super, 1957, 1963). As an example, consider the need to carefully navigate the educatio-employment system as one makes key career decisions. Given the growing challenges of our educatio-employment system, the period from around age sixteen to the mid-twenties is fraught with anxiety and apprehension. Indeed, decisions made during this crit-ical juncture in an individual's life might be viewed as "practice" or preparation for other key turning points that will undoubtedly be faced later in life. Socializing young people to believe that transitional experiences are potentially periods of re-newal can hopefully be an opportunity to instill a positive psychological outlook.

Role-playing can sound negative, as if someone shoved a script in our hands and demanded that we perform. A patient once stated to me that "I got lost in decades of role-playing," presumably meaning that he became used to presenting inauthentic selves. Others often spoke of "breaking out of roles" imposed upon them; one linked this statement "to leaving the system" (meaning the revolving door of therapy, recovery, and more therapy). But under therapeutic guidance, a patient can role-play some problematic facet of themselves (or even someone else) and thereby gain self-objectivity.

Psychodrama: The Inherently Theatrical Self

The therapeutic tradition that most closely resonates with RSP is psychodrama. This was originally associated with the system developed by J. L. Moreno (1889-1974) (1959, 1964, 1987) and Zerka T. Moreno (1917-2016) in the mid-1930s, but many of its techniques are now utilized in many therapeutic interventions. This therapy teaches patients how to examine the roles they have internalized and to develop the ability to discard those roles that are no longer useful or to modify them. Psychodrama stresses spontaneity, creativity, the "here-and-now," and the authenticity and intensity of encountering others.

Psychodrama and role-playing demonstrate the limits of just "talking" (and perhaps over-intellectualizing problems) since they encourage individuals to embody, act out, and express their thoughts and feelings in a visible manner that they themselves can witness. This enhances self-monitoring. Psychodrama is very experiential, as is apparent in the use of catharsis, or the release of pent-up emotions. Role-playing can evoke a surprisingly emotional impact. Individuals can enthusiastically put themselves into their roles (I remember as a student being impressed with how the other students—the "audience"—were visibly moved by the "performance"; they were not mere passive spectators). However, it should be noted that emotional expression is not necessarily enough, as group members also require cognitive reframing of maladaptive thought-feeling patterns. As in other therapeutic treatments, psychodrama is processual, unfolding over three phases: (1) warm-up or preparation, during which trust and cohesion among group members is built; facets of what troubles the protagonist are explored; (2) the action or acting out the events in question; a cathartic resolution may result; and (3) sharing and closure; in a nonjudgmental manner, a relaxed discussion about the performance ensues and a debriefing and "de-roling" conclude the performance.

"Classical psychodrama" requires much training and a deep familiarity with its constellation of techniques.[7] An arsenal of interventions and notions are utilized that allow the "protagonist" (as well as, presumably, the "audience members" of the group) to step out of their habitual daily roles and question life scripts that might be causing problems. Psychodrama allows an individual to re-experience past events or to engage in future projection by expressing thoughts about what might happen. Therapists utilize a highly interiorized, subjective technique called "surplus reality." This is an inner mental stage where a protagonist can covertly act out a scene that in the real world would be uncomfortable, impossible, or unlikely. If carried out in a group setting, the group facilitator acts as the "director," who functions as the producer, observer, and analyst of performances. The protagonist is the group member undergoing therapy, and the "audience" is the other group members. The "double" is the protagonist's inner self, or another aspect of the protagonist's self that is not adequately articulated or recognized. There may be more than one double, each representing various personas of the protagonist. "Auxiliaries" (supporting roles performed by other group participants) might: (1) play out the perceptions or express feelings of the protagonist; (2) explore the interaction between the protagonist and their own roles; (3) interpret relations and interactions; or (4) act as therapeutic guides in assisting the protagonist to develop an improved relationship. An auxiliary may play the role of double. A participant might shadow the protagonist; this shadow reflects the emotional signals that the protagonist gives off. The facilitator might pause the scene and ask the protagonist if the shadow is accurately indicating their emotions. This assists the protagonist in identifying behaviors and nonverbal cues of which they are not conscious. In the "mirror technique" a group member reflects the protagonist's movements, gestures, and speech, thereby helping the protagonist engage in self-reflection and self-assessment, thereby enhancing self-reflexivity.

A number of other techniques afford psychodrama's theatrical impact: role reversal (looking at oneself through the eyes of another);[8] role training (allowing a patient to experiment with and rehearse new, more adaptive behaviors); learning how to select a role (pick a script that one identifies with or one that is alien to one's sense of self); "warming-up" (rehearsing); and picking a center spot ("stage"). Other relevant concepts are the "magic shop" (a place containing bottles filled with aspects of the protagonist's personality); empty chair; and the "soliloquy" in which a protagonist shares their innermost thoughts and feelings (this might occur in dialogue with a double). An individual counseling session can be regarded as the offstage where one can let one's more intimate facets of selfhood be displayed. It may also be regarded as the backstage where one freely rehearses new roles or behaviors.

The Multi-Roled Person

Watching my autistic brother suffer from severe epileptic fits—which would sometimes manifest themselves as extremely violent, adrenaline-charged psychomotor seizures—made me think about how the mind was put together. His personality would undergo a radical alteration, and I wondered how his mind could fragment so that he would suddenly acquire super-human strength and spew demon-like foul language. The mind, I concluded, is not unitary, despite the strange illusion that it is. From a young age, this piqued my interest in how the mind is constituted. Years later, I would pursue research in Japan on spirit possession and witness a similar segregation of the psyche (but rarely so violent).

Psychic partition is not inherently dysfunctional, and of course we all experience something similar, but to a far lesser degree and not as dramatic, i.e., controlling impressions by wearing different personas, managing self-presentations, performing different social roles, acting, etc. More severe forms of the compartmentalization of mentation allow self-deception, a central leitmotif of psychotherapy. From a positive perspective, the partitioning of the psyche allows one part to step back, take a deep breath, observe, scrutinize, and analyze the reactions of other aspects of one's selfhood. This meta-framing ability is a crucial aspect of RSP, which highlights how different psychological components make up the person—the self is a compound and is constituted by smaller selves that together form a "complex self." This is illustrated by what a patient, frustrated by the challenge of making a decision, told me: "There's a committee in my head that keeps making excuses." Another patient said, "I'm a walking contradiction," to express the same sentiment. Individuals lack a "unitary, fixed view of the self"; rather, they possess multiple conceptions of the self (Dodgson & Wood, 1998, p. 179).

One way to conceptually grasp our multi-roled nature is to search for its origins in our very socioaffiliation, i.e., how we interact with others and how such exchanges build our sense of selfness. Social life is a choreography of "doing things to others" or "having others do things to us." From these dynamic, interactive encounters, agentive and passive modes of selfness are generated: an "I" or self-as-subject that acts on others, as well as a "me" or self-as-object that accepts/receives actions from others. While only one "I" exists, many "me's" or smaller role-selves come into existence as circumstances demand; in other words, the "I" is the "director" while "me's" are "actors" that follow stage directions. "Me's" can be understood as interself roles we play toward ourselves (intrapersonally) as well as vis-à-vis others (interpersonally). Communication between the "I" and the "me" is the crucial issue for understanding how we function as self-staging, self-transforming social beings.

Our "me's" or role-selves are constituted by numerous partially completed scripts "written" by society and internalized. However, as the particular life challenges for each individual will differ, the mind, in an attempt to adapt to changing circumstances, will utilize, fill in, and rewrite the scripts as conditions demand. These scripts, or schemas, are then enacted by role-selves. Sometimes scripts can become burdensome and oppressive, so that an individual ends up playing a role for the benefit of others, leading to feelings of inauthenticity and disaffection. A corollary of the complex self-premise is that one's relationship with oneself (intrapersonal) is just as important as any relationship with other individuals (interpersonal). This is why the value of self-respect, self-compassion (Neff, 2011), and self-forgiveness (or of letting go of resentment toward oneself for some past transgression) (Wohl, DeShea, & Wahkinney, 2008) should be acknowledged.

Selves versus Personalities

We need to take a detour and distinguish between the presentation of different selves versus the emergence of distinct personalities within the same individual. The former concerns playing roles, "me's," personas, putting on fronts, and impression management. Personality, in conventional usage, refers to a suite of relatively enduring traits, so it is somewhat out of the ordinary to conceive of "personalities" within the same individual. In any event, it describes stand-alone, separate subpersonalities and is often considered maladaptive and pathological, as in dissociative identity disorder (or in negatory "spirit possession"). A subpersonality typically possesses its own views, wishes, motives, feelings, and memories.

Most likely a continuum exists. At one end are mask-like performances and façades of convenience. At the opposite end are independent, autonomous self-entities with a high degree of agency that can exhibit radically different identities. In between are role-selves. Assuming there are subselves (sitting somewhere on the aforementioned continuum) leads to a number of theoretical questions: (1) Is the organization of sub-selves "tight" or "loose"? (2) Can mental content move between subselves? (3) Are subselves conscious or unconscious, or can each subself have conscious and unconscious content? (4) Are subselves organized hierarchically or transversely? (5) Can subselves intrude upon one another (Lester, 2015, p. 168; see also Ryle & Fawkes, 2007)? Here I will not answer these queries; I merely delineate the problem.

Integrated and Fragmented Selves

"What do you think is holding you back?" I asked a patient struggling with enacting meaningful change in his life. "I can't tell [the patient's own name] anything," he responded, indicating an intuitive recognition of his multi-component nature. An integrated self is a state in which our "I" and "me" are united (or self-immersed); the "I" identifies with "me." In a sense, this stable role-self is the default condition. When confronted with a problem, a gap grows between the "I" and "me"; such self-distancing is a function of heightened interiority. This instance of meta-framing is ordinarily healthy, affording objectivity and perspective, since it allows one part of a person to "see" another part.

Other reasons for a distal relationship emerging between one's "I" and "me" might be to monitor one's self-presentation or self-performance while trying to make a good first impression, lying, or theatrical role-playing for artistic purposes. Dishonesty does not benefit social relations, of course, but more intense forms of "I"-"me" detachment, such as routine mendacity or seriously disjointed, disaffected selves, can characterize mental disorders (Table 7.1).

Table 7.1 Modes of Self-Presentation

←Integrated Roles and Self→		←Roles and Self Disjointed→
"I" fused with "me"	"I" manages "me"	"I" estranged from "me"
Expressed self	Acting	Duplicitous self
Being oneself	Pretending self	Alienated self
Authentic self	Deceiving others	Deceiving self
Honest	Dishonest	Inauthentic self

From McVeigh, 2002; modified.

Self-Distancing Strategies

Recent research demonstrates the value of several self-distancing strategies. For example, the "fly-on-the-wall" perspective allows one to become an observer ("I") and imagine an event as if it were happening at a distance from oneself, so one does not get enmeshed in one's own negative proclivities. Such an approach helps with anxiety-provoking future events. Another intervention is the "not me" approach in which one addresses oneself in the third person, by using either one's own name or the pronouns "he" or "she" or "you" rather than "I" or "me." In other words, the psychological distance between subject-self and object-self is greatly increased. In a third intervention called "time travel," one imagines a "future me" so as to decrease distress about an event that is causing one anxiety. Time travel appears to work because of "impermanence focus," i.e., one persuades oneself that current feelings are temporary and will eventually diminish over time (Kross & Ayduk, 2017; White et al., 2018).

Psychodrama, Positive Psychology, and the Role-Self Perspective

A key difference between RSP and psychodrama is that in the former, patients would be taught to regard their own "I" as a "director" (rather than having the therapist perform this function), thereby granting them more self-autonomy and self-determination. Another important difference is that though the doubles of classical psychodrama are the various "me's" of RSP, in the latter approach the intrapersonal and interpersonal impacts of doubles are afforded more of a reality, i.e., inner selves are not aspects of self but semi-agentive personas. The aim of RSP is to increase the number of roles/"me's"/smaller selves, so that the patient is equipped with more adaptive modes of interaction.

RSP is grounded in the positive psychological cultivation of assets and inner strengths. Concretely, for RSP this means that in the same way an actant (actor) can change, select, refuse, or develop new role-selves, the individual possesses the ability to choose, reject, and rewrite scripts to fit more positive and healthful life trajectories. RSP assumes that individuals are naturally resilient and therefore, when necessary, ready to be transformed for the better.

Young (2015) relies on a Jaynesian perspective to explain why negative self-statements and overly critical self-appraisals are so strong, persistent, and impervious to correction. He contends that these internally self-originated claims possess the authority of a god in directing our self-evaluations (i.e., vestiges of bicameral mentality). He proposes "dialogical disputation." This occurs by using role-playing in order to shift the locus of discourse from "self-generated" to "other-generated," i.e., the therapist reflects the problematic statements back to the patient from a position of "other-originated."

Transactional Analysis: Acknowledging Our Diverse Nature

It is worth a brief digression to show how one type of therapy, transactional analysis (TA), explicitly acknowledges our mutli-roled nature. TA, as developed by Eric Berne, is derived from psychoanalytic theory and postulates that each individual has three "ego states."[9] The first, the Parent state (exteropsyche), describes a style of treating others modeled on how one's parents (or other authoritative figures) behaved, felt, and thought. The second state, Adult (neopsyche), works to make objective, rational assessments of reality. The processes of meta-framing and self-introspection are operating at full capacity, and self-autonomy and self-authorization are unclouded by irrational, emotional turmoil. The third or Child state (archaeopsyche) is grounded in an individual's very early experiences. Though this state can behave immaturely and irresponsibly, it has a positive side since it is the origin of the ability to experience emotional intimacy and to lead a life full of spontaneity, enjoyment, and creativity.

Unhelpful styles of interaction, shaped by early life experiences, each have their "scripts" that one relies on to guide one through "games" and navigate interpersonal relations. Individuals communicate—often nonconsciously—with the other ego states of others, making for complicated dynamics; often these transactions lead to crossed lines of communication. TA therapy analyzes how an individual moves in and out of these states and gives and receives "strokes" (units of recognition). TA focuses on developing skills required to strengthen the Adult state that in some ways appears to correspond with Freud's ego and has a meta-framing function, objectively mediating between the games of the Parent and Child.

Taking Stock

This chapter has described the self as an entity: (1) systemized, i.e., the networked psyche as informed by a systems theory approach; (2) serialized and narratizable; and (3) staged and dramatized. This was done to set the groundwork for the role-self perspective (RSP), i.e., how we enact scripts that are potentially rewritable. Such reauthoring can help the mind repair.

The implicit philosophical presuppositions of Plato, Aristotle, Descartes, and Kant shaped a view that the mind is self-reflective, passive, and timeless; it mirrors the outside world. However, another view is that the mind is experiential, active, and changing. Indeed, the mind is a moving target whose complexity is due to its temporal nature; it is constantly updating, interacting, goal-directed, and future-directed (Buzsáki, 2006). Its Gestalt nature is temporal and its neurological plasticity allows great transformability.[10] The next chapter explores the psychotherapeutic implications of the unfolding nature of self-change.

Notes

1. Another example: trade networks of the Neolithic period seem impressive given the lack of modern techno-communications.
2. Though pharmacotherapy can be a vital intervention.
3. Or "excipients," also called bulking agents, fillers, diluents; these facilitate a drug's effect, e.g., helping with absorption, reducing viscosity, enhancing solubility, and ensuring long-term stabilization.
4. In "The Totalitarian Ego," Greenwald (1980) posits an analogy between the self and a dictator. Like the latter, the self fabricates and revises history, and cognitive biases and distortions correspond to thought control and propaganda.
5. Brown notes the resonances between the Buddhist notion of "no self" and the modern, secular idea that the self is a constructed representation (2016, p. 452).
6. However, playing the role of the patient seemed as educational as being a counselor, since while talking, I could observe the subtle behaviors of the "counselor." I wondered what he or she might say in response to my performance.
7. Psychodrama resonates with role theory in anthropology and "self-presentation" and "self-management" in sociology (e.g., Goffman, 1959).
8. Two types: reciprocal or between one's self and another person; and representational or between roles, objects, or parts of the self.
9. Rather than beginning as an extension of individual therapy, TA started as a group therapy model.
10. Of which there are three types: (1) replacement of neurons by neurogenesis; (2) the slow growth of dendritic spines even in adults (wiring-based plasticity); and (3) strengthening or weakening synapses with each other (synaptic plasticity) (Buzsáki, 2006).

8

The Self-Organizing Mind

Rhythms, Routines, Rituals

I had just arrived at the agency where I was working when a house attention—a sort of emergency meeting to deal with the occasional urgent matter—had already been called. The issue was an incident in the kitchen involving a patient of mine. I tried to be objective but had sympathy for my patient, who was ordered by the staff to stand against a wall and face his peers who one by one asked him to account for his behavior. Some expressed critical comments. At first he was angered by the questioning and stated, "I'm looking at that exit sign above that door over there. That sign looks like a good idea to me right now" (i.e., to leave the facility and give up on treatment). Soon, however, he gained his composure and seemed to realize that perhaps he did have to self-reflect on his behavior and that others had a valid point. I considered how I should discuss his reactions to what the others had said to him in our next scheduled session.

Later that day, the individual who had was the focus of attention came into my office unannounced. "I know I'm breaking the chain of command [not putting his want or need on a list to be run up to staff for permission to speak to someone], but I have to say this. I wonder if the staff here can really help us, but I'm willing to give it a try. I was a counselor myself years ago, and back then you could help people. Now you can't because of all the paperwork demands from OASAS [Office of Alcoholism and Substance Use Services, NY State]." He continued to confidently offer his opinions. He was so energetic in his presentation that he stood up and approached my desk as he gesticulated, and then quickly jumped back, saying "Oh, sorry, I didn't mean to come so close." And he said, "Oh, about this morning, I know I was wrong. I really needed that check-in with others."

What struck me was how this same individual who had experienced a painful emotional crisis was now bubbly, almost cheerful. I wondered if the morning meeting had stabilized him, or was his frenetic presentation masking something? It then occurred to me that maybe I should just take his own words at face value and accept the fact that, perhaps humiliating in the eyes of some, being put on the spot by one's peers and encouraged to self-introspect was a type of healing experience. "Some think treatment is a microwave, but it takes time," one patient told me. And the time it takes is structured, following a trajectory of: (1) a destabilizing issue; (2) instability of one's thinking leading to some insight; and (3) re-stabilization of psychosocial processes.

In this chapter I explore how patterned activities help reset the mind, both in its intrapersonal and interpersonal aspects, by adjusting to transitions and transformations. I provide examples by looking at stages of change.

Adaptive Phasic Structurations: Resetting the Mind

Evolutionary mutations, sociohistorical upheavals, life-span developments, or periodic psychological resettings in therapeutic settings[1]—adaptation defines and continually redefines *Homo sapiens*. The complex flow of social life demands that we take a processual approach; i.e., being goal-oriented, individuals are constantly adjusting to reach their aims and pursue socially sanctioned developmental sequences. Whether at the societal or psychological level, we must confront change, transitions, and transformations. Some of these are welcomed, others feared, while still others, existing in the realm of everyday life, are given little attention. But whatever our attitude toward these breaks with routine, as a species we prefer some measure of predictability and control while negotiating the challenges—whether minor or major—of daily living. Taken together, these adjustments can be understood as adaptive phasic structurations (APSs); they help us navigate through life. The APS perspective accepts that the psyche is inherently temporal due to the brainwave oscillations that underlay it. Describing how routines act as a form of self-care and help him stay healthy, a patient stated, "My body is like the House [the community residence in which the patient resided]. Tasks need to be done, there's a schedule, chores, responsibilities."

The individual mind, as it moves through time (whether measured in hours, days, months, or longer), must strike a balance between negentropy (order) and entropy (chaos). Too much of the former, inflexibility results. Too much of the latter, and the consequence is under-regulated mentation (these fluctuations of dysregulation and regulation represent general mentation and are not necessarily related to conscious or nonconscious cognition). Ideally, then, the psyche should operate in the window between overly organized and disorganized emotional–cognitive patterning. The function of APSs is to ensure that psychological processes continually readjust, thereby driving adaptive regulation (Figure 8.1).

The APS approach coincides with what is called "predictive coding" (or predictive processing). This theorizes that the mind is incessantly updating and generating models of the environment. Such models produce predictions of sensory input that are compared to actual, incoming sensory input. This contrast leads to prediction errors that are then utilized to revise and update how we navigate through the environment.[2] The mind is tasked with disambiguating the constant incoming stream of stimuli while simultaneously organizing an action response. In the words of Bill Rowe, the mind must always be "ahead of the game," as it were. Like APS, predictive coding follows a tripartite trajectory of: (1) perturbation: stimuli (which might be external/physical or internal/psychological) that act on an equilibrium and trigger an inclination to action; (2) process: the neurophysiological reordering of that action;

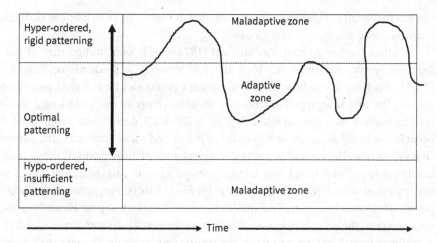

Figure 8.1. Adaptive and maladaptive zones of mental operations.

and (3) resolution: either a return to the prior equilibrium or the settling into a new equilibrium. The second phase, process, can be subdivided into prediction, expectation, and confirmation (Bill Rowe, personal communication).

Rituals, Ceremonies, Psychosocial Change: Adaptive Phasic Structurations

Anthropologists call APSs "rituals." For many of us, these are usually associated with religion and evoke images of the "traditional" or unchanging customs steeped in the past that have frozen earlier practices whose original purpose has been long forgotten. Some of us also tend to assume that rituals are characterized by unthinking and automatic behavior; they are associated with repetition, routinization, and regularization. However, rituals should be understood as instances of dynamic adaptation to changing circumstances. It should be stressed that, besides religious ceremonies, ritual behavior may characterize political, economic, educational, leisure, or mundane (e.g., daily greetings) activities. If understood as attempts to pattern and order the commotion and turmoil of psychosocial life, APSs can be found everywhere—changes in social status; life crises; falling outs; stitching together newly learned material; patching up problems; digesting powerful feelings; resolving conflict.

All organizations have their own list of daily routines, regular activities, and special events that pattern their operations. Usually the more restrictive a facility is, the more rituals it will have. For example, a therapeutic or residential community uses intakes and assessments, and, depending on the place, orientations; morning staff meetings; treatment team meetings; closing ceremonies; house attentions (to work out interpersonal problems; to "hear yourself talk" when in crisis); house closings; individual sessions; and process groups.

The ethnographer Arnold Van Gennep (1873–1957), who studied rites of passage (baptisms; confirmations; b'nei mitzvah; marriages; graduations; funerals) (1977), theorized about how socially significant events can be analyzed into three phases. The first is segregation from the social structure or one's old social status (pre-liminality): activities symbolizing an individual's detachment from a fixed point in the social structure or from a set of prescribed social attributes. The person "leaves" society. The second phase is a marginal state or suspension of status (liminality): stripped of features that normally define a person, an individual comes to occupy an indeterminate, ambiguous state. The final phase is aggregation and reincorporation into social structure or acquisition of new social status (post-liminality): the person rejoins the normal structure of society, perhaps assigned with a new identity.

Building upon Van Gennep's work, the anthropologist Victor Turner (1967, 1969, 1974) explored how socially meaningful events (which may be brief or lengthy) expose social conflict and tensions at the collective level. He elaborated on Van Gennep's rites of passage and proposed three phases: (1) initial (introduction of issue or presenting problem, preparatory activities, separation from ordinary life); (2) liminal (confrontation of problem, adjustment, alteration); and (3) ending (resolution, concluding activities, return to ordinary life). Turner focused on the liminal stage. When individuals pass through this phase, they enter a disruptive "betwixt and between" state, transitioning from a stabilized "structure" to a re-stabilized "re-structuring." This intermediate "anti-structure" stage upsets social arrangements. The individual is stripped of old attributes, becoming a "blank state" on which characteristics of a new status can be inscribed. A crucial feature of the liminal phase is communitas, which describes common experiences, sentiments of equality, and a strong sense of community that levels social status so that the ascription of new attributes proceeds more readily (communitas is in opposition to structure, which is associated with the first and third stages). From an educatio-socialization perspective, the individual passes through: (1) conditioning (socializing/learning); (2) deconditioning (desocializing/unlearning); and (3) reconditioning (resocializing/learning anew).

Liminality: From Order, through Chaos, to Reordering

The liminal stage is in a sense the most pivotal since this is when actual transformation transpires—though sometimes not for the better. A patient, who had seemed enthusiastic when he showed up for treatment, struggled with sorting out his problems over a number of sessions; he told me that "I'm too comfortable in chaos. I'd rather be in chaos than be happy," meaning that he was stuck in the transitional phase.

Of the three parts of a ritual, the liminal phase is the crux of the matter because this is when conscious interiority, triggered by challenges and difficult decisions, is usually mobilized. The liminal period is a process of shifting. The old and familiar have been left behind. However, the new has not yet emerged. During the liminal stage, a "letting loose" destabilizes rigid mindsets, thereby allowing a new perspective on maladaptive habits to emerge; hopefully more adaptive cognitions, through restructuring processes, can replace distorted thought patterns. Paying attention to the liminal phase, then, is crucial, as this is when conscious interiority is at its most active and promises the potential for progress and change. Therapeutically, the liminal phase is the most uncomfortable part of therapy, often filled with unsettling feelings (Bussolari & Goodell, 2009). In the case of mental disorders, the larger and more chaotic the liminal zone has grown, for whatever reason, the more likely the mental disorder will be severe; thus the importance of affording support and careful monitoring during any type of transition.

For instance, a patient described how while in prison (which became his individualized APS), he had everything stripped away. However, in his view this was helpful, as it allowed him to "check-in" on himself, rebuild his self-identity, and gain perspective. Another example: in a therapeutic community in which I interned, during the first thirty days of the twelve-month program patients would learn the rules and size up their new situation; they were hopeful, optimistic, and enthusiastic. But as they entered the second phase and their cognitions were challenged and emotions unsettled, the honeymoon period ended and the reality of treatment hit them.

Rupture and repair processes, originally theorized by Sandor Ferenczi (1931), are a good example of what happens during the liminal phase. He believed that breakdowns and disruptions in the therapist-patient relationship are inevitable. But such therapeutic impasses are an important part of positive change, allowing the patient to restore a healthier form of interaction with the clinician (Safran & Muran, 1996, 2000, 2006). Also relevant here is Frederick C. Thorne's work (1904-1994). He viewed mental illness as disorders of integration. Therapy works through the "principle of unification." But before this can transpire, a "positive disintegration" precedes the reorganizing and reintegrating of what were disorganized psychic components (Thorne, 1950; Thorne & Pishkin, 1968).

Residents in a mental health facility or members of a group who, experiencing the emotional turmoil that often characterizes a phase transition, can be sensitive to perceived slights:[3] "Stay in your own lane!" (mind your own business); "If you let the pressure out of your tires, then the ride is smoother" (do not be so full of yourself); "Watch your mouth, save your teeth"; "I won't cosign your bullshit" (will not enable another substance user); "You're just another stop sign" (addressed to a group member accused of interfering in a patient's recovery); "Residents play Battleship too much" (the predilection of peers to react excessively to the teasing and taunting by others in a community residence). Some display obstinacy: "If it ain't my way it's no way." Others interact with others in a guarded fashion: "I have to keep my BS radar turned on." One patient, befuddled by the questionable behavior of another, told him, "What you eat doesn't make me fat" (your bad decisions do not impact me). Some feel the need to warn others: "There's a chick called karma" (what goes around comes around). Some engage in sarcasm: "You not being there for Christmas is your gift to me" (addressed to a girlfriend with whom the patient was having strained relations). Others, passing through the liminal period, reframe their past personal experiences in a positive light or gain an insight, e.g., "Close friends are the trunk of the tree while acquaintances are the twigs and branches."

Psychotherapy as Ritual

We are not continually conscious throughout the day; that we believe we are in an illusion. But when confronted with a novel problem, challenge, or stressful situation, FOCI are activated. The triggering of these abilities helps us meta-frame, reframe, and hopefully overcome any obstacles (Figure 8.2). Occasionally FOCI are not properly deactivated, leading to runaway or hyper-interiorized consciousness (Figure 8.3).

Humans possess inherent rhythms of healing, not only within their bodies, but also within their psyches. But sometimes, the obstacle-transition-restoration process goes awry for some reason, or our natural ability to repair is overwhelmed by circumstances. This is when the guidance of a therapist is required to collaboratively and thoughtfully bring the patient to a mental state that is open to modification and positive change.

Frank delineated four elements common to all healing therapies (1991). As explained by Jørgensen, these are: (1) an emotionally charged relationship that solidifies the patient–therapist bond; (2) the healing setting or its institutional context that are "socially sanctioned and legitimized," thereby enhancing the "patient's expectations of help" (Jørgensen, 2004, p. 516); (3) a believable rationale for change that "offers an explanation of the patient's problems and methods for eliciting change" (Jørgensen, 2004, p. 517); and (4) a corresponding set of therapeutic rituals, or the specific tasks and procedures that signal the healer's competence and provide patients an alibi for change (Jørgensen, 2004, p. 517).

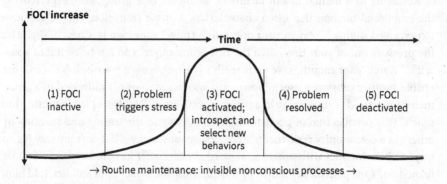

Figure 8.2. Routine activation of FOCI.

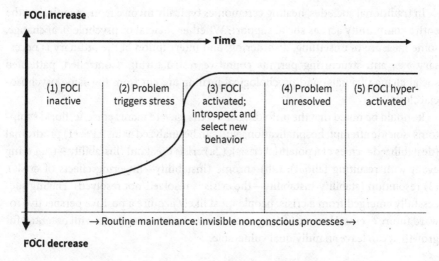

FOCI increase

→ Time →

| (1) FOCI inactive | (2) Problem triggers stress | (3) FOCI activated; introspect and select new behavior | (4) Problem unresolved | (5) FOCI hyper-activated |

→ Routine maintenance: invisible nonconscious processes →

FOCI decrease

Figure 8.3. Runaway consciousness: when FOCI are not deactivated.

Frank's last factor cited above—therapeutic rituals—can be broken down into three parts if understood as an APS. First, psychotherapeutic treatment is initiated, and together patients and therapist begin to explore the presenting problem(s). In the second stage, patients are invited to honestly confront their issues and hopefully cultivate insight. It is during this phase that patients are more than likely asked to reveal themselves and intensify their upsetting emotions. Ideally, the togetherness of communitas enhances the facilitative conditions of the working alliance with the therapist. Finally, assuming the patient has made progress, they return to "normal" society and begin maintaining a program of healthy action.

Much of therapy is "just a set of beliefs," i.e., arguably much of what works in psychotherapy has never been "proven" to work. In a sense, then, one must be open to the idea that much of psychological healing transpires in ways we do not yet fully understand. Healers, who may be shamans or clinicians, guide seekers of care through their "culturally established mythic world" whose curative symbols can be manipulated (Dow, 1986, p. 56). Such "symbolic healing" is grounded in the cognitive imperatives of a mythological worldview. Some systems locate restorative symbols in the supernatural realm, while others place them in the shiny certainties of modern science. The cultural mythic world possesses knowledge that is experientially—but not necessarily empirically—true. Together the healer and patients construct individualized symbols imbued with healing potency (Dow, 1986, p. 61). Symbolic healing possesses a universal structure: (1) the "experiences of healers and healed are generalized with culture-specific symbols"; (2) the healer convinces the patient that their problem can be defined in mythic terms; (3) the "healer attaches the patient's emotions to transformative, transactional symbols," leading to catharsis; (4) the healer manipulates transactional symbols to help patients transact their own emotions (Dow, 1986, p. 56).

In traditional societies, healing ceremonies typically involve many people, i.e., the entire community acts as social support. Whether societal or psychological change, some measure of unsettling, disordering, and interruption of the ordinary is necessary, i.e., anti-structuring permits cognitive restructuring. Controlled, patterned social change (rituals) and psychological healing are cut from the same psychosocial cloth.

It should be noted that the unfolding of a crisis (severe manic episode, florid symptoms, suicide attempt, hospitalization, etc.) can be analyzed as an APS: (1) prodromal (destabilized—clues of a potential crisis); (2a) crisis breakout (instability—triggering event with resulting fallout); (2b) chronic (instability—lingering effects of crisis); (3) resolution (stability/instability—the crisis is resolved/not resolved). Having successfully emerged from a crisis, people most likely acquire a positive perspective toward future events. However, though a crisis may be a turning point with potential for growth, it can leave an individual vulnerable.

Therapy: Repairing the Psychosocial System

During therapy, certain FOCI may need to be switched off and then turned on again, like a computer, in order to reset the system. Automaticized or habitual parts of maladaptive thinking are de-automaticized. In this way a molding of chaotic cognitive magma transpires. In some cases hyper-interiority needs to be decelerated (Figure 8.4).

To make my case that intervention can be conceived as an APS, an approach borrowed from any psychotherapeutic system would suffice. Below I begin with a brief discussion of the intake session, which can set the tone for the following sessions. Then, to provide an example of the first stage, I rely on Hill's idea of "exploration." In her approach the second and third phases, respectively, are insight[4] and action (Hill, 2014). In practice, these three states do not necessarily progress in a neat order and may follow alternate paths (for Hill her three stages correspond to client-centered,

(1) Maladaptive behaviors/ cognitions interfere in daily life	(2) Treatment begins	(3) FOCI utilized to address issues perspective OR Hyper-interiority arrested	(4) Adaptive behaviors/ cognitions acquired	(5) Maintenance of adaptive behaviors/ cognitions

→ Routine maintenance: invisible nonconscious processes →

⟶ **Time** ⟶

Figure 8.4. Resetting FOCI through therapy.

psychoanalytic, and behavioral therapy, respectively). For the second and third stage, I borrow examples from my own experiences.

Before proceeding, a recap of some key points: We are all naturally actors, some better than others. We manage the impressions we give off, learn new life scripts, rehearse in our minds our actions, and regularly take off and don new masks when engaging with others. APSs expedite our dramatizing tendencies, permitting us to process unforeseen stresses and navigate life's crossroads (Appendix H).

Exploration as Initial State and Problem: Intake and Assessment

Ideally, an intake should gather accurate information and establish rapport with the patient. Remembering all the requisite questions and making sure to cover all the bases can be challenging. These range from risk assessment (suicidal/homicidal ideation, substance use/abuse); details of the presenting problem; mental health status; relationships and support; medications; medical records; prior counseling experiences; physical health; employment status; cultural background. All this should be done while observing a patient's general demeanor and behavior (to look for any incongruence between what is said and self-presentation). Then, the therapist should go over the goals of therapy, ask the patient how he or she felt about the intake session, and provide an opportunity for the patient to ask any questions. Meanwhile, an attempt at building therapeutic rapport should be made. Ideally, a therapist should attend to what is happening with the patient, especially to what seems to be most important at the time, i.e., the primary presenting problem, while being aware of other secondary problems.

A key issue concerns striking a balance between what is essential and what spontaneously emerges but may be significant. The challenge is not to appear to be interviewing—or worse, interrogating—a patient as if one were a mere agent of a bureaucratic organization. The goal is to be empathic and caring. Enough attention should be given to "how" a person is giving information (rambling, incoherent, disorganized, guarded). Close attention should also be afforded to any unintended signals that the therapist might be giving off that can impact the therapist–patient interaction. Another concern is being up on the latest research for a particular population and their problems.

The stage of exploration establishes rapport and helps patients investigate their own thoughts and feelings (Hill, 2014, p. 203).[5] This stage is informed by the major elements of Rogerian client-centered therapy, and the focus of this initial step is to have the patient acknowledge their feelings.

To help facilitate this stage, the therapist should begin by taking some time to get "centered" (focusing on the patient; monitoring one's feelings; relaxing; deep breathing). Wrapping up a session should be a joint effort with the patient. Time should also be devoted to properly conceptualizing the patient, i.e., what is motivating the patient to obtain help now? Some difficulties implementing the exploration stage might be: inadequate attending and listening; asking too many closed questions; talking too much; not allowing silence; having an urge to disclose too much; giving too much advice; trying to be "buddies"; discouraging intense expression of affect; and feeling discouraged about one's counseling skills.

Instability and Alteration: An Example of the Transition Stage

The director of the agency warned the residents at a meeting that if their attitude did not change, she would "close the House" (i.e., the substance use agency). She sternly warned them: "On the street there's a saying—'My word is my bond. Try me.'" A house closing was a sort of lockdown. A house closing is a response to a breach in group relations or a crisis. Residents were not allowed to have visitors (reserved for the second and fourth Saturday of the month); could not attend self-help meetings; watch TV; listen to music; use the computer; or make phone calls. They were only permitted to attend medical, dental, probation, parole, or drug court appointments. A few days after her warning, she carried out her promise. After calling a house attention, she ordered the staff to collect DVDs; put away the entertainment equipment; take down speakers; and collect cell phones from residents as they forlornly stood around. The "House Is Closed" sign was hung on the front door. We had entered a liminal period.

Though a number of incidents were behind her decision, the final straw was the discovery by staff that a resident (who happened to be my patient) was in possession of contraband (a cell phone). He would not admit it (nor was he formally accused by the staff). This was concerning, as previously he had been put on therapeutic contract because he was found with a cell phone once before. Even more troubling, before he was put on contract he "broke the chain" by running up to the director and vehemently and self-righteously denying the charges. The director was hoping that residents would persuade the possessor of contraband to come clean and give it up. We were told that the closing was "indefinite." The pressure increased daily.

For the next week or so, the atmosphere in the House was tense and emotions were running high, to say the least. It was "betwixt and between" normal structure and renormalized structure. This became apparent in a group I facilitated during the house closing; it also demonstrated how psychological and social processes cannot be disentangled. The topic was how residents were going to deal with the closing. A resident (who happened to be my patient) became very upset and angry that the House was shut down; he said he had a hard time trying to accept a situation that was not "transparent" and could not see the reason behind the policies of the facility. He was disturbed by how he had to pay the price for what others did. He stated that certain residents did not respect the regulations and listed several residents who he believed were responsible for the closing. Another resident stated that the house closing encouraged "snitching" and since some of them are legally mandated to be at the facility, the House was always "shut down anyway." He also angrily demanded to know why I was taking notes, whom they were for, and the point of the group. I calmly listened to him and tried to answer his questions while trying to remain in charge of the situation.

The house closing only had a day or two to go. The director came into the common room to announce that "one of your peers is in crisis." In a soft voice, she asked the troubled resident to tell everyone why he was upset. The patient in question, who despite his age and complaints of arthritis was muscular and very much from the "street," broke down and cried. The other residents responded by drawing on their own life journeys that were often full of distressing detours that brought them to treatment. Their words were highly expressive and moving, almost lyrical, e.g., "There are only two things worse than addiction—cancer and death." Some residents made it clear they would always be available to lend a sympathetic ear. This all from a crowd that, being self-described "real ball busters," regularly goaded, provoked, and made fun of each other. As their routines were suspended by the house closing, they seemed to have had the opportunity to reframe their differences as not that significant and to pull together as a group, the very definition of a therapeutic community in action, even in the midst of tensions of the house closing. The emotional turmoil experienced had led to positive transformation.

Termination as an Example of Restoration and the Final State

A patient that I had been working with for about half a year said good-bye to everyone in the agency. This patient, a heavily tattooed bear-like man and a fan of hip-hop who typically sported a large silver cross, loud jewelry, and other bling, was moving to another facility to begin several months of supportive living. Since he was my patient, the staff asked me to call a "listen up" to gather all residents together to begin the "closing" (a meeting in which each resident and staff member offers comments for and about the departing resident). There were lots of "man hugs," back patting, and hearty "Good luck, bro's!"

For a few days before the patient's departure, I had to move fast to ensure all the paperwork was in place for the upcoming transition. A couple of hours before the closing, my supervisor asked me how I felt about a patient of mine finally finishing the program. I responded that I felt somewhat concerned that eventually he might suffer a relapse even though he had made substantial progress. I also mentioned that I wondered what, if anything, I would say to him if I ran into him out in public. My supervisor also asked what I would have done differently with this patient. I did not have a good answer, except to say that if I could do it over, I would have made more of an effort to ask about his personal life and family relations. It was not that I did not inquire about these topics, but looking back I felt I could have attempted to get to know him better, perhaps coming across a clue that might shed light on his personal challenges and worldview. I pointed to the patient's four-inch-thick chart and commented on how it was a bit concerning how a person can be reduced to paperwork shoved into a binder.

Ending a therapeutic relationship with an individual who had shared so much with a therapist and sometimes had relied on that therapist to arrange certain things for them over such a long time (i.e., case management) can be a mixed bag for both parties.[6] Termination, as the final part of the three-phase process, is necessary for emotional closure. Hopefully, if the treatment has been successful, the patient can build upon any insights obtained and begin anew when re-entering society.

A few points about termination. First, the crucial differences between terminating therapy and ending other types of relationships (e.g., among intimates) is that in the latter we do not necessarily completely cut ties (even in romantic relations, the potential for reconnecting always exists). People know that the chance of meeting up again is a distinct possibility. Concluding a therapeutic relationship is different, as it carries a sense of finality. A therapist–patient relationship is at once professional and personal, i.e., it is highly intimate but at the same time, therapists must work hard to maintain objective distance between themselves and the patient.

Second, termination is a two-way process, affecting not just the patient but the therapist as well. This point relates to how the person of the therapist becomes a tool in a therapeutic setting, and thus must be ready to function as an instrument able to "pick up" emotions. By examining one's own affects, one can attempt to step into the shoes of the patient and sensitively consider how they might experience certain emotions. Composing a summary of progress and sharing it with the patient may allow both therapist and patient to come to a mutual understanding of what has been accomplished and afford a sense of closure. Since some patients struggle with a loss of socially meaningful relationships, this part of the termination can let the patient know that their meeting with the therapist has had an influence on the therapist.

The third issue is how challenging terminations could be; indeed, compared to the initial stages of therapy, they seem to be more of a task. Given the issues surrounding termination, we need to consider that it actually starts at the first session. Terminating appears difficult because of the many topics that deserve attention: the therapist should inquire about the patient's thoughts and feelings concerning concluding therapy; ask if it was helpful; goals that were met or unmet; explain why a friendship is not allowed post-therapy; review available resources; revisit coping skills; enumerate post-therapy goals; discuss ground rules if the therapist and patient meet in public; when do patients know if they might have to return to therapy (symptoms, triggers, warning signs); and finally, the therapist might share some of his or her own feelings about the ending. And the last point concerns how therapists should always remind themselves that the therapeutic endeavor is not about them. This especially applies during the termination process since a therapist is more likely to register affects when saying good-bye for good to a patient.

Discerning the Stages of Change

No one can talk another individual into self-change. Making a commitment when one is emotionally unprepared often does not end well. As a patient once told me, "If you're not ready for it, it's not ready for you." On the other hand, a patient in a group I facilitated reminded other members not to rush through their treatment: "When in recovery, don't take the elevator, take the stairs." Another advised members to slow down and ask questions while in session, but first they need to "Press the chill button." Timing is everything. This is why coming to terms with knowing when to gently push, hold back, or to more assertively try to persuade an individual to engage in self-change thinking and behaviors is vital.

An influential therapeutic approach that resonates with how anthropologists view rituals, rites of passage, and healing ceremonies is the "five stages of change" (Norcross, 2013; Norcross & Beutler, 2014; Norcross & Godlfried, 2005; Prochaska & Norcross, 2013). "Stages of change" comprise one of the six traits of patients delineated by Norcross and Beutler (indicating which treatment makes a good fit between patient and technique) (Norcross & Beutler, 2014, pp. 511-514). The approach of stages of change is useful since self-modification is an inherent feature of the human organism. Such adaptation occurs sequentially, so a careful counselor must discern how ready an individual is for change. The stages of change model can be used to gauge a patient's readiness for change: (1) precontemplation: patients lack the intention to change; most patients are unaware they have a problem; (2) contemplation: patients begin to seriously consider making a change but have not yet made a total commitment; (3) preparation: patients have made some minor changes but have not yet reached the threshold for effective action; (4) action: patients start to noticeably modify their behavior and become confident that they can overcome their problems; (5) maintenance: patients continue to make progress and take actions to prevent relapse (Norcross & Beutler, 2014, pp. 510-512).[7] It is most likely during the preparation and action stages—the transitional, liminal phase—that an individual is at a crossroads and transformational processes begin. Of great import is Norcross and Beutler's suggestion of how to integrate psychotherapy systems with the stages of change, as well as matching the therapist's relational stance (Table 8.1). Different strategies are most likely appropriate at different stages or phases of treatment (Parloff, 1986, p. 526).

In principle, any treatment system can be viewed through the lens of APS, though some seem more amenable to the tripartite structure than others. For example, consider the three stages of stress inoculation therapy (SIT), which loosely follow the three-phased process. Developed by Donald Meichenbaum (CBT), in SIT patients learn about stress and what they can do to avoid negative outcomes caused by anxiety. In the first stage, "initial conceptualization," the therapist educates the patient about the nature of stress, as well as concepts such as appraisal and cognitive distortion that shape stress reactions. Obstacles are identified. Stressors are reframed as opportunities for growth and puzzles to be solved, not as troubling problems to be

Table 8.1 Integration of Psychotherapy Systems within the Stages of Change

Stages of Change				
Precontemplation	Contemplation	Preparation	Action	Maintenance
Therapist relational stance to patient				
"Nurturing parent"	"Socratic teacher"	"Experienced coach"		"Consultant"
Suggested psychotherapy systems				
MI, FT, PAT	ADT, JT, PDT	CBT, EXT, REBT, IPT. GT		BT, SOLT, EMDRT

Source: Norcross and Beutler (2014), pp. 511–512; with modifications.

overcome. The patient is taught to discern the difference between what can and what cannot be changed in their lives; for the latter, acceptance-based coping is appropriate (ACT).

In the second stage, "skills acquisition and rehearsal," interventions are individually tailored for each patient, taking into account their unique strengths as well as their particular vulnerabilities. Techniques that unsettle one's affective and cognitive patterns are targeted through emotion regulation; relaxation; appraisal of one's thinking; problem-solving; and communication and socialization skills.

The final stage is "application and follow through." What was learned is put into action, and the patient practices coping skills. Simulation methods may be utilized to increase the realism of coping practice, e.g., visualization exercises; modeling; vicarious learning; role-playing; and repetitious practice of skills. At the conclusion, the patient should be ready to handle any unforeseen events that might trigger anxiety by developing an individualized plan.

Stages of Change: An Example

In an unsourced document entitled "stages of treatment for substance use," four stages are described. A clear-cut tripartite division of destabilize–instability–restabilize is lacking. However, it seems that if self-change does occur, it most likely transpires in stages two and three, which possess liminal, transitional elements.

Stabilization and Crisis Intervention (First Two Weeks)

Immediately stop all drug and alcohol use; break off contact with dealers and users; recover from acute aftereffects and drug "withdrawal"; stabilize daily functioning; stabilize or resolve immediate crisis situations; establish a positive connection to the treatment program; formulate a treatment plan.

Early Abstinence (Month One and Two)

Learn about addictive diseases; admit that the addiction exists; establish a support system; begin involvement in self-help; achieve stable abstinence for at least two weeks.

Relapse Prevention (Month Three to Month Six)

Progress from verbally admitting to emotionally accepting that the disease exists; learn about the relapse process, warning signs, relapse risk factors, and how to counteract them; make positive, lasting changes in lifestyle; learn how to deal effectively with problems, adjustments, and setbacks; learn how to identify and handle negative feelings; learn how to have fun without drugs; deepen involvement in self-help; maintain stable abstinence for at least six months.

Advanced Recovery (Post-Treatment to Six Months)

Achieve more lasting changes in attitude, lifestyle, and behavior; change addictive thinking styles and personality traits; address issues of arrested maturity; solidify adaptive coping and problem-solving skills; work through emotional, relationships, and self-esteem problems; continue and deepen involvement in self-help.[8]

Lessons from the Theatrical Arts

Though Schechner's framework is primarily concerned with theatrical performances, his appreciation of the value of "me behaving as if I am someone else" carries tremendous therapeutic implications, and his view overlaps with psychodrama (1992, p. 41). Schechner puts aside the commonsensical ontological hierarchies of what is real, not real, and fantasy (1992, p. 75). His discussion of performance studies and acting deeply resonates with the positive as-if-ness potential of the virtual, imaginative, fictive, and make-believe (Schechner, 1992, pp. 62, 76).[9] More specifically for our purposes, Schechner treats how a sense of selfness is regenerated from the interplay of the "me" and "not me," i.e., how elements that are "not self" become "self." Not only is the "not self" crucial to regenerating ourselves, but the double negativity of "not not self" is also important.

In what Schechner calls "workshop-rehearsals," a performer, in preparation for a performance, passes through three steps that basically coincide with the ritual process: (1) separation, stripping away, reducing, eliminating, or setting aside "me"; (2) initiation or revelation or finding out about one's "not me and not not me" and new, undisclosed aspects of one's self; (3) reintegration or building up longer and

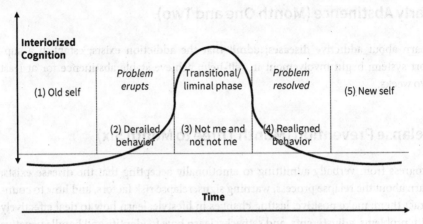

Figure 8.5. How a renewed self emerges from the transitional phase.

meaningful strips of behavior; making something for the public—preparing to re-enter the social world but as a new and/or different self (Schechner, 1992, p. 66). This ritual can elicit alienated or objectified aspects of the performer's selfhood (Schechner, 1992, p. 65). Schechner's workshop-rehearsal shares underlying socio-psychological process with a therapeutic intervention in that an individual, confront-ing a life challenge, passes through a transitional and transformative "not me and not not me" phase and acquires a new outlook in a "potential space." Figure 8.5 illustrates this process.

As Jørgensen contends, psychotherapy comprises a "potential space" (cf. Winnicott, 1971) where patients are afforded the opportunity to "play with reality." Interiorized mental states are manifested in the "safe world of psychotherapy—an 'as if' world that is decoupled from everyday reality." The world is experienced in a "pre-tend mode" (Fonagy et al., 2002) in which the contents of the individual's psyche—fantasies, thoughts, worries—are defanged and "become less dangerous than they are in the real world" (Jørgensen, 2004, p. 531). The hypothetical nature of psychotherapy allows the cultivation of meta-framing capacities, i.e., separating mental representa-tions from external reality; becoming aware of the representational nature of experi-ences; stepping beyond the immediate reality of one's own experience; entertaining different perspectives; appreciating the distinctions between immediate experience and the underlying mental states from which it emerges; and acknowledging that "emotions and fantasies are communications from and to the self" (i.e., interself in-teraction) (Jørgensen, 2004, p. 529).[10]

I conclude this chapter with a summary of the phases of psychosocial restabiliza-tion (Table 8.2).

Table 8.2 Phases of Psychosocial Restabilization

	(1) Destabilized/Obstacle		(2) Instability/Transition	(3) Restabilized/Restoration	
	Presenting problem/introduction of issue, preparatory activities, leaving ordinary life		Adjustment, alteration, confrontation of problem	Resolution, concluding activities, return to ordinary life	
	Initial state	Problem	Transitional state	Restoration	Final state
Psychological Level					
(1)	Formation	Orientation	Transition / Working	Consolidation	Evaluation and follow-up
(2)	Precontemplation	Contemplation	Preparation / Action	Maintenance	
(3)	Exploration		Insight	Action	
Societal Level					
(4)	Preliminary: separation and segregation		Liminality: marginal state	Post-liminality: incorporation and aggregation	New or renewed social structure
(5)	Breach in relations	Crisis	Redressive actions / Anti-structure and communitas	Acts of reintegration	New or renewed social structure
	Original or normal social structure / Old status	Breach in or challenge to social structure	Intermediate Period / Suspension, elevation OR Reversal of status	Repair of or return to social structure	New status OR return to original status

Examples:

(1) Corey (2012)
(2) Norcross and Beutler (2014)
(3) Hill (2014)
(4) Van Gennep (1977)
(5) Turner (1967, 1969, 1974).

Taking Stock

This chapter offered examples of how the mind psychosocially adjusts to transitions through adaptive phasic structurations (APSs), e.g., rituals, ceremonies, and in clinical settings, stages of change. The next chapter builds upon the psyche's inbuilt propensity to self-heal by examining how particular systems of psychotherapy effect positive self-change.

Notes

1. I witnessed this processual approach while conducting fieldwork in Japan on "spirit possession" (McVeigh, 1997a). This dissociative trancing was arguably a ceremony in which afflicted individuals progressed through a series of healing experiences.
2. I am grateful to Bill Rowe for pointing out to me the resonances between APSs and the predictive coding modeling. See Barrett (2017a); Barrett (2017b); Clark (2013); Hohwy (2012); Kogo & Trengove (2015); Lethin (2002); Rao & Ballard (1999); and Seth (2013).
3. Note that the introduction of new personalities (whether patients or staff) into a system (e.g., group or therapeutic community) might destabilize (even if temporally) interpersonal dynamics, thereby challenging communitas.
4. Hill notes that typically it takes students many years to master the skills for the insight stage. The skills for the exploration stage are easier to acquire because it is more about gathering information from the client by listening rather than making conceptual linkages or interpretations, which can seem riskier.
5. Arguably, some clients just need exploration, while others need action but not necessarily insight.
6. But it is the patient's reaction to termination that should be the focus.
7. Stages of change are elaborated by Schottenbauer et al. (2005).
8. For a specific example of how the stages of change model works, see Prochaska, DiClemente, & Norcross (1997), who apply it to addictive behaviors.
9. Cf. Gregory Bateson's "play frame" (1972). The British psychoanalyst D. W. Winnicott (1896-1971) theorized about an intermediate state between "me" and "not me" that infants discover as they acquire their own identity.
10. McCallum and Piper refer to these abilities as "psychological mindedness" (1997).

PART IV

APPLICATIONS, APPROACHES, AND INTERVENTIONS

9

Using Conscious Interiority as a Therapeutic Tool

"I now look at my time in jail as a vacation," explained one individual, who found benefit in being imprisoned. "Rehab is not prison," said another patient. Another patient redefined "snitching" from "ratting out others" to informing staff about other patients who need help. "I now realize that my thinking was shaped by a jailhouse mentality" (i.e., deeply socialized by long stays in the judicial system and "being institutionalized"). Patients struggling with addiction would rethink "telling each other war stories" and realize that romanticizing their previous lifestyle, a common deflection tactic in groups, is not beneficial to their recovery. Other examples from the area of substance use illustrate reframing: "I don't have a drug problem but a thinking problem"; "I try to have love from a distance" (when dealing with family members who continue to use substances); "This is not a drinking game; it's a thinking game"; "The biggest amends we can make is staying sober for others, if not ourselves." To describe the interpersonal challenges his substance-using wife presented to him, one individual said, "I now think of my wife as my special needs daughter."

These aforementioned instances of reframing an issue by looking at it from a different angle (thereby giving it an alternative meaning) can be a powerful cognitive maneuver. Cognitive restructuring is about instructing individuals how to interrogate their irrational beliefs, perfectionism, maladaptive behaviors, unrealistic goals, and grandiosity by adopting more rational (preferential) thoughts and deploying logico-empirical and pragmatic approaches (REBT, CBT). Meta-framing undergirds specific techniques: decatastrophizing (a "what-if" technique to help patients prepare for feared consequences); reattribution (challenging automatic thoughts and core beliefs by considering alternative causes of events, especially if patients view themselves as causes of a problem); stopping and monitoring (establishing cues to stop and notice thought processes throughout the day); modeling (asking a patient to emulate someone who demonstrates a desired behavior); and decentering (to counter an unhealthy self-focusing and social anxiety in which in one's mind one becomes the center of attention). One patient, who suffered from social anxiety and consequently had a difficult time in groups, explained to me how he got through the sessions by pretending to be "looking at reality TV" while observing other members.

Reducing Hyper-Interiority by Utilizing FOCI

This chapter examines how conscious interiority operates as a therapeutic tool in various psychotherapeutic systems. A useful intervention is educating patients about FOCI, thereby demystifying the processes behind their own recovery and encouraging them to mobilize their own inner resources and strengths and alleviating the symptoms of mental disorders within a FOCI perspective. The first two systems examined fall squarely under the general cognitive therapeutic paradigm, while CCT, GT, EXT are grounded in the humanistic tradition.

A crucial principle of third wave BT is mindfulness; this is the inspiration for ACT and DBT, which are also examined. These systems, rather than explaining and attempting to "solve" our problems or becoming entangled in worrisome thought patterns, emphasize mindfulness which allows one to meta-frame by taking a step back from the world, allowing experiences to occur nonjudgmentally, and describing what is happening to ourselves. One's "I" is tasked with merely "observing" and monitoring one's reactions as if from a distance.

Rational Emotive Behavior Therapy: An Active-Directive Approach

Albert Ellis (1913-2007) was inspired by the Greek stoic philosopher Epictetus (50-135 CE) who reportedly said, "People are disturbed not by things but by the views they take of them." REBT views human nature from different aspects: (1) physiological—we have a built-in tendency to rely on irrational thinking to make sense of the world; (2) social—we are concerned about what others think of us; and (3) psychological—individuals sometimes permit their irrational beliefs to over-emotionalize the reasons they have encountered adversity. REBT's goal is to effect a profound philosophical change in one's outlook, thereby making a person less susceptible to future disturbances.

While REBT certainly pays attention to emotions, it emphasizes cognitions because they are easier to evaluate than feelings; core irrational beliefs often affect several areas of thought, so that altering a distorted cognition can often change several dysfunctional viewpoints. Moreover, changes in thought patterns require less insight than emotionally charged ideas and are more likely to be readily understood and processed.

Common core irrational beliefs (which can reinforce each other) include: absolutistic "demands, musts, and should"; "I-can't-stand-it-ism"; condemning oneself or others; and "awfulizing." The latter is illustrated by a patient who advised griping group members that a negative incident should not be allowed to color their entire day: "You don't have a bad day. You have a bad five minutes that you carry with you all day." Three common irrational beliefs are: (1) "I absolutely must under all conditions do important tasks well and be approved by significant others or else I am an inadequate and unlovable person"; (2) "other people absolutely must under all conditions treat me fairly and justly or else they are rotten and damnable persons"; and (3) "conditions under which I live absolutely must always be the way I want them to be, give me almost immediate gratification, and not require me to work too hard to change or improve them, or else it is awful, I can't stand them, and it is impossible for me to be happy at all!"

Though people have a natural ability to change themselves, REBT uses an active-directive approach to effect improvement. In this sense it differs somewhat from CBT, which in principle is not necessarily as directive. An active-directive intervention may be effective for patients who: (1) may be biologically predisposed to mental disorders; (2) have low frustration tolerance; (3) view change as threatening because it robs them of their excuses; (4) prefer to interact with a caring therapist rather than to confront their problems; (5) are hostile to others who are pushing them to change; and (6) do not agree with certain therapeutic approaches.

In order to help the patient replace a self-defeating outlook with a realistic and acceptable worldview, an REBT therapist identifies and strongly challenges the patient's irrational beliefs. The individual needs to see what difficulties result from those beliefs, instead of focusing on antecedent causes and conditions. Although problems do not go away by themselves, they can be minimized through rational emotive thinking and action. The primary technique of REBT is to dispute irrational beliefs. The different kinds of disputations include: (1) functional, or questioning whether the belief helps accomplish desired goals; (2) empirical, or questioning whether the "facts" are accurate; (3) logical, or questioning the logic of thinking processes; and (4) philosophical, or suggesting that despite dissatisfaction, some pleasure can be derived from life, no matter our present circumstances. After disputing the irrational beliefs, the patient is asked to verbalize more reasonable coping statements. The deeper and more profound the statements, the more helpful they are likely to be.

Cognitive Behavior Therapy: Evolution and Learned Behavior

CBT is grounded in the basics of human evolution. Evolutionary theory, if broadly understood, regards the human organism as incessantly adapting to a changing environment by modifying a constellation of different systems that constitute the psyche; this is the first premise of CBT. CBT then is grounded in the idea that the processing of information is vital to an organism's survival. While CBT recognizes environmental influences, it stresses the role of the individual's cognitive-emotional apparatus in initiating change. One's thoughts drive one's feelings and behaviors, not just external events, people, or circumstances. As one changes his or her thoughts, one's symptoms diminish, despite the situation or what one can or cannot control. Maladaptive behavior is associated with patterns of thinking and responses which do not result in mentally healthy outcomes. CBT aims to change or substitute these patterns with more realistic and useful thoughts and responses. It is used to treat depression, anxiety disorders, specific phobias, and other mental disorders. It takes seriously the varying symptomology of different disorders and proposes that each one possesses its own "cognitive profile." Medication is often used in conjunction with this approach to treat depressive disorders and bipolar and related disorders. Though CBT can appear nomothetic ("scientific" and "rational"), it is actually idiographic, as it advocates the notion that each individual possesses a set of idiosyncratic vulnerabilities and sensitivities which should be taken into account when administering treatment.

The mental mechanisms bequeathed to us by evolution are usually adaptive. However, the many working parts of the psyche can also, if pressed to function overtime, result in misperceptions and a dysfunctional view of one's circumstances. The result is a "cognitive shift." Certain attitudes, assumptions, or core beliefs contribute to such shifts. Consequently, an individual comes to perceive their interactions with the world through a systematically biased lens. One's life's circumstances may set in motion cognitive distortions or underlying maladaptive assumptions that generate negative thought patterns. Patients with distorted thinking misattribute causes, mistakenly define events, misinterpret circumstances, and "catastrophize" (Beck & Weishaar, 2014). This is driven by hyper-interiorization.

CBT does not deny the role of physiological processes or neurochemical predispositions. However, its second premise is learning theory; it stresses how individuals respond to specific stressors because of acquired experiences and how they process information as the best ways to understand the workings of human nature.

CBT and BT rely heavily on three types of exposure-based interventions: (1) in vivo exposure, or controlled contact with a real-life fearful or anxiety-inducing situation; (2) interoceptive exposure, or purposely experiencing unpleasant sensations until they are no longer unpleasant; and (3) imaginal (introceptual) exposure, or evoking and visualizing feared mental imagery. These techniques facilitate the individual's objectifying of negative affects so that they become excerpted as an entity separate from the experiencer ("I") and so more controllable. They also may be thought of as memory reconsolidation-based treatments that lead to new insights and learning; this occurs via the rewriting or the self-renarratization of unsettling or traumatic experiences.

All things considered, in vivo exposure is more effective than imaginal exposure, as it more comprehensively engages perceptual, conceptual, and conscious interiorized dimensions of the psyche. However, for practical reasons, imaginal exposure may be the only exposure-based intervention that can be utilized to treat certain irrational fears that, from a commonsensical perspective, are highly unlikely. Sometimes imaginal exposures can be used as "warm-up" exercises prior to patients engaging with in vivo exposures.

Schemas and Core Beliefs

Cognitive change transpires at several levels: voluntary thoughts, automatic mentation, underlying assumptions, and core beliefs. These "layers" of the psyche differ in degree of accessibility and stability, with voluntary thoughts being the most the ame-nable to change (conscious and preconscious) and stable and core beliefs being the least (quarantined nonconscious).

From socialization, individuals acquire schemas. An individual's learning history, an array of accumulated experiences, shapes how he or she perceives, interprets, and assigns meaning to events. Early traumatic childhood experiences can play a key role in the formation of mental disorders (Beck & Weishaar, 2014). Significantly, if much of human behavior (understood as something configured by controlling and consequential forces within the environment) can be learned, then it can also be un-learned (Beck & Weishaar, 2014). The basic goal is to have patients identify the dis-torting schemas that need to be altered through treatment, and then to consciously override—meta-frame—maladaptive modes by questioning underlying assump-tions. This is done by treating unhelpful conclusions as testable hypotheses, providing alternative interpretations, generating contradictory evidence, and adopting more adaptive beliefs. The systems or schemas (knowledge forms that allow people to in-terpret their circumstances and structure their fundamental beliefs and assumptions) work together and form networks of cognitive, affective, motivational, and behavioral patterns that make up one's personality. Modes may be primary (nonconscious au-tomatic and reflexive responses) or under voluntary control (conscious, deliberate thinking, problem-solving, long-term planning).

Granting Self-Autonomy to the Patient

In CBT patients are viewed as active co-participants in their own treatment; they are "practical scientists" who cooperate with the therapist in finding their own answers. Such "collaborative empiricism" fosters a sense of self-autonomy and self-authorization. Self-agentive control can make an individual feel as if they "own" the solution, thereby empowering them (Yapko, 2012, p. 516). In this way they can accomplish more when they are guided and encouraged to use homework, skill-building tasks, bibliothera-pies, and behavioral experiments. Guided discovery, by finding threads that form pat-terns in the patient's misperceptions, helps patients engage in "active learning," which requires: (1) "activating or constructing appropriate knowledge to be used for making sense of new incoming information"; and (2) "integrating new incoming information with an appropriate knowledge base" (consilience) (Mayer, 2004, p. 15).

A step-by-step Socratic method can be utilized in order to discern the issues. This can be accomplished in a variety of ways: (1) the therapist can show patients how to monitor their negative thoughts that automatically arise (excerption); (2) patients can learn how to recognize linkages among thinking, affect, and behavior (understanding how consilience works); (3) they can be instructed on how to come up with evidence for and against automatic, distorted thoughts and acknowledge the sometimes un-helpful role of spontaneous nonconscious processes; (4) they can be taught how to substitute more reality-oriented interpretations for biased cognitions; and (5) they can learn how to identify and change dysfunctional core beliefs that predispose them to distort their thought patterns (Beck & Weishaar, 2014).

Disputing the A-B-C-D Chain of Cognition

Before beginning interventions, patients should understand the A-B-C-D model and recognize that they are primarily responsible for their own reactions to life events (self-autonomy). Discussing with patients how excerption, consilience, and other FOCI can distort thinking patterns may go a long way in permitting them to see how their symptoms are intrinsic to their own mentation. Acknowledging the import of FOCI highlights the potency of self-conditioning, self-reconditioning, self-righting, and self-regulating capacities. REBT and CBT aim at disrupting distorted thinking by working through the A-B-C-D chain. Typically, from an individual's point of view, an activating event (A) causes a highly charged emotional consequence (C). However, in reality, A does not result in C. Instead, the emotional reaction is created by an intermediating link: the individual's belief system and expectations (B). Reactions are informed by a person's interpretation of the events and opinions about those events or adversities. People acquire schemas that structure an individual's fundamental views and assumptions. An individual's learning history (or array of accumulated experiences) shapes how a person perceives, interprets, and assigns meaning to events (A), which may contribute to but do not directly cause emotional consequences (C). The ultimate goal of therapy is to teach patients about their mistaken premises by having them consciously evoke and then challenge and dispute the interiorized cognitions that cause distress (D) (E, meaning effort and exercise, might be a final link).

Ruminating leads to problematic secondary symptoms. Many patients clearly recognize that they are depressed or anxious, but they increase their distress by becoming depressed about being depressed or anxious about being anxious (hyperinteriorization). For example, one may be worried about an upcoming event (A); this leads to anxiety (C). Then comes another emotional response: "I feel anxious" (A2). Then one concludes, "Aren't my feelings of anxiety awful!" (B2). Next comes even greater feelings of anxiety (C2). The sequence of A–B–C spirals out of control.

Client-Centered Therapy: Highlighting the Interiorized, Subjective Contents of the Mind

According to Carl Rogers, the essentials for therapeutic change come about through three "core conditions." The first is congruence, or attaining a state of wholeness such that a person's actual experience coincides with their idealized self-concept ("I" coincides with an improved "me" or role-self). The second is unconditional positive regard, or an open-minded acknowledgment of the client as an individual, irrespective of the therapist's own values. This core condition is one of acceptance of and respect for the client's individuality (appreciating their self-individuation), stemming from trust in the client's self-directing (self-autonomous) capacity for positive change. In order to value the client's inherent capacity for and right to self-determination, the counselor needs to adopt a nondirective attitude. The third condition is an empathic understanding of the client's frame of reference. While sympathy implies a position of power and pity and emotional contagion (experiencing and sharing feelings with the client), empathy is a deep and genuine understanding of how clients experience their subjective world.[1] The client-centered perspective of Rogers intends to rectify the loss of personal power by enhancing a sense of control over one's own person. CCT recognizes the highly individuated elements of the client.

The counselor's genuineness drives empathic understanding. To convey genuineness, Rogerian counselors draw upon their own interiorized experiences during counseling and the authenticity of their own feelings. Since present experience provides the means to personal growth, the client-centered counselor serves as facilitator, helping the client to find meaning in inner experiences. By freely showing responsive warmth while avoiding evaluative judgments and overly intrusive, probing questions, the therapist encourages a permissive atmosphere without pressure or coercion. The therapist assumes that a client has the potential to develop "self-regard," or that aspect of selfhood that develops from the esteem or respect accorded to oneself. Self-regarding capabilities allow an individual to differentiate between positive and negative inner experiences. Such differentiation requires self-reflexivity. Impacted by the reactions of others and by introjection of external conditions, an individual encounters conflict when personal needs and desires run counter to those of significant others. Intervention is needed when environmental needs routinely eclipse self-regard needs. Client-centered counseling seeks to allow conflicted individuals to incorporate these negative organismic needs (once denied) into their self-concept. Through "symbolization," a life event or experience (this may mean sensory and visceral experiences) is acknowledged in such a way that it coincides with one's self-concept. If experiences are not interpreted in such a way to fit with the individual's self-definition, a person can become psychologically maladjusted (a disjunction between "I" and "me"). The goal is to have individuals experience a greater openness and flexibility to one's self and the world, reducing defensiveness and instilling a self-directed, self-authorized expansion of self-awareness. This can occur when an individual's self-understandings and feelings about themselves change. Clients gain self-esteem when, on the dimension of locus of evaluation, the basis for their standards and values shifts from other people to themselves (internal frame of reference). In other words, a movement toward an interior locus of evaluation allows an immediacy of experiencing and changes in self-acceptance.

CCT is used for moderate to high-functioning clients and helps them to unlock blocked feelings. Rogers believed that everyone possesses an innate, internal guide—"organismic valuing process"—that leads individuals to self-actualization (self-individuation). All people seek "unconditional positive regard" (more concretely, acceptance, respect, warmth); an individual wants to be loved merely for who he or she is without any "conditions of worth" (COWs). But COWs give rise to an incongruence between a person's actual experience and their ideal self-concept. When one's self-worth becomes dependent on COWs, inauthenticity, self-alienation, and an inability to experience genuine affect result. Defenses are deployed, such as perceptual distortion and denial. These in turn lead to subjective interiorized experiences becoming incongruent with reality, a rigidity of perception, and discrepancies between the ideal (future "me") and real self (current "me"). As one client told me, "If I feel good about myself, then I won't want to numb that good feeling" (by using substances).

Some therapists, perhaps not appreciating the nuances of Rogers's viewpoint, might convey to the client that the only thing that matters is the person's "self," understood as what the person feels or desires minus a meta-framing distancing from one's "me" and mental contents. Related to this is the issue of to what degree a client should be regarded as an expert in their own treatment. A co-creator or participant in the therapeutic alliance, yes, but an "expert"?

Existential Therapy: Confronting our Self-Individuation

Existential isolation is the fundamental and inescapable feeling of separation from others, the world, and one's self (too much self-individuation). Though such isolation can certainly be minimized, it can never be completely eliminated. One way to reduce one's sense of isolation is through "fusion" or the surrender of oneself to become part of another person or a group, e.g., a fervent political movement or religious fanaticism. Existential isolation, which is a consequence of a very modern form of conscious interiority, resonates with heightened versions of FOCI. Consider that we pay a heavy price for the gift of FOCI. Though they can propel humans forward as psychological beings, in their hyper-forms they highlight our seclusion from an ultimate grounding, both as a species and as individuals. The individual's private psychoscape can feel like a desolate terrain abandoned by the gods. Self-autonomy can lead to the weighty responsibility of making choices; self-reflexivity can result in one's "I" silently staring at one's "me" waiting for a response; self-individuation can cause feelings of detachment from the comfort of socioaffiliation; self-authorization can end up making one long for answers and direction that never come.

In EXT, techniques are secondary in the therapeutic process; the client's subjective understanding is primary. Indeed, EXT lacks a set of standard techniques and is tailored to the needs of the client. A distinction exists between standardized "recipes" of treatment and "throw-ins" or unscripted "off-the-record extras" that can make a profound difference in moving therapy in a fruitful direction (Yalom, 1980). It is this possibility of spontaneous genuineness and authenticity (humor and paradox might be used) that just might allow a client to stare down the void and become self-transcendent (adopt a meta-framed view of their predicament). EXT attempts to show clients an authentic mode of living.[2] This describes a way of being in which one understands and appreciates the fragility of one's existence while acknowledging responsibility for one's own life (self-autonomy, self-authorization).

A distinction between the "why" and the "what-is-wrong" perspective regarding psychoemotional health problems relates to an existential outlook that is often lost in perfunctory and hurried sessions, clinical examinations, impersonal tests, and laboratory reports. The "why" concerns the cosmomoral order into which one is born and an individual's total individual–environment system; as such, it evokes existential questions. The "why" perspective can also relate to interpersonal relations and underlying emotional difficulties that do not readily present themselves for whatever reason. The "what is wrong" perspective involves modern scientific knowledge applied to health problems and attempts to treat symptoms (Rappaport & Rappaport, 1981, p. 780).

Gestalt Therapy: Focusing on the Experiential Self

Gestalt therapy (GT) puts center stage the affective and experiential, focusing on the client's experience and bringing the past into the here and now. Another central concept of GT is self-regulation, i.e., humans are inherently self-adjusting and growth oriented. In more prosaic terms, we might say that humans are, like all animals, always naturally adapting. However, self-adjusting is a form of meta-framing. In terms of actual therapy, GT advocates intersubjectivity or mutual, reciprocal emotional influences between the therapist and client, which implicates a search for shared meanings. From a positive psychological perspective, Steger (2009) sees meaning as grounded in two components: (1) comprehension of one's trajectory through life; and (2) purpose, i.e., highly motivating, long-term goals (self-narratization).

A number of innovative techniques characterize GT interventions. "Contact" (being in touch with what is occurring presently); conscious awareness (focused concentration on habitual modes that are not working); and experimentation (trying something new by leaving one's comfort zone). As the client increases present-centered awareness, unfinished business emerges, which is then dealt with to assist the client in living more fully in the present. Gestalt techniques are designed to help the client express the self freely and in a way that provides congruence with inner conflicts and to unlock blocked feelings.

"Dialogue (game of)," meaning here inclusion and empathetic engagement, can be enacted by the therapist being fully present and joining with the client in a heartfelt back-and-forth conversation while ensuring that the therapist does not control the discussion. The "internal dialogue exercise" sees the client act out a personal conflict, simultaneously role-playing the controlling ("I") as well as the controlled ("me") aspect of self (internalized behavioral rehearsal). The use of psychodrama can enliven the experience with genuine feelings, sentiments, and anything else the client believes is relevant to their therapeutic encounter.

The "empty chair" technique sees the client address a chair as if another person (typically a significant other), or even an aspect of themselves (i.e., feeling, personality facet, role, "me"), were present. The client will talk to their personified anxiety or even practice different confrontations that may need to take place in the future between the client and another person or a future "me." The client may assume more than one role, and move back and forth between chairs. The client can thereby explore some aspect of their selfhood. A related method is the "two chair" technique in which a client moves back and forth between two chairs while engaging in a dialogue with another person or while acting out their own role-selves.

In the "reversal technique," the therapist asks the client to do the opposite of their targeted problem behavior, acting out a counter-scenario. This allows a client to step back (meta-frame) from their usual patterns of activity to better self-observe and obtain insight, understanding, and entertain hypothetical possibilities. In "exaggerating a behavior," the therapist has the client exaggerate specific movements to aid in understanding feelings. For example, if the client is talking about his teenage son, he is instructed to move like he does, which will intensify the client's awareness and feelings about his son.

GT explores "five major channels of resistance." The first is "introjection," or an uncritical acceptance of the standards of others and what they believe about one's self (weak self-individuation). It can also mean to passively incorporate whatever the environment affords and being unconcerned about what one personally needs or wants (weak self-autonomy). The second is projection. This indicates several things. It means to disown aspects of one's self by assigning them to external forces (undeveloped self-authorization). Or it denotes a difficulty in distinguishing between the "inside" world (one's psychoscape governed by an autonomous self) and the outside world. It also means to deny aspects of one's self that do not match one's self-image and attributing them to others. Finally, it signifies self-alienation, or how one avoids responsibility for one's own feelings and how one defines oneself. The third is retroflection, or doing something to one's self that one really wanted to do or would have done to someone else. The fourth is deflection (or distraction). This may mean not sustaining a realistic connection to reality or diminished authentic emotional experience. The final channel of resistance is confluence, which means a blurring of the differentiation between one's person and the environment. More specifically, confluence might be expressed as an obsession with fitting in, avoiding conflict, a need for acceptance and approval, and seeing no need for self-expression (underdeveloped self-individuation and self-autonomy).

GT is typically used with moderate- to high-functioning clients. Its big bag of tricks—body awareness, breathing techniques, enactment, guided fantasy, and imagery—is what makes it flexible and open to creative application. Notably, its experiential-orientation attempts to bridge the mind–body gap.

Dialectical Behavior Therapy

Dialectic is a type of reasoning in which propositions (theses) and counter-propositions (antitheses) are exchanged. Three outcomes are possible: (1) an argument is refuted; (2) the opposing assertions are combined to produce a synthesis; or (3) the direction of the dialogue is transformed. DBT is founded on the idea that life is about balancing the need to adapt, change, and accommodate with an acceptance of the way things actually are. In other words, we must learn to find a middle ground when we engage in the incessant self-arguments and self-debates that cause such a cacophony of voices in our heads. We must be neither overly pessimistic nor overly optimistic, but judiciously realistic.

The roiling mentation of our psyche throws up positions, propositions, or problems (and their possible solutions). But often, when our "I" weighs in, it prefers categorical conclusions and chooses either a thesis or an antithesis. Wedding arguments with counter-arguments is more of a challenge, as is changing the very premises of the debate. However, these are healthier options. Assuming that the "I" is able to take the meta-framed middle ground, the resulting synthesis becomes a new thesis or antithesis as circumstances change. Then the process is repeated, without end.

Radical Acceptance

Fighting reality is quite an endeavor. But if we choose to "radically accept" whatever comes our way, we grant ourselves a certain freedom to embrace whatever the situation presents to us. Here "radical" means all the way. This is a tall order, but such acceptance (which does not mean approval of a stressful situation or judging it to be good) just means acknowledging that it is what it is. Acceptance of reality demands "turning the mind" or making a choice. This needs to be rooted in a strong sense of self-autonomy. Though making such a commitment does not equate with full acceptance, it is the first step. Teaching patients the value of unconditional self-acceptance and unconditional other-acceptance (ACT) is a type of meta-framing.

The Emotional, Rational, and Wise Mind

DBT posits "three minds." The first is the "emotion mind," which is useful as it motivates us to action, keeps us attached to others, and builds relationships that satisfy our innate need for socioaffiliation. But the emotional mind also describes occasions when we lose control of our feelings, which can influence or control our thinking and behavior. So emotion regulation is another key tool in the DBT toolbox. It is essential to appreciate how emotions work so that we (our purely aware, nonjudgmental "I") is in charge, and not our negative emotions. This reduces vulnerability to affective disruptions. When feeling overwhelmed by emotional flare-ups, four useful crisis skills can be utilized: (1) distracting oneself; (2) self-soothing; (3) improving the moment; and (4) thinking of pros and cons (of the situation).

The second mind is "reasonable" or "rational." It is necessary for making mature, logical decisions, evaluations, and plans, and is associated with cool cognition. When we are doing fine, we see the world through the lens of the reasonable mind. However, when we do not feel well or are overwhelmed, staying in the reasonable mind is difficult.

We cannot completely turn off or overcome emotional mind using the logic of reasonable mind, and the latter cannot by itself create a healthy emotional life. So we must balance our cool/cold and warm/hot cognitions with "wise mind." The integration of emotional and reasonable mind leads to knowledge that is centered and balanced, i.e., it is an instance of meta-framing above extremes.

Willfulness and Willingness

DBT practitioners speak about the difference between willfulness (trying to impose one's will, regardless of reality) and willingness (acting skillfully, from a realistic understanding of one's present circumstances). The former denotes resistance to making changes that are needed. It discourages one from accepting potentially useful suggestions or advice that might be helpful. Indeed, it can mean giving up on oneself. Willingness, on the other hand, is acknowledging that one must take appropriate actions to effectively change one's situation. It means allowing one's "I" to meta-frame above one's challenging circumstances, listening carefully to one's wise mind and thereby connecting with and opening up to the wider world of which we are all a part.

Mindfulness Skills

Mindfulness skills denote a foundational concept that informs the techniques taught in DBT, as it assists individuals to accept and tolerate powerful feelings of resistance when confronting die-hard habits or being exposed to upsetting situations. "One-mindfully" means simply to do one thing at a time (to avoid the perils of "multi-tasking"). One-mindfulness is not just about focusing one's attention. Rather, it concerns zeroing one's interiorized attention into one point, i.e., the FOCI of concentration. This minimizes distractions and makes each experience richer. When eating, eat; when walking, walk; when working, work; when listening, listen; and when worrying, worry.

"Participate" means to enter into one's experience by dropping ruminations or distracting thoughts. "Becoming one with your experience" and "forgetting yourself" sound a tad mystical, but they are antidotes to overthinking; only do what is required in each situation. Think of a skillful skater, dancer, or martial arts competitor whose actions seem to naturally flow from their bodies. We sometimes allow self-narratization to take us too far back into the past or forward into the future. Self-consciousness becomes hyper-consciousness. We become overly attached to excerpted thoughts that distract us, pulling us away from what needs to be accomplished.

Another key mindfulness skill is being non-judgmental. We should strive to allow an impartial "I" to stand above a situation and observe just the facts, without assessing whether what is occurring is good or bad. And if you find yourself judging, do not judge your judging.

To "observe" means to take notice of something without getting caught up in the experience; in other words, experiencing without reacting to your experience or allowing one's "I" to monitor a situation from a distance. Common metaphors to describe allowing feelings and thoughts to march in and out of one's mind include: having a "Teflon mind"; watching one's thoughts come and go like clouds in the sky; observing one's feelings rise and fall like waves in the ocean. Paying attention to how others are reacting or what sensations one's eyes, ears, nose, and skin perceive is one method of controlling one's concentration without, as counterintuitive as it sounds, becoming attached to distractions. Simply "describing" or "putting words on one's experience" when an unsettling feeling or thought arises and withholding evaluation can lead to a calmer acknowledgment of one's circumstances.

Distress Tolerance Survival Skills

Tolerance survival skills are intended to have individuals accept, in a non-evaluative manner, a stressful situation and one's immediate reaction to it. This allows one to utilize wise mind and make judicious decisions and avoid falling into extreme, desperate, and destructive emotional reactions. Distress tolerance skills include "distracting." The goal is to reduce exposure to emotional stimuli, and this is accomplished when wise mind ACCEPTS: activities, contributing, comparisons, (opposite) emotions, pushing away, (other) thoughts, and sensations. Other distress tolerance skills are self-soothing; drawing our attention away from an unsettling situation using the five senses of vision, hearing, smell, taste, and touch; and IMPROVE: imagery, meaning, prayer, relaxation, one (thing in the moment), vacation, and self-encouragement.

Acceptance and Commitment Therapy

The primary aim of ACT is to increase "psychological flexibility." This designates the ability to be fully aware of the present moment (engaged FOCI), to be open to whatever experiences transpire, and to take action guided by our values. The greater our ability to be present, open up, and do what matters, then the more readily we can respond effectively to life's problems, challenges, and quandaries. This improves our quality of life as we acquire a sense of meaning and purpose and develop "vitality." This term means being fully alive and welcoming the here and now, regardless of what feeling we might be experiencing at the moment. The point is to accept living itself, in spite of its darker moments.

Psychological flexibility involves a number of core therapeutic processes, and though for pragmatic purposes they can be enumerated, they actually are not separate processes. The first is "acceptance," or opening up and making room for painful emotions. Patients are encouraged to stop confronting, interrogating, and struggling with negative experiences. I tell my patients to regard the latter as annoying neighbors; the more you complain to them, the more trouble they will cause you. Better to drop by, get to know them, view the neighborhood from their yard's perspective, and perhaps suggest a different way of doing things. If they are a particularly troublesome neighbor, we probably will not end up liking them. But that is not the point; the idea is to acknowledge their existence without making matters worse by resisting, fighting, running away, or becoming overwhelmed by them.

The second core process is "cognitive defusion," which means to step back and separate or detach from one's thoughts, images, and memories. This is a type of meta-framing. This technique views thoughts as mere words or pictures (excerptions) that can be watched, rather than as things in which we must become entangled ("hold them lightly, don't clutch them tightly"). The third core process is "self-as-context." Though we often speak as if there were a singular mind, in fact it can be divided into a "thinking self" and the "observing self." We are familiar with the former (generating thoughts, beliefs, memories, judgments, fantasies, plans, etc.), but we are less familiar with the latter. This is the facet of our mind that is aware of whatever we are thinking, feeling, perceiving, or doing at any given moment. Another term for the "observing self" is "pure awareness" (transcendent "I"). Though we physically, intellectually, and emotionally change as we age, something in our psyche appears not to change—the "observing self." This is the part of "you" that is able to survey, monitor, and notice what changes and what does not change as we journey through life.

Values—or "knowing what matters"—are the fourth core process. These are desired qualities that describe what inspires us, what we stand for, and what at the end of the day is truly significant to us. Clarifying how we want to behave in a continual manner is a crucial step in creating a meaningful life. Values are chosen—ideally in a self-autonomous manner—life directions. The fifth core process, which follows from the fourth, is committed action ("do what it takes"). Values need to be put to be into operation, and this occurs when committed action is governed by our values. Putting our values on the table may lead to discomfort, but only through values-congruent behavior does life becomes rich, full, and meaningful. Tried and tested traditional interventions of BT (e.g., goal setting; exposure; skills training for assertiveness; time management; problem-solving; self-soothing; coping with crises; humor; diversion techniques; activity scheduling; activity-based homework; graded-task assignment) can be utilized to ensure one is able to follow through on committed action.

The sixth core process is "contacting the present moment." We find it hard to stay present and often live our lives in the past or the future, as victims of overactive self-narratization. It is very difficult to "be here now." And it is sometimes much easier to operate on automatic pilot. But consciously connecting with and engaging in whatever is happening at this very moment make us profoundly psychologically present. This means concentrating our awareness on either the physical world around us or the interiorized landscape within us (or both, for that matter).

FOCI and Self-Improvement

A patient of mine talked about leaving treatment and rationalized about how the facility was inappropriate for him as his crime was merely smoking cannabis. I pointed out that this was not true; he was mandated to treatment because he violated his probation and had a string of drug-related offenses. He then argued that he only needed a few months in a program to get help. I gently countered: "You have serious mental health challenges, are a registered sex offender, lost your father to suicide, and were sexually abused. I think many people would say you should take advantage of your time here and work on your problems." He stared back at me and I sensed my words were possibly having an impact. He then called his probation officer. After he hung up, he said, "I'm surprised my PO has faith in me. He okayed a pass for me to see my family." "That's interesting," I said. "He seems to have more faith in you than you do in yourself. It seems to me that perhaps you want to leave treatment because you lack faith in yourself—you don't think you can handle the hard work. And yet here's your PO, the guy whose job is to enforce the law, expressing confidence in you." He sat back in his chair and gazed up at the ceiling. Suddenly he somehow seemed at ease with himself.

Genuine self-reflexivity (not the basic sense of replaying one's recent behaviors in one's head) can be challenging and often quite difficult since it can open up emotional wounds, old and new, and trigger painful memories. Self-introspecting in a sustained manner entails being humble, accepting oneself as vulnerable, and learning to become more interpersonally connected by acknowledging one's socioaffiliative nature.

Self-Change through Self-Reflexivity

Convincing individuals that change itself does not necessarily present danger can understandably be quite challenging, as some recognize their problems with cockiness and overconfidence: "I am the great 'I am'"; "My problem was that I believed in myself too much"; "My ego is not my amigo." One patient described his egotism as "pumping air into my head." Others were indecisive and afraid of making hard decisions: "I'm tired of people giving me options"; "I'm scared of myself." "Can the Devil be reformed?" asked a patient, seemingly unsure if he himself could alter his behavior.

Others clearly recognize and acknowledge their particular challenges: "There should be special treatment for 'people pleasing'"; "I have martyr syndrome." The sense of wasted or unused potential is sometimes heard: "I have a full box of tools, but refuse to use them." Confronting temptation is another issue: "I know the Devil is busy because I deal with him every day." The theme of being too hard on oneself and unleashing one's inner critic is common: "I'm my own Siskel and Ebert" (the famous move critics). The patient from whom these words came then expanded this trope, noting that he had starred in many movies (i.e., many bad experiences), but so far has not won any Oscars. Related to these sentiments was being one's own worst enemy: "I'm the best self-sabotager in the world." Attempts at slowing down, changing an unhealthy lifestyle, or being more mindful of one's actions were also commonly heard: "I have to move over to the slower lane. The passing lane is too fast"; "I have to learn to pump my brakes," said another patient. One individual, struggling with strained interpersonal relations, said, "I need emotional training wheels." Another realized he had to focus on treatment rather than devoting time to the problems of others and distracting himself from his own self-care: "In recovery you have to be selfish."

With hopefulness, some clearly recognize their desire for improvement: "I want to reprogram myself like a robot"; "I used to think 'change' was a dirty word"; "I'm sick and tired of being sick and tired"; "What's my biggest room? The room for improvement," commented one patient. Understanding one's self and confronting falsehoods and denial are often mentioned: "Honesty is the beginning of change. The truth may set you free. But first it will piss you off"; " 'Never' is a swear word in addiction recovery." Life-changing insights were captured in declarations such as "I turned into my father and married my mother." Another discussed how he learned from the past but realized he can now move on: "I can look back but I don't have to go back." Realizing that mistakes are not evidence of worthlessness, one individual learned how to turn adversity into success: "When you stumble, make it part of the dance." I once commented on a patient's new definition of sartorial self-presentation. He responded by saying, "Why do drug dealers swarm around me? I have to change my appearance." One patient said, "I feel like a reincarnated new self." Confidence and self-efficacy, as well as self-autonomy, were evident in statements such as "I know I can change because my dreams keep tapping me on the shoulder"; "I'm the biggest part of the medicine"; "There's freedom in acknowledging what we can't change." In a sudden surge of self-confidence, an individual declared in a group, "I won't wait until a miracle happens. I am the miracle!"

For certain individuals, making progress can seem futile at times: "I felt like I had a parachute on my back, dragging me back, and I had weights on my feet," one patient told me. But overcoming hardships and accounts of resilience were just as common: "You're looking at a miracle. I survived prison, violence, and trauma." Job-like, a patient said, "I fought with God, but didn't die." A patient described his inner strength by saying, "I bounced back like a basketball." Another described his acquired coping mechanisms as "ammunition." Another portrayed his persistence in asking the supreme power for support by saying, "I've prayed and asked God for help so many times that I'm waiting to get a phone call from him telling me, 'You're a pain in the ass, buddy.' "

The import of planning for and controlling one's own destiny (self-autonomy) is a common theme: "If you don't have a plan for yourself, somebody else will." In a heated group discussion, one member snapped at another, annoyed at how he kept allowing himself to fall into verbal traps and overreacting: "Why do you keep giving me the power to control you?"

Taking Stock

In order to illustrate the integrative psychological approach of this book, this chapter has examined the interventions and techniques of the various systems to demonstrate how they incorporate FOCI for healing purposes. But such interventions and techniques need to be acquired by the provider of care.

Beginning drivers are panicky because they are overwhelmed with all the tasks that must be attended to, but over time, with enough practice, the necessary skills recede into the background and become automatic and habitual. Counseling becomes less tiring in the same way that novice drivers lose their tight, tense grip on the steering wheel and learn to relax. But what skills need to be acquired? What roles internalized? The next chapter examines the art of counseling from a dramaturgical perspective, listing the requisite skills and techniques.

Notes

1. Rogers developed a 19-proposition theory of therapy, personality, and interpersonal relationships that concretely codifies these aforementioned principles.
2. As described by the philosopher Martin Heidegger (1889-1976).

10

Key Therapeutic Skills and Conscious Interiority

Learning the Therapeutic Role

Though my internship was not a full-time position, I sometimes found that after a day at my site I ended up feeling surprisingly tired. Part of the answer was the stress of such an environment. One could argue that counseling is as much a physical as it is an intellectual endeavor, for both patients and therapists. Whether in individual sessions or groups, counseling itself can run down one's batteries. There is something taxing about balancing two different modes of interpersonal engagement. On the one hand, therapists must intensely focus on what patients say so as to appear engaged and empathic; they must be attentive enough so that care and concern are conveyed in a genuine manner. On the other hand, therapists must not come off as being too sympathetic; he or she must give off some measure of objectivity and avoid making unfair judgments. Patients must be put at ease by injecting the warmth of human emotion into the session, but it should not be overly emotionalized. This balancing act comes about by constantly monitoring one's own body language and controlling one's facial expressions—this is why it can be so draining.

One must wonder if all those minimal encouragers result in, at least from the point of view of patients, inauthentic expressions of concern, or if a poker-faced countenance appears unsympathetic. The ability to apply one's skills as a therapist while playing the role of observer of one's own emotional reactions is crucial. Mental health providers must be attuned to their own selves as these, during the psychotherapeutic session, ideally become the tools that can mend social disconnection or act as a compass offering reorientation and new directions. If the instrument of healing is not well sharpened, then it cannot aid in the treatment process. Just as therapists ask patients to scrutinize their psychological and physical processes, it is crucial that therapists themselves monitor their own psychophysiological reactions (self-reflexivity). Therapists, of course, are not the only ones balancing, rehearsing, and practicing roles; indeed, we are all beings with multiple roles, who perform, enact, and dramatize our social existence.

This chapter enumerates the skills and techniques and how these are learned as roles. It also introduces the significance of the therapeutic alliance and the importance of socioaffiliative presence.

Adopting the Appropriate Role

Therapists need to tailor treatment for each patient, from those with severe disabilities or special needs, to those who are well-educated and articulate. One also needs to take into account where an individual is developmentally (physiologically, neurologically, cognitively, and emotionally) and in terms of conscious interiority: Do they rely on terminology that evidences self-introspective proclivities? Would zeroing in on such tendencies help advance treatment goals? In the case of children, for example, toys might be utilized, language should not be clinicalized, and attempts should be made to compose a story that allows the therapist to get down to their level without sounding condescending. Adolescents may be awkwardly reluctant to share, so being open and transparent, minus, of course, any sermonizing or lecturing, goes a long way in facilitating communication (this applies to adults as well). It is better to talk about sex in a matter-of-fact manner with adolescents. In the case of family therapy, a therapist needs to pay attention to which family members sit near whom, who talks to whom, their tone, etc. The importance of adopting an appropriate communication style is necessary, not just with children or adolescents, but with any population. A therapist should be aware of the limitations of the techniques used; monitor the reactions of patients; be prepared to change techniques; and be equipped with a flexible attitude.

Consider the formality/reserved/prescribed versus informality/casualness/relaxed styles of social interaction. These styles are not necessarily due to cultural distinctions; they may be due to generational differences. Within my own lifetime and in "my culture" the boundaries separating the public and private realms have altered considerably. Usually we attribute such changes to our increasingly technologically networked society, but arguably the transformations are deeper than that. So the careful therapist, at least during the initial interview when the tone of the therapist–patient relationship is established and first impressions formed, should pay close attention to the type of interaction with which a certain patient is comfortable. As the sessions proceed, presumably the patient will gradually let their own guard down, but the important point is that this should happen at a pace they determine.

For those who were abused (whether physically, emotionally, verbally, or sexually), therapists should not tip-toe around issues of trauma. When a patient recounts some painful experience, sometimes all the therapist can do is rephrase what patients say and reflect it back to them. Therapists, primed to help others in need, may feel the impulse to say something useful in order to alleviate distress. But sometimes just allowing an individual to "see" (via the therapist) whatever feelings they are experiencing can be helpful, i.e., "listening is doing."

Basic Counseling Skills

There is no one "correct" way to counsel—when to explore, when to reflect, when to summarize, when to normalize, etc. This can be a relief and a challenge for the novice therapist. No "best" method characterizes delivering psychotherapy (though arguably one's response to a patient can always be tweaked and improved). A therapist is afforded many directions in which he or she can go during a session in response to what a patient says, and multiple tracks of inquiry readily pop into one's mind. This multi-tracked way of thinking can get in the way of carefully attending to what patients are saying, and a therapist cannot completely erase his or her emotional reactions. But with practice, a seasoned therapist learns to not let their own excerptions interfere with the healing process.

Active Listening

Everyone wants their feelings acknowledged, so it is not a bad way to begin a first session by assuming that a patient is "hungry to be heard," as one individual put it to me. In a therapeutic community where I worked, I frequently heard patients tell one another, "God gave us two ears and only one mouth for a reason"; "Take the cotton out of your ears and put it in your mouth"; and "Use your ears not your mouth." Communication, defined broadly, actually defines our drive to socioaffiliation; that is, being a social being means exchanging ideas, and more fundamentally, transmitting emotional messages and being open to their import. With this said, the most basic skill is to attentively listen, capture, and understand what patients are conveying, while granting patients an invitation to continue.

Techniques of Active Listening

One technique involves simply paying attention. Patients deserve undivided attention, so focusing on nonverbal communication (body language and paralinguistic behavior) can be just as significant as any verbalization. Repeating in one's own mindspace what patients have verbalized is an effective method of focusing attention and remembering what was spoken. Making clear to patients that they are being heard by appearing interested and engaged is vital. This can be accomplished by utilizing body language, appropriate facial expressions, open posture, and gestures.

Attentive listening means to treat individuals with dignity. This is especially important in the mental health field since more than a broken limb or painful bodily part is at issue—the psyche is deeply linked to the person in a way that transcends physicality.[1] A desire for respectful recognition by others should drive much of our behavior. Here "recognition" is more than a formal, legalistic respect of others; it means an empathetic understanding of what a person brings to others, regardless of social position and background. The tendency to reduce human motivation to economism has led to much misinterpretation of social problems. "Honor," "dignity," and "face" sound old-fashioned (at least in the modern American context), and while by themselves they cannot put food on our tables or roofs over our heads, they go a long way in maintaining our emotional well-being as well as, to see the larger picture, stabilizing sociopolitical relations. If you respect someone, he or she will rise to the occasion. This demonstrates how individuals respond positively to having their own "culture of self" validated.

Also, what is trivial to someone may be of great significance to someone else. Again, this resonates with the idea that what one person regards as unimportant can possess great personal (or cultural) worth to someone else. This is why acknowledging differences can so powerfully affirm another's dignity.

Listening to the Feelings of Others

A crucial skill is asking a patient about their feelings without asking about feelings; the idea is to inquire without coming off as predictable or stale—in other words, avoid becoming the caricature of the psychotherapist who asks how someone feels about what might seem to an individual the inconsequential details of life or something blindingly obvious. Helping patients experience feelings at a deeper level begins with affect labeling, or a "statement that explicitly labels the client's feelings" (Hill, 2014, p. 179). Much of therapy demands putting feelings into words and "emotional re-experiencing" so that patients are able to gain mastery over their sentiments and thereby increase self-autonomy. Denying emotions is in fact ignoring parts of ourselves (whether we like or dislike certain aspects of our selfhood). One challenge is how to discern if a patient is truly exploring their emotions or merely ruminating. Is the patient putting too much distance between their "I" and their feelings? Or is he or she recounting episodes with an attitude of acceptance (ACT, DBT)? Often if the former is the case, the patient will pause, vary tone of voice, and narrate an account without much repetition (Hill 2014, p. 150). The claim that "people rarely know why they do things" (Hill, 2014, p. 162) shows how multilayered and opaque the individual psyche can be.

The Self-Presentation of the Therapist and Providing Feedback

The therapist should monitor their general demeanor, facial expressions, and consider when to smile (or not). They need to physically attend and orient themselves to patients (so they know the therapist is focused on them); maintain steady eye contact (without staring); speak in a soft tone; and occasionally reassuringly nod. Ideally, a therapist should strike a balance between sitting up straight (appearing serious and professional), leaning forward slightly (to exhibit more of an attitude of attending), and not getting too comfortable in one's chair (to avoid looking overly relaxed). Undoubtedly patients have heard many times, "Thank you for sharing. I know it must have been hard. I'm sure it took a lot of courage." And the therapist, often repeating this, might appear condescending, insincere, or fake. This is why developing a demeanor of sincerity is so important.

Healthcare providers must be wary of how their own beliefs, assumptions, and daily distractions can distort what a patient presents. Therapists in particular must monitor their own emotional responses and avoid judgments; they must refrain from jumping to conclusions when providing feedback. Thus the therapist must ensure their monitoring and observing self ("I") is excerpting (paraphrasing) what is relevant, thereby reflecting back to patients their own thoughts and feelings ("What I'm hearing is ..." or "It sounds like you are saying ..."). This also ensures proper preparation for asking appropriate questions and clarifying points: "Is this what you meant?" "What do you mean when you say ... ?" In particular, it is important to discern the emotional state of patients. Summarizing the comments of patients from time to time requires concentrating on one's own (i.e., the therapist's) train of thought and that of patients.

People have an automatic inclination, when interacting with others, to pose questions rather than simply rephrase what another stated (probably because asking questions feels helpful as it is a way to search for an answer to another's problem). But therapists must resist the urge to query patients too much, at least initially, since (especially during the exploration stage or intake) it is important for patients to gain the therapist's trust by expressing their thoughts. Though therapists need to gather information, they must do so with a minimum of interruption, by keeping statements to a minimum, and asserting one's opinions respectfully and with tact. This brings us to an important technique: facilitating effective listening by the use of restatements. These are done concisely so as to avoid sounding repetitive; these reflect feelings back to patients. Restatements are more concise than summaries and should focus on patients' thoughts rather than emotions. In other words, restating does not mean summarizing (a longer version of a restatement). The purpose of restating is to have the therapist become a sounding board for patients so they can "hear themselves think" and notice key excerptions or patterns of consilience.

Staying Focused

Being distracted by their own thoughts and feelings can erode a clinician's active listening. These include thinking about something unrelated to patient issues; countertransference; overthinking a topic and paying too much attention to something that was stated; thinking of what to say next; wondering about current events; not liking your patient; being attracted to your patient; not being in the mood to attend to a patient; ruminating about one's own concerns; apprehensions about being recorded or supervised if being trained; and personal biases. Needless to say, admitting that we all have personal biases and stereotypes and managing them are crucial.

Active listening demands focusing on multiple aspects of a therapeutic encounter involving patients, the therapist, and the resultant interaction between them. Therapists need to divide their conscious concentration into how their "I" attends to (1) the patient; (2) the interaction between the patient's "I" and "me" (here "me" may mean presenting problem, excerpted elements, repressed materials, roles); and (3) the therapist's own emotional reactions, distractions, etc. ("me's"). Visualizing the "I's" and "me's" standing in for different parts of the therapist-patient interaction can assist in active listening.

Observation Skills and Collecting Information

Needless to say, being able to take in relevant information about patients and making useful observations are crucial.[2] People often traffic in messages at more than one level, so it becomes particularly important to notice discrepancies in the self-presentation of patients. It can be difficult to simultaneously pay attention to patients' facial expressions, general demeanor, incongruences between what is stated and body language, and the tone of what is verbalized (not just the words themselves). It is necessary, obviously, to carefully interpret what a patient "means," not just what he or she says. This means being sensitive to how messages can be conveyed via different modalities and how individuals utilize nonverbal communication ("back channel," e.g., demeanor, gestures) as well as explicit verbal communications.

Besides listening, therapists need to know how to pose questions and probe (asking a patient to explore feelings in more detail) without looking insensitive (especially if cultural differences are involved). A therapist must decide how much exploration is necessary before moving into the stages of hypothesizing, looking for insights, and formulating (or at least suggesting) to patients an action plan. Emphasizing open (rather than closed) questions ensures that patients do most of the talking and demonstrates an attitude of humility. Therapists must know how to respond when a patient brings up a topic with which a therapist cannot identify. They must also gently challenge what patients say when needed ("carefrontation") and perhaps occasionally self-disclose when appropriate.

When confronted with a patient from a different culture, a therapist should (1) continually engage in their own cultural self-assessment while learning about other traditions; (2) recognize the significance of diverse cultural identities and how these impact a patient's perspective; (3) consider the interaction between the therapist's identity and that of the patients; and (4) establish meaningful connection with patients. These suggestions are obviously themes that fall under the umbrella of one meta-theme: we should be keenly aware and open to how human diversity relates to mental health counseling (MCT).

The Usefulness of Silence

Silence serves a function. However, one must obviously develop an intuition to be able to discern when not talking is not appropriate. This relates to another concern some might have when facilitating a group: whether leaders should call on group members who are overly shy or for some reason just do not want to contribute to the group endeavor. To what degree should a group leader encourage ("push"?) a reluctant and reticent member (since, of course, therapeutic progress can only be made if members themselves become actively involved in group discussions)? Where does one draw a line between reticence and recalcitrance? Particularly in group settings, some patients will have to be reminded to play their role in a give-and-take dialogue (recognizing that our words impact others). At the same time, a never-ending monologue does not constitute a meaningful and worthwhile conservation; rather, it conveys a lack of mindfulness and not caring about giving other group members the opportunity to share.

Advantages and Disadvantages of Self-Revelation

Self-disclosure brings up the perils of telling "too little" or revealing "too much." The former tactic, motivated by an attempt to "appear professional," runs the danger of coming off as aloof, distant, and detached. If the latter approach is followed, perhaps by a desire to seek approval by "paying membership dues" (i.e., giving information about one's self and background), one may look unprofessional, even desperate. Excessive self-disclosure may lead to confusing one's role as a therapist with that of being a friend. Disclosing oneself should not be about "exposing secrets," "letting everything hang out," or "expressing every fleeting reaction to others" (Corey, 2012, pp. 103–104).

Ideally, of course, a therapist should first ask if self-disclosure is meant to help themselves (the therapist) or those seeking help. Then, keeping in mind that judicious self-disclosure is about gaining a patient's trust by demonstrating a certain level of honesty and openness, timeliness and selective self-revelation should be the order of the day. Self-disclosure can be a powerful aid for patients as it normalizes their experiences, affords modeling, strengthens the therapeutic alliance, validates reality, and offers alternative ways to think or behave (Corey, 2012, pp. 20–22). The disclosure of feelings—a "statement about a feeling that the helper had in a similar situation as the client" (Hill, 2014, p. 194)—can at times move the session along.

Do a therapist's sexual identity, race (visible physical attributes), ethnocultural background, religious background, political beliefs, being physically or sexually abused, addictions, or committing immoral or illegal acts matter?[3] The real concern is not so much issues of "when" and "how much" to disclose, but the question of "what" should be exposed. The Golden Rule appears to be "it depends." In other words, the therapist's own intuition, cultivated by experience, is the best guide. Self-disclosure is a wide-ranging concept. How one decorates one's office is a type of self-disclosure, as is one's manner of dressing, demeanor, and style of social interaction (warm, informal, casual, formal, stiff).

Not unexpectedly, patients want to hear from the therapist, who understandably is granted authority by their search for guidance. But the careful therapist should also ask him- or herself "why" certain patients want them to self-disclose; i.e., is it a means of resistance? A way to deflect attention away from relevant but painful issues? A therapist should also keep in mind that different individuals react differently to self-disclosure by therapists. This relates to the importance of moving at the right pace, which ideally should be determined by patients.

Other more nitty-gritty, technical aspects of counseling skills include: kinesics (relationship between bodily movements to communication); emblems (behaviors that substitute for words); illustrators (gestures that accompany speech); regulators (head nods, posture); and adaptors (unconscious habitual acts without communication content); minimal verbal behaviors (i.e., minimal encouragers that convey reassurance and avoid appearing judgmental) (Hill, 2014, pp. 130-146). Checking if a patient's body language (physical reactions) and verbalizations are congruent is also important.

The Therapeutic Alliance

In the realm of everyday social life we are forced to deal with dishonesty, and indeed, being honest can sometimes get one in trouble. We need safe havens where we can just be ourselves, for our sake and for that of others. A therapy session is one of the few places people can encounter the truth. The intention is to relax patients, to let them know they are in a nonjudgmental space and can reveal themselves, to provide a place where both patients and therapists can visit and view the problem from different angles. Patients and therapists "play with reality" in the space between their individual minds (Jørgensen, 2004, p. 531). A therapy session allows patients to "hear themselves think" and to freely stage scenes from their own mental world that they ordinarily would not. Properly establishing a therapeutic alliance instills within patients self-autonomy and self-authorization. "Alliance" concerns the contributions of both the deliverer of care and the recipient as they work toward the patient's goals (Bordin, 1979). The quality of the alliance itself is an active factor (Gaston et al., 1991). The therapist–patient relationship generates beneficial changes (Lambert & Bergin, 1994) and the positive impact of the alliance is backed up by one thousand findings (Orlinsky et al., 1994). Krupnick et al. (1996) concluded that the alliance was the most predictive variable for success. In a major study of various therapies for alcohol use disorder, the alliance was notably predictive of success (Connors et al., 1997). Charuvastra and Cloitre (2008) describe therapeutic alliance as: (1) the presence of a feeling of mutual warmth and understanding between therapist and patient; (2) agreeing on the goals of treatment; and (3) agreement on the means by which these goals will be attained.

A therapist is a "bearer of secrets" who must guard confidentiality.[4] In addition to being the basis of the therapist–patient relationship, confidentiality prioritizes the self-authorization of patients, i.e., they decide with whom they share interiorized mental content. A therapist should also be comfortable with the stress of uncertainty; they should not withdraw when a patient expresses strong emotions. Not a few people have a natural tendency to pull back in the face of intense feelings, so therapists should be ready to accept and attempt to process patients' affective states; this effects a deeper understanding for those seeking help. And being prepared to expend some emotional energy requires mindful attending. Conveying empathy and warmth is vital. Therapists are also advised to have a sense of humor and to know that it is sometimes acceptable to laugh in session.

Some therapists might have a tendency to rush in and provide an interpretation or a hypothesis. Of course, this must be resisted since it is better to have patients themselves obtain insight so as to make them feel more self-autonomous. One must be mindful that the goals of the therapist and patients are not necessarily the same. And therapists must avoid the trap of trying to "fix" someone's personal problems. Being patient allows help-seekers to set the terms of the interaction. It is not "what" we say, but "how" we say it—via bodily language, how one sits, tone of voice, countenance, etc. (this applies to patients as well, of course, who can reveal their discomfort discussing certain matters when body and mind are not in sync). It is through the "how of delivery" that one can utilize one's own strengths and personality traits for persuasive healing. Counseling is a collaborative "dance" or "duet" which demands not rushing a patient, allowing what was said to "sink in," and not jumping to conclusions. Finessing such coordination demands a number of skills.

The Healing Power of Presence and Socioaffiliation

There have been times when we have visited someone in the hospital who for some reason could not talk so that no conversation occurred. But we sensed that just being there made a difference. Related to this point is that people are sometimes desperate for an uninterrupted opportunity to express themselves. Being sociorelationally present, in and of itself, can be healing. After all, we are only a person in relation to others.[5] In a psychotherapeutic context the relationship is an active element of change. Merely sitting in a room with someone and not necessarily verbalizing anything can be viewed as a type of communication. In many situations, certain individuals cannot communicate directly (e.g., individuals with severe autism), but just knowing you are there nevertheless conveys communicative impact, at least at the affective level.

No dichotomy exists between technique and therapist since treatments and interventions work only if a relationship has been established. Mental healthcare providers need to avoid assuming the "white coat" posture, i.e., acting as the "objective" professional who might inadvertently put a distance between themselves and patients, or becoming "technical" when they feel out of their depth.[6] Rosenzweig went so far as to write that observers intuitively seem to sense the "characteristics of the good therapist time and again in particular instances, sometimes being so impressed as almost to believe that the personality of the therapist could be sufficient in itself, apart from everything else, to account for the cure of many a patient by a sort of catalytic effect" (Rosenzweig, 2002, p. 7). Moreover, it is of "comparatively little consequence" what particular techniques therapists employ (Rosenzweig, 2002, p. 8).

The overriding task of a therapist, then, is to "be there," to convey a sincere effort to understand, even if a therapist initially gets things wrong. Being present is much more important than persuading patients of something. In other words, being emotionally present for someone else, without necessarily saying anything, is an act of acknowledging another's humanity. Despite all the talk of the need to recognize diversity and the role of a multicultural perspective, it is worth keeping in mind that at the end of the day we all share a fundamental humanity; i.e., despite any cultural differences, we need to remind ourselves that our basic human-ness makes us more similar than different from individuals in need.

Third-Person Psychotherapy

Normal psychological development entails learning how to understand one's self-hood and that of others in terms of mental states, or what is known as theory of mind. Fonagy et al. (2002) refer to this as the capability to mentalize (to interiorize and to impute interiority to others). Knowing the thoughts, feelings, beliefs, and the desires of others allows one to "predict and explain other people's actions by inferring and attributing causal intentional mind states to them" (Fonagy et al, 2002, p. 347). Psychotherapeutic techniques contribute to the cultivation of mentalizing (Fonagy et al., 2002, p. 368). This occurs when the therapist sees patients as intentional and mentalizing agents (develops self-autonomy and self-authorization). Mentalization, then, allows patients to discover within themselves the therapist's view of them. Such internalized representations permit them to develop a healthier, more self-objective definition of self. Encountering a processed version of their own mental states in the mind of the therapist allows them to redefine themselves. In this regard, mentalization and self-regulation are intimately related (Jørgensen, 2004, p. 529). The key elements in this interpersonal processing of interiorized states have been conceptualized by Melanie Klein (1946) and Wilfred Bion (1963) as "projective identification" (Jørgensen, 2004, pp. 529–530; see also Ogden, 1979, 1982). Winnicott (1971) wrote that the point of "psychotherapy is not making clever and apt interpretations; by and large it is a long-term giving the patient back what the patient brings" and "if I do this well enough the patient will find his or her own self, and will be able to exist and to feel real" (Winnicott, 1971, p. 117).

It is often said that a couple is more than the sum of its parts; this could be said for any collectivity, including the therapist–patient dyad. "One-person psychology" describes a situation in which the therapist is an impartial, objective observer upon whom patients project their transference and desires. This is more of a hierarchical relationship in which patients are evaluated and have their treatment prescribed. This "one-way street" dynamic is associated with earlier forms of psychoanalytic psychotherapy. But in "two-person psychology" (later systems of behavior, cognitive, and humanistic therapies) it is understood that the influence is mutual, with the therapist and patient working on a "two-way street." Therapists must be sensitive to their own contributions since their very self is a tool for intervention. When therapists become confused about developments they are advised go back to patients and ask for additional information or clarification. The therapeutic encounter is a mutual, collaborative endeavor. Patients are thus empowered (self-empowered).

But in what might be called "three-person psychology" a third "person" emerges at the intersection of therapist–patient interaction. This third person is the product of the complex dynamics of the therapist's "I" and "me" and the patient's "I" and "me." Both therapist and patient learn to be aware of how their active subject-selves and passive object-selves become intertwined.

The Therapist–Patient Feedback Loop

"Other men are lenses through which we read our own minds," wrote Ralph Waldo Emerson (2015, p. 5). Third-person psychotherapy, since it takes into account inter-self relations, offers a more complicated exchange of information. Together, the therapist and patient form a reciprocal sociopsychological system, or a feedback loop. This describes how the therapist sends communication back to a patient, and vice versa, establishing a recursive input–output process. Ideally, assuming that "two heads are better than one,"[7] the more information exchanged, the more the self-reflexivity of patients is enhanced.[8] The therapist–patient dynamic establishes an interpersonal field. But interpersonal relations are grounded in intrapersonal interactions, and in the same way an atom needs to be broken down into subatomic particles, an individual's psyche needs to be analyzed into its interself elements: subject-self and object-self. With this stated, a patient might be advised that a therapist–patient interaction actually involves three "persons": (1) therapist; (2) patient as "I" (therapizer); and (3) patient as "me" (therapized). Such a perspective might at least suggest the possibility of increasing self-autonomy and alert patients that they, to a degree, are responsible for their own treatment.

Taking Stock

This chapter has explored the techniques of active listening; paying close attention to the feelings of others; the self-presentation of the therapist; providing feedback; staying focused; observation skills and collecting information; the usefulness of silence; the advantages and disadvantages of self-revelation; third-person psychotherapy; and the therapist–patient feedback loop. How do such skills play out in group settings?

I once heard a patient say, on his way to group, that he was going to "the shed to sharpen my tools" (attending group to hone his skills). Another described his group as "my own psychologist." Still another called his group his "watcher of my thoughts." Eager to begin treatment, one patient said, "I was like a kid with a bag of candy" when selecting which groups to join. Some group discussions can be emotionally riveting: "Everyone better buckle up!" stated one patient at the start of a group. Others have their self-reflexivity enhanced: "My [mental health] disease told me the group leader is full of s---. But I told my disease, 'no, you're full of s---.'" With their life scripts and expectations challenged, members can begin to interrogate their habitual roles. Some members recognize the high stakes: "What you say in a group may save someone's life."

The next chapter highlights the power of group work, while examining the processual, transitional, and systems-theoretical facets of group and family therapies and how they relate to FOCI.

Notes

1. Many complaints, whether formal or informal, could often be precluded if those in the healthcare industry made more of an effort to provide better service by putting their patients at ease, being more polite and respectful, and overall, treating people like people, rather than as a case number or a disease that just happens to be connected to a person.
2. Different opinions exist about taking notes during therapy sessions. Note taking can become a crutch and divert focus away from the skills that need to be cultivated.
3. Or even if a therapist has relatives or friends who have had such experiences or behaviors— a type of "extended self-disclosure."
4. Though the presumption of confidentiality is not legally absolute and is qualified by mandatory reporting laws. Related to confidentiality is testimonial privilege, or the patient's right to keep confidential communications from being disclosed in a legal proceeding.
5. Ironically, given our socioaffiliative instinct, the more we interconnect with others, the greater the risk of emotionally enmeshing in ways that are unhealthy.
6. Indeed, it is still surprising in this day and age how some working in the medical profession could use some training in bedside manners.
7. This expression can be described in other terms that, while not exactly synonymous with a cognitive circuit, resonate: shared cognition; collective cognition; co-cognition; coupled cognition; distributed cognition.
8. Recursive functions are a fundamental feature of our nervous system. The output of a nerve cell feeds back to the same cell to further modulate its activity.

11
Groups and Families as Therapeutic Systems

A therapeutic community illustrates well the complexity of group dynamics. Consider how within a therapeutic community facilitation transpires not just vertically between patients and staff, but also horizontally among patients. Though each resident is typically assigned a staff member who becomes their primary counselor, clinicians are expected to pay attention to the behavior of all residents and to be aware of what is occurring in the facility. So rather than being able to focus just on their patients, clinicians must be cognizant of all residents—their medical issues, recent developments in their personal lives, mood swings, sleeping patterns, drug changes, etc. This can be a bit overwhelming, but the challenges of tracking things become easier over time as one gets to know each individual. Constantly updating the communications log throughout the day to keep track of resident matters can be challenging, as one must decide what needs to be recorded and what does not. Staff must also pay attention to the interactions of individuals. Rather than focusing on the responses of just one individual in a circumscribed situation behind closed doors, interactions in the facility are shifting, transpiring among cliques (or "teams," as the residents in one facility where I worked sarcastically described such groupings) that form and then fall apart, adding much drama to social dynamics. Some residents make alliances, while others are easily triggered and set off by the unwelcome behaviors of others. Such dramatics demonstrate how individuals can be emotionally enmeshed in group dynamics.

This chapter analyzes group dynamics, which can be quite convoluted, from a systems theory approach. Such an approach can be applied "upward" (the psychological level) or "downward" (the societal level). The latter conceives society itself as a meta-system with educational, political, and economic subsystems.[1] But between the downward and upward perspectives are intermediate levels, two of which relate directly to therapeutic interventions—groups and families. These are the focus of the following sections. These systems expose and elicit roles, illustrate how operations of the psyche utilize adaptive phasic structures (APSs), and are defined by their changing, processual nature.

Groups as Systems

A group is a social system in microcosm that functions as a therapeutic agent of change (Yalom, 1995). Group dynamics are a product of group size, setting, formats, duration, meeting intervals, participation (voluntary or mandated), techniques, objectives, rules, norms (which may be implicit or explicit), and the psychotherapeutic system to be utilized. Smaller groups, which means a smaller audience, often see members open up more and the quality of exchange increase. But this is not necessarily true, as a small number of people may be too intimate for some, who perhaps counterintuitively prefer to have a larger, more anonymous audience. Individual preferences, personal beliefs, values, and particular expectations of members also play a role. For example, an individual's out-group status (e.g., occupation) might shape behavior within the group, thereby configuring the in-group hierarchical ranking of members.

The Stages of Group Work

All things being equal, groups seem to develop in a regular and predictable pattern and display increasing levels of interactional complexity. They may regress and reverse back to earlier stages. Group work, as it progresses, usually unfolds in a structured pattern. The stages of group work—initial, working, final—can be broken down into more detail and expanded upon (Corey, 2012, pp. 70-71):

1. Formation: This pregroup stage concerns preparation, announcing the group, screening, and selecting members. During this stage each prospective member may be interviewed to see if they will make a good fit and benefit from the group. An interview may be necessary to screen out those who may be mentally unstable, may have serious disorders, or who may be overtly hostile, domineering, or suicidal. It also allows prospective members to meet and discuss the group with the facilitator. The potential member is also given a chance to learn about confidentiality, members' rights and responsibilities, and group goals.
2. Orientation: The initial sessions involve exploration of members' expectations and having them become familiar with each other.
3. Transition: It is during the third stage, or the phase of "dealing with resistance," in which opposition and defiance often manifest themselves (though resistance can crop up during any stage of treatment). This makes sense if the transition stage is understood as a liminal phase when members express anxiety, defensiveness ("that won't work for me" or "I already tried that"), and ambivalence about being in the group. Members may become judgmental, or initiate power struggles with the facilitator or other members to establish a pecking order.
4. Working: During the fourth stage more cohesion among group members becomes apparent. They become productive in terms of taking concrete action, dealing with significant personal issues, and translating insight into behaviors, both in the group and outside of it.
5. Consolidation: The fifth stage is one of termination and applying to everyday life what has been learned in group.

6. Evaluation and follow-up issues: In the final stage, post-group concerns are addressed. Feelings of ambiguity and sadness might emerge as the group breaks up.

The ending phase of a group is significant as it might evoke a resurgence of presenting symptoms or unresolved conflicts. But it is also a time to remind, review, and reinforce any positive growth among patients and to encourage them to practice their newly acquired coping skills. Termination activities help group members to reflect on their past experiences, process memories, evaluate what was learned, and acknowledge any ambivalent feelings. Through their participation in these activities, group members are able to integrate and use information gleaned from the group experience and apply it to outside situations. This helps members generalize their group experience and put into action what they have acquired.

Other Descriptions of Group Stages

Irvin Yalom (1995) sees four group stages: (1) orientation; (2) conflict; (3) cohesion; and (4) termination. Conflict and cohesion constitute the transitional, transformative phase. After reviewing the relevant research on team dynamics and building, Tuckman and Jensen (1977) concluded that there are five stages:

1. Forming: Members are introduced, get to know each other, and rules are discussed. Members are uncertain about roles and may look to the group leader for guidance.
2. Storming: Members compete with each other and conflict, so that discord, tension, and anxiety may emerge, but importantly, participants learn to freely disagree with each other. This is when de-structuring of emotional and cognitive patterns may occur.
3. Norming: Members begin to work more effectively as a team and trust, cohesiveness, and rules are established. Like the storming stage, norming is a transitional phase during which communitas and group spirit emerge.
4. Performing: The group functions at a high level and members focus on tasks, exchange feedback, experiment, and achieve goals.
5. Adjourning/mourning: During this termination stage, members say good-bye, celebrate the group's success, and consider how to implement what has been learned.

Transition: Communitas, Cohesiveness, and Changes

During the transitional stage the groups' culture will both solidify and on occasion be challenged by the anti-therapeutic maneuvers of unwilling patients. An important part of group solidification is communitas—common experiences generated by being a part of a community of equals—and a crucial aspect of communitas is cohesiveness. This should be considered a key factor for a successful outcome and is in itself a therapeutic factor. Cohesiveness encourages a person to remain in the group since it affords an atmosphere of openness, warmth, comfort, a sense of belonging, and the feeling of being unconditionally accepted. Being accepted, despite one's faults, transgressions, or past life experiences, is a powerful healing force, as it taps into our deep need for socioaffiliation. Members may even form meaningful relationships within the group. The group itself, along with its procedural norms, become valued. Cohesiveness correlates with attendance, participation, mutual support, and upholding group norms. Solidarity facilitates the internalizing of the group's attitudes and standards. Ideally, therapeutic transformations endure because members are disinclined to disappoint other group members (Yalom, 1995).

Communitas creates a group atmosphere in which an individual's dysfunctional thinking and behaviors, rooted in past experiences (trauma, distorted family dynamics), are more readily evoked and start to manifest themselves. Other members then have the chance to point out the individual's maladaptive behaviors. The member hopefully recognizes that they have been unfairly and nonconsciously projecting their distorted thoughts onto others and a corrective recapitulation occurs (or they may leave the group).

Jacob Moreno, the founder of psychodrama, used "tele" to describe a dynamic similar to rapport; this refers to a two-way flow of feelings and attraction between people (Moreno, 1959). This describes the emotional bond that holds a group together and may facilitate healing through a reciprocal empathic feeling. This dynamic may operate at a preconscious or even nonconscious level. Acknowledging tele helps people to become more explicitly cognizant of their interpersonal preferences and is a major component of developing self-awareness.

Transference and Countertransference as Elements of Transformation

If we consider the group to be a microcosm of society, it should not be surprising that our own relations are replicated in group dynamics; it is a strong human predilection to see one's self reflected in others. Given enough time, people usually begin to act in group as they do in life. This occurs during transference, or when a patient projects onto the group leader past feelings that they had toward important people in their life. Some relive significant family relationships. Also, it is not uncommon for group members to see characteristics of someone they know in another group member. Like resistance, transference is not necessarily detrimental, since it allows group members to identify their own emotional triggers and unresolved issues.

Countertransference occurs when group leaders project their attitudes about significant others onto group members. If not properly acknowledged, countertransference can prevent the therapist from seeing group dynamics and personal interactions clearly (though of course group work itself is not supposed to be an opportunity to deal with a therapist's personal issues). Such feelings may concern unresolved conflict from past or present relationships (i.e., not the therapeutic relationship with this particular patient). The judicious therapist will discuss with a colleague or supervisor any persistent emotional reactions that tend to recur. It is crucial to obtain the viewpoint of others in these situations and to cultivate self-knowledge via self-reflexivity so as to ensure that the group is not negatively impacted.

Group members, not surprisingly, are all different as performers on the group stage. Some seem to need to listen first, then share. At times silence can be so prolonged and deafening that a facilitator is relieved when a member pipes up with any comment. "If you're new to sharing it can be hard"; this was commonly stated by more experienced members trying to encourage others. Members can be heartwarmingly sincere; in one group with a particularly reticent member, another individual told her, "If you have a story to tell, someone will help you." Some members feel the need to keep the group on track, sometimes by assisting the facilitator with encouraging comments to recalcitrant participants. Others, as a form of resistance, attempt to disrupt the group by telling inappropriate jokes, smirking, or sarcastically commenting on the remarks of other group members. Some just refuse to participate. Such negative behavior can easily hinder the progress of the entire group. Some use the group setting to dominate and hold the group hostage, turning the meeting into their own individual session at the expense of other members. Some individuals are selfishly at odds with group goals and need to be reminded of the virtues of allowing everyone to contribute. Other countertherapeutic roles include the blocker, aggressor, recognition seeker, follower, and victim.

At times, subgroups will form within a group. This typically occurs as a defense mechanism and can subvert a group's goals. During a particularly rowdy group I was facilitating, one member gleefully shouted, this is like "watching a TV show!" I realized that it was this member who was egging on other members, in effect stage directing his own show for his personal entertainment and enjoyment.

Group Facilitators as Stage Directors

Group facilitators or leaders perform many roles: information seekers, mediators, conciliators, compromisers, and neutralizers. In sum they are stage directors, encouraging others to do their best. They must discern patterns of exchange by attending to verbal and nonverbal communication, build a healthy group culture, be relaxed

but firm, and have a sense of humor. They should unify the group without domi-
nating it. Therapists are advised to keep in mind CHASE, or the core conditions of
charm, honesty, acceptable self-disclosure (with a large dose of prudence), and empathy. To prevent an anti-therapeutic atmosphere from developing, facilitators must
occasionally point out tardiness, absences, scapegoating, subgrouping, and other disruptive behaviors. Group therapists need to be sensitive to opportunities for therapy
intervention and discourage automatic conforming responses. The group facilitator
should uncover and encourage the expression of feelings, agency (self-autonomy),
insight (self-reflexivity), and personal perspectives (self-individuation).

Matters can become complicated in a group setting where, from the perspective
of the group leader, members, each with their own "I's" and "me's" (e.g., ideal and actual selves) are communicating with the leader and other members at different levels.
If the group leader is not being honest with him- or herself, and if members are not
being self-honest, then the therapeutic endeavor will be hindered.

To initiate a group, a facilitator may make the rounds, asking each member to check
in: "How are you doing? Anything interesting happening with you lately?" Beginning
each session with this ritual (and perhaps concluding with a check-out) and peri-
odically updating information about members are significant because they: (1) let
the group leader know what is on the minds of each member; (2) allow the leader to
set the agenda; (3) alert the leader if someone requires more support; (5) ensure that
everyone is working toward being on the same page; and (6) enhance group bonding.
Check-ins ensure that each member has an opportunity to say something since some
may be reluctant to share. Concisely rephrasing what a member said is a way to alert
all group members to what the group leader may regard as crucial.

Group facilitators need to gauge the progress of members. Are they able to relate to
the topic or discussion? Do they only ask questions of others, or do they make meaningful contributions themselves? Do they disclose therapeutically useful information
about themselves? Do they offer opinions, suggestions, or feedback useful for other
members? Do they participate in exercises? Complete homework?

The Family as a System

Family therapy (FT), which is both a theory as well as a treatment method, describes a
collection of various approaches. A number of psychotherapeutic traditions have fed
into FT: "mainstream" FT (Bowen, 1976); classical-psychoanalytically inspired object
relations theory; psychodynamic; Gestalt, transgenerational family therapy; structural family therapy; NT; social constructionist family therapy; cognitive-behavior
family therapy; a focus on communication and emotional experiencing (Satir &
Baldwin, 1983); an exploration of the structure or organization of the family so that
its relationships can be reframed and stereotyped patterns modified (Minuchin,
1974); and solution-focused "strategic FT," that is, viewing problems as real and solv-
able (i.e., problems are not mere symptoms of deeper dynamics) (Haley, 1971). The

common and defining feature of all these approaches is how the family itself is viewed as the basic unit of analysis, rather than the individual. In other words, rather than premising its treatment on intrapsychic conflicts, FT focuses on interpersonal disputes. The "identified patient"—the family member considered to be the problem in the family—is regarded as manifesting troubled or troubling behavior maintained by problematic transactions or maladaptive, self-defeating, and self-limiting belief systems that result in repetitive relationship patterns (Goldenberg, Goldenberg, & Goldenberg Pelavin, 2014).[2]

FT is premised on systems theory, which means that family members mutually define and shape each other's identities as well as their problems. Though a family may be regarded as one system, subsystems (permutations of alliances of spouses, parents, siblings, children, etc.) can in a sense constitute a single family (Goldenberg, Goldenberg, & Goldenberg, 2014). It seems commonsensical that any disturbance in one subsystem (e.g., between spouses) can reverberate throughout the entire familial psycho-emotional system. There are times when it is simply more appropriate to view psychological disorders in a less individualistic way and within the context of a family's transactional patterns. In other words, sometimes the termination of individual intrapsychic conflicts should be regarded as secondary to improving overall family functioning. FT teaches us, besides the limitations of pathologizing the individual, how the individual is part of a complex dynamic. Specifically, it shows us how psychological processes concern fundamentally the exchange of information and how problems arise when communication becomes distorted and overly emotionalized.

Different Approaches to Family Therapy

Though for the sake of convenience we can speak of "family therapy," in fact a number of therapies have developed that emphasize different facets of a systems approach. For this reason they deserve a brief treatment. Structural FT views problems rooted in the context of family transaction patterns. Issues are addressed by restructuring these patterns and integrating subsystems (i.e., the roles of members). Key techniques include reframing and creating flexible boundaries among family members (Minuchin, 1974; Minuchin & Fishman, 2009). Narrative FT encourages family members to meta-frame and question the stories individuals tell themselves that organize their experiences and interpretations (self-narratization). Then they are asked to re-author their problem-saturated narratives and develop options for dealing with other family members. The past is regarded as a possible repository of successful efforts to overcome problems (Epston, 1994; White, 2000, 2007). Strategic FT searches for redundant communication patterns that lead to dysfunctional behaviors. Symptoms among family members point to strategies for controlling a relationship while simultaneously claiming that one lacks control over one's unwelcome behavior. Change is sought through following directives rather than cultivating insight. Relabeling, paradoxical interventions, and prescribing the symptom are employed (Haley, 1971;

Jackson, 1957; Keim, 1999; Madanes, 1981; Watzlawick, Weakland, & Fisch, 1974; Weakland, 1977).

Explaining how family members are guided by belief systems that do not reflect reality and end up being trapped in destructive "games" is the goal of Milan FT. Its techniques include reframing, circular questioning, paradox, and invariant prescription (Boscolo et al., 1987; Tomm, 1984a, 1984b). The focus of experiential FT is free choice, self-determination (self-autonomy), and growth of the self (self-individuation). One matures and thus relates better to other family members by gaining personal fulfillment. Inspired by the Gestalt perspective, bodily awareness, and emotion-focused techniques, therapists might confront an individual in order to provoke self-discovery and utilize family sculpting (Greenberg, 2004, 2007; Greenberg & Johnson, 1988; Greenberg & Paivio, 1997; Greenberg & Safran, 1987; Johnson & Bradley, 2009; Kempler, 1981; Satir, 1967, 1972; Whitaker, 1975, 1976; Whitaker and Keith, 1981). In transgenerational FT, one's emotional attachments to one's family of origin are explored and discussed. Commonly used techniques are (self-)individuation, differentiation, and taking "I" stands (Boszormenyi-Nagy & Framo, 1985; Boszormenyi-Nagy & Spark, 1973; Bowen, 1959, 1967; Epston, 1994; Kerr, 2003; Papero, 2000).

Communication and Information Flow within the Family

Sometimes problems result from a family's lack of adequate communication skills. The flow of information within a family, since it is a system, must circulate so as to maintain homeostasis. Sometimes what is communicated are "stories families tell themselves"—these may be myths, unspoken assumptions, secrets, etc.—which convey distorted views (a type of communal narratization). Mystification, or the masking of problems among individuals, may occur. Also, like all systems, a family is rule-governed and possesses boundaries. If the rules are not adequate for accommodating changing conditions or serious threats, the family structure itself can be destabilized. A family's boundaries may be rigid or flexible, closed or opened to extra-family forces and influences that might restore a healthy homeostasis. Ideally, members should strike a balance between separateness and togetherness. However, they may become disengaged (members feel isolated from each other) or enmeshed (members are intertwined in one another's lives, thereby fostering dependency, i.e., loss of self-individuation) (Minuchin, 1974). If too many "cross-connections" bind a family unit together, no space is available for members to find solutions to the problems they might confront (Hoffman, 1981, p. 77). Other system-level problems are pseudomutuality (members dread genuine expressions of individuality, fearing that this will destabilize a fragile structure); pseudohostility (members bicker in order to avoid becoming deeply affectionate or deeply hostile to each other); and scapegoating, in which one member is singled out for blame in an attempt to shift responsibility for any dysfunction. Members might adopt defensive stances in coping with stress, or they might placate or engage in distraction. Ironically, some families seem to function best when someone is ill or has a serious problem (Minuchin & Fishman, 2009, p. 6).

Depending on their specific emphases, family therapists might utilize various tools: reframing (of problematic behaviors); challenging outdated or rigid family rules; making boundaries clearer; realigning dysfunctional relations; modeling more flexible family interactions; enactment (role-playing); cognitive restructuring; family sculpting; family mapping; de Shazer's "miracle question"; externalization (i.e., problems are recast as being outside the family) in order to effect positive change. Some take a more psychoanalytical approach (e.g., work to gain insights into how introjects are re-projected onto present-day family members to compensate for unsatisfactory early-age, formative object relations). Others try to develop a "secure family base" from which individuals can explore new solutions to problems, both during and post-therapy (Byng-Hill, 1995). Some therapists might focus on behavioral change (typically highly directive and focused), while others give more attention to experiential change, i.e., instead of manifesting defensive or coercive secondary emotions, having hidden primary emotions or "real feelings" expressed.

One might wonder if in the case of a pending divorce, remarriage (from the point of view of children), alternative lifestyles, etc., family systems therapy is adequate or appropriate, as the family structure itself is being radically configured (or even dismantled). Moreover, for whatever reason, some may not want to repair or even maintain family relations. Also, in some cases one member of a family may be able to persuade the unwary therapist of "their story" at the expense of the accounts of other members, especially if the therapist possesses (nonconsciously) a biased agenda (i.e., what is the therapist's view of marriage?).

While in therapy, family members might encounter a therapeutic dilemma and be forced to decide between continuing to live with distressing symptoms or facing the challenges and consequences of recovery. The "purpose" of a symptom must be discerned, e.g., is a family member's drug addiction a problem in itself, or is it symptomatic of a deeper problem that has destabilized the family?

Parenting Styles and Conscious Interiority

Though no one right way exists to raise children, psychologists divide parenting styles into four major types. The first is authoritarian. Parents emphasize demanding standards, rigid rules, obedience, and rely on repressive, punitive methods to ensure compliance. Even threats, deprivation, and physical punishment may take the place of judicious rearing. Control trumps warmth. Authoritarian parents come off as irritable and aggressive. Parents may suffer from low levels of esteem, poor academic achievement, and a limited sense of responsibility. Harsh, inconsistent discipline and parental power assertion ensure that the source of self-authorization becomes linked with aggression and other antisocial behaviors. A lack of clear explications hinders self-reflexivity. Children of authoritarian parents often turn out to be socially with-drawn, hostile, and rebellious.

The second style is authoritative. The overriding approach is rationality, warmth, and responsiveness. Self-authorization becomes associated with independence, a set of clear rules, and high standards. Parents explain their rationales for family rules and decisions and encourage discussion. The use of reasoned praise not only reduces aggression and antisocial behaviors, but enhances confidence and a self-reflexivity bolstered by rational explanations. Children mature into assertive, self-confident, so-cially responsible, and achievement-oriented individuals. The third style is permis-sive. Though warm and caring, permissive parents are unconcerned with control or rules, provide little direction, make few demands, and shy away from punishment. Poor supervision and indulgence lead to a lack of clear self-other boundaries, i.e., poor self-individuation and self-autonomy. The children of permissive parents might grow up to be self-centered, easily frustrated, impulsive, and low in achievement and self-independence.

The final style is uninvolved. Parents exhibit low levels of warmth, caring, and con-trol. They devote little effort to raising their children, who develop low levels of self-esteem and end up being impulsive, moody, aggressive, delinquent, and rebellious. Detached parenting, not surprisingly, does not cultivate the capabilities needed for healthy self-individuation (few familial resources upon which to build stable self-identity); self-reflexivity (lack of positive parenting means little experience in de-veloping self-communication skills, i.e., between "I" and "me"); self-authorization (uncertain about from where one's impulses come); or self-autonomy (lack of bound-aries between self and others).

Taking Stock

This chapter looked at how changes experienced within systems can be perceived as transitioning through distinct stages. Also explored were the relation of conscious in-teriority to the dynamics of positive change and transformation via communitas and cohesiveness; transference and countertransference as elements of transformation; group facilitators as stage directors; and communication and information flow within the family.

Western philosophy and thought, at least since the Enlightenment, has had a strong bias against emotions. The legacy of mind as rational was solidified in the 1800s when science and technology greatly altered the socioeconomic and political landscape of industrializing societies. Human nature, in order to accommodate the demands of a rationalized technoscientific worldview, was reconceptualized so that sentiments and feelings should take a backseat to the primacy of intellectual capabil-ities. We still live in a social environment that prizes detached, dispassionate objec-tivity. Mainstream culture socializes us to believe that people are, for the most part, self-understanding and clear-headed beings. Emotions can interfere with our train of thought that ordinarily should interlock in "commonsensical," "rational" logic; strong sentiments distort a healthy, balanced engagement with the world. The next chapter attempts to balance this view by showing how emotions are at the center of psychological well-being.

Notes

1. This has important implications for community psychology. Cf. Bronfenbrenner's ecological systems theory (1979). He envisioned society as composed of: (1) the individual; (2) microsystems (family, school, peers, church, health services); (3) the mesosystem, or the interrelations among a constellation of microsystems (moving among two or more settings); (4) the exosystem (industry, mass media, local politics, neighbors, social services); (5) the macrosystem, or ideologies and attitudes of one's culture; (6) the chronosystem, or the pattern of environmental events and transitions throughout one's life course as well as changing socio-historical circumstances.
2. We should also mention filial therapy, which provides caregivers (typically parents) with training in basic play therapy techniques so they can use these with their own children. This modality was one of the first systemic FT interventions. Founded on the belief that parents can learn the necessary skills to become therapeutic catalysts in their children's lives, filial therapy incorporates family members as the main agents of change. Trained professionals educate primary caregivers in the method and then provide supervision and guidance as families begin to navigate and resolve challenges.

12
Emotions and Conscious Interiority

One day one of my patients was seriously talking about leaving the facility where I worked and was planning to ask his probation officer if he could be transferred to another short-term facility. Recently, in a group I had facilitated, he had complained so much about the facility that other group members were being robbed of their opportunity to share; the group eventually deteriorated into a "blame and bitch" session in which residents criticized staff and policies. Then two residents began listing the problems with the program. I stayed calm and tried to steer the discussion in a more positive direction by emphasizing how, as individuals, they could spend more time on their own problems (rather than discussing the failings of their peers and staff); utilize "house attentions" and "listen ups"; participate more constructively in groups; and exercise more self-advocacy in their individual sessions. I said that though legally mandated to the facility, all residents were free to leave if they were unhappy but would suffer the consequences. I took great pains to explain to the residents the thinking of the staff, i.e., if they did not like the program they could leave anytime as the door was not locked. But my words only agitated the complaining residents. One accused me of "smirking" and "judging" him; another launched into a verbal assault, claiming that I did not care about helping him, saying "You just said to all of us, 'f--- y--!' " I responded that he was mischaracterizing what I meant. I interpreted his outburst as an expression of resistance, put up because my words presented him with a stark choice: stay in treatment and do the difficult work of self-change, or just leave, give up, and face the legal consequences.

The next day in group the resident who said I was smirking at him began the discussion with "by the way, I think we had a good group yesterday. I really learned a lot." I asked him to elaborate. "Well, I feel we reached an understanding." Other group members, nodding in agreement, concurred. The change from outright hostility to a more positive attitude took me off guard. It seemed as if the members had to pass through a somewhat tumultuous session, with emotions running high, for them to have their thought patterns cathartically reset.

In this chapter I delineate how confronting emotional problems in a therapeutic setting follows a processual trajectory and possesses positive implications. I also contextualize the role of feelings within a FOCI perspective inspired by Jaynes's two-tiered theory of emotions (1982).

The Meanings of Emotions

"You have to get out of your head" was a common expression I heard in groups—residents would advise other residents to take a meta-framed, objective perspective on their predicament and not allow their distorted, emotionally driven thinking to mislead them. Some patients advised those easily bothered by others to not let them "rent space in your head." "You sit between your ears too much" captures the same sentiment.

Deep down we viscerally feel the reality of emotions—we are often conflicted and confused, unsure as to why we end up behaving in a certain way. Such a perspective calls for an open attitude toward the complexity of the human condition. After all, feelings are to be treasured, as they provide the flavors and colors of a fulfilling life. They inspire, agitate, enflame our cherished passions, and rouse us to righteous action. Coming to terms with one's emotional currents is crucial to experiencing a rich and healthy existence. It leads to better self-understanding and more self-reflexivity; lowers defensiveness, guilt, and insecurity; encourages more positive interpersonal relations; and elevates our capacity to experience and express feelings as they arise within us. We must confront the hidden, enduring pull and push of sentiments. Arguably, we are emotional beings first and "thinking" beings second.

Various psychotherapeutic systems have different views of the role of emotions. Some view them as hindrances to insight, instinct-driven reactions that should be put on hold, or as impulses that should just be ignored. REBT and CBT recognize that people, equipped with powerful affects, possess an irrational side—our emotionalized perspective of events needs to be scrutinized since our feelings can fog our better judgment.

Other psychotherapeutic systems view emotions as innate, natural processes that require healthy expression (GT). It is commonly believed that if our emotions are not adequately expressed, they erupt somatically. I witnessed firsthand the power of bottled-up feelings: my father's face literally melted during a meeting with my sister, myself, and a nurse conducting a nursing-home assessment of my mother. His mind, weighted down with worry and anxiety, burst through his body and caused a stroke, dramatically showing how psyche and physiology are one and the same.

Other systems see emotions, especially negative ones, as parts of ourselves that need to be accepted and accommodated (ACT). Some have highlighted the importance of bodily experiences (in which emotions are grounded). Gendlin's (1962) experiential therapy, intended to facilitate a felt-shift by monitoring experiential components (i.e., sensations, visceral flows within the body, and tensions), allows one to get in touch with one's underlying sentiments. We associate emotions, unlike cognitions, with distinct bodily expressions, and often confuse visceral experiences with low-intensity feelings or strong sentiments, which do not necessarily carry discernable physiological responses.

Feelings and thoughts are very difficult to disentangle, as they form a sort of emotional-cognitive magma. However, evolution's gift of meta-framing allows us to separate them. For the sake of argument, we can tease out mentation along a continuum of emotionally hot, warm, cool, and cold cognition. Probably most of the time we operate in the areas of warm and cool cognition. Hot cognition is regarded as too messy and unpredictable and a sign that one is weak and has lost control. Cold cognition, associated with impartiality, unbiased thinking, and disciplined self-control, is often difficult to achieve, especially when circumstances cause our thoughts to swing wildly from being coolly logical to colored and overheated by affect. Nevertheless, often the best place from which to view matters, especially in a therapeutic setting, is the position of cold cognition.

The Positive Aspect of Emotions

Emotions are the glue that holds socioaffiliative systems together. Recent research has focused on human connections as aspects of positive psychological processes. For example, Harvey and Pauwels (2009) examined how to achieve a constructive relationship. They looked at "minding," which creates stability and closeness. It is defined as a reciprocal knowledge process that occurs nonstop throughout the history of the relationship and involves a complex package of interrelated thoughts, behaviors, and feelings. Though "attachment theory" is usually associated with the very young and children, it is useful to also acknowledge findings on adult attachment. F. G. Lopez (2009) links adult attachment to hope, optimism, positive feelings, parenting and care-giving competence, educational and career-related motivation, altruistic behavior, and existential well-being.

Like everything else involving humans, relationships are a double-edged sword. They can lead to conflict, rejection, and criticism, but also to support, intimacy, and companionship (Maisel & Gable, 2009). But rather than focusing on the negatives that unhealthy relations often generate, Maisel and Gable (2009) explore the beneficial processes in relationships, such as positive emotional expressions, shared novel experiences, intimacy, and the benefits of sharing pleasant events. Hendrick and Hendrick (2009) point out that given its centrality in many dimensions of human life, romantic love is the "giant elephant" in psychology's living room, and they discern the need for a "relationship science" with implications for a positive psychology.

Meta-Framing Emotions

Being able to simultaneously experience an emotion while stepping back and cognitively introspecting it from different angles is surely a positive feature of our complex mind. In what follows, I present some examples of meta-framing emotions. Niederhoffer and Pennebaker (2009) have explored linkages between the "writing paradigm" and healing transformation. Articulating emotional events into textual form can result in positive sociopsychological and neural changes. This is accomplished by putting our lives (or at least their significant events) into a story-like format (self-narratization); such an activity affords a sense of completion and even control. Arguably, written narratives function as meta-framing in how they reify significant information from which we can stand back from, look at, read, and process. They also adhere to the APS tripartite structure: (1) the appearance or beginning of a problem; (2) attempts to deal with the problem and accompanying emotional turmoil; and (3) resolution and closure ("the end").

Stanton, Sullivan, and Austenfeld's (2009) Emotional Approach Coping (EAC) scale is another example of meta-framing. It is the intentional use of emotional processing and expression to manage stressful, adverse situations. This scale is composed of two subscales: (1) attempts to acknowledge, explore, and understand emotions; and (2) verbal and/or nonverbal efforts to communicate or symbolize emotional experience. The EAC scale has been used to enhance adjustments to stressors such as infertility, sexual assault, and breast cancer (Stanton, Sullivan, & Austenfeld, 2009).

Isen (2009) has demonstrated how mild positive affect facilitates problem-solving and social interaction. Positive emotions lead to an openness to potentially useful information, reduce defensiveness, and allow one to see multiple angles of one's circumstances and concentrate on resources that might be helpful. Broadly understood, emotional intelligence can be conceptualized as an instance of meta-framing. It has four interrelated abilities that concern emotional information processing: (1) perceiving emotions; (2) using emotions to facilitate cognitive activities; (3) understanding emotions; (4) managing emotions within one's self and among others (Salovey et al., 2009).

The purpose of positive emotions differs from that of negative ones. The latter were evolutionarily designed for rapid response to an imminent threat, while positive emotions transpire in relatively safe and controllable circumstances and lead to useful and novel resources (Cohn & Fredrickson, 2009). While negative affects narrow and restrict options, positive emotions are nonspecific and have the potential to generate new and adaptive "thought-action tendencies." In the "broaden-and-build theory of positive emotions" Fredrickson (2009) and Cohn and Fredrickson (2009) contend that positive emotions expand repertoires of thoughts and actions. Positive emotions work by a type of meta-framing—they "broaden" our awareness (spread out for introspection) and then "build" upon resultant learning to create future psychological resources. In this way we elevate above our situation and utilize what is inspected.[1]

Feelings as Interiorized Affects

During a group, a patient became quite angry over what another member said. Both I and the other patient were baffled about why he was so upset. At first the irate patient blamed the member who supposedly insulted him, and then he turned his anger toward me, falsely accusing me of all sorts of odd things. One part of me (the objective, observing self) remained calm as I attempted to "talk through" and "talk out" with him why he was so agitated. But another part of me was upset at the inexplicable irrationality of the patient's outburst. My "I" monitored the physical sensation in my stomach as he accused me of "lying" and colluding with the other patient. It took a good ten or so minutes, but he eventually calmed down and then apologized to me and the other patient. I was able to project myself into the future, somewhat bothered by what the patient said about me. But when I "saw" my future self, this covert behavior seemed petty, immature, and uncalled for.

There is nothing particularly special about the aforementioned experience; it merely illustrates something many of us do all the time, sometimes successfully, sometimes not: having our "I" ensure that a raw affective reaction (anger) does not mutate into something worse, such as hatred. This is an example of meta-framing and becomes particularly important in clinical settings when individuals are taught to identify, monitor, accept, and perhaps reconfigure their affective reactions. Such meta-framing might be termed meta-emotion, meaning an individual's emotions about their initial emotions (or somebody else's emotions).

Jaynes offered a "two-tiered theory" of emotions. He argued that all mammals (including *Homo sapiens*) possess a basic set of genetically organized affects that are specific aptitudes that respond to "characterizable classes of stimuli or events in certain characterizable ways" (Jaynes, 1982, p. 147).[2] However, "our present affectional experience consists of far more than the basic affects of mammals" (Jaynes, 1982, p. 150). For one thing, unlike other mammals, humans occupy an intensely rich, nuanced, and complex universe of emotions that carry a heavy symbolic load. And second, when consciousness entered the historical scene about 1000 BCE, affects were interiorized and turned into narratizable emotionalized events. This new human capability stretched affects out over mentally spatialized time, allowing us to dwell on or review completed past behaviors or on possible future behaviors and "respond to them as if they were presently occurring, with copies of the affects themselves" (Jaynes, 1982, p. 149). Unlike other mammals, human beings introceive themselves as embedded in their own narratized stories, which are infused with collective as well as personal meanings. Reminiscing about the past and imagining the future turn affects into conscious feelings.

Phrased differently, Jaynes's two-tiered theory of emotions describes a historical meta-framing of emotions, i.e., historically building upon and interiorizing affective systems at the societal, interpersonal level, beginning some three thousand years ago. This constructed a socializing environment in which, at the psychological, intrapersonal level, more nuanced and complicated feelings that enhanced communication were produced via linguistic forms. The conscious interiorization of emotions meant that shame became guilt; anger, hatred; fear, anxiety; excitement, joy; disgust, contempt; affiliation, love; and sexual emotions, erotic fantasies.

Viewing feelings as interiorized affects has practical applications. Therapists may have patients check or monitor their feelings, thoughts, and bodily sensations at a crucial junction during a session by requesting that they characterize what they are feeling as they describe something, or conversely, have them verbalize what they are thinking as they experience an emotion. Among other benefits, such techniques allow individuals to remain in the present moment, thereby increasing self-awareness and an acknowledgment and acceptance of one's actual array of affects.

A Caveat: The Dangers of Emotion Worship

Despite the success of the Enlightenment, with its stress on cold rationality, order, and objectivism, it did have to compete with the powerful contender of romanticism, which put a premium on emotional subjectivism, free expression, and individualized inwardness. Romanticism, among other things, suggests the "danger of emotion worship" (Pittman, 1994). Therapists, who sometimes are already working with someone who hyper-emotionalizes their circumstances, must not fall into the trap of further over-emotionalizing the patient's condition. Some, perhaps in reaction to the over-rationalizations of scientism, give primacy to an emotionally supercharged subjective reasoning that becomes detached from objective reality. They push the belief that feelings are equivalent to facts and amplify emotions in unhealthy ways (Pittman, 1994). But feelings are not necessarily the most important determinant of action. An over-focus on emotions may distract those who need help learning how to prudently test reality and explore and observe the world around them. It also breeds "opinionitis," i.e., an individual's viewpoint, no matter how faulty, misguided, or inaccurate, has an inherent value (this is the dark side of too much self-individuation). Such a hyper-interiorized, overly emotionalized introspectiveness leads to narcissism and loneliness since one's own feelings become confused with the feelings of the people who share our lives (Pittman, 1994).

With this caveat stated, we can explore the role of emotions by examining emotionally focused therapy (EFT) which explicitly addresses issues of emotional engagement.

Emotionally Focused Therapy

Often used in couple and family therapy and inspired by bonding and attachment theory, EFT concentrates on an individual's ability to first stabilize and then alter their feelings. EFT acknowledges the importance of seeking secure interpersonal relations whereby a healthy emotional life can be stabilized. Empirically validated (Johnson et al., 1999), its basic premises include: (1) emotions serve adaptive purposes and are linked to our most essential needs (Greenberg & Paivio, 1997; Greenberg & Safran, 1987); (2) emotions do not inhibit therapeutic processes; this is why even unpleasant feelings can be adaptive and useful (Johnson & Greenberg, 1987; Johnson et al., 1999); (3) interpersonal relations from the past configure our emotional outlook (Yalom, 2011); (4) individuals must first arrive at a certain place before they can depart from it, i.e., they must "own" powerful sentiments before such affective experiences can be understood (What is emotion focused therapy? 2009); and (5) people can modify their affective states (Goldman & Greenberg, 2006; Johnson & Greenberg, 1987).

The Stages of Emotional Re-regulation

Emotion regulation is the process by which individuals determine which emotions they experience, when they have them, and how they express these sentiments (Gross, 1998, p. 275). Regulating emotions is not an inborn capability. As a person develops, they learn to identify and express their emotional states in an appropriate manner. Since this is an interpersonal, socializing experience, this developmental process is one of co-regulation (Jørgensen, 2004, pp. 527-528). EFT interventions, like APSs, transpire over three phases (which, taken together, have nine steps), thereby allowing the re-regulating of dysregulated emotions: (1) de-escalation (preparation, exploration); (2) restructuring (transformative, transitional); (3) consolidation (resolution, restabilization) (Johnson, 2011).

Phase 1: De-escalation—Steps One to Four

A friend from Hungary used to wonder, in a critical manner, why Americans felt they had to "act happy" at all times. Indeed, it does seem that in the United States, people are socialized in such a way that they should always be cheerful. Many reasons for this could be offered. Perhaps it relates to how individuals unthinkingly model their expressions on a sunny "consumutopian," shop-till-you-drop ideology, reflected by enticing media images. The fulfillment of our every need is waiting just around the corner. Or maybe this forced cheerfulness allows us to conceal more realistic and honest appraisals of our situation. Or very possibly this over-optimism suggests a poverty in the repertoire of expressions. Indeed, it is not uncommon for patients to state, "I don't know how I feel." It is not that they are completely incognizant of their feelings, but often they lack the terminology to convey their sentiments. What is needed is the development of a more sophisticated, nuanced vocabulary to convey emotional states to others. Certainly this is the case in psychotherapeutic settings in which communicating one's emotion-cognitions are vital.

"You looked worried," stated a patient in a concerned tone as I entered the room to begin a group. His remark surprised me, as I thought I was doing a good job of keeping my personal worries under wraps. We emit emotional vibes without even knowing it. But many people instinctively prefer not to talk about their emotions. Some affect an off-putting bravado to hide their reluctance: "Don't let my appearance fool you. I'm just a scared little boy," one patient told me. Some struggle with vague, existentialist issues: "Deep down I'm scared, really scared. I'm scared of life, scared of success," one woman told me. Many regard feelings as very private, something "owned" by an individual; they should be guarded and only circumspectly shared, even with intimates. A patient explained that he used to "put a cage around my head" to describe how he avoided discussing his feelings. Another said he used to "seal my feelings off in a vault in my head." Still another stated, "there were guards at my mind's door. They didn't want to open up and barricaded my real feelings." This is why giving someone "permission to feel" can be empowering. This may sound strange, as many people assume that the self-authorization to experience one's own emotion arises naturally. But we are socialized—like Dr. Spock from Star Trek—to believe that the display of emotion can be problematic, e.g., too much emotion is ill-mannered and somehow disruptive to polite society (which of course sometimes it is). And individual sessions can be draining. One patient characterized them as an "internal workout," analogizing emotional expressions to the physical exertions of an exercise routine.

Given how hard it is for many of us to articulate our feelings, the first step of the de-escalation phase is crucial. Not only are an array of presenting problems and issues explored, but an attempt is made to identify one's most relevant emotions. I always feel a bit self-conscious handing out a feeling chart to an individual. Though effective, they sometimes appear to patients as a tad childish, and we might assume that labeling our emotions is something restricted to children. But in fact adults may struggle with this, too. Moreover, people are often uncertain as to how they feel about something, presumably because we have so many ambiguous sentiments about our personal relationships. Such ambiguity becomes problematic when it interferes with daily functioning. To change a disruptive emotional pattern, we must first give the pattern a name that governs our cognitions. The identification of feeling is needed before a modification can transpire.

In the second step the negative cycles of hurt-reaction-hurt caused by insecure attachment issues are identified. Obtaining secure attachment is the foundation for optimal functioning. People strive for safe, stable, and predictable emotional connections with others. Parenting matters. When this does not happen, individuals often behave so as to elicit reactions from others to meet their needs. This configures their emotional worldview. "I was raised by a professional f---up," one patient told me when asked to describe why he struggled to have healthy relations with others. Another patient, describing the lack of parental maturity of the part of his mother, told me, "She was my sister, not my mother." If maladaptive and insecure attachments develop, emotions drive negative interactional cycles. The working premise is that an individual, never having developed secure attachments while growing up, has adopted unhelpful strategies, such as easily triggered anger and free-floating anxiety. Lacking emotional awareness, some individuals cannot readily make sense of what they feel. They become stuck in an unhealthy habitual approach to engaging with others. This is because the primary emotions (presumably anger and resentment), buried deep in the past, though acknowledged, have not been adequately processed. Nevertheless, the core emotions generate secondary emotions that take the form of defensive coping mechanisms. The patient's anxiety and depression can be viewed as methods of defense.

Processing negative emotions can be challenging, to say the least. "I had so much pain it would make the devil get down on his knees and cry," said one patient about his emotional hurt. Feeling hopeless and despondent, another told me "today I have a big bucket of f---its." Anxiety "lies to you"—i.e., it distorts one's rational thought patterns—exclaimed one patient. Another expressed her worsening rate of anxiety as if "there's a hamster wheel in my head." One patient portrayed the spiraling nature of fear by saying it is "like bacteria, it grows if not stopped." "From sugar to shit" is how one patient with bipolar described her quickly altering emotions. "I'm a fire-cracker!" declared another, characterizing his volatile, unpredictable manner of inter-acting with people. The comment "I'm like a raw egg" conveyed feeling emotionally unstable and hyper-sensitive; "I want everything microwaved" depicted impatience; and "words just puke put of my mouth" indicated feeling so upset that a patient could not control his speech. "Don't look at the big picture. Look at what's in the picture" said a patient who struggled with ADHD, while another, having problems with gain-ing perspective on his troubling thoughts, explained, "I have to step outside the box."

The third step focuses on accessing and exploring the underlying emotions. The role of the therapist is to disentangle and highlight for patients the various emotions they experience, to teach them to become aware of how they affect their mental out-look, mood, and behavior, and to have them clearly discern the linkages between their primary (readily identified) and secondary emotions (not as easily identified; often following from primary emotions). Choreographing new, healthier interac-tional patterns results in a new dance, bringing about positive emotional experiences as well as their expression.

As it may be challenging to access a person's deeper feelings using probing ques-tions, the "circle of feelings" is a very useful schema for viewing how sentiments are, like sediments, deposited and layered over each other with time. The circle of feelings conceptualizes outermost emotions as being on the "surface" and more innermost ones as closer to the core of our emotional lives. The deepest emotions inform the more surface-level ones and drive cognitions and behaviors. Significantly, as patients become more emotionally vulnerable, they open themselves up to positive change. This drives home the centrality of feelings in our daily lives, whether we consciously acknowledge those in the core of our being or not.

Techniques to be utilized include evocative responding, open-ended questions, en-actment, and re-experiencing key moments. Heightening salient emotions, the crea-tive use of imagery and metaphors, and the two-chair and empty-chair techniques, may also be pressed into service (Greenberg, 2004).

In the fourth step the therapist discusses with patients how to reframe their pre-senting problems in terms of their underlying emotions.

Phase 2: Restructuring—Steps Five to Seven

Identifying the emotional needs of patients is the fifth step. In the sixth step, the new perspectives vis-à-vis their relations and how these relate to new behaviors are pro-moted. Change will occur once patients are able to access and process primary emo-tions and increase emotional awareness and connect the dots between their problems. Patients can hopefully develop new perspectives, positive responses to others, and more stable social interpersonal patterns by reframing, reshaping, and restructuring their repertoire of feelings and sentiments. Positive interactional patterns will be reinforced and replace maladaptive patterns.

In the seventh step the therapist and patients explore how the latter can express their emotional needs and wants in productive, adaptive ways. The lesson is that insight must be emotional as well intellectual. The latter type of insight is typically easier, since people are often wary of expressing emotions to others or consciously registering emotions even to themselves. Even if individuals do not seem to express their emotions in an obvious way, they nevertheless possess them. Indeed, people have emotional currents and countercurrents that configure their behavior in ways of which they are often unaware. It is not uncommon for couples (and people in general, for that matter) to "love" each other in strange, unhealthy, codependent ways; dysfunction can keep people together.

Phase 3: Consolidation—Steps Eight to Nine

Consolidation begins with the eighth step. Armed with a rehabilitated viewpoint on the "why" of the roiling passions that have until now often overtaken their more reasonable self, patients will now consider new solutions to their problems, minor and major, that have afflicted their life and will monitor these negative feelings when they arise (self-autonomy). The final step sees patients further solidify and strengthen their new outlook.

Taking Stock

This chapter took as its theoretical linchpin Jaynes's two-tiered theory of emotions, i.e., a layer of feelings culturally constructed over basic mammalian affects. More nuanced feelings come with a price: meta-framed emotions become unnecessarily prolonged and distressful since our narratizing selves may extend them into our past or "futurize" them, so they sometimes preoccupy our worldview and distort our cognition.

One of the most humbling experiences I have ever had was the first time I attempted to practice meditation among Tibetan Buddhists. When I would sit still and attempt to "think without thinking," I quickly learned I was not the captain of my soul. I felt as if my mind were a vast ocean, raging and roiling, churning powerful waves filled with mental debris. But surely, I thought, something can be learned from this practice about the workings of psyche. I reached the same conclusion about hypnosis. The next chapter explores the theoretical underpinnings and clinical implications of anomalous psychological experience from a Jaynesian perspective.

Notes

1. Note that at very elevated levels, positive emotions might be detrimental (Cohn & Fredrickson, 2009).
2. Mammalian emotions are evolved from the overt behaviors of reptiles. In mammals, these behaviors become "inhibited by more recently evolved parts of the brain, leaving them more diffusely related to actual overt behavior in a more general energizing way." In other words, "most emotional behaviors of mammals are paleoreptilian behaviors, transformed on both the stimulus and the response side by limbic and cortical selective inhibition" (Jaynes, 1982, p. 147).

13
Hypnosis and Meditation
Suspending and Modulating Conscious Interiority

Can research that compares "altered states of consciousness"[1] shed light on "ordinary" consciousness? A specific and recently popular route to accomplish this is by comparing hypnosis with meditation. Investigating these anomalous phenomena will improve our understanding of cognition and conscious interiority, as well as allow the development of better therapeutic techniques. The purpose of this chapter is to examine these topics. For example, explorations of hypnosis and meditation help us better understand a central topic in psychology, namely, differences between controlled (voluntary, slow, effortful) and automatic (involuntary, fast, effortless) mental processes (Lifshitz & Raz, 2012, p. 6). Importantly for any therapeutic implications, Lifshitz and Raz point out that like hypnosis, meditative practices provide an effective method of gaining control over automatic processes. For example, "specific forms of meditation appear to override habitual responses associated with spontaneous thought" (Lifshitz & Raz, 2012, p. 7).

Comparing Hypnosis with Meditation

Generally categorized as anomalous psychological phenomena, it is not surprising that some have searched for commonalities as well as differences between hypnosis and meditation. Lifshitz (2016) notes how hypnosis and meditation both share phenomenological and neurocognitive features, as well as having potential therapeutic effects. Evidence indicates that they draw on "overlapping functional neuroanatomy, neural circuitry, chemical modulators, and cellular structure" (Lifshitz & Raz, 2012, p. 5).[2] Ott (2016) points out that though hypnosis and meditation seem diametrically opposed, they both show a strong correlation with attentional absorption, suggesting neural commonalities. However, this similarity is only between hypnosis and concentrative meditation, not mindful meditation. Mooneyham and Schooler (2016), drawing on work in attention and meta-awareness, suggest how to examine the specific functional changes that occur within the executive process (monitoring) for both hypnosis and meditation. Yapko (2016) notes that processes of focus, dissociation, and suggestion overlap in mindful meditation and hypnosis. Viewing matters from the perspective of personal transformation, Farb (2016) sees hypnosis as "concentrative" and directing perception and/or action toward a particular end. Mindfulness, on the other hand, reduces reliance on habitual self-appraisals and enables open-ended

inquiry and exploration. Yapko (2016) urges caution when utilizing mindful meditation as a therapeutic technique, since its goals may not coincide with personal or spiritual growth (i.e., spiritual practice and clinical application are not the same). Zeidan
and Grant (2016) contend that hypnotic and meditative states reduce pain through
overlapping but unique mechanisms involving attention, cognitive control, appraisal
processes, and suggestibility. By relying on a predictive coding approach, Jamieson
(2016) attempted to delineate a unified theory of diverse mental states that account
for hypnosis and meditation. From a practical perspective, Lynn et al. (2016) tried to
integrate our understanding of hypnosis, meditation, and acceptance-based strategies for smoking-cessation intervention.

Holroyd (2003) contextualizes hypnosis by looking at it from the perspective of two
aspects of Buddhist meditation—concentration and mindfulness (CNT). The conclusion is that an understanding of hypnosis needs to accommodate "altered states" as well
as the capacity for expectations and imaginative involvement. Halsband et al. (2009)
contend that both hypnosis and meditation share focused attention, concentration, and
letting go of thoughts. But differences are apparent in processing sensory input, memory,
and a sense of time.[3] Lifshitz and Raz (2012) submit that "suggestion" and "concentration" (often referred to as "attention" in the literature) represent two key processes that
need to be investigated to discern the relation between hypnosis and meditation.

From a neuroanatomical perspective, Raz (2016) contends that the anterior cingulate cortex seems to be a key node in hypnosis and some forms of meditation, while
the dorsolateral prefrontal cortex appears to be engaged in hypnosis. Tang and Posner
(2016) show how hypnosis lessens activity within the anterior cingulate cortex,
thereby preventing goals from activating the executive attention network; this allows
control by external input and prior instructions. Meditation may work to enhance executive attention, resulting in improved self-control.[4]

To analyze hypnosis and meditation, Dienes et al. (2016) apply the framework of
first-order mental states (mindfulness of the world) and second-order mental states
(meta-cognitive mindfulness of one's mental state; this definitionally resonates with
FOCI). Hypnosis is associated with self-deception, and meditation with self-insight.
They conclude that hypnotic response is a failure of meta-cognition, while meditation enhances meta-cognition. When under hypnosis a person does intend to act,
imagine, or pretend; however, they are not aware of that intention (Dienes et al., 2016,
p. 3). That is, while the first-order state of intending is normal, when hypnotized an
individual inaccurately forms a higher order thought to the effect that they are not
intending, despite any sustained reflection on the volitional nature of the behavior
(Dienes et al., 2016, p. 3). This "cold control" theory, that we can have executive control without accurate higher-order thoughts, intuitively sounds right but does not
seem to capture all the dimensions of the hypnotic trance.

Dienes et al. (2016) contend that, despite any similarities, hypnosis and meditation
are essentially different. The latter aims to cultivate meta-awareness, while the former
transpires due to a lack of awareness of intentions, i.e., hypnosis is really a form of

self-deception. Thompson et al. (2016), while acknowledging that hypnosis and meditation overlap, also stress that they are distinct experiential and neurophysiological processes. To analyze them, they utilize five dimensions: (1) effort (trait versus practice); (2) attention (narrow versus broad); (3) continuity of awareness (dissociation versus integration); (4) imagery/visualization (prominent versus minimal); and (5) agency (the "hidden observer" versus "no self").[5]

The wisdom of Buddhist spirituality has inspired the view of not a few researchers vis-à-vis anomalous psychological states (CNT).[6] For instance, Tart (2016) integrates what we know about meditation and hypnosis with Buddhist understandings of mental states and compares "consensus consciousness," hypnosis, quieting meditation, and insight meditation.[7] Toneatto and Courtice (2016), adopting a psychoanalytic approach, discuss how mindfulness meditation and hypnosis facilitate a reorganization of the personality through the dissolution of narcissist ego functioning, a process that resonates with Buddhist ideas. Veissière (2016) explores interphenomenality, or the shared experiences of "what it feels like" which are generated by "joint attention," a process that resonates with hypnosis. To illustrate his points, he explores *tulpa* (sentient imaginary companions) that are conjured via "thought-form"[8] meditative practice. Jinpa (2016) investigates "visualization meditation" used in the Tibetan Buddhist tradition. This practice heavily relies on a robust introceptual ability, a key feature of FOCI. Deely (2016) looks at the Chod (*gcod*) and discerns links to hypnosis. This is a meditation practice in which, through the act of self-offering, gods and demons consume the practitioner's body. It is used to cultivate the Buddhist goals of compassion and non-attachment.

Table 13.1 compares typical and atypical cognition. Figure 13.1 shows how hypnosis occurs when FOCI are suspended while one enters a meditative state when certain features of FOCI are focused.

Figure 13.2 shows the different permutations of mentality produced by selective concentration and suggestibility.

Table 13.1 Typical and Atypical Cognition

Cognition	Conscious Interiority	Adaptive ←——————————→ Maladaptive	
Typical cognition	Conscious interiority	Routine conscious mentation	
Atypical cognition	Certain features of conscious interiority highlighted	Meditation	Hyper-conscious
Atypical cognition	Features of conscious interiority suspended	Hypnotherapy	

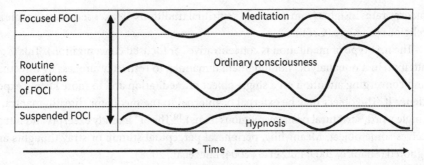

Figure 13.1. Meditation, hypnosis, and ordinary consciousness compared.

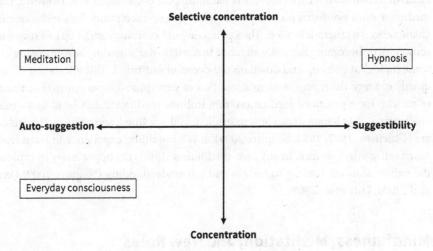

Figure 13.2. Permutations of mentality.

Meditation as Meta-Framing—Regulating Conscious Interiority to Promote Insight

Meditation can help some patients learn how to better regulate their attention and concentration. This contemplative practice cultivates insight, objective observations about experience, and self-reflexivity. Meditation (which is not the same as deep relaxation) belongs to a family of techniques with a long history (CNT). It comes in two types: concentrative and mindfulness.[9] Whatever the type, meditation is an ambitious meta-framing mental exercise. Research beginning in the late 1970s on meditation tended to focus on its physiological aspects, with symptom reduction and alleviation being major interests. Researchers gave little attention to topics such as personal development, enhancement, or cultivation of qualities that might lead to positive growth (PPT) (Shapiro, 2009). More recently, however, meditation-related research can be considered part of a larger and welcome trend in psychology that incorporates insights from the world's spiritual traditions. It takes seriously the role of religious practices (CNT).

The first type of meditation is concentrative (or focused concentration). This is an attempt, in a nonanalytic, nonjudgmental manner, to restrict awareness by directing and converging attention on a single object of meditation and to more keenly experience it. The object may be external or internal to the meditator (breath, mantra, a single word, scriptural passage, religious icons).[10] The "I" intently excerpts and introceives some object. Meanwhile, peripheral perceptual stimuli or stray thoughts are ignored (Shapiro, 2009; Lutz et al., 2004; Lutz et al., 2008).

The second type is mindfulness meditation. The goal is to observe all stimuli in both one's exterior perceptual field and interiorized psychoscape. One attends in a calm, detached manner to whatever is parading past one's mind's eye. However, the meditator does not focus on one particular object or excerption. This technique is characterized by meta-attention. The key is to avoid becoming caught up in a singular sensation, or becoming mentally attached to a particular stimulus, or ruminating on some topic that bobs up and down on the ocean of our mind. This allows our "I" to quietly observe the moment-to-moment flux of perceptuo-introceptions. For those of us who have practiced meditation, mindfulness meditation can be at first quite challenging, as it demonstrates how unbridled, undisciplined, and noisy our thoughts are (Goleman, 1972, 1988; Shapiro, 2009). It is a humbling experience to learn how much self-control we lack. In any case, meditation affords the opportunity to explore the nature of mind, leading to insight and self-understanding (Shapiro, 2009; Lutz et al., 2004; Lutz et al., 2008).

Mindfulness, Meditation, and New Roles

The soothing balm of mindfulness can be understood by considering what it is like to have a head full of racing thoughts, as described by patients recounting sentiments of agitation: "There's a party going on inside my head"; "My head has a hamster wheel in it"; "When I try to go to sleep it's as if I was trying to write a book"; "I can't make up my own mind because my head's committee lacks a chairman"; "My head is like a logjam of thoughts." Mindfulness, or paying attention to one's ongoing experience, can enhance openness and cognitive flexibility. Within the context of positive psychology, Langer (2009) links mindfulness, which is associated with openness to novelty, sensitivity to context, and engagement with the present moment, to learning experiences. Being mindful allows patients to: (1) create new categories of experience; (2) be open to new information; and (3) see situations more clearly from various angles (Langer, 1989).

"Learning how to control one's mind without allowing one's mind to control you" can be viewed through the FOCI lens and reformulated as learning how to have one's "I" objectively observe one's thoughts so that other parts of one's mind (various "me's" or excerptions) do not usurp one's objectivity and what is actually occurring all around us. "Thinking before you think" (not spiraling rumination, but a more self-objective "thinking about what you are thinking about and why") and considering "what are you feeling and why" are crucial to the self-healing endeavor. While in session, therapists, of course, must also step back and meta-frame their own thinking patterns so as to better gauge their impact on those who are seeking aid.

Mindfulness can facilitate a growing awareness within the individual of all possible parts ("me's") of their self, thereby revealing unknown but potential assets (Jourard, 1971). It is a preparatory step toward meditation, whose one purpose in RSP might be to allow patients to take an inventory of their roles. This is done by using mental imagery in order to call up a "behavioral mental space" (the counterpart of behavioral physical space) where our different role-selves can be viewed. Meditation is the mental practice of attending in an unemotional manner to whatever passes before one's eyes or one's mind's eye. For RSP, the "I" becomes the disinterested observer, while "me's"—one's roles—parade past this impartial witness.[11] During meditation, patients might be asked to be mindful of the assorted roles they perform. RSP encourages patients to adopt a neutral, calm, and mindful standpoint of the observing "I." Patients should then become self-objective by first considering their current roles, e.g., spouse, parent, sibling, worker, etc. Then, they will reflect on their past role-selves. Finally, they can then be requested to contemplate on what is needed to meet the demands of their future selves, e.g., successful entrepreneur, faithful spouse, good parent, civic-minded citizen, etc. After meditation, patients are invited to comment on the advantages, disadvantages, and meaning of the roles that define their intrapersonal and interpersonal relations. In order to monitor and enact their roles, patients can be educated on the uses of mindfulness, or closely paying attention to their own ongoing immediate experiences (whether perceptual, conceptual, or introceptual).

We can appreciate mindfulness by describing its opposite—mindlessness: being inattentive; reacting habitually without consideration; relying on worn-out concepts; and being overly anxious or ruminating about one's past (e.g., what someone did to me; my failures) or future (Will I succeed in my endeavors? What happens to me if … ?). Mindlessness is a cognitive process that is habitual, prematurely committed to categories, and focused on the future rather than one's immediate surroundings or circumstances (Langer, 1989). Being mindless means responding unreflectively, cruising through the day on automatic pilot, and applying outdated or inappropriate framework. In other words, the individual swallows the rush of information without properly digesting it.

Buddhism sees mindfulness as attention to "experience without attachment to one's experience," i.e., one's transcendent "I" merely observes without engaging one's churning thoughts. The quote, "with meditation I found a ledge above the waterfall of my thoughts," captures the sense of how this practice allows us to meta-frame above the riotous circus of unruly ideas passing before our mind's eye (Pipher, 2009). Needless to say, stress increases mindlessness and, consequently, anxiety.

Hypnosis—Pausing the Noise of Consciousness to Reboot the Mind

I have dealt with how utilizing FOCI can be therapeutically useful. But can shutting them down via hypnotic trance have any utility—in the same way we turn off an uncooperative technological device to reset it? If our modern mentality is an "immutable genetically determined characteristic evolved back somewhere in mammalian evolution" (Jaynes, 1976, p. 380), how can it be so readily altered by the mere words of another? How can the verbalizations of another become so persuasive, causing us to ignore pain, redefine ourselves, and do things we ordinarily would not? In other words, if the basics of our mentality are prewired, what explains the effects of hypnosis? We need to jettison the conventional view that consciousness is genetically innate. We can begin to comprehend hypnosis when we appreciate that consciousness is an array of learned cultural abilities superimposed over earlier vestigial substrates for individuals who unhesitatingly obeyed social dictates (Jaynes, 1976, p. 380).[12] The very existence of hypnosis reveals our inherent neurocultural plasticity.[13] Indeed, beliefs about hypnosis have radically changed through history, indicating, like human cognition in general, its remarkably malleable and unfixed nature (Jaynes, 1976, pp. 383–384).[14]

Hypnosis deserves careful consideration, not just because it challenges our core assumptions about self-control, but because of its great therapeutic merits. It has been used for all types of problems, including age regression,[15] age progression (pseudo-orientation in time), and anesthesia (Yápko, 2012, p. 345). While "put under," one can radically alter one's self-identity, ignore pain and sensory stimulation, change one's emotional reactions at the drop of a hat, and control automatic responses when commanded to do so by a hypnotist.

Jaynes wrote that we live in a "buzzing cloud of whys and wherefores," filled with "purposes and reasonings of our narratizations, the many-routed adventures of our analog 'I's'" (Jaynes, 1976, p. 402). However, this "constant spinning out of possibilities is precisely what is necessary to save us from behavior of too impulsive a sort." The "I" and "me" are "always resting at the confluence of many collective cognitive imperatives. We know too much to command ourselves very far" (Jaynes, 1976, p. 402). Hypnosis is a way to temporarily shut down our uncertainties, hesitations, and reservations.

Defining and Delineating Hypnosis

Volumes have been written about hypnosis and the effective uses of hypnotherapy. An examination of hypnosis implicates an array of psychological processes related to the influence of expectancies; beliefs; attitudes; suggestibility; attention; fantasy and imagination; the role of rapport in relationships; memory; automatic, spontaneous versus goal-directed thought (cited in Brown, 2016, p. 454; see also Lynn, Rhue, &

Kirsch, 2010; Nash & Barnier, 2008). Numerous theories compete to explain what it is and why it works.[16] For instance, the French neurologist Hippolyte Bernheim (1840-1919) used "ideodynamism" to refer to the conversion of an idea or suggestion into an automatic and actual response (subtypes are ideoaffective, ideocognitive, ideomotor, and ideosensory). A more modern perspective views hypnosis as a dissociated state—the psyche's subsystems become segregated from each other and thus respond independently to a therapist's suggestions. Hilgard's (1977) theory of neo-dissociation updated this approach.

Yapko summarizes the major theoretical perspectives that have also been used as a theoretical framework to explain hypnosis: as a psychobiological phenomenon; an altered state of consciousness; a passive or permissive state; a special interactional outcome; a sociocognitive phenomenon; social-role playing; reality testing; the result of conditioning; the potent property of words (Yapko, 2012, pp. 48-60). These theorizings, each in their own way, certainly shed light on certain dimensions of hypnosis. However, none of them is completely satisfactory. Some seem to describe, rather than explain, the nature of hypnosis, and they do not fit hypnotic experiences into a larger explanatory framework that includes other forms of cognition.

Let us start to disentangle the complex web of this strange behavior with some definitions and descriptions. Halsband et al. characterize hypnosis as "focused attention, a heightened compliance with suggestion, an awareness of internal images and a reduced ability to think critically" (2009, p. 195). They add attentional control; concentration; imagination; mental relaxation; altered perception of the environment; and disengagement of discursive and critical analytical reasoning (Halsband et al., 2009, p. 198). Other associated phenomena are amnesia; catalepsy; dissociation; hallucinations;[17] sensory alterations; time distortion; increased or decreased affect; cognitive and perceptual flexibility; and fluctuations in level of absorption. Physical and physiological changes include muscular relaxation; muscular twitching; lacrimation (watering eyes); eye closure with fluttering eyelids; changes in breathing rate and pulse rate; jaw relaxation; catalepsy; and bodily sensory shifts (Yapko, 2012, pp. 192-194). A more therapeutically oriented definition of hypnosis reads: a "focused experience of attentional absorption that invites people to respond experientially on multiple levels to amplify and utilize their personal resources in a goal-directed fashion" (Yapko, 2012, p. 523).

A Jaynesian Perspective on Hypnosis

Authorization and Suggestibility—Granting Permission to Self-Heal

At its barest, hypnosis can be defined as a mental state involving: (1) selective concentration along with reduced peripheral perception; (2) an enhanced capacity to respond to suggestions (i.e., self-authorization is suspended); and (3) a weakening of conscious interiority or its loss. Below I comment on these key aspects by contextualizing them within the four aspects of what Jaynes termed the "general bicameral paradigm." This hypothesized structure is behind a class of anomalous phenomena of diminished FOCI—spirit possession, glossolalia, hypergraphia—that are partial holdovers from an earlier mentality (Jaynes, 1976, p. 323).

The Power of Culture: The Collective Cognitive Imperative

The collective cognitive imperative, or a "culturally agreed-on expectancy or prescription which defines the particular form of a phenomenon and the roles to be acted out within that form" (Jaynes, 1976, p. 323), grounds and shapes how hypnosis is socially manifested. Accepted notions and metaphors of the day, embedded in a society's belief system, have been used to account for hypnosis. The late eighteenth century witnessed Mesmerism (an "animal magnetism" pervades the cosmos that can be tapped into to restore one's health) and in the nineteenth century hypnosis was considered a type of sleep, a common misconception still in circulation (from Hypnos, the Greek god of slumber). However, what is called "active and alert" hypnosis dispels such a misunderstanding. The twentieth and early twenty-first centuries saw more scientific attempts to explain hypnosis. Some researchers merely attempted to explain it away; this, of course, is a common reaction when confronted with a phenomenon that simply cannot be easily accommodated within the prevailing paradigm. Key tropes still shape our understanding: the ego's ability to test reality (how an individual can rationally function interpersonally); different levels and orders of thought and executive control (as if the mind were a miniaturized bureaucracy); role-taking (a theatrical analogy of being directed and directing others; not "role-faking"); systems theory (dissociated parts of the psyche branch off from each other); acquiring a social role (learned social behavior). And while the findings from neuroscience about the physical aspects of hypnosis are informative, research into neurophysiological changes and interhemispheric relations, being part of a modern mythology of the brain-as-computer model and neurological localism, needs to be approached cautiously.

Suspending FOCI through Induction

Procedures designed to induce trance increase selective concentration ("attention"). This means the "ability to voluntarily focus on one portion of an experience while 'tuning out' the rest" (Yapko, 2012, p. 84). The focusing on a specific stimulus while excluding others is the "foundation upon which hypnotic experience rests" (Yapko, 2012, p. 184). Like APSs, hypnotherapy is typically delivered in a staged, structured manner in which an individual leaves ordinary consciousness, enters a transitional, liminal state, and then returns to ordinary consciousness, hopefully with an altered mentality: (1) trance induction; (2) transition into trance; (3) direct statements or suggestions regarding the source and/or solution of the problem; (4) metaphorical or anecdotal guidance toward the source and/or solution of the problem; (5) trance termination (rehearsal review; ratification; reorientation; distraction); (6) follow-up evaluation (Havens & Walters, 2012, p. 42). Here we might note that Yapko outlines the "stages of hypnotic interaction,"[18] the "stages of hypnotic induction,"[19] and the "generic structure for a hypnosis session."[20]

A formally ritualized procedure, "whose function is the narrowing of consciousness by focusing attention on a small range of preoccupations" (Jaynes, 1976, p. 323), is the typical entry to hypnotic trance—i.e., induction. The ability to deactivate FOCI involves the inherent power of verbalization, or the "conditioning property of words." This describes how we can firmly attach words to experience. However, the resulting physical, emotional, and sensory changes that transpire actually happen in all kinds of nonhypnotic contexts (Yapko, 2012, pp. 58–60).[21] Hypnosis greatly intensifies such changes to such a degree that it appears to be a remarkably different mental state. It is through the "paralogical compliance to verbally mediated reality" (Jaynes, 1976, p. 393) that radical psychological alterations transpire. During hypnotherapy, when an individual's suspicious self-conscious guards are off duty, patients more readily attach particular significance to the clinician's words. Consequently, such verbalizations have potential therapeutic benefit.

In their attempt to reformulate the mindfulness construct, Vervaeke and Ferraro conceive ritual as a key behavior in our cognitive evolution. Ritual seems to "functionally integrate mindfulness practices with hypnosis; it binds the manipulation of attention and suggestion together" (Vervaeke & Ferraro 2016, p. 264). During the liminal state of a ritual, crucial frame-breaking and frame-making strategies allow new reframings to emerge. In this way, ritual "optimizes the machinery of both insight and self-regulation in a highly coordinated and integrated manner" (Vervaeke & Ferraro, 2016, p. 263).

Trancing as a Diminution of FOCI

A direct response to induction is trance. But here note that merely describing hypnosis (as well as meditation) as some type of "trance" is tautological. Moreover, we need to inquire about the nature of trance—one phenomenon or many? Something pathological or an elevated, health-enhancing state? (Harrington, 2016). In any event, the uses of trancing are shaped by the collective cognitive imperative. For our purposes, trance can be understood as the lessening or suspension of FOCI or their loss, such as the diminishing of the analog "I" or its effacement. The result is a "role that is accepted, tolerated, or encouraged by the group" or the culture at large (Jaynes, 1976, p. 323). Note that individual and circumstantial variables impact which and to what degree certain FOCI are diminished. As self-authorization is weakened, the hypnotist (or hypnotherapist) becomes the *perceived* source of authorization, since strictly speaking, the hypnotizer ("I") and the hypnotized ("me") are the same person, i.e., no one can be hypnotized against their will. As Jay Haley stated, "I can hypnotize you only by you hypnotizing yourself" (Haley, 1963; cited in Yapko, 2012, p. 29). During hypnosis, a hypnotherapist facilitates trance by encouraging a person to suspend, or at least lessen, the workings of conscious interiority. Such suspension occurs when the hypnotherapist temporarily deactivates FOCI. Note, however, that anyone encul-turated to be conscious can never permanently or completely suspend FOCI; though suppressed during trance, traces of FOCI will always lurk in the nonconscious under-ground, waiting to be reactivated.[22]

A key trait of trancing is "time distortion," or the loss of a clear sense of temporal unfolding. Usually we consciously narratize a "row of happenings" that are time-tagged (Jaynes, 1976, p. 391). But like schizophrenic patients or preconscious indi-viduals from an earlier period, for the hypnotized, inner subjectivity and its resident, the analog "I," are either inhibited or absent, thereby severely restricting narratization (Jaynes, 1976, p. 387).

The State-versus-Nonstate Debate

The key theoretical dispute about hypnotic trance revolves around "special state" versus "nonstate" explanations. In other words, is hypnosis a special mental opera-tion (the most common position), or is it continuous with other mental operations? Here is a good place to join the debate. Special-state interpretations stress differences between hypnosis and "ordinary psychological processes," while nonstate approaches highlight their basic similarities. Both sides of the debate have merit. Hypnosis, for anyone who has witnessed it, is a singular psychological phenomenon that deserves to be regarded as a distinct state. At the same time, it cannot be totally disentangled from the fabric of other forms of mentation. In this sense it is nonstate. Arguably, then, the terms of the debate are misleading, and "special state" versus "nonstate" can be applied to any manifestation of mental functioning.

The state-versus-nonstate debate does not seem so unsolvable if hypnosis and nonhypnotic states are positioned at either ends of a continuum. After all, the "core structures of hypnotic methods"—selective concentration and suggestion—are not unique to hypnosis and can be found to varying degrees in other therapeutic tech-niques (Yapko, 2012, pp. 515–516). As consciousness increases, hypnotic trance decreases, and as hypnotic trance increases, FOCI decrease. Occupying the middle of the continuum are hypnoidal states that resemble mild hypnosis but are usually induced by nonhypnotic means. Many states we consider "normal waking" are prob-ably hypnoidal to some degree, or if put another way, overlap in significant ways with hypnosis (daydreaming, visualization, guided imagery, EMDR, deep relaxation, au-togenic training).[23]

What is described as "flow," or experience of complete absorption in the present moment, may be hypnoidal (Nakamura & Csikszentmihalyi, 2009).[24] The charac-teristics of flow are: (1) intense and focused concentration on the present moment; (2) merging of action and awareness; (3) loss of reflective self-consciousness (or loss of awareness that one is a social actor); (4) a sense that one can control one's actions (or a sense that one can in principle deal with the situation because one knows how to respond to whatever happens next); (5) distortion of temporal experience (often time passes faster than normal); (6) the experience of the activity as intrinsically rewarding, such that often the end goal is just an excuse for the process (Nakamura & Csikszentmihalyi, 2009, pp. 195–197).

Suggestion: Granting and Receiving Authorization to Change One's Self

The most salient trait that characterizes hypnosis is arguably an increased responsiveness to suggestion; such receptivity to promptings happens because of authorization. It needs to be stressed that such responsiveness is not the same as gullibility or noncritical acceptance of suggestions; indeed, hypnosis "actually amplifies a person's range of choices" and some suggestions may be rejected (Yapko, 2012, pp. 184–187).

Jaynes used the term "archaic authorization" to describe the fourth aspect of the general bicameral paradigm. The original context of his argument was religious, so that trancing was "directed or related to, usually a god, but sometimes a person who is accepted by the individual and his culture as an authority over the individual [e.g., healthcare provider], and who by the collective cognitive imperative is prescribed to be responsible for controlling the trance state" (Jaynes, 1976, p. 323). But to whomever or whatever one directs one's trance (a healer or therapist), the operative word here is authorization, so that during trance the interself process of self-authorization is suspended. The feeling of hetero-authorization (control by another) emerges; the hypnotherapist usurps the "I" and takes over a person's "me." It is as if "someone else were doing things through us. And why is this so? And why is this easier? Is it that we have to lose our conscious selves [nagging and interfering self-doubts] to gain such control, which cannot then be by us?" (Jaynes, 1976, p. 402).

The effectiveness of suggestions transpires due to "trance logic," or the ability to accept incongruities or inconsistencies without question—suggestions that one would not tolerate while conscious (Orne, 1959). Jaynes refers to this unreflective attitude as "paralogic": the routine rules of everyday reasoning are set aside to conform to assertions about reality that are untrue. Paralogical behavior infuses mythological thinking and certain religious activities. However, it is particularly pronounced in hypnosis. Paralogic compliance explains why hypnotized individuals walk around a chair that they have been told is not there, rather than crashing into it (logical compliance). They do not hallucinate the chair out of existence. They find nothing illogical in their actions (Jaynes, 1976, pp. 390–391). Hypnosis affords a doorway into a world of as-if-ness; but this heightened hypotheticality also comes with a suppression of "it-isn't" (Jaynes, 1976, p. 389).

Whether described as trance logic or paralogic, the as-if/it-isn't perspective establishes the groundwork for metaphoric thinking. As in therapy in general, metaphors perform a key role in hypnotherapy: making or illustrating a point; suggesting solutions; having individuals recognize their own thoughts; seeding ideas; increasing motivation; embedding directives; decreasing resistance; reframing and redefining a problem; increasing accessibility to personal resources; encouraging a search for relevance; discovering alternate responses (Yapko, 2012, pp. 442–443).

Suggestion as Therapeutic Communication

Broadly understood, suggestion is the influence a therapist can have over patients. Any suggestion in and of itself can be therapeutic since it can mitigate anxiety and afford hope to the person in need (Dow, 1986; Frank & Frank, 1991). However, a narrower definition of suggestion involves a special type of verbalization. Indeed, hypnosis can be theorized as a problem of interpersonal as well as interself communication. Halligan and Oakley (2014, p. 105) describe suggestion as a "form of communicable ideation or belief" (transpiring intrapersonally), while suggestibility facilitates or enhances the probability of a suggestion being accepted and believed.

In a healing context in which patients seek out the reassuring authorization of a healer, "therapeutic communication" transpires. This is defined as what happens when a person in distress is influenced "to think, feel, or behave differently in a way that is considered more adaptive or beneficial" (Yapko, 2012, pp. 16, 17). Certain "patterns of influence" characterize all types of social interaction—everyday relations, paratherapeutic (self-help groups), or therapeutic. Hypnosis escalates these patterns, and in this sense it can be conceptualized as an issue of communication. It is easy to command others (telling others what to do). However, issuing an order, for a variety of reasons, does not necessarily mean controlling another. A "sender" may be another person, society in general, or oneself. A "receiver" is whoever "hears" and processes the directive. A command is issued by a sender; if a receiver obeys (i.e., is controlled), the command-control circuit is closed. The degree of suggestibility is the likelihood of obtaining closure. Resistance to suggestions or commands interferes with closing the communicative loop. Hypnosis is a special type of communication as it increases suggestibility by dispersing bothersome preoccupations, distractions, and the inattentiveness of our wandering consciousness ("noise").[25] This permits the focusing and concentrating of the powers of self-control. The hypnotized grants permission to the hypnotherapist to facilitate change of some aspect of themselves (Table 13.2).

A key goal of suggestion in the therapeutic setting is the de-automatization of habitual processes (Lifshitz & Raz, 2012, p. 6). Throughout life, effortful tasks become automatized after repeated and extensive practice. But once automatized, the processes underlying the task's execution become "resistant to control and largely imperturbable." What is noteworthy is that such "overlearned habits form the backbone of many mental disorders; consider, for example, the centrality of ruminative thinking in depression" (Lifshitz & Raz, 2012, p. 6).[26]

Table 13.2 Permutations of Hypnosis

Suggestibility	Command-Control Circuit	Type of Social Interaction	Sociopsychological Process
Counter-suggestibility	Not closed	Defiance	Other does not control me
Counter auto-suggestibility	Not closed	Resistance	"I" cannot control/change "me"
Authorized suggestibility	Closed	Allowing others to tell us what to do	Other controls me
Self-authorized suggestibility	Closed	Telling ourselves what to do; ordinary decision-making	"I" controls "me"
Enhanced suggestibility (hypnosis)	Closed	Telling ourselves what to do while mitigating "noise" with assistance from another	Hypnotist aids hypnotizer ("I") to control hypnotized ("me")
Enhanced auto-suggestibility (self-hypnosis)	Closed	Telling ourselves what to do while mitigating "noise"	Hypnotizer ("I") controls hypnotized ("me")

In order to facilitate therapeutic communication, scripts might be utilized. Besides used for trance-induction and trance-termination procedures, scripts can be utilized for problems in living; direct approaches to change; managing pain; recovering from trauma and grief; medical issues; enhancing relationships; dealing with depression; alleviating unwarranted fears; concentration and success in work, school, and sports; overcoming sexual problems; impulse control; smoking cessation; habit or addiction problems; childbirth and pregnancy issues; identifying one's core values (Havens & Walters, 2002; Nongard, 2012). Note, however, that Yapko warns the therapist against an overreliance on scripts (2012, p. 43).

Taking Stock

This chapter was premised on the idea that understanding hypnosis and meditation enhances our conceptualization of cognition and conscious interiority. A Jaynesian perspective on hypnosis allows us to view it as a suspension of conscious interiority, while meditation was seen as a type of meta-framing. All this has important clinical implications.

The next chapter is inspired by the notion that "every person is a culture," i.e., each person is a dynamic, complex intersection of identity factors. Therefore, *all* counseling is cross-cultural. While exploring the intersection of multiculturalism, conscious interiority, and therapy, the next chapter also analyzes the meaning of "identity" in order to investigate its uses and misuses, as well as what is required to be a multiculturally sensitive therapist.

Notes

1. See Beischel et al. (2011) and Vaitl et al. (2005) for literature reviews on altered states of consciousness.
2. For instance, "motivation and effort may account for much of the improvement in attention usually ascribed to mindfulness practice" (Lifshitz & Raz, 2012, p. 6).
3. See Halsband et al.'s chart detailing changes that occur in two types of meditation and hypnosis (interaction; input/processing; concentration; memory; sense of time; stress coping (2009, p. 196). Note that "suggestibility" is missing.
4. McGeown (2016) provides a review of the explosion of recent research in brain network functional connectivity.
5. Polito and Connors (2016) explore the methodological problems in analyzing hypnosis and meditation by formulating four conceptual issues: (1) distinguishing the procedures participants follow from what they report; (2) separating participants' trait capacities from contextual influences; (3) considering the interplay between cognitive and social processes; and (4) controlling for demand characteristics.
6. But note that Brown (2016) judiciously distinguishes between the different schools of Buddhist thought.
7. Tart provides a useful chart that compares the effects of four states/practices on basic subsystem of consciousness (2016, p. 159).
8. An interesting term that transcends mind–body dualism.
9. Tart refers to concentrative as "insight" and mindful as "quieting" meditation (2016, pp. 152–153).
10. This resonates with Leary and Guadagno's intriguing ideas about the "hypoegoic state" in which self-awareness is low and attention is focused on concrete rather than abstract stimuli. During the hypoegoic state, "self-talk" decreases, i.e., flow-interfering self-monitoring and self-observing are minimized, thereby decreasing anxiety and distraction (Leary & Guadagno, 2011).
11. To go one step further, some patients might also be encouraged to meditate on who or what is observing the "I" (which in fact is another or transcendent "I"; this continual stepping back proceeds ad infinitum). Hopefully, the concatenation of sensations, thoughts, etc., that feed into self-identity can be monitored, thereby leading to the mystical-sounding "self-less awareness" (Rahula, 1974).
12. See Krause (2019) and Kuijsten (2012b) for an exploration of the Jaynesian approach to hypnosis.
13. On neuroplasticity see also Doidge (2007); Simpkins and Simpkins (2010); and Yapko (2011). Some are interested in the neural mechanisms that subserve hypnosis and meditation. Using electroencephalography (EEG), positron emission tomography (PET), and functional magnetic resonance imaging (fMRI), Halsband et al. (2009) investigated plasticity changes in the brain during hypnosis and meditation.
14. See Green et al. (2014) for the historical context of hypnosis.

15. Much disagreement surrounds "age regression," and over the years heated arguments have raged over the "false memory debate," the "memory wars," and "repressed memory controversy." These disputes highlight the clinical challenges surrounding the relationship among trauma, memory, and suggestibility. Some have charged, with merit, that clinicians have implanted memories. True regression does not take place, but rather a form of play-acting occurs. This is why patients present with symptoms but lack any recollection of the relevant trauma; they come to believe they were abused though no maltreatment actually occurred (of course, though rare, submerging very painful events does happen) (Yapko, 2012, pp. 346–348). Yapko succinctly clarifies a reasonable stance on the issue: "If individuals know now and have always known they were abused, then the issue is moot; such memories can be believed and considered as reliable as any other" (Yapko, 2012, p. 348).

16. Recent research that highlights the importance of hypnosis includes Cardeña (2014); Kihlstrom (2014); Lynn et al. (2014); and Mazzoni et al. (2014). See Yeh et al. (2014) for a discussion of issues concerning the dissemination of hypnosis to healthcare settings.

17. Though Jaynes contends that these are not true hallucinations (Jaynes, 1976, p. 389).

18. (1) preparing patients, building expectancy, psychoeducation, aims and methods; (2) orienting to the experience and securing attentional absorption; (3) hypnotic induction or mindful focusing (building focus, selective attention); (4) building a response set with an increased tendency to respond positively as the session progress; an intensification or deepening of the experiences; (5) therapeutic utilization or suggestions given directly or indirectly with an intent to alter patients' experience in some presumably therapeutically beneficial way based on a treatment plan; (6) contextualization of new behaviors or establishing an association between new experiences gained in session with other aspects of patients' lives (consilience); (7) disengagement and reorientation; guiding people out of the experience into their "usual" awareness (Yapko, 2012, p. 523).

19. (1) rapport building; (2) attentional absorption; (3) hypnotic induction; (4) deepening (intensification); (5) building a response set (increasing responsiveness); (6) hypnotic utilization (therapy); (7) posthypnotic suggestion; (8) closure/disengagement (Yapko, 2012, p. 302).

20. (1) orient patients to hypnosis; (2) perform induction procedure; (3) build a response set; (4) introduce therapeutic theme #1 (problem, goal); (5) provide suggestions addressing the theme; (6) ask about derived meanings; (7) introduce therapeutic themes #2 (#3, etc.); (8) provide suggestions addressing the themes; (9) ask about derived meanings; (10) provide posthypnotic suggestions (contextualization); (11) provide closure; (12) suggest disengagement (Yapko, 2012, p. 302). See also "general structure of a critical incident process" (Yapko 2012, p. 302) and a "general age progression strategy" (Yapko, 2012, p. 358).

21. Theoretically inspired by the linguistic notion of transderivational search (Yapko, 2012, p. 59).

22. Submerged but active traces of FOCI cause this writer to speculate that Hilgard's (1977) "hidden observer"—a part of the hypnotized individual still possessing a relatively realistic and objective appreciation of what is occurring during trance—is the "I" or observing subject-self still operating semi-consciously while trancing. However, in later writings Hilgard modified his view, describing the hidden observer as the "information source capable of a high level of cognitive functioning, *not consciously experienced* by the hypnotized person" (Hilgard, 1992, p. 77, italics added).

23. A form of relaxation therapy involving autosuggestion.

24. From a positive psychological perspective, understanding flow can have educational and employment implications (Nakamura & Csikszentmihalyi, 2009).

25. Though note that "elements of any piece of communication can have hypnotic qualities associated with them without formally being called hypnosis" (Yapko, 2012, p. 17).

26. Connors et al. (2014) discuss how they utilized hypnotic suggestions to model psychopathology in the hypnosis laboratory.

14
Human Diversity, Social Adaptation, and Psychotherapy

In the early 1980s, while an exchange student at Beijing University, I lived in an "international" dorm segregated from the Chinese-student living quarters. In order to improve my Mandarin I requested a Chinese roommate. Diligent, studious, helpful, and forthcoming, he told me he was instructed to monitor my activities. Having a not-too-friendly Iranian student next door and sharing a cafeteria table with North Koreans and PLO-affiliated youth focused my thoughts on where I stood on the political spectrum. I learned to express my political views carefully. But I also learned not to judge prematurely.

One afternoon, a North Korean female student cagily accosted me in the dormitory's stairwell and in broken English asked if I had any American dollars. In one brief moment a person boldly peaked out from underneath the stiff party-mandated attire and well-coiffured hair. I was awed by the brazenness of an offense that, if found out, would result in severe punishment for her. Insuppressible individuality and authentic identity—these define, in spite of political divisions and cultural gaps, our common humanity. This chapter explores the intersection of multiculturalism, conscious interiority, and therapy.

The Uses and Misuses of Identity in Counseling

Rather than an explicit theoretical framework, multicultural theories are grounded in the value of celebrating human diversity. They are premised on the notion that human differences are valuable and that they matter. This perspective enhances awareness, respect, cultural sensitivity, and the appreciation of human variety for its own sake. Unlike monocultural, dominant psychotherapies, which are sometimes decontextualized, ahistorical, and apolitical, multicultural approaches see a complex constellation of identity features constituting the individual (ethnic, racial, socioeconomic, age, sex, gender, etc.). The workings of the psyche cannot be understood unless it is placed in political, economic, and ideological context. In other words, a multicultural perspective is absolutely required to understand the human condition as it recognizes that mental disorders can be aggravated, or even caused by, cultural trauma, systematic oppression, institutional discrimination, learned helplessness, and daily indignities.

Some "mainstream" psychotherapists may interpret a client's expression of identity features, whether ethnic, gendered, socioeconomic, etc., as resistance, inferiority, or some sort of deviance, when in fact, from the client's point of view, they are normative behaviors and expected reactions to their circumstances. The American Psychological Association, American Counseling Association, and the National Association of Social Workers have all issued much-needed guidelines on multicultural issues. Due to increased communication among different nations and peoples, the importance of culturally sensitive and positive psychological approaches has become paramount (Teramoto Pedrotti, Edwards, & Lopez, 2009).

Ironically, in the rush to grant dignity to and care for individuals who belong to what are perceived to be disadvantaged minorities, questionable intellectual maneuvers may be taken. Terms that pepper multicultural writings—white privilege, microaggression, microassault—while well-intentioned, in a subtle way end up establishing new forms of victimhood. The sociopsychological processes that encourage such suppression run the danger of robbing individuals of self-autonomy and self-determination. One must wonder if categorizing individuals as either "not privileged" or "privileged" actually empowers individuals to be autonomously self-defining and does justice to the not easily observed, distinctive, and intriguing features that constitute that most important minority, the individual.

Beginning and Ending with the Individual

Too readily sorting, slotting, and shunting individuals into groupings cause problems. Over-categorizing and pigeon-holing persons, and assuming that anyone who is not part of the "majority" is in desperate need of help, can result in an unhealthy condescension. When dealing with anyone (whether in a therapeutic or everyday context), we should begin with the individual and end with the individual. Attempting to readily classify people without hearing their personal narrative overlooks individuality. The consequence is stereotyping or using the "grossly misfocused lens through which one group views another" (Goleman, 1985, p. 188). This mutates into identity fundamentalism, which may be of the ethnocultural, racial, religious, sexual, gendered, or political variety.[1] We need to avoid assumptions that specific groups are culturally homogeneous or possess uniform characteristics (Hays, 2008, p. 67; Pope & Vasquez, 2011, p. 262) and that a person is "either a minority or not" (Hays, 2008, p. 67). Identity, being multidimensional, varies tremendously across context (Hays, 2008, p. 83).

Besides stereotyping others, we often self-stereotype groupings to which we claim membership. For example: Americans are supposedly, compared to other groups, highly individualistic. But in actuality many Americans, in terms of behavior and practice, are very group-oriented. Examples include how many Americans typically identify with an ethnocultural or racial group by hyphenating their identities; "teamwork," whether in the boardroom or on the sports field, is as American as apple pie;

and the patriotism on display during a parade can mobilize and organize "individ-ualistic" Americans very effectively. The lesson here is that we should thoughtfully explore our own cultural background and daily activities with an objective eye and avoid simplifications and uninformed categorization while appreciating the role of contextualization.

Biases and Nonconscious Cognition

Most of us probably assume that getting to know others is more difficult than under-standing ourselves. However, being familiar with one's own background and identity and their impact on others, one's biases (especially if we like to believe that we do not have any), and one's preferences, likes, and dislikes (which may not be obvious even to ourselves), is actually a daunting task. Becoming familiar with one's set of values, especially if one has never explicitly considered what they are or from where they came, can also be a taxing endeavor. Moreover, to make matters even more compli-cated, one's values may evolve in reaction to our changing life circumstances as we mature. "Knowing one's values" is not enough. One must be firmly grounded in one's values, as this is a crucial part of being prepared to discuss with people difficult issues and informing them of things they may not necessarily want to hear (or standing up to one's colleagues if one's feels they are misguided or engaged in untoward behavior).

Nonconscious cognition is the most salient part of our psyche. Most of our actions occur without our conscious thoughts, allowing us to function in an extraordinarily complex world. Learning about ourselves is as much as a challenge as getting to know others. This applies to both clients and therapists. The myth of self-objectivity, that we are open books, transparent to ourselves, is actually a type of self-deception driven by introceptual experiences that fool us, convincing us that our mind's eye somehow possesses a clearer view than our physical eyes. But like the nose on our faces, often it is not that easy to clearly "see" ourselves. To understand our own values more clearly demands incessant self-introspection. The best way to gain such insight is not necessarily by shutting oneself off from social engagement and meditating, but by listening to what others have had to say about oneself. This can be an uncomfort-able task.

Acknowledging the role of nonconscious mentation permits clients to view un-welcome impulses in a new light. Moreover, discussing how biases are formed una-wareness is crucial. Stereotypes may be consciously recognized (explicit) or they may be implicit. The latter are highly problematic since they configure attitudes toward social identity categories (racial, ethnocultural, sexual, gender, class, generational, political affiliation, etc.) (MCT). "Implicit" here means that we are either unaware of or somehow mistaken about our thoughts or feelings. Obviously, if we are unaware of our sentiments then we cannot report about them if asked. Stereotypes, attitudes, and social cognitions (thoughts about particular groups) can be implicit (Greenwald & Banaji, 1995). Upon self-reflection we may not verbally endorse nonconscious, hidden thinking and feelings. Significantly, implicit biases often predict how people will behave more accurately than explicit, consciously expressed values.

Identifying "Identity"

A definition of identity might be that one's selfhood relates to, is affiliated with, linked to, associated with, or defined by some collectivity. In other words, a person and a group both share a type of "sameness." Such commonality takes numerous forms and shapes our assumptions about sexual experiences, gender preferences, ethnocultural understandings, racial relations, political affiliation, citizenship, religiosity, class status, occupational aspirations, educational level, linguistic usage, views on immigration, and social movements.[2] Period and place shape one's identity. In premodern times, one's religious affiliation and kinship ties defined one's identities, while in modern times, as far as the state is concerned, political affiliation (national citizenship) supersedes religious and familial relations. In American society, one's bioraciality plays a predominant role in everyday interactions, while in other places ethnocultural identity or religious denomination is considered more important. And identities can be ranked. Depending on the situation or our own preferences, we may conceal certain identities, such as economic class, educational level, and occupation, while highlighting others (e.g., racial). The term "identity" sums up affinities; affiliations; forms of belonging; self-identification; and experiences of cohesion. Consequently, we press into analytical service a term—identity—that is less than useful; we are encumbered by a "blunt, flat, undifferentiated vocabulary" (Brubaker & Cooper, 2000, p. 2). To rectify this, identity needs to be untangled into: (1) identification and categorization; (2) self-understanding; (3) commonality; (4) connectedness; and (5) groupness. It is important to note these usages, as they "point in sharply differing directions" (Brubaker & Cooper, 2000, p. 8).

Identification and Categorization by Others

As an exchange student in China in 1982, I was sensitive to how others viewed me—how they were making certain assumptions about me—whether I agreed with the classification or not. Not a few wondered if I were a spy and some wanted to know if I knew anyone who had killed their relatives in the Korean War, fought about thirty years before (two of my uncles had fought in that conflict). More than race or ethnocultural identity, my views as an "American capitalist" were the center of discussion. One's political beliefs were either "correct" or "incorrect," and little room for political debate was allowed. Not too many years before my time in China, individuals with whom I discussed matters had relatives killed for voicing the wrong "opinion."[3] This was all serious business. In such a political environment, one pays close attention to who is identifying and categorizing whom.

To speak of identification is to invite us to "specify the agents that do the identifying. And it does not presuppose that such identifying (even by powerful agents, such as the state) will necessarily result in the internal sameness, the distinctiveness, the bounded group-ness that political entrepreneurs may seek to achieve" (Brubaker & Cooper, 2000, p. 14). This raises important political questions: Who assigns us our identities? Some of our identities, whether we agree or disagree with a certain categorization and despite attempts at self-definition, are assigned by others (political authorities, the state, religious authorities, kinship members, etc. So we should be wary of official projects bent on too readily categorizing peoples. Identity varies significantly depending on who is doing the classification.

Identification does not necessarily lead to a stable set of defining features. Identification is the reification of an "identity." This concerns the issue of immutable or mutable identities. Some identities are readily changeable, others difficult to alter. For instance, bioraciality and one's biological sex are difficult to change (though due to medical advances, the latter is not impossible to modify). Modern technologies allow individuals to easily alter their identities, e.g., identity theft and plastic surgery. One can join a different spiritual community with relative ease, and work hard to improve one's socioeconomic status. But in the premodern world, one's caste or estate was very difficult to change. Many expressions of identity exist somewhere on an immutability-versus-mutability continuum.

We need to note two types of identification. The first are "relational modes" which position an individual in a relationship. Examples include being a member of a family, in a partnership, or a citizen of a national state. The second type are categorical modes of identification. These provide classificatory attributes that place one within a group, e.g., race, ethnocultural community, or a sex.

Interiorizing Identity and Self-Understanding

Identity may be objectively perceived or subjectively experienced. The former is relatively easy to classify and demonstrate (e.g., citizenship, biological sex). The latter, however, concerns self-understanding and what someone believes or feels about their self-identity and so is obviously more difficult to measure. The subjective dimension of one's identity has increased with modernity and is driven by interiorization. In other words, as conscious interiority has expanded (especially in the past half-century or so), one's sense of self-autonomy (choosing and shaping one's self-identity to one's personalized preferences) has grown. Indeed, self-identity has acquired the features of a consumerist good, so that one's "I" is afforded the opportunity of choice from a menu of "me's" or different identities. Advances in medico-technology allow us to physically modify our identity, permitting the acquisition of postmodern identities.

How we view ourselves, then, and how others see us, can differ substantially. Like identification, "self-understanding" does not possess the reifying connotations of "identity." Self-understanding is an internal, subjective, auto-referential term.

Attributions, definitions, understandings, or descriptions externally imposed by others on oneself may overlap with self-understanding, but they are not synonymous.

Commonality and Sameness

Any individual shares features with some collectivity, e.g., ancestral homeland, customs, language, cuisine preferences, physical (racial) appearance. However, it does not necessarily follow that an individual within a certain group is deeply connected to others in the same group. Indeed, despite the sharing of sameness, individuals usually do not personally know other members of the same aggregate of individuals.

Moreover, people lack singular, all-defining identities. Rather, they have identity complexes, i.e., a person is an intersection of numerous identification features, both manifest and hidden; there is no overriding sameness that members of a group all share in common. We should always take into account the inherent ambiguous nature of identity. Identities overlap, interact, and interrelate in complicated ways.

Emotional Connectedness

Connectedness describes strong sentiments of being linked to others, and we are all familiar with the emotional bonds tying us to family members. However, though situations certainly occur when we form affective links to extra-kin or large extended groups (e.g., fighting for one's nation), we cannot assume that "identity" always characterizes the emotionally charged relational ties that interconnect people within the same group.

Groupness: Belonging to a Distinctive, Bounded, Solidary Group

Consider the use of "Asian" in the American context. This is an unfortunate tendency to supercategorize "Asians" under the rubric Asian-Americans. "Asian" is a term whose use in a practical sense is meaningless—it is used to describe individuals associated with Korea, Japan, China, Southeast Asia (Vietnam, Thailand, Malaysia, etc.), and South Asian countries (India, Sri Lanka, Pakistan, Bangladesh). Chinese-Americans I have known are proud to be US citizens, but ethnoculturally consider themselves Cantonese, Fujianese, Hakka, etc. Arguably, "Chinese" can only be understood in the most abstract civilizational sense (e.g., perhaps the vague precepts of Confucianism and a relatively common written, but not spoken, language). Some Chinese-Americans are suspicious of individuals from different parts of China and often are dismissive of their customs, cuisine, languages, and dialects. Other supercategorizing terms are the "black community" and "Hispanic"; these are so broad in application as to be useless for purposes of becoming acquainted with an individual.

Neither commonality nor connectedness alone necessarily engender "groupness" or the sense of "belonging to a distinctive, bounded, solidary group" (Brubaker & Cooper, 2000, p. 20). Of course, belongingness may involve varying degrees of commonality and connectedness. Nevertheless, groupness does not equate with identity, and it demands other ingredients. These may include common experiences of the past, particularly memorable historical events, a motivating political agenda, or the inspiring principles of a social movement. Groupness, then, is the "emotionally laden sense of belonging to a distinctive, bounded group, involving both a felt solidarity or oneness with fellow group members and a felt difference from or even antipathy to specified outsiders" (Brubaker & Cooper, 2000, p. 19). At the same time, we must be wary of the "illusion of uniform group characteristics with which to stereotype the client. Neither variation between groups nor within groups can be discounted or ignored" (Pope & Vasquez, 2011, p. 262).

Not appreciating the aforementioned aspects regarding identity leads to misunderstandings about others, strained intergroup relations, and perilous politics. Unless a sophisticated social-scientifically informed understanding of identity is adopted, identity fundamentalism takes root, leading to intolerance, discrimination, bias, bigotry, and misguided therapy.

Individualizing the Collectivity and Collectivizing the Individual

In the 1960s I spent much time traveling through the South on annual family car trips to Florida. This allowed me to witness the tumultuous "American cultural revolution" as hope and idealism challenged racism and resistance to change. Decades later, it is interesting to see how attempts to grant everyone justice have played out.

Our great cultural revolution, which, like a lumbering steam locomotive, began slowly moving not long after World War II and then gained explosive momentum by the 1960s, branched off down two very different lines: individual rights and collective rights. The former, informed by the Constitution, is associated with liberty, while the latter is linked to a type of group liberation. Ideally, one's race or ethnicity was but one element of one's individuality. Suffering discrimination meant that someone, motivated by hatred and ignorance, gravely insulted this aspect of one's being and violated one's legal rights as well as one's dignity. The civil rights movement aimed to restore one's inherent rights as a self-autonomous being.

The collective-rights movement, on the other hand, assumes that one's identity constitutes one's core being so that this form of identity trumps all other affiliations (whether racial, ethnocultural, class, religious, political). A restoration of rights comes from an acknowledgment by others that one belongs to a certain group that has suffered historically and systemically. In a certain sense the individual *is* the group, or it can be said that the individual is collectivized.

When it comes to multiculturalism, not a few counselors, political policymakers, and social activists usually treat the social landscape in one of two ways. They collectivize the individual (work toward the individual), i.e., they begin with an identity category and attempt to slot an individual into a preset classificatory scheme. Or they individualize collectivities (work toward the collectivity), i.e., they treat huge aggregates (of individuals) as if they all shared the same feature(s). Over the centuries, the individual has become more psychologically interiorized (increased FOCI). This has led to a tendency to individualize collectivities, i.e., treating large of aggregates of individuals as if they were persons writ large. We end up, in subtle ways, psychologizing collectivities, imputing to entire groups personal characteristics. This in turn makes it easier to collective individuals. Individualizing a collectivity occurs when an entire group is characterized as possessing certain traits usually associated with an individual; a whole group purportedly shares certain commonalities.

Whether individualizing collectivities or collectivizing individuals, and whatever the purpose or motivation, both maneuvers are misleading idealizations.

Collectivizing the Individual—The Misuses of the Group

My experience living in Japan was an instance of being clearly categorized into a group: either an individual is Japanese or not (i.e., a foreigner racially, ethnoculturally, and citizenship-wise). I was often asked, "Can you eat rice and sushi?" and "What do *gaijin* (foreigner, literally "outside person") think?" about some issue, or was told, "You use chopsticks so well!" I did not consider these "microaggressions." They were rather minor annoyances, and I always tried to consider the intention behind such comments; they were never malicious. I had many occasions to feel physically conspicuous—public bathing, getting strange stares when walking through a neighborhood, or even riding a crowded train. More serious irritations were being discriminated against while looking for housing, working under unfair labor practices, not being treated equally as an employee, expected to always carry a foreign resident card ready for presentation if demanded by the police, and dealing with surly immigration officers when having my visa annually renewed.[4]

Groups may seem like "substantial things-in-the-world" (and in some senses they are). But overreliance on group identification and forcibly subsuming individuals into overly categorized groupings run the danger of swallowing up the unique personhood of each individual. Such collectivizing encourages people to over-identify using vague super-aggregates. The consequence is that pressing problems and immediate obstacles that are difficult to articulate (economic inequities, inadequate healthcare, substandard education) are not usefully conceptualized when simplistically tied to group identification. Is there a danger of the individual over-identifying with and being subsumed by the collectivity? Specifically, where do we draw a line between the individual and group? When does the political (macro-level interests) become personal (micro-level concerns), and vice versa?

People are socialized too readily to make distinctions motivated by groupism or a "tendency to take discrete, sharply differentiated, internally homogeneous and externally bounded-groups as basic constituents of social life, chief protagonists of social conflicts, and fundamental units of social analysis" (Brubaker, 2002, p. 164). Groupism subsumes individuals into collectivized entities which supposedly possess clear, explicit boundaries. This ideology assumes that agency and interests can be readily attributed to entire collectivities that in fact possess tremendous diversity and complexity. Under groupism, an individual, due to obvious but sometimes misleading identity markers (e.g., color, sexual features), too easily indexes an entire group defined by race, sex, ethnoculture, class, etc. But no individual can be defined by a singular identity.

Under certain circumstances, practical reasons dictate the reasons why collectivizing an individual may be expedient. However, since the interaction between collectivity and individuality is so complex, I argue that, at least in the realm of the helping professions, for most purposes it is more productive to start with an individual and end with the individual. Between point A (initiating a therapeutic endeavor with an individual) and point B (concluding a therapeutic endeavor with the same individual) is an entire constellation of identities and experiences that can potentially manifest themselves; these have shaped, empowered, or been used against—i.e., discrimination—the client. The elements making up this constellation may concern pride, personal resources, bigotry, stigma, and pain. Singling a few of these elements out and using them to frame or index the untapped richness of a person seem shortsighted. Different identities all converge in one person, creating a unique and irreplaceable individual that cannot be reduced to a representative stand-in or a token for some imagined "community." Allow me to elaborate on the aforementioned points.

First, the most immediate unit of analysis is the singular person. This is not necessarily an argument that the most basic unit of society is the individual, just a recognition that usually in the counseling setting the actual delivery of direct care is to the individual. While community psychology contributes to our understanding of how policies and local-level facilities can be changed to better deliver services, mitigate institutionalized discrimination, and fight economic inequities, at the end of the day it is the individual counselor and individual client who directly interact.

Second, some individuals, for whatever reason, highlight certain identities while overlooking the significance of others. In any case, we should *ideally* be aware of how an array of social forces and not-so-obvious personality traits configure our identities. But the fact remains that an individual's identities are very personal. Of course, we cannot be so naïve as to believe that we can escape from the pigeon-holing of others (whether from officialdom or from people we encounter in daily interactions). But this does not mean we should readily accept the sorting, cataloging, and taxonomies imposed by others. We need to be wary of what happens when we allow others to write the scripts of our identities and permit supercategories to subsume an individual's self-individuality.

Third, collectivizing the individual can lead to identity fundamentalism. Besides ethnocultural and bioracial identifications, identity fundamentalism can also be about sexual or gender self-definitions. This often comes as a surprise to many, as not a few assume that sex and gender are innate and biologically predetermined. Any introductory anthropology or upper-division "history of sexuality" course clears these matters up by teaching us the following: first, natural essentialism—i.e., Mother Nature establishes the categories with which we live—is a myth. Second, we should begin with a clear distinction between sex ("nature": innate physical features) and gender ("nurture": how we are enculturated about sex and masculinity/femininity). Third, this sex/gender distinction, though a useful analytical starting point, is in itself misleading since the interplay among our biology, socialization, cultural customs, and personal preferences is so complex. Moreover, economics has a role since for the most part, like kinship structures, sexual/gender identities are to no small degree configured by economic demands. Finally, we should note that given the richness of human diversity and our sociopsychological malleability, sexual/gender variation should not be surprising, and for the benefit of all, welcome.

Individualizing the Collectivity—How to Avoid Monolithic Characterizations

The supercategorization of peoples, needless to say, should always be avoided.[5] It is important to understand the uniqueness of each individual and their presenting issues, despite their membership, affiliation, or association with some group. Therapists should be wary of over-pathologizing—as first-year anthropology students learn about "cultural relativism," what is abnormal "here" may be quite normal "there," and vice versa.[6] This may transpire when pathological and nonpathological behaviors and beliefs are not carefully distinguished. This sounds very in nice in theory, but in actual practice many helpers confront situations in which the line between the pathological/ nonpathological is unclear. Assessing unusual perceptions and experiences (e.g., hallucinations) can be challenging. This is a salient issue in the realm of religiosity. While studying "spirit possession" in Japan, it was clear to me that a number of members suffered from some form of mental disorder. I was not there to counsel or diagnose anyone, of course, but watching the "possessed" did make me wonder about when an individual's behavior should be classified as either abnormal/pathological or normal/ nonpathological.[7]

One needs to balance one's own scientific approach and identity with the strong beliefs of others who engage in activities that they believe are personally beneficial but that may not be part of mainstream "scientific" thought. And speaking of religion, note that traditionally, psychologists have either tended to ignore spirituality, view it as pathological, or treat it as a process reducible to more basic underlying psychological, social, or physiological functions (Pargament & Mahoney, 2009). But religion is central to the lives of countless individuals around the world. In the words of one client,

"God is in the passenger seat. He takes the steering wheel when I go off the road." For its part, the American Psychological Association now defines religion as a "cultural variable" (Pargament & Mahoney, 2009).

A strengths-oriented approach can be productively employed to highlight abilities that a monolithic perspective may overlook. The different "places" where strengths and supports can be found may be: (1) within the individual; (2) interpersonally, e.g., among family, friends, group-networks, special events and occasions; and (3) in physical and environmental conditions, e.g., a special place of gathering, such as a community center, park, church, temple, or mosque. Rather than assuming that differences are obstacles, the inherent benefits and advantages of diversity need to be recognized and culture itself should be mobilized as a resource for healing and self-help.

"Every Person a Culture": Multicultural Therapeutic Interventions

The need to develop cultural competencies that inform clinical practice and counseling is inherently an enlightened perspective as it grants more knowledge about an individual to the therapist. In other words, a multicultural approach, since it acknowledges the configurative power of macro-level forces, social status, political ideologies, and identity features that are locally and culturally inflected, provides the therapist with more contextual information about a client. Additionally, any approach that takes into account insights and knowledge from transcultural psychiatry, psychological anthropology, cultural psychology, and the studies of folk healing will undoubtedly provision psychotherapy's armamentarium.

Multiculturalism, at base, is about always being aware of potential power differences that categorization, social positioning, and stereotyping produce. Such an approach is vital for alerting the practicing therapist to the impact of economic inequities, powerful institutions, hidden networks, and unspoken assumptions that shape the therapeutic experience. Feminist therapy (FET) illustrates an approach that explicitly acknowledges power differentials and the inherent multiculturalism of any therapeutic encounter. It argues for a specialty in counseling and treating women. Due to society's assumptions and biases, it is necessary to move beyond the inadequacies of "traditional" therapy and offer alternative counseling models. This can be done via "empowerment" FET, which is a positive and enabling intervention for the particular concerns that motivate women to seek help. But FET and its theoretical and psychotherapeutic implications are not just for women—they also apply to men. Cultural prescriptions of femaleness and maleness—femininity and masculinity—mutually define and co-construct each other. In this sense it can be used for self-edifying purposes to educate both men and women. FET is not merely about symptom reduction; rather, it has the therapeutic goal of self-autonomy and, in this regard, resonates with positive psychology.

FET directly concerns managing multiple roles ("I" reconsidering one's socially sanctioned "me's" and roles); negotiating dual careers; coping with role conflict (work versus family); role strain (work and family stress); "nontraditional" career development; employment discrimination; sexual harassment; etc. On a related note: to deal with the growing diversity and complexity of kinship arrangements, Sheridan and Burt (2009) propose a strengths-based perspective.

The Multiculturally Sensitive Therapist

A culturally sensitive therapist needs to be humble and familiar with "-isms"—racism, sexism, classism, heterosexism, ageism, ableism, colonialism, etc.—that plague society. He or she should be open to self-exploration and an appreciation of how culture impacts one's worldview and assumptions. Therapists must avoid becoming "culturally encapsulated therapists," i.e., if the people surrounding healthcare providers share the same identities and privileges, they may end up seeing matters from the viewpoint of an assumed "universal" worldview. They should support an "intercultural, critical, and transdisciplinary praxis" when it comes to dealing with clients. Basic multicultural counseling competencies include: (1) being aware of assumptions, values, and biases; (2) understanding the worldview of the culturally different clients; and (3) developing appropriate intervention strategies and techniques (Wang & Kim, 2010, p. 395).[8] More specifically, this may be accomplished by: (1) developing intercultural competencies (e.g., learning a second language); (2) examining the history and politics of a community; (3) expanding community psychology's theoretical and methodological repertoire; and (4) creating spaces and opportunities for critical reflexivity to explore and challenge our positions in power hierarchies (Cruz & Sonn, 2011, p. 212).

Self-Autonomy: Putting the Client in Charge

It is important to be sensitive to what types of identities clients themselves want to discuss. Some therapists may assume that a client's ethnocultural, racial, sexual, or gender identity may be a salient variable in treatment when in fact for that particular individual their identity is irrelevant to the presenting problem. It is important to keep in mind that while some idealize the past and the place from where they came, others may want to forget their previous lives due to painful and traumatic experiences (immigrants and refugees). Some reject or even condemn their traditions for personal reasons. For some, ethnicity is "optional" (Gans, 1979).

Obtaining the Client's History

Even something as fundamental as eliciting information from a client during an initial interview requires careful attention to cultural differences. Some clients may come from a tradition in which a circuitous manner is preferred over a more straightforward, linear style of speaking. Also, some clients may be reluctant to answer certain questions due to cultural prohibitions, while others insist on including family members in therapeutic sessions. The systems perspective is useful in this regard. It takes into account the networks formed by extended families, non-kin relations, and the cultural and political contexts, thereby allowing the therapist to collect possibly relevant information from different sources and influences. This is especially true of elderly clients, who most likely are taking medications. Also, it is essential to gather medical and other healthcare information. The role that cultural differences in the conceptualizations of health, illness, and disability play should always be considered.

How much is too much when the therapist self-discloses? Some helpers may believe that revealing too much about oneself can lead to an unwelcome dialogue about identity. This has obvious but important implications, i.e., how much does a client really need or want to know about how a therapist defines his or her identity? Also, is the mission of therapy liberation from political oppression or from a mental disorder?

Finally, we should consider the interaction between the therapist's and the client's identities. Rather than assuming that a wall of ethnic, racial, or socioeconomic differences separate the therapist and client that must be overcome, it is better to view each therapist–client meeting as an intersection of identities that leads to moments of creative engagement, self-edification, and self-enrichment.

Paying Attention to the Power of Words

Given how linguistic codes rapidly change, we should not overreact to elderly or not terribly educated or cultured clients who might use (offensive) outdated language. Moreover, it behooves us to be mindful of commonly used terms, especially those appearing in multicultural writings, whose glib use can be misleading (e.g., confusing race with ethnoculture).

As an example, consider the problematic use of "West" and "Western." These words are weighed down with many unhelpful connotations (this applies to the equally ambiguous terms "European" and "white," or any color, for that matter). From the context of many readings on multiculturalism, a more appropriate term might be, as unwieldy as it is, the "highly industrialized democracies of the North Atlantic." Moreover, the overuse of the "West" resonates for many with the division of the world's cultures into the "West" and the "rest," or "victimizers" and "victims." There is an assumption that something conveniently called "Western thought" worked to establish Eurocentric colonialism along with a progeny of hierarchical differentiations (civilized vs. uncivilized; modern vs. primitive; expert knowledge vs. general knowledge; development vs. underdevelopment; saved vs. condemned; European vs. other; white vs. people of color) (cf. Cruz & Sonn, 2011, p. 206). While the historical validity of these differentiations cannot be denied, the overuse of "Western ways" can nevertheless lead to essentializing and stereotyping.

People from the powerful North Atlantic national states—the "West"—often assume that "minority" individuals can be subsumed under overarching groupings, e.g., "people of color." But we must be careful viewing any individual as a singular representation or stand-in token for a collectivity. From the majority's point of view, a person may index a group, but from a "minority" individual's perspective, he or she is an individual first, not a member of some vague aggregate. Many in North America confuse individualism (a political economic philosophy that views the individual as the basic unit of social functioning) with self-individuality (the unique constellation of characteristics constituting a person). While societies worldwide do not necessarily value the former, they do put much stock in the latter.

Acknowledging Macro-Contextual Forces

One year spent as a university exchange student in the People's Republic of China taught me that in some places, one's political ideology (e.g., Marxist-determined economic class) trumps racial, ethnic, sexual, and gendered identities. When I returned to university to pursue a degree in mental health counseling, I was struck by how American-centric classroom discussions were, focusing on an individual's raciality. This is not surprising given American history. On the other hand, such a unidimensional definition of our humanity distorts the issues and ends up neglecting more fruitful conversations.

A reading of "Principle E: Respect for People's Rights and Dignity" reveals a surprising omission: psychologists should respect and be aware of cultural, individual, and role differences, as based on age, gender, gender identity, race, ethnicity, culture, national origin, religion, sexual orientation, disability, language, and socioeconomic status.[9] Interestingly, one of the most important and consequential differences people may have—political beliefs and opinions—is missing from the list. More individuals were killed in the twentieth century's great Eurasian bloody upheavals, most notably the Russian and Chinese Revolutions, because of ideological identity rather than cultural or racial or differences. Questions of political ideology have been much more consequential for most people in the twentieth century; this continues to be true in the early twenty-first century. The overly ambitious plans of egotistical leaders, overbearing bureaucrats, and self-important officials continue to push individuals around like hapless billiard balls in many parts of the globe.

Larger political economic forces do shape our identities. But the sensitive therapist will be careful to avoid encouraging clients to engage in self-focused narratives on why they are victims and have been completely robbed of any self-autonomy. Such "indulgent therapy" may prevent a therapist from being able to discern the difference between actual victimization and victimism. The challenge is how to strike a balance between assuming that an individual in need possesses liberating self-autonomy versus the idea that they are doomed prisoners of powerful ideologies and politico-economic forces.

Notes

1. Politics, incidentally, being the most deadly; in the twentieth century alone, both right-wing (European fascism) and left-wing (Eurasian communism) slaughtered more than other hate-infused ideologies.
2. Researchers into identity sometimes confuse "political practice" [i.e., activism] and "academic analysis" (Brubaker & Cooper 2000, p. 4).
3. Being polite while sticking to one's beliefs in a politically charged foreign environment definitely makes one consider what type of impact one's words and general countenance have on others. It also teaches one the value of humility, i.e., rather than becoming defensive, it is of course crucial to at least attentively listen to where people are coming from, no matter how offensive and disagreeable their views may be.
4. Being an outsider can have its "benefits." In China, just before it took off economically and opened up politically (relatively speaking) in the 1980s, non-Chinese "guests" might be afforded certain privileges. For example, I was allowed to jump ration lines because I was a "guest of the People's Republic of China" and once was given special accommodations on a train reserved for party cadres.
5. Especially when they seem to reflect a questionable agenda of the political establishment.
6. Related to over-pathologizing is how to assess "insidious trauma." This is associated with characteristics of a person's identity that are devalued by the dominant culture (e.g., race, gender, sexual orientation, disability) and may be passed down via intergenerational transmission. See Fasta and Collin-Vézina (2010).
7. I also wondered how to balance my own scientific approach and identity with the strong beliefs of others who engage in activities that they accept as something personally beneficial but are not part of mainstream "scientific" thought.
8. As developed by Sue et al. (1982), revised by Sue, Arredondo, and McDavis (1992), and further operationalized by Arredondo et al. (1996).
9. American Psychological Association's Code of Ethics, General Principles (2010).

Epilogue
Final Thoughts

The Challenge of Obtaining Proper Mental Healthcare

Imagine going to a hospital in search of help. One has heard that this particular facility, a large, impressive, and well-appointed building with the latest equipment, is well known for recent breakthroughs in care and advances in medical knowledge. But looking for treatment, one becomes lost in its long, confusing corridors. Multiple information desks provide different directions and contradictory instructions. One ends ups wandering from unit to unit, receiving some measure of care but never really satisfied or restored to health. Providing the same information and filling out endless forms and paperwork waste valuable time and increases one's stress. The point is that no matter how much expertise exists or the quality of care, these do little good if individuals cannot access them. Another problem is that whether one receives adequate care depends on the point of initial contact and assessment, as it is here that one may be misdiagnosed, over-diagnosed, or referred to another unit for inappropriate treatment.

The aforementioned analogy is meant to highlight the "good news, bad news" about the current state of the mental health field, i.e., a tremendous amount of research and development of effective interventions, but a poor record in building systems of efficient delivery and public education. A number of problems vex current practice of mental healthcare (e.g., division into systems, lack of specificity in formulating treatment goals, excessive length of treatment, limited accessibility by some, and an excessively individualistic ideology). It is worth noting the larger forces that hinder genuine patient-centered mental healthcare: the tendency in certain circles to medicate, manage, control, and correct what is deemed "irrational behavior"; how much research ignores difficult-to-conceptualize topics and focuses only on the easily measurable; the preference for readily manualized treatments and empirical-based evidence; and neglecting the suffering of the underprivileged and ignoring other issues inconvenient to the public.

Below I offer some context on these problems by looking at the: (1) social ecology of mental health; (2) what has been called the "illness ideology" that for many practitioners governs treatment and approach; (3) challenges of diagnosing; (4) the suppression of "it-isn't"; and (5) the practical implications of mind–body dualism, informed by conscious interiority, that continues to configure the delivery of care.

The Social Context of Mental Health

I have attempted to abstract out the features of subjective, interiorized mentation and show how FOCI can be therapeutically mobilized—as in fact they are, every day, in clinical settings for self-healing purposes. My claim that conscious interiority itself is a salutary force in its own right is grounded in the idea that FOCI developed in response to major upheavals about three millennia ago. Many therapeutic techniques work the way they do because of the nature of FOCI—mental maneuvers that meta-frame and reframe one's circumstances, thereby offering us new perceptions and perspectives. This makes sense given the reasons why FOCI historically evolved in the first place, i.e., as a set of cognitive capabilities to enhance sociocognitive interaction in the face of massive social stresses. This project, by examining processes that we take for granted (FOCI), hopefully advances our knowledge of the self-repairing mind. But the mind, though a system in and of itself, is part of suprasystems whose workings may be conducive (or not) to self-healing individuals.

To what degree do social and contextual factors trigger, exacerbate, or even cause mental disorders? Should therapists and clinicians even concern themselves with environmental issues that do not necessarily seem directly related to the manifestation of mental illnesses? There are good reasons for raising such questions. First of all, it is very difficult to dispute the fact that social factors play a salient role in the development and maintenance of mental disorders. Indeed, an entire field, community psychology, is devoted to researching the social environmental conditions, broadly understood, that negatively impact the delivery of services to those in need of mental healthcare. In fact, many practitioners of community psychology take a more activist role vis-à-vis institutions and authorities involved with the provision of mental healthcare.

But to what degree should practitioners devote their limited time and resources to disentangling social factors from the psychological causes of mental illnesses? Should practitioners attempt to "fix" political and economic conditions that aggravate mental illness? Or should they devote themselves to resolving the more immediate psychogenic or organic "root causes"?

Such questions have practical implications. For example, given that the subculture of college-age individuals are at greater risk for heavy alcohol consumption and its consequent problems (Martens et al., 2011), it behooves concerned practitioners to acknowledge the social factors constituting the subculture to which these young people belong in order to design and implement more adequate protective behavioral strategies.

Or consider the "social ecology of posttraumatic syndrome disorder." As Charuvastra and Cloitre (2008) point out, both PTSD risk and recovery are highly dependent on social phenomena. Humans possess an "innate psychobiological system" that motivates them to search for closeness to significant others in times of danger, stress, or novelty (Charuvastra & Cloitre, 2008, p. 309). This is why the role of social networks is crucial. Linking their research to developmental psychopathology, attachment theory, social neuroscience, and the "social brain," Charuvastra and Cloitre note how support is effective as an "emotional regulator," i.e., the "behaviors of others can soothe or exacerbate trauma-driven fears" (2008, p. 302). This is why interpersonal traumas are worse than those generated by accidental or impersonal causes. In other words, given our socioaffiliative nature, pain resulting from social agents is registered more deeply than that visited upon us by nonsocial forces.

In a study that investigated the impact of comorbid anxiety disorders (PTSD and generalized anxiety and panic disorders) on health-related quality of life among patients in a collaborative care depression intervention study, Mittal et al. (2006) found that patients often ranked "improved quality of life" as more important than the alleviation of symptoms. Social support (along with depression severity and the number of chronic medical conditions) was a key predictor in the QWB-SA (Quality of Well-Being Scale, self-administered version). Social support also significantly predicted MCS-12V (mental component summary) scores. In a study of the quality of life among patients, Olatunji, Cistler, and Tolin (2007) pointed to the role of demographic variables. They commented on how marital and financial problems among those with panic disorder unsurprisingly hindered recovery.

The Enabling Power of Positive Institutions

PPT seriously considers cultural differences and environmental influences, recognizing these as resources, rather than just obstacles. This has significant implications for education, industrial organization, and other domains where counseling might be needed (Linley et al., 2009; see also Lopez & Gallagher, 2009). Huang and Blumenthal (2009) look at positive institutions, law, and policy. These implicate highly valued benefits such as free inquiry, free press (self-expression), and democratic and civic participation. Cultivating strong families, schools, businesses, communities, and work can foster human flourishing. Positive education can promote student well-being, engagement, and school satisfaction (Huebner et al., 2009). In the context of higher education, this might specifically involve academic advising: student leadership development; promoting student psychological well-being; and psychotherapy services: preventive outreach; talent development approach; engaged learning; strengths-based education; and consultation services (Schreiner et al., 2009). Positive psychology in the workplace concerns organizational behavior, human resource development, and what is termed "psychological capital" (Luthans & Youssef, 2009). Wright and Lopez (2009) consider the significance of "widening the diagnostic focus" by considering person–environment interaction; both deficits and strengths of the person as well as the environment need to be taken into account. Handelsman,

Knapp, and Gottlieb (2009) look at "positive ethics." This concerns global awareness (multicultural sensitivity, political sensitivity, and civic virtue); self-awareness (self-care and cultivating personal virtues); and professional awareness (the importance of understanding one's own values and motives). In her discussion of the future of positive psychology, Lopez (2009) suggests three "big" aspirational goals: (1) the psychological reform of schools; (2) strengthening families; and (3) ensuring that work is imbued with meaning. Resilience, or positive adaptation in the face of significant adversity, is examined by Masten et al. (2009). They suggest strategies for promoting resilience in children and youth, such as advocating self-regulation skills; good parenting; community resources; effective schooling; and common but powerful "ordinary protective processes" that foster resilience.

To conclude this section: mental disorders can be viewed from two, rather admittedly idealized, angles. The first is the "mental disorder in and of itself" (MD-in-itself or historically context free). The second angle is "mental disorder in social context" (MD-in-society or historically contextualized). This concerns a number of configuring forces: political (government regulations, policies, programs); economic (class, educational credentials); cultural (ethnic and racial identity, values, norms, implicit assumptions); and spiritual (religious beliefs and existential concerns). MD-in-society highlights how environmental stressors, such as poverty, discrimination, war experiences, dysfunctional family life, and a detrimental lifestyle can elicit or intensify mental disorders that under more positive circumstances may not present themselves, e.g., if personality disorders are understood as extreme variants of general traits we all possess, then perhaps certain social pressures may elicit them (De Fruyt & De Clercq, 2012). After all, the idea that "psychopathology and treatment can be detached from their societal and cultural context is an illusion" (Jørgensen, 2004, p. 534).

"Illness Ideology"

Maddux, writing within the context of positive clinical psychology, argues that much of mental healthcare is rooted in early psychiatry and medicine, making clinical psychology an "illness ideology." The very language commonly employed—symptom; disorder; pathology; illness; diagnosis; doctor; patient; normal-versus-abnormal; clinical-versus-nonclinical problems—delineates this array of ideas. Illness ideology (1) categorizes and pathologizes humans and human experience; (2) assumes that "so-called mental disorders exist in individuals rather than in the relationships among the individual and the culture at large"; (3) accepts that "what is worst and weakest about us is more important than understanding what is best and bravest" (Maddux, 2009b, p. 68). Illness ideology needs to be replaced with the pursuit of happiness and satisfaction; interpersonal skills; perseverance; talent; wisdom; what makes life with living; and personal responsibility (self-autonomy). The iterations of the DSM (now at edition five) are manifestations of illness ideology. It assumes that categories are themselves facts about the world, that normal and abnormal can be readily distinguished, and that labeling facilitates clinical judgment and intervention (Maddux, 2009b). Though illness ideology is officially rejected, the contents themselves of the DSM are inconsistent with this disavowal (Maddux, 2009b, p. 63). Moreover, the DMS provides a false sense of progress, as classifying is not necessarily understanding, and labeling is not explaining (Maddux, 2009b, p. 65). Duncan recommends that therapists eschew the "five Ds" of "patient desecration": diagnosis, deficits, disorders, diseases, and dysfunction. Health providers should instead search for ways to inspire patients to pursue their goals. The point is to look for what help-seekers already possess (Duncan, 2002b, p. 38), such as FOCI.[1]

The Challenges of Diagnosis

One's ethnic, racial, or religious identity, depending on how such an identification is received or positioned in larger mainstream society, is a crucial social factor that impacts the type of therapy one is afforded (or not). It also concerns diagnosing. Sue et al. (2007) noted that racial microaggressions, the covert, subtle, but insidious forms of discrimination (microassault, microinsult, microinvalidation), can result in the underutilization or premature termination of therapy among certain populations.[2] Gender and sexual identity and issues of adequate treatment also implicate social factors. The APA recognizes that social factors, such as access to transition-related healthcare, access to appropriate legal documents, and proper placement and treatment within sex-segregated facilities, is vital for delivering adequate treatment for individuals who identify as transgender or gender variant (APA Report of the Task Force on Gender Identity & Gender Variance, 2008).

One relevant lesson concerns the dangers of over-pathologizing. This may transpire when pathological and nonpathological behaviors and beliefs are not carefully distinguished. This sounds very nice in theory, but in actual practice many therapists confront situations in which the line between the pathological and nonpathological is unclear. Mental health, then, must be understood within the context of the conditions in which it occurs. Elements of this context include the functional (what an individual can or cannot do); existential/identity ("who am I?"); cultural (crucial norms and values we live by); social relational (how we coexist with others); and spiritual (how we are nourished by the awe-inspiring wonder and humbled by the awful terror of the world around us).

Suppressing "It-Isn't" and the Social Environment

In the 1979 movie *Being There*, simple-minded Chance the gardener (Peter Sellars) is forced to move out of a townhouse after his employer dies. Chance has spent his entire life tending the townhouse's garden but has never left the property and is completely inexperienced in the ways of the world. Through a series of fortuitous events, he is taken in by the wealthy and well-connected Ben Rand, who mistakes "Chauncey Gardiner" for an upper-class, highly educated businessman who has fallen on hard times but is endowed with profound if unassuming insight. Chauncey's enigmatic utterances pave the way for his rise to the top of high society. At Rand's funeral, a group of powerful elites who act as pallbearers are heard deciding that Chauncey should eventually become president of the United States. In the very last scene, Chauncey is seen wandering away from the burial service and walking, Jesus-like, across a lake. He dips his umbrella into the water and then continues to walk on the surface of the lake while the president of the United States is heard quoting Rand's favorite saying in his eulogy: "Life is a state of mind."

The lesson here is that because Chauncey was unfamiliar with the properties of water, he did not know he was supposed to plunge through the lake's surface when he stepped out onto it. It was not so much an "as-if" but rather a denial of "it-isn't" (it is not possible to walk on water), i.e., walking on water is possible.

Why is meta-framing above ourselves and authorizing ourselves into becoming what we really want to be, perhaps by changing an unwelcome trait, so difficult? After all, hypnosis sometimes seems able to accomplish this. Why is change, "in and by ourselves," so hard? Why is it that whatever we refer to as will, standing "master and captain over action with as sovereign a hand as the operator over a subject" (Jaynes, 1976, p. 402), often does not follow our commands? Partly the answer is in the limitations of learned conscious interiority. We are creatures of "self-doubt, scholars of our very failures, geniuses at excuse and tomorrowing our resolves." And so we "become practiced in powerless resolution until hope gets undone and dies in the unattempted." To step above this "noise of knowings and really change ourselves" requires an authorization that is difficult to evoke (Jaynes, 1976, p. 402). Conscious interiority has replaced those simpler, more absolute methods of control that characterized our earlier preconscious mentality. But to self-transform we still need some potent authorization. In preconscious times, this authorization was provided by the gods and ancestors, while conscious individuals require an updated self-control, but one, for better or for worse, authorized by grand political ideologies, self-absorbed charismatic leaders, difficult-to-understand scientific specialists, and psychotherapists with all those probing and discomfiting questions.

So how can our struggling better selves overcome so much doubt, suspicion, and skepticism? If afforded appropriate opportunities (a safe, inviting environment and rapport), an individual's inherent self-repairing powers have a good chance of kicking in, especially if he or she has faith in the skills of the therapist. But in addition to one-on-one caregiving, more attention should be given to positive institutions, or what can be called the facilitative potential of the social environment.

We are endowed with great, inborn potential (PPT), i.e., a remarkable neurocultural plasticity. Cultivating and enhancing awareness is about educating individuals to make their own conscious choices. The idea of focusing attention on habitual modes of living that are not working is decidedly phenomenological as it assumes that subjective experience is central to human nature (GT). Recognizing that particular aspects of cognition themselves can be curative encourages mature, self-actualized individuals to unconditionally accept themselves, others, and the world itself (REBT). This demands to some degree an existentialist outlook since, as individuals, we are responsible for and can direct our own thought processes (EXT).

The Great Cosmic Split: Mind–Body Dualism as a Result of Consciousness

A major legacy of the emergence of conscious interiority after approximately 1000 BCE was the instilling within individuals an introcosmos, a quasi-sensory world that, though imperfectly, corresponds to physical reality. We live in parallel universes, one somehow localized within us and in quality differing strangely from external existence. The other one we perceptually experience in direct terms and share with others. The powerful sense that one is fundamentally split between an interior, introspectable realm that is more "me" than anything else, and an exterior, bodily, sensate experience, is, if one reflects upon it, quite mysterious. This cosmic split is called mind–body dualism. It is a vexing philosophical problem that still shapes—and haunts—research. As it is something we all experience, such a rupture is not just an arcane, philosophical debate. Arguably, the modern incarnation of mind–body dualism was *the* philosophical quandary that, beginning in the seventeenth century, acted as the catalyst for the eventual establishment of modern psychology some two hundred years later. In a survey of the first 100 terms/concepts learned in psychology (history/systems), the "mind–body problem" ranks 15th (Boneau, 1990).

Mind–Body Dualism as an Instance of Internal versus External Epistemology

The basic spatial metaphors of what is "internal" and "external" to the person are applied to various phenomena in order to organize the world and our relation to it. Indeed, many of our key ways of configuring reality are grounded in the internal versus external epistemology. The contours of the bifurcated worldview, besides being a deeply rooted folk theory, shapes research agendas, intellectual endeavors, and disciplinary dualisms that have spawned a large family of twins (Table E.1). Conventionally (though not categorically), the internality perspective is associated with meaning, interpretation, translation, understanding, and intentions, while the outside perspective resonates with measurements, experiments, causality, predictability, and facts. A number of disciplinary agendas have admirably attempted to bridge the internal versus external divide (e.g., social psychology, social cognition, neuropsychology, neurophenomenology).[3]

Table E.1 Permutations of the Internal versus External Epistemology

Internal	External
Mind	Body
Psyche	Soma
Individual	Collectivity
Self	Other
Intrapersonal	Interpersonal
Subjectivity	Objectivity
Mind	Society
Psychological	Sociological
Mental	Material
Belief	Behavior
Knowledge	Practice
Phenomenological	Noumenonological
Experiential	Experimental
Unobservable	Observable
First-person view	Third-person view

A specific instance of this spatialized epistemology is mind–body dualism, a dichotomous way of thinking that archaic preconscious individuals, lacking interiorized consciousness, could not experience. After the emergence of conscious interiority, individuals began witnessing not just the world as events occurring outside themselves, but they also experienced a personal introcosmos invisible to others. The entire intellectual edifice of psychology is premised on this separation.

Mind–Body Dualism and Its Challenges to a Scientific Psychology

Conscious interiorization, then—sharply segregating the external from the inner world—explains why dualism has been so central to philosophical debates. Mind–body dualism, related to the "hard problem" of consciousness, challenges the very foundations of modern, scientific psychology. The absence of a clear-cut mind-body dualism in premodern or "non-Western" societies[4] may be related to the strength of FOCI. The academic disciplines that determine how we conceive the world and shape research agendas follow a formatting—i.e., psychology/individual/cognition versus sociology/society/culture—grounded in Cartesian mind-body dualism. For some, certain aspects of psyche seem to threaten the scientific foundations of modern psychology. Not solving the mystery of our inner lives just means that we have not been able to use the "hard" (read "serious") natural sciences to clearly understand the mental side of the mind–body unity. Despite these challenges, conscious subjective experience should be a key target of inquiry. Overcoming the bifurcation of the human condition remains an unresolved challenge in psychology. Once place to start would be to acknowledge a triality of interiority-mind-body since such a perspective at least clarifies some of the issues.

In its modern incarnation, mind–body dualism is traced back to René Descartes (1596–1650), one of the great rationalist thinkers who, in his insistence on thinking logically and without biases, led the march in setting the groundwork for modern science.[5] He contended that two different "substances" constitute our being: (1) thought (unextended, indivisible, immeasurable); and (2) physicality (extended, divisible, measurable). The first substance, or mind, possesses a special role as it is autonomous and, being more immediately known than anything material, becomes the starting place for analyzing reality. By cleaving mind from body and linking the former to the soul, Descartes ironically placed the mind off bounds to scientific investigation.

Since the seventeenth century, many thinkers may not have explicitly attempted to come to terms with mind–body dualism. However, their work was often an implicit endeavor aimed at solving the bifurcation of human existence. In any case, Cartesian mind–body dualism has generated a number of variations of how psyche and physicality relate and interact. But in order to illustrate how dualism has been variously interpreted, I propose three basic trajectories that have informed, often implicitly, research agendas in what by the late 1800s would evolve into psychology: (1) materialism; (2) mentalism; and (3) monism. Materialism postulates that neurological, chemical, or physiological events cause psychological processes; indeed, the latter are often considered mere epiphenomena of more "real" physical events. Mentalism grants a causative role to mind. In its more extreme forms, mentalism has readmitted the material world in a "dematerialized" or "mentalizing" form. The subjective idealism of George Berkeley (1685–1753) represents this view that not only is mind a spiritual substance, but bodies are reduced to sensations of our minds. Monism rejects dualism and postulates only one "substance." The Dutch philosopher Baruch Spinoza (1632–1677) adopted this "substance monism," arguing that minds and bodies are not really substances, but modes or manifestations of one reality.

Many thinkers adopted dualism but rejected mind–body interactionism and combined mentalism and materialism. The physician David Hartley (1705–1757) adopted psychophysical parallelism: psychological and physiological processes exist separately but function alongside each other.

For many, the first component of mind–body duality limits scientific psychology since certain aspects of psyche cannot be measured and quantified as readily as our physiology can be. We cannot observe another's thoughts, though we assess such phenomena indirectly and are evolutionarily well-equipped to decipher their intentions, i.e., mind read. Mind (often linked to religio-metaphysical entities, e.g., soul) is positioned beyond the purview of objectivity, which has come to mean ridding the scientific endeavor of any trace of subjectivity (difficult to interpret invisible intentions and messy motivations). Immanuel Kant (1724–1804) believed that the mind was transcendent, does not occupy space, and is therefore not measurable. Consequently, there could be no scientific study of mind. It would take major intellectual advances of the nineteenth century for researchers to begin to attempt to scientifically measure the mind.

Nevertheless, the ghost of mind–body dualism still haunts the psychosciences and has practical implications. For example, though perhaps implicitly, mental health professionals employ a mind–body dichotomy when reasoning about the causes of mental illness. The more a behavioral problem is seen as originating in psychological [mind] processes, the "more a patient tends to be viewed as responsible and blameworthy for his or her symptoms; conversely, the more behaviors are attributed to neurobiological causes [body], the less likely patients are to be viewed as responsible and blameworthy" (Miresco & Kirmayer, 2006, p. 913).

The Value of an Interdisciplinary Paradigm

The conundrum of mind–body dichotomy may never be solved. This is perhaps due to the very workings of psyche itself, i.e., it has built-in limitations, preventing us from cracking the "hard problem" of conscious experience. In any case, for practical purposes, the mind–body problem is why we need to adopt an interdisciplinary approach; this allows us to take a holistic view of the person. After all, very few people can claim the necessary expertise in the several fields constituting the all-encompassing "biopsychosocial" approach; it is at once hopeful but overly ambitious. But it at least acknowledges the multidimensional nature of what it means to be human. This is why, as Tillman (2008) advocates, a team approach is vital. Such an integrated interdisciplinary treatment recognizes that a disorder can compel an individual, a complicated multi-systemic system, to attempt to lessen symptoms by acquiring maladaptive behaviors that worsen the situation. Therefore, depending on the mental disorder, a combination of psychodynamic psychotherapy, psychopharmacology, family systems approaches, and psychosocial engagement may be required. Consider, as an example, schizophrenia, which most likely lacks a single etiology (this is probably true of most mental disorders). Environmental causes, such as childhood molestation and physical abuse, have been associated with increased incidence of schizophrenia (Tillman, 2008). Stein et al. (2006) point out that as of now, no FDA-approved medication or standardized cognitive-behavioral manual exists to treat impulse-control disorders. Perhaps this is because such disorders are biopsychosocial in nature.

Some psychiatrists, particularly the more biologically oriented, assume that mental disorders can be reduced to biology, i.e., "mental diseases are brain diseases" (Huemer, Hall, & Steiner, 2012, p. 40).[6] Certain brands of biological psychiatry might encourage a consumerist, quick-fix mentality that leads to over-prescription. One patient complained to me that "I was like a guinea pig on too many medications. I'm not a science experiment." Another told me that he was convinced he needed "a whole prescription pad to recover." Of course, there are limitations to medications, which may only treat the symptoms and not the underlying psychological causes. But an anti-medication stance can be harmful for those individuals who do need them. One patient equated taking mental health medications with "hit the mute button" (to control his manic episodes). Another told me he found "Jesus Christ in a prescription bottle" for mental health medications, while still another, impressed at how effective they were for controlling his manic episodes, described his medication as "be cool pills."

Some make valiant efforts to integrate very different research methods that bridge mind-body dualism, as in work on psychophysiological functioning. For example, McCraty and Rees (2009) studied heart rate variability generated by the interaction between the heart and brain via the neural signals flowing through the afferent (ascending) and efferent (descending) pathways of the sympathetic and parasympathetic branches of the autonomic nervous system. Their research has implications for understanding how shifts occur in perception, mental clarity, and heightened intuitive awareness when heart-centered, positive emotion-refocusing and restructuring techniques are practiced. In their research on toughness as a positive psychological phenomenon, Dienstbier and Pytlik Zillig (2009) look at how the body impacts the mind. More specifically, they examine how the effects of toughness are mediated by neuroendocrine systems (pituitary-adrenal-cortical system and the central nervous system). In her work on the neuropsychology of positive affects, Isen (2009) argues for an integration of behavioral cognitive and neuropsychological levels of analysis. Cardeña (2016) calls for a neurophenomenological approach in the study of hypnosis in which third-person neuroimaging data and first-person methods are integrated. Dickerson and Zoccola (2009) examine the "stress-buffering hypothesis" and how physiological functioning and supportive social ties are interrelated. Better functioning of the immune system lowers the levels of neuroendocrine activity, causes a downregulation of stress responses, and dampens sympathetic and neuroendocrine activity. On the other hand, deficient social support and conflict have been associated with negative biological profiles.

In physics the great challenge is to unify Einstein's theory of general relativity with quantum mechanics, two levels of reality that appear to play by very different rules. Psychology has a similar challenge: how to marry objectivity to subjectivity. It appears as if, due to the inherent nature of conscious experience, we cannot discern how introspection emerges from neurological processes. Introspectable subjective experience is not a mere sensory reflection of the world; it seems to defy empirical science with its ghostly quasi-perceptions. Perhaps in the same way that recently discovered dark energy and dark matter challenge physics, introspection—as something misunderstood but potentially promising—will provide psychology with unexpected revelations.

Notes

1. Hubble et al. (1999) provide practical suggestions for mobilizing patient factors.
2. Tillman (2008) also noted the saliency of increased incidence of psychotic disorders associated with discrimination.

3. For instance, Markovic and Thompson (2016) compare hypnosis and meditation by using the "phenomenological and neurocognitive matrix of mindfulness" (PNM). See also Cardeña (2016).

4. Whose views on healing are not due so much to "cultural" differences but rather are explained by a lack of modern techno-science.

5. Though usually associated with Descartes, this philosophical problem can be traced back to the ancient Greeks.

6. Related to this is the hope that neuroimaging technologies will someday solve the riddle of mind-body dualism.

Synopsis of Positive Psychology

Though often considered a relatively new therapeutic approach, PPT actually has many precursors. However, its predecessors lacked an integrated framework that explicitly brought the various findings together (Diener, 2009). PPT is grounded in the humanistic tradition which sees value in well-being and self-empowerment. The term "positive psychology" was first used by Abraham Maslow (1908–1970), who wrote that psychology had "voluntarily restricted itself to only half its rightful jurisdiction, the darker, meaner half" (Maslow, 1954, p. 354). Other humanistic well-known psychotherapists, such as Carl Rogers and Erich Fromm, can be credited with advocating positive psychological approaches. The psychiatrist, neurologist, and psychotherapist Nossrat Peseschkian (1933–2010) postulated that two core capabilities ground our inherent abilities to self-heal (1987). The first is the "capability of perception," or finding and infusing meaning among the various domains of our lives, as well as seeing significance not only in our own existence but in the existence of what is around us. The second is the "capability of love," or our ability to grow emotionally and enhance our interpersonal relationships.

PPT has attempted to shift therapeutic focus from what is negative, wrong, or deficient to what is positive, right, and admirable about an individual. For instance, Fava (1999), Ruini and Fava (2004), and Fava and Ruini (2003) developed "well-being therapy" that looks at how to build personal mastery across different domains of one's life (i.e., environmental, personal growth, life purpose, self-acceptance, and positive relationships). Diener developed the "tripartite model of subjective well-being" in which cognitive, emotional, and contextual factors contribute to positivity: (1) frequent positive emotions; (2) infrequent negative emotions; and (3) cognitive evaluations of one's life situation (Diener, 1984; Diener & Suh, 2000; Tov & Diener, 2013). Ryff's (1989) model of psychological well-being has six factors: (1) self-acceptance; (2) personal growth; (3) purpose in life; (4) environmental mastery; (5) self-autonomy; (6) positive relations with others (see also Ryff & Keyes, 1995). Ong and Zautra (2009) deal with how contemporary theories of well-being may be empirically evaluated using a variety of research designs and analytic techniques that can fully capture the complexity and dynamics of positive human health (Ong & Zautra, 2009).

Consider "happiness," which at first blush for some does not seem like it belongs in a serious discussion of mental illness. In their work Diener, Oishi, and Lucas (2009) review the challenges of measuring life satisfaction, subjective well-being, and happiness. Fordyce (1977) developed a "happiness" intervention for students (socializing, engaging in meaningful work, deepening close relationships with loved ones, managing expectations). Boehm and Lyubomirsky (2009) have presented evidence that three factors lead to sustainable happiness: (1) the set point (an individual's range of happiness) (50% of variance); (2) life circumstances (10% of variance); and (3) intentional behaviors or effortful strategies (40% of variance). Dunn, Uswatte, and Elliott (2009) demonstrated how many adjust reasonably well and do not suffer depression or other expected problems from physical disabilities.

Many PPT principles are subsumed under Seligman's (2011) PERMA (positive emotions, engagement, relationships, meaning and purpose, accomplishments). One core principle of PPT is individual empowerment (self-autonomy). This encourages people not just to acknowledge their weaknesses and faults, but also to self-reflectively take stock of their own skills and character strengths so they can cope with and overcome life's challenges (Peterson & Park, 2009). Empowering individuals grants them a sense of self-direction, heightened awareness of their capabilities, and a more active role in the therapist–patient relationship (Rashid & Seligman, 2018). Related to self-empowerment is reframing one's negative symptoms. Despite criticisms that it only concerns itself, in a Pollyanna-ish manner, with the positive, PPT actually takes into account an individual's dysfunctional features, since it attempts to have individuals accept their troubling past as well as their pleasant memories. PPT is about more than just eliminating negative symptoms or feelings; it is also about cultivating positive emotions. The goal is to balance one's vulnerabilities with an honest appraisal of one's assets to produce a realistic assessment. Note that psychosis (Schrank et al., 2016), suicide (Johnson et al., 2010), depression (Seligman, Rashid, & Parks, 2006; Carver, Scheier, & Segerstrom, 2010), and borderline personality disorder (Uliaszek, 2016) have been effectively treated with PPT interventions.

Synopsis of Common Factors

Attempts at psychotherapy integration emerged from dissatisfaction with single-school therapy systems and "pure form" approaches. Integrative psychotherapies come in four flavors: (1) technical eclecticism (selecting the best treatment method for the person and the problem); (2) theoretical integration (uniting two or more theories); (3) assimilative integration (a grounding in one system but with a willingness to incorporate ideas from other systems); and (4) CFs (identifying "core ingredients" shared by different therapies) (Norcross & Beutler, 2014, pp. 500–502). While the three other integrative psychotherapies all have something important to bring to the table of intervention, the emphasis in this work is on CFs. Some important ingredients that have been identified include the therapeutic alliance (therapist–patient partnership geared toward agreed-upon treatment goals); a therapist's skills (ability to engage the patient, degree of empathy, genuineness);[1] and positive expectations of the patient. To this list I add FOCI.

Historical Perspective on Common Factors

The works of a number of individuals have fed into integrative psychotherapies. For example, Frederick Thorne, the "grandfather of eclecticism," encouraged psychotherapists to equip themselves with various techniques borrowed from different approaches (1957, 1967). The first formal recommendation for an integrative therapeutic model was proposed by Thomas French (1933). He saw salient similarities between Freudian psychoanalysis and Pavlovian conditioning (French, 1933). The psychiatrist and psychoanalyst Laurence Kubie (1896–1973) also saw parallels (1943). The psychiatrist Alfred Meyer (1860–1955) suggested that the potential for convergences between different approaches were worth pursuing.[2] More recently, Paul Wachtel (1940–) has attempted to integrate psychoanalysis and behavior therapy (1977).

But the one thinker who is often regarded as the father of the CF approach is the psychotherapist Saul Rosenzweig (1907–2004). In a groundbreaking 1936 article, he wondered if first the factors "alleged to be operating in a given therapy are identical with the factors that actually are operating"; and second, if the factors that "actually are operating in several different therapies may not have much more in common than have the factors alleged to be operating" (Rosenzweig, 2002, p. 6).[3] He observed that all forms of psychotherapeutic healing can claim a fair measure of achievement.[4] He then concluded that such success is not in and of itself a reliable indicator of the validity of a theory and that powerful implicit CFs account for the uniformity of success of seemingly diverse techniques (Duncan, 2002b, p. 12). Rosenzweig summarized what he took to be CFs:

> (1) the operation of implicit, unverbalized factors, such as catharsis, and the as yet undefined effect of the personality of the good therapist; (2) the formal consistency of the therapeutic ideology as a basis for reintegration; (3) the alternative formulation of psychological events and the interdependence of personality organization as concepts which reduce the effectual importance of mooted differences between one form of psychotherapy and another. (Rosenzweig, 2002, p. 9)

Rosenzweig contended that whatever system a therapist utilizes, relatively speaking, is unimportant. What matters is the "formal consistency with which the doctrine employed is adhered to, for by virtue of this consistency the patient received a schema for achieving some sort and degree of personality organization" (Rosenzweig, 2002, p. 7). Four years after Rosenzweig wrote his influential 1936 article, members on a panel ("Areas of Agreement in Psychotherapy") concurred that "more similarities existed between approaches than differences" and proposed four areas of agreement: (1) therapeutic objectives are similar; (2) the therapist–patient relationship is central; (3) ensuring that the responsibility for making decisions is the patient's; and (4) expanding the patient's understanding of self (Duncan, 2002b, p. 12; Watson et al., 1940).

Next in line for making crucial contributions to a CF approach is the psychiatrist Jerome Frank (1909–2005). He recognized the value in age-old healing techniques and noted how diverse healing practices, including every form of psychotherapy, share four essential factors or strategies. The first is an emotionally charged but close and confiding relationship with the healer (1974).[5] The therapeutic alliance, charisma of the healer, and interpersonal dynamic enhance the confidence of those seeking care in the helper's competence. Therapists offer a special type of relationship—they show concern for the welfare of patients and encourage the formation of a trusting interrelationship. The goal is to foster hope and expectations of receiving help (Parloff, 1986, p. 527). The second factor is a healing setting. The trappings, paraphernalia, or equipment used in a ceremony or medical intervention afford the theatrical props that persuade recipients of help to believe they are in a safe place, a sanctuary "presided over by a tolerant protector" (Frank, 1975, p. 124). The third factor is the conceptual scheme that prescribes certain procedures and treatments. The cultural rationale or myth of why an intervention works resonates with what Jaynes called the collective cognitive imperative (1976). The formulations must be linked to the "dominant cosmology" of the help-seeker's culture (Frank, 1975, p. 124). Patients are provided with an explanation for their distress and dysphoric subjective states and are told how the treatment will relieve their symptoms (Parloff, 1986, p. 527). The final factor is the actual therapeutic ritual.[6] In some cultural contexts this might involve inducing trance for hypnotherapy or communicating with "possessing spirits." Whatever the particular cultural setting, those in need are more likely to engage in the process of healing or treatment if a prescribed set of procedures, informed by conceptual schema, are clearly delineated.

More recent contributors to CF research include Goldfried (1980). In his discussion of "therapeutic change principles," he noted a "therapeutic underground" that may "appear in the literature but which nonetheless reflects those informal, if not unspoken, clinical observations on what tends to work ... clinicians are starting to acknowledge its existence more openly and are beginning to recognize the contributions from orientations other than their own" (Goldfried, 1980, p. 992).[7] The transtheoretical approach of Prochaska and DiClemente (1984) proposes "common change principles" that can be tracked through "stages of change" (see also Norcross & Beutler, 2014, p. 502). Parloff noted the vital role of suggestion, nonspecific elements, placebo, and how CFs address demoralization (helplessness, inability to cope, self-blame, feelings of worthlessness, hopelessness, alienation) (Parloff, 1986, p. 522).

Omer and Alon propose healing strategies that operate as unifying concepts for different psychotherapies and offer the "rudiments for a common psychotherapeutic language" (1989, p. 282): (1) delineate a corpus of strategic rules for choosing and defining goals; (2) use small interventions to test the patient's reactions and introduce an initiating change relevant to the problem area; (3) avoid focusing on major points of resistance unless certain they can be overcome; (4) "exploit propitious timings," i.e., life transitions, crises, the beginning of therapy, or create points of transition by unexpected suggestions; (5) center therapeutic interventions so as to obtain maximum impact at a strategic point; (6) mobilize allies who can advance therapeutic goals; (7) solidify partial achievements and successes; (8) if progress is hindered by competing therapeutic goals, follow a direction that may advance therapy either way; (9) prepare a line of retreat to allow for continuing therapy if interventions fail; (10) if a strategy does fail, redefine goals or alter the therapeutic framework (Omer & Alon, 1989.[8]

Building on Lambert's proposal (1992), Miller et al. (1997) expanded the use of CFs from their earlier meaning of nonspecific or relational factors to include four more specific elements: patient, relationship, placebo, and technique. Barth et al., in their discussion of a "common elements framework," conceptualized "clinical practice in terms of generic components that cut across many distinct treatment protocols" (2012, p. 109).

Also relevant is the work of Theodore Millon (1928-2014), whose "personality-guided synergistic therapy" (1999) viewed the person as the "crossover point," and the "intersecting medium" that brings interventions together to address behaviors, cognitions, nonconscious processes, sociopolitical conditions, or biological defects. DBT, developed and promoted by Marsha Linehan (1943-), is also highly integrative in its approach (Linehan, 1993).[9]

The Scientific Validity of Common Factors

Wampold notes that a common criticism of the CF approach is that it is an "atheoretical collection of commonalities." He counters this claim by contending that a theoretical basis can be discerned if one knows where to look (Wampold, 2015a). He proposes the "contextual model" in order to flesh out CFs by focusing on three "pathways" that produce change: (1) the real relationship between patient and therapist (the cultivation of social support, belongingness, attachment); (2) the creation of expectations through the explanation of the disorder and the relevant treatment involved (remoralization, sense of self-control, self-efficacy, self-autonomy); and (3) the enactment of health-promoting actions (specific ingredients create *expectations*—certain interventions do not just target certain psychological deficits—among patients so that their own actions have a positive effect). Before these pathways can be activated, an "initial therapeutic relationship must be established" (Wampold, 2015b, p. 270). The mechanisms undergirding these pathways are grounded in "evolved characteristics of humans as the ultimate social species" (Wampold, 2015b, p. 270). As such, psychotherapy is a special case of social healing, i.e., we are able to self-heal because of our inherent socioaffiliative nature.

Wampold utilized meta-analyses to present evidence of CFs: (1) alliance (therapist-patient bond, consensus about the goals of therapy, and agreement about the tasks of therapy; these are needed for pathways 2 and 3); (2) empathy (being affected by and sharing the emotional state of another); (3) expectations (relatively small but statistically significant relationship between rated expectations and outcome); (4) cultural adaptation (accommodating a certain group's rituals and worldview); and (5) therapist effects (differences among therapists within a treatment) (Wampold, 2015a, 2015b).

Some Specifics of Specific Factors

Grencavage and Norcross (1990) reviewed 50 articles from the CF literature in order to discern commonalities. They found that the number of factors per publication ranged from one to 20, with a total of 89 different commonalities found across the reviewed corpus. The most agreed-upon commonalities were the development of a therapeutic alliance, opportunity for catharsis, acquisition and practice of new behaviors, and positive expectancies of patients. They retained only commonalities mentioned by at least 10 percent of the reviewed sources. The result was 35 commonalities. They then organized these 35 commonalities into five superordinate categories: (1) patient characteristics (3 commonalities); (2) therapist qualities (6 commonalities); (3) change processes (16 commonalities); (4) treatment structures (7 commonalities); and (5) relationship elements (3 commonalities). Here we might note that among the 35 commonalities, two in particular resonate with FOCI: (1) foster insight/awareness (no. 13, superordinate category of change processes); and (2) focus on a patient's "inner world"/ exploration of emotional issues (no. 27, superordinate category of treatment structures).

Building upon the work of Grencavage and Norcross (1990), Tracey et al. (2003) utilized multidimensional scaling and cluster analysis and came up with two dimensions. To do this they rewrote the 35 commonalities to represent general concepts, rather than perspectives. "To achieve this, each of the 35 commonalities was translated into one perspective," that of the patient (Tracey et al., 2003, p. 404). The first dimension concerns two processing modes—"hot" (closeness, warmth, emotional experience) versus "cool" (thinking, techniques, persuasion). The second dimension concerns therapeutic activity, i.e., a difference between role and activity. The former focuses on theory and healer, while the latter focuses on insight and feedback (Tracey et al., 2003, p. 406). Three clusters can be mapped onto the resulting four quadrants: (1) bond (warmth, seeking help, partner, alliance, tension reduction, insight, emotion); (2) role (theory consistency, positive expectation, healer, techniques); and (3) information (persuasion, information, feedback) (Tracey et al., 2003, p. 407).

Concluding Thoughts

The integrative approach, specifically CFs, can help advance psychotherapy (Paris, 2013). Curative cognitive processes involve restorative, rectifying, and self-directed operations in which conscious interiority are controlled in complex ways. Indeed, certain FOCI may even be switched off to reset the cognition machinery (via hypnosis). The methods of mental rectification vary depending on whether the goal is insight- or experiential-oriented healing.

Some urge caution with CF approaches. Chwalisz (2001) notes that they have encountered robust scientific and institutional resistance, and he explored the economic and professional forces lined up against the CF perspective. Castelnuovo et al. compare RCTs and CF approaches; see their convenient chart comparing "features of RCTs" and "criticisms of RCTs" (2004, p. 213). They offer a critical review of the epistemological and methodological issues involved and recommend possible solutions to the relevant debates. They suggest that there may be advantages of shifting from evidence-based practices to practice-based evidence (Castelnuovo et al., 2004, p. 221; see also Margison et al., 2000). Constantino and Bernecker write that in order to combat the perception that CF approaches are "prescientific," researchers need to rely more on empirically supported treatments. Moreover, if advocates of CFs want to understand which elements are most significant under what conditions, they need to hypothesize and test plausible mechanisms through which factors lead to change (Constantino & Bernecker, 2014, p. 509). Beutler (2014) believes that some have inadvertently equated CFs with nonspecific elements and therefore have excluded moderating variables that produce specific and differential effects but which are really not nonspecific. Asnaani and Foa (2014) contend that more empirical comparisons and testing are needed before CF approaches can be safely considered legitimate forms of treatment.

Despite misgivings, the role of nonspecific factors cannot be ignored. Wampold's meta-analytic review estimated that specific effects account for 8% of the variance in psychotherapy outcome, while CFs account for 70%. The remaining 22% is attributable to unexplained effects (Wampold, 2001).[10] Laska and Wampold (2014) contend that CF approaches do have scientific backing. Among other points they make, CFs are embedded in scientific theory and there is no "common factor treatment" (as there is no specific FOCI treatment). They also note that RCTs, often considered the gold standard of research, are not the only path to knowledge. Jacobson and Christensen point out that RCTs are able to only assess existing treatments and what is more, they cannot develop new ones (1996, p. 1038).[11]

Notes

1. The therapist may be at least eight times more influential than the theoretical approach or specific technique.
2. Also relevant are Heine (1953) and Hoch (1955).
3. See Duncan (2002a, 2002b) and Kaufamn (2007) for discussions of Rosenzweig's contributions.
4. Rosenzweig's 1936 article was republished in 2002. See also Rosenzweig (1933, 1937, 1938, 1940, 1949, 1951, 1954, 1978, 1987, 1992).
5. See also Frank and Frank (1991).
6. This resonates with what Jaynes termed "induction" (1976).
7. See also Klein et al. (1969) and Wachtel (1977).
8. Relevant here is Gottfried (1980).
9. See also Ahn and Wampold (2001); Wampold (2015b); and Tryon and Tryon (2011).
10. Note the results of a much earlier study: though we must cautiously approach any estimation, perhaps only 15% of patient improvement may be due to specific techniques, while 40% is attributable to individual patient variables and extratherapeutic factors, 30% to the therapeutic relationship, and 15% to expectancy effects (Lambert, 1992).
11. In the research community a tendency exists to exclude studies on treatments that are not BT or CBT oriented; this limits clinical innovation (Chwalisz, 2001, p. 266).

The Historical Birth of Conscious Interiority

The Roots of Consciousness in Historical Upheaval

The controversial theorizing of Julian Jaynes offers an explanation for the origins and purpose of consciousness. He contended that supernatural visitations of the ancient world were adaptations to demographic pressures and technological developments. Auditory hallucinations were a side effect of language comprehension that evolved by natural selection as a method of behavioral control. Such social management became necessary because early *Homo sapiens* lacked the ability to stay on task for time-consuming undertakings (stalking or chasing down prey, chipping away at stone tools to make them sharper, etc.).

> Let us consider a man commanded by himself or his chief to set up a fish weir far upstream from a campsite. If he is not conscious, and cannot therefore narratize the situation and so hold his analog "I" in a spatialized time with its consequences fully imagined, how does he do it? It is only language, I think, that can keep him at this time-consuming all-afternoon work. A Middle Pleistocene man would forget what he was doing. (Jaynes, 1976, p. 134)

Language provided humans with the capability to remind themselves by means of repeated hallucinated looping auto-communication of how to complete enduring tasks. Articulate speech then became unilateralized in the left hemisphere, thereby freeing up the brain's right side for hallucinated voices that could maintain prolonged activities.

How Population Pressures Configured Cognition

Population pressures changed language, which in turn altered cognition. As group size increased, more and more social control-at-a-distance became necessary. Hallucinated voices eventually were attributed to absent clan leaders, ancestors, and supernatural beings. As populations expanded and urbanization took root, verbal hallucinations provided social control and divine authorization and propped up hierarchies. Note that hallucinations were usually unnecessary before approximately 1000 BCE as most human behavior was habit-determined, prescribed, and routinized. Nonconscious schemas, ritualized patterns of activity, and scripts were adequate for most decisions—as is the case, incidentally, for modern humans. But when confronted with a particularly novel, stressful, or challenging situation that required cautious deliberation, individuals in the Bronze Age would hear the guiding "voices" of gods, ancestors, or divine rulers. These voice-volitions originated in the right hemisphere (the commanding "god") and would communicate with the left hemisphere (the obeying "mortal"). Preconscious individuals relied on supernatural entities to authorize immediate control of their behavior. Now our selves serve this authorizing function, enmeshed as they are in collective cognitive imperatives, political ideologies, and charismatic leaders that provide sources of legitimization.

A New Mentality—How Social Complexity Scaled up Cognition

Jaynes argued that the roots of introspectable self-awareness are not in our evolutionary past, but rather in historical turmoil. Rather than a neurological process, consciousness is better understood as a product of historico-cultural change. As civilizations became larger and more complicated, people gradually had to learn a new type of "interiorized" cognition, i.e., consciousness. This was a consequence of sociodemographic expansion. This cultural psychological adaptation allowed people to "spatialize" and "see" (via mental imagery) problems and solutions "in" their heads. This interiorization of behavior positioned agency within the individual, and with it, that indefinable experience of being subjectively self-aware and able to mentally "see" oneself and plan for the future. This led to a more efficient decision-making process, i.e., it permitted people to simulate possible outcomes of choices without actually having to act them out in the real world. Overall, it gave the human psyche the ability to interconnect its neurological components in a more efficacious way, forming novel neurocultural pathways that sped up information flow. The cultural development of an inner mental space led to mind-body dualism, a puzzle that has, though with great variation, haunted the world's philosophical traditions since the mid-first millennium century BCE (but not, intriguingly, during the Bronze Age).

In a sense, conscious interiority greatly aided humankind in the same way that scientific developments did. People had to learn and cultivate consciousness in the same way they acquired and developed new political arrangements, ideologies, and bodies of knowledge (e.g., mathematics).

Table Appendix C.1 is intended to illustrate linkages between the recent upgrading of our psychological abilities and disruptive historical changes that strained our mental abilities. Social complexity precipitates adaptive mental modifications. The latter then fuel and drive population pressures, economic expansion, political organizations, and proto-scientific advancements. These become both causes and consequences of historico-psychological changes, fueling spiraling feedback loops.

Table Appendix C.1 FOCI as Mental Adaptations to Social Complexity

Social Complexity → Configures → Mental Adaptations (FOCI) ↖ Reinforce ↗	
Examples of social complexity	Examples of how FOCI upgraded mentation
Population pressures	
Enlarged demographic scale: larger settlements, urbanization	Objective perspective-taking; acceptance of other-role diversity
Multiple roles and their diversification	
Extra-familial friendships: "strangers"	
Interpreting behavior of others: "mind-reading"	
Challenges of communicating with diverse peoples	
Economic expansion	
Need to distribute growing wealth (surplus) and improve storage more efficiently	"Picturing" problems to be solved from different angles

Table Appendix C.1 *Continued*

Social Complexity → Configures → Mental Adaptations (FOCI) ↖ Reinforce ↗	
Enhanced communications for long-distance trade	"Time-traveling"; past, present, and future are more clearly delineated; retrospective and prospective abilities bolstered
Indirect reciprocity, expanded exchange circuitry, and networks: more trade	
Problems of long-term planning	
Increased occupational specialization	Acceptance of other-role diversity
Political organization	
Steeper, less stable command-and-control hierarchies	Decisional capabilities
Longer, perilous communication lines among centers of power	Higher-order conceptualization
Forming alliances with unfamiliar groups	Objective perspective-taking; acceptance of other-role diversity
Larger groupings: supra-kinship relations	
Complex proto bureau-administration	Higher-order conceptualization
More elaborate religio-ideologies requiring abstraction	Bringing mental objects together; higher-order conceptualization; abstraction and generalization
Proto-scientific advancements	
Technoeconomic innovations: calendrics, irrigation	"Picturing" problems to be solved from different angles; conjectural mentation; using mental imagery to "see" different perspectives
Spread of literacy and numeracy	Abstraction and generalization

What Conscious Interiority Is Not

Consciousness Is Not Thinking

Many of us assume that consciousness is thinking. The equation of thinking with consciousness (or being "aware") is part of a powerful folk psychology that has persuaded early researchers in psychology to equate thinking with conscious cognition. Very little of what transpires within an individual mind is open to conscious introspection. As many research psychologists have demonstrated experimentally, conscious processes that transpire during socialization internalize the regularities of one's actions and reactions to the world, and eventually incorporate them so that the conscious mind is no longer burdened with having to process each and every routine psychological operation (Bargh, 1997, p. 10). Most of the thinking, feeling, and doing things in everyday life occurs automatically and is "driven by current features of the environment (i.e., people, objects, behaviors of others, settings, roles, norms, etc.) as mediated by automatic cognitive processing of those features" (Bargh, 1997, p. 2). Mediation by conscious choice or reflection plays a very minor role. Thus, although "we may be aware of the goals of and the conditions or procedures and the products of their executions [consciousness] we are not aware of the operations themselves [nonconsciousness]" (Khilstrom, 1987, p. 1446). In other words, most of our thinking is nonconscious, and what is called "introspection" is in fact the *product* of cognitive processes (that are not directly accessible). We accept for the most part the "pervasive illusion" that "we dictate the scope and direction of awareness." However, what we experience is a "final, finished version" of "invisible stagehands." The "stuff of experience from moment to moment is concocted for us just beyond the periphery of awareness, in realms of mind which scan, select, and filter the array of information available from the senses and memory" (Goleman, 1985, p. 75).

Many of our actions and much of thinking are automatic, habitual, reflexive, and are better described as cognitively prescribed, rather than consciously monitored—whatever the conscious mind decides and the nonconscious mind executes (Goleman, 1985, p. 71).[1] Indeed, the more institutionalized knowledge becomes, the more "invisible" and nonconscious it becomes. For example, Vera and Simon (1993) discuss the "functional transparency" of skills: the concrete and specific details needed to carry out an act become nonconscious as one becomes more familiar with a skill; e.g., driving a car or learning to type (Cooper, 1983) are oft-cited examples, but there are countless others. Indeed, "there is insufficient evidence to support the position that conscious mediation of situational effects is the rule rather than the exception" (Bargh, 1997, p. 5). Consciousness is not only unnecessary for many actions, sometimes it is counterproductive (Baumeister & Sommer, 1997, p. 76); consider what happens if one attempts to be conscious of every step when running down a staircase or gives attention to every finger movement when playing the piano.

To illustrate that indeed most of our mental labor is automatic, we do not have to rely on arid philosophizing removed from reality or the artificial confines of psychological experimentation. All we need do is investigate mundane and banal practices where so much of the labor of mentation is carried out in order to legitimate, maintain, and inform daily life as well as the institutions of the socioeconomic and political order. Certain practices become particularly powerful when they form patterns of social life, turning habitual or routine: "One might describe this process of routine-formation as *enhabitation*: thoughts, reactions and symbols become turned into routine habits and, thus, they become *enhabited*" (Billig, 1995, p. 42, emphasis in original). Such routine-formation disguises the true nature of consciousness.

Consciousness Is Not Perception

The equation of consciousness with perceptual experiences is another common mistake. We fall for this misattribution because in the same way that we metaphorically use "wakefulness" to describe consciousness, we also employ perception to try to understand consciousness. Jaynes labels perceptual processes "reactivity," which includes:

> all stimuli my behavior takes into account of in any way, while consciousness is something quite distinct and a far less ubiquitous phenomenon. We are conscious of what we are reacting to only from time to time. And whereas reactivity can be defined behaviorally and neurologically, consciousness at the present state of knowledge cannot. (Jaynes, 1976, p. 22)

Note

1. Though Goleman notes that at the same time the "unconscious can also execute its own intentions" (1985, p. 71).

Psyche—Biological Hardware or Cultural Software?

Evolutionary psychology/psychiatry has attempted to answer questions that involve biological "hardware" that took hundreds of millennia to unfold. However, such fields are greatly hampered in explanatory power when it comes to developments with briefer timescales. Better suited to understanding sociocultural adaptation are historico-cultural psychology—the "software" of the mind—and archaeopsychology. Indeed, research psychology has a desperate need for an intermediate temporal scale. Mainstream, conventional psychology typically utilizes two types of time: (1) developmental, i.e., the trajectory of the human life span; and (2) evolutionary or the unimaginably long passage of many millennia. But certain perspectives on human nature demand a third type of temporality measured in several centuries or even a few generations.

Evolutionary Psychology versus Historical Psychology

In his discussion of the advantages of adopting an evolutionary view for mental illnesses, Nesse (2019) points out that two kinds of explanations are required. The first are proximate explanations (how a system functions), while the second are evolutionary or ultimate explanations. Nesse is interested in evolutionary psychology/psychiatry. However, his use of "proximate versus evolutionary" and "slice-in-time versus sequence-across-time" to frame Tinbergen's "four questions" is a useful starting point for a discussion of the historicity of FOCI (Nesse, 2019, pp. 11-12; Tinbergen, 1963) (Table Appendix E.1).

Table Appendix E.1 Tinbergen's Four Questions, Organized

	Proximate	Evolutionary
Slice in time	What is the mechanism?	What is its adaptive significance?
Sequence across time	How does it develop in an individual?	What is its evolutionary history?

Source: Nesse (2019, p. 12).

Table Appendix E.2 is a modification of Nesse's conceptualization, altered to envisage FOCI as sociohistorical rather than as bioevolutionary phenomena.

Table Appendix E.2 Types of Explanations for FOCI

	Proximate/Immediate	Sociohistorical/Distal
Slice in time	What is the nature of FOCI and how do they operate?	How have FOCI helped societies adapt to particular problems?
Sequence across time	How is the individual socialized/enculturated to be conscious (life span development)?	What is the cultural history of FOCI? When did they first emerge?

Examples of Metaphoric Creativity

In order to illustrate the power of metaphors, I offer expressions that I heard while working as a substance use counselor. These examples demonstrate that by objectifying and anthropomorphizing substances, patients were able to better confront their fears, hopes, and challenges, as well as rob their addictive proclivity of the hold it had over their lives.

"Addiction will lie to you."

"Alcohol is like Little Miss Alcohol, all dressed up, nice and sexy, trying to seduce me."

"Alcohol was my friend."

"Alcohol whipped my ass!"

"Cocaine was my doctor" (self-medication via substances).

"Crack was my God. I worshipped crack. I prayed to crack."

"Drinking can handle me but I can't handle drinking."

"Drinking was my buddy. It wouldn't argue or reject me. It didn't care if I put my recovery on a back burner."

"Drugs kept calling my name."

"Drugs were my wife."

"Heroin use became my full-time job."

"Heroin was my new girlfriend."

"I cheated on my wife. With my mistress, heroin."

"I don't want it (heroin), but it wants me."

"I gave my drug of choice an eviction notice. I'm changing the locks."

"I had beer muscles" (describes how when intoxicated the patient became recklessly brave).

"I had no social relationships. But with drugs, well, they loved me back."

"I like drugs but they didn't like me."

"I love to drink but it doesn't like me."

"I partied like a rock star."

"I said to cocaine 'I'm here if you need me.'"

"I was a party animal from hell."

"I was milking the cow for one year and getting away with it (using substances). But I realized I was not getting my own milk" (describes not living a fulfilling and healthy life).

"I was my own party when using."

"I was off to the races" (describes going off on a bender).

"I was smoking like Choo-choo Charlie."

"I've been in and out of treatment like a hamster on a wheel."

"It's Miller time!" (describes the decision to give in to the urge to use alcohol).

"My addiction is a mean, nasty, demonic ghost, waiting for me on other side of a door."

"My job is to keep my side of the street clean" (stay self-focused on my recovery and mind my own business)

"Relapse is just a comma, not a period."

"Relapse is like Ground Hog Day."

"Relapse is like walking ten miles into the woods, then ten miles back, plus one extra mile to get out of the woods."

"She (alcohol) won't sign the divorce papers."

"Substances were my best friend."

"Taking a vacation without taking a vacation" (describes living in a community residence for treatment).

"That's the disease talking" (a patient apologizing during group after he raised his voice in anger).

"The disease (substance use disorder) wants me dead."

"The highs are not always so high, but the lows are not so low" (describes sobriety).

"The liquor store was a cemetery for me."

"The streets are calling me" (describes memories, associations, triggers related to substance use).

"Using drugs was like a job that I didn't want to go to" (describes why the patient wanted to stop using substances).

"Using drugs would turn me into a savage hyena."

"When it comes to the urge to use, it's like muscles running from your mind."

"When I drink I break out in handcuffs" (ends up being arrested).

"When I felt like using, it was like my old lover coming and knocking on my door."

"When I start drinking, it's like a liquidation sale. Everything goes (money)."

"When sober my emotions came over me like a flood."

Five Perspectives on Conscious Interiority: A Summary

(1) Nonconsciousness: Deactivated Conscious Interiority

Many of us mistakenly assume that our consciousness is always "switched on"; in fact, throughout the day we are typically not as conscious as we assume. Indeed, when engagements with our environment are predictable, ordinary, and uninterrupted, or if no difficulties tax our problem-solving abilities, automatic habit is all that is required for daily navigation.[1] Nonconscious background operations and a type of automated perceptual reactivity—think of how many movements are required to drive a car that are actually consciously registered—suffice to get us from one task to another. Such behind-the-scene processes are always turned on and possess an automaticity that can go quite far in getting us through the day, as if we were on autopilot. Think of a large house. Barring any unforeseen troublesome repairs, major renovations, or structural damage, the cleaning staff are all that is needed for regular upkeep and housekeeping.

(2) Everyday Conscious Interiority

When confronted with the unpredictable, extraordinary, or unexpected, or if the demands of the environment overwhelm our problem-solving abilities, a type of meta-cognition kicks in. Such meta-framing developed over history to deal with increasing social complexity and can also be referred to as interiorized cognition or conscious interiority (FOCI); it is only occasionally switched on. It allows higher-level neurological components to better communicate with each other. Conscious interiority is episodic and occurs when a chain of behaviors is interrupted, disrupted, or when an individual faces the burden of a major decision.[2] It aids us in navigating daily predicaments and making decisions; these may be relatively mundane or critical (though we are typically most conscious when confronted with major choices).

Keeping with the aforementioned metaphor of a large house, everyday conscious interiority is the janitor who takes care of tasks that are beyond the purview of a building's cleaning staff. He is charged with routine maintenance and minor repairs.

(3) Developmental Conscious Interiority

Throughout the ages, parents and collectivities have been concerned that children learn socially appropriate roles. Crucial life transitions were marked by rites of passage, usually imbued with religious significance. However, it was only recently that, due to schooling designed to expand abstract reasoning, hypothetical capabilities, literacy, and numeracy of whole populations in a lockstep manner, role transition became mental transformation. This was driven by the global spread of industrialization in the nineteenth century. Life-span developmental conscious interiority, then, has been configured by historical forces. In addition to formative socio-educational experiences, being interconnected via modern communications technology (with social media being only its most recent manifestation) has also shaped our mentality in ways that are now just beginning to be recognized. Consciousness, then, has had to adapt to the cultural imperatives of the socio-collectivity. Life-span development is a series of socializings, desocializings, and resocializings (APSs), much of it mediated by educational institutions. Or we might say that our large house, in need of structural expansion and major renovation due to a growing family, requires contractors: electricians, plumbers, masons, roofers (i.e., teachers, coaches, school counselors, tutors, professors).

(4) Therapeutic Conscious Interiority

As we navigate through our environment, corrective cognition continuously operates unawares all the time. On the other hand, corrective consciousness—self-directed or self-controlled consciousness facilitated by a therapist—is the prescription for a higher dosage of FOCI. This can lead to insights, the acquisition of a new understanding, or experiential-oriented healing. Therapeutically directed consciousness, then, is restorative in how it enhances healthier communications and commands (between "I" and "me"), targets maladaptive thoughts (controlling excerption and consilience), and concentrates mindfulness (attention) where it is needed. Such maneuvers, originating in everyday types of mentation, are not necessarily limited to clinical settings and can be utilized in paratherapeutic settings (self-help groups, meetings with priests, ministers, rabbis, imams).

To return to the large house analogy: no matter how conscientious the cleaning staff or competent a janitor, sometimes a house suffers serious damage (mental illness/disorder). Even contractors may not be able to deal with emergency repairs due to some calamity. Major reconstruction is the order of the day, and an architect or engineer (mental healthcare provider) is needed.

(5) Suspended Conscious Interiority

FOCI are culturally learned. If they are acquired via socialization, then they should exhibit plasticity. And this is the case—features of consciousness can be temporally "shut off," allowing an individual to trance and be hypnotized (though variability in hypnotizability exists). Table Appendix G.1 summarizes some of the aforementioned points.

Table Appendix G.1 Types of Conscious Interiority

Type of Conscious Interiority	Purpose and Features	Analogy
(1) Deactivated conscious interiority	Nonconscious background operations; behind-the-scene processes, always switched on*	Housekeeping, regular upkeep (cleaning staff)
(2) Everyday conscious interiority	Navigates daily predicaments, from mundane to critical decision-making; occasionally switched on	Routine maintenance, minor repairs (janitor, superintendent)
(3) Developmental conscious interiority	Adapts to demands of socio-collectivity, cultural imperatives; life-span, socio-educational experiences	Structural expansion, renovation (contractors: electrician, plumber, mason, roofer)
(4) Therapeutic conscious interiority	Addresses mental illnesses/disorders; interventions: mobilizes features of conscious interiority	Emergency repairs due to damage, major reconstruction (architect, engineer)
(5) Suspended conscious interiority	FOCI are diminished or suspended while nonconscious processes operate (i.e., trancing and hypnosis)	N/A

* A point of clarification: "Deactivated conscious interiority" simply means one is not self-aware; however, this does not mean nonconscious mentation is not in operation (i.e., it is "always switched on").

Notes

1. This is not to deny that the cognition underlying habits is neurologically complex.
2. According to Jaynes in preconscious times, meta-cognition took the form of commanding, hallucinatory "voice-volitions" from the gods and ancestors, while for post-bicameral individuals, self-authorization and self-autonomy (i.e., volitional, intentional, and deliberative behavior) are important features of meta-cognition.

Developmental Stages of the Life Span and FOCI

The Psychosocial Stages of Development

Recounting his dysfunctional socializing experiences, a patient once told me, "I had no teenage life because my parents weren't around. I had to grow up too fast." Passing through the requisite socializing stages, especially in techno-economically complex societies, is vital for *Homo sapiens*.[1] There is much debate about what these stages are, and unsurprisingly they vary by culture, but basic phases can be delineated as they concern psychosocial and physiological developmental transitions.

Life-span stages are conceptual cousin to APSs. The latter are often repetitive, usually temporally delimited, circumscribed, and sometimes more routine in nature (the exception would be rites of passage). Life-span stages are one-and-done, longer in duration, cover an entire period of a person's life, and are often of great significance. However, both APSs and life-span stages are fundamentally processual and speak to the regulation of adaptive processes, phase adjustments, accommodating changes, and pursuing goals and objectives. Both are meta-framing maneuvers. Below I offer several glimpses into well-known conceptualizations of life stages and their relation to FOCI, but first a few comments on development from a positive psychological perspective.

By looking at "intentional self-regulation optimization," Lerner (2009) sets the theoretical and empirical groundwork for a strengths-based approach to adolescent development. The healthy development of children and adolescents can be promoted through "hope" and "benefit finding" (Kirschman et al., 2009). Scheibe, Kunzmann, and Baltes discuss how to acquire wisdom about one's progress through life (self-narratization) within the context of *Sehnsucht* (life longings), or the "recurring and strong desire for ideal (utopian), alternative states and expressions of life" (2009, p. 171) and how these contribute to personal growth and meaning. Williamson and Christie (2009) examine how to maintain self-control (self-autonomy) so one can age successfully and highlight the importance of engagement in personally meaningful endeavors.

Psychoanalytic Stages

Probably the best known—though the most theoretically problematic—are the Freudian stages of psychoanalytic development. Classic psychoanalysis aims to enable the client to discover unconscious conflicts (that were caused by not adequately graduating though certain stages), with the idea that once they have been revealed, such conflicts respond to rational approaches. In this way, neurotic behaviors may be controlled and abated. According to Freud, individuals pass through: (1) an oral stage (birth to about eighteen months); (2) an anal phase (about eighteen months to age three); (3) a phallic phase (from age three to age six); (4) and a latency period (from the phallic phase to puberty).

Object Relations Theory and Stages of Development

Using psychoanalytic concepts, Margaret Mahler (1897-1985), a Hungarian psychiatrist, developed the "separation-individuation theory of child development" (Mahler, Pine, & Bergman, 1973). In this view, development is divided into three stages of the "preoedipal phase" of an infant (first two or three years): (1) normal autistic (newborn to one month)—the baby is only aware of his or her needs; (2) normal symbiosis (one to five months)—fusion with mother occurs; (3) the separation-individuation stage, which is broken down into four subcategories: (a) differentiation (five to ten months)—the infant may develop separation anxiety; it needs reassurance that the mother is still there even when not in view; (b) practicing motor skills (ten to sixteen months)—the baby attempts crawling and exploring short distances away from its mother; though the baby is most comfortable playing with its mother in view; (c) rapprochement (sixteen to twenty-four months)—"ambitendency," i.e., the child discovers that he or she is an individual distinct from the mother, which is both exciting and frightening, e.g., the child may run away from the mother and defy her instructions but then come running right back and want to be held; (d) constancy of self and object (twenty-four to thirty-six months)—the child develops "object constancy," i.e., even though an object is not viewable, it still exists; separation from the mother becomes somewhat easier. The development of ambitendency is an instance of meta-framing, while the discovery by an individual that he or she is distinct from the mother lays the groundwork for later developments of self-autonomy, self-individuation, and self-authorization.

Jane Loevinger's Ego Development System

Jane Loevinger (1918-2008), influenced by Erik Erikson and Harry Stack Sullivan, theorized various stages of ego development: impulsive; self-protective; conformist; self-aware; conscientious; conscientious-conformist; individualistic; autonomous; integrated (and a possible tenth stage). The individualistic and autonomous stages resonate with the FOCI of self-individuation and self-autonomy, respectively. Loevinger's "integrated stage" is similar to Maslow's self-actualization and Kohlberg's universal ethical principles.

Erik Erikson's Eight Stages and Meta-Framing

Erik Erikson's (1902-1994) more sophisticated modification of Freud's psychosexual stages is potentially useful from the perspective of lifespan development. According to Erikson people pass through eight stages of psychosocial development. Each phase presents the individual with a certain type of conflict or crisis that demands resolution within one's social environment. More specifically, individuals need to negotiate each phase by striking a balance between the characteristics that give the life stage its name. They must neither completely accept nor reject one characteristic; rather they must confront the challenge of holding both extremes of each life-stage challenge. Only when both extremes are balanced can the optimal "virtue" (potency) for that stage surface. Successfully navigating the stages provides people with a strong sense of "ego identity," thereby allowing positive potentialities to become permanently part of one's repertoire of personal strengths. Erikson's perspective sees individuals meta-framing through a series of progressive steps of maturation.

The eight stages of Erikson's life-stage virtues are: (1) hope or "basic trust vs. mistrust" (infancy to one year of age); (2) will or autonomy vs. shame (one to three years); (3) purpose or initiative vs. guilt (three to six years); (4) competence or industry vs. inferiority (six to eleven years); (5) fidelity or identity vs. role confusion (twelve to eighteen years); (6) love or intimacy vs. isolation (eighteen to forty years); (7) care or generativity vs. stagnation (forty to sixty-five years); (8) wisdom or integrity vs. despair (sixty-five years and older).

Jean Piaget and the Meta-Framing of Childhood Development

Jean Piaget (1896-1980) theorized that four developmental stages characterize children's development. The first is the sensorimotor stage (from birth to age two) during which children experience their environment via their senses and movement. During this stage children are egocentric (they cannot perceive the world from the viewpoint of another). This stage is divided into six substages: (1) simple reflexes; (2) first habits and primary circular reactions; (3) secondary circular reactions; (4) coordination of secondary circular reactions (origins of intentionally; they can now combine and recombine schemata and attempt to obtain goals; they begin to understand object permanence or to understand that objects continue to exist even when they cannot be seen); (5) tertiary circular reactions, novelty, and curiosity; (6) internalization of schemata. Conscious interiority is still completely absent.

In the second state, preoperational (until the age of seven), children neither understand concrete logic nor can they mentally manipulate information. Centration, conservation, irreversibility, class inclusion, and transitive inference characterize preoperative thought. Moreover, they still have trouble seeing things from different points of view. However, an increase in manipulating symbols, playing, and pretending becomes evident. These—especially pretending—signal that hypothetical "as-if" cognition, the grounding of conscious interiority, are emerging. Though stable concepts and "magical beliefs" are apparent, mental operations cannot yet be adequately performed (indicating a lack of FOCI, especially an imaginary mind-space, excerption, and consilience). The preoperational stage is divided into two substages. The first is the symbolic function substage (from two to four years of age) during which children are able to understand, remember, and nonconsciously represent objects in their mind without having the object in front of them (I doubt they can at this early age introceptually "picture" things in their mind). Children are able to use symbols to represent physical models of their surrounding world. In the second substage of intuitive thought (from about the ages of four and seven), children become curious and begin to ask "why?" indicating a step-up in hypotheticality. They intuit that they possess knowledge but are unsure how they acquired (nonconsciously) it.

In the third or concrete operational stage (from ages seven to eleven), children become more aware of conservation, logic (e.g., they understand reversibility), and improve their classification skills due to the enhancement of FOCI. However, they are still limited to what they can physically manipulate. Egocentricity has by now greatly diminished—as children internalize the viewpoints of others, their own selfhood is enriched by the perspective of others. By the fourth stage, formal operations (from age eleven to sixteen and onward), children's abstract reasoning drastically improves (excerption, consilience, self-narratization). Robust meta-framing allows logical connections to become easier. This leads to better problem-solving skills.

Robert J. Havighurst's Contributions

Mention should also be made of the important work of Robert J. Havighurst (1900-1991), who focused on developmental tasks related to physical maturation, personal values, and social pressures. He identified six stages of the life span: (1) infancy and early childhood (birth to six years; learning to walk and eat solid foods); (2) middle childhood (six to thirteen years; learning to get along with peers or developing a conscience); (3) adolescence (thirteen to eighteen years; preparing for marriage, an economic career, and the tasks of early adulthood); (4) early adulthood (nineteen years to thirty years; selecting a mate and starting a family, and the tasks of middle age); (5) middle age (thirty to sixty years; assisting teenage children to become responsible adults and developing leisure-time activities); (6) later maturity (sixty years and beyond; dealing with the death of a spouse and adjusting to retirement).

Kohlberg's Stages of Moral Development

Influenced by Jean Piaget, Lawrence Kohlberg's (1927–1987) investigated stages of moral development. He argued that a person passes through three levels (altogether six stages). These steps cannot be skipped, and each stage, meta-framed upon the previous one, is a new and necessary perspective, more comprehensive and complex than its predecessors, though it incorporates previous elements so that the understanding obtained in each stage is retained in later stages. Level 1, or pre-conventional, contains (1) obedience and punishment orientation ("how can I avoid punishment?") and (2) self-interest orientation ("what's in it for me?" and "paying for a benefit"). Level 2, or conventional, contains (3) interpersonal accord and conformity ("social norms" and "the good boy/girl attitude") and (4) authority and social-order maintaining orientation ("law and order morality"). Level 3, or post-conventional, contains (5) social contract orientation and (6) universal ethical principles ("principled conscience").

Abraham Maslow's Hierarchy of Needs

Abraham Maslow's "hierarchy of needs" can be conceptualized as a stage model. Each need, once fulfilled, is meta-framed upon the previous need. This theory of psychological health is predicated on fulfilling innate human needs by priority, culminating in self-actualization. Maslow's approach has greatly influenced positive psychology. The first need is physiological (breathing, food, water, sex drive, homeostasis, excretion). The second is safety (security of body, employment, resources, morality, family, health, property). The third is love/belonging (friendship, family, sexual intimacy). The fourth is esteem (confidence, achievement, respect by others), and the final need is self-actualization (morality, creativity, spontaneity, problem-solving, lack of prejudice, acceptance of facts). These all relate to self-individuation.

Stages of Identity Formation

An individual's relation to their own racial, ethnocultural, or other identity-affording group can be conceptualized as passing through stages. This implicates self-individuation and self-autonomy. Atkinson, Morten, and Sue (1998) provide a "minority identity development model." It consists of five stages: (1) conformity (one's reference is the dominant culture; feels negatively toward one's self and one's own group; perceives one's self as the dominant culture does); (2) dissonance (one experiences a racial/ethnic-related experience; this stage represents transition and mixed feelings toward one's self and others); (3) resistance and immersion (complete acceptance of one's group while completely rejecting "white culture"; mixed feelings toward other racial/ethnic groups); (4) introspection (increased comfort with one's racial/ethnic identity allows for more flexible views of other groups; one begins to differentiate between self-identity and group identity; "whites" are not seen as monolithic); (5) synergetic articulation and awareness (racial/ethnic identity is secure and positive; one sees one's racial/ethnic identity as only one aspect of one's being; one respects and appreciates other groups).

Cross (1995) has offered an ethnic development model for African-Americans: (1) pre-encounter-assimilation (pro-American values and low salience to one's racial identity; mis-education; negative stereotypes about being African-American; self-hatred, negative attitudes about self due to racism); (2) encounter (occurs after an experience that changes awareness of one's race; characterized by confusion, depression, or alarm); (3) immersion/emersion (over-romanticized immersion into and intense involvement with African-American culture; strong feelings against "white culture" and values); (4) internalization (working to empower the African-American community; self-acceptance of African-American identity with other cultural variables emphasized; bi-cultural or multiculturalist attitudes).

Phinney's (1996) ethnic identity model acknowledges that individuals raised between cultures might experience identity confusion and adaptation problems. The therapist should be sensitive to notions such as "self-categorization" (self-identifying with a particular ethnic group); "commitment and attachment" (sense of belonging to a certain group); "exploration" (becoming involved in a range of activities and learning about cultural practices and attending cultural events); "behavioral involvement" (if applicable, speaking the language, eating the food, associating with members of one's own group); and "in-group attitudes" (developing a positive attitude toward one's own group and its values and beliefs).

Note

1. The family life cycle is constituted of stages—adolescence; leaving home; joining of families through marriage; having children; launching of one's children into adulthood; midlife crisis; perhaps starting another family in later life; and possibly divorce (McGoldrick, Carter, & Petro, 2011). We must acknowledge the diversity of today's kinship dynamics. Obviously there is no "typical" version of the family life cycle and many variations exist.

Glossary: A Jaynesian Therapeutic Perspective on Techniques and Interventions

The goal of this glossary is to view common interventions, techniques, and therapies through the lens of a Jaynesian psychotherapeutic paradigm. This is intended to add some theoretical coherency to the vast body of psychotherapeutic tools. I have taken the license of adding to and revising descriptions in order to fit their underlying processes into the FOCI perspective. This list is by no means comprehensive.

Acceptance (ACT): One of ACT's six core therapeutic process. Making mental room for painful feelings, sensations, urges, and emotions. Instead of resisting, running from, being overwhelmed by, struggling against, (not) liking, or (not) wanting them, we become open to them, rise above them, and allow them to be meta-framed just as they are.

Acting "as if" (ADT): Encourages and motivates patients to be the way they want to be (idealized self) by dramatizing the desired change "as if" it has already occurred. This form of cognition transpires when one's observing self ("I") monitors the hypothetical behavior of one's observed self ("me") on one's introspectable stage.

Active imagination (JT): One excerpts and identifies an entity (e.g., shadow figure, anima, maternal figure) and focuses one's attention on the figure (this may happen while meditating or dreaming). One's subject-self ("I") initiates a dialogue with the entity (object-self). The point is to confront and access aspects of one's person that have been rejected or repressed, thereby bridging the gap between the conscious and unconscious. These aspects are brought from the backstage of nonconsciousness to introceptual center stage, and new role-selves are enacted and integrated. This technique may be played out via writing, sculpting, dancing, or other artistic mediums.

Active listening (CCT): The bedrock skill of any counseling encounter. This skill can be broken down into a number of abilities, but in essence, effective active listening requires focusing not just on what patients verbalize, but also on the therapist's own reaction.

Activity scheduling (BT): Useful in the treatment of depression, this technique is done with a chart using short descriptions (typically one to three words), according to a hierarchy of easiest to hardest; both necessary and enjoyable tasks are excerpted. Patients adhere to the planned activities and record any behaviors that were not pre-planned and rate activities according to level of enjoyment. This enhances self-reflexivity, self-direction, and self-determination. Eventually patients resume their normal schedule.

Altering the dominant negative story (NT): An individual's life narrative (or perhaps smaller narratives constituting a master narrative) might be permeated with negative experiences, problems (real or perceived), or crises, orienting the individual toward a pessimistic outlook.

Therapists assist patients in rewriting their life story through a careful investigation of patterns of negative excerptions and consiliences (revising one's personal timeline). Negative mental representations from one's stream of thought can be mentally selected out. Patients might be asked to compare and contrast two lines of self-narratizations, one negative, the other positive, highlighting excerptions to better discern differences. Patients can be asked to focus on key turning points in their personal series of events, thereby enhancing self-direction and feelings of control of one's destiny.

Altruism (PAT): Defense mechanism protecting the ego (self-definition) from anxiety by satisfying one's internal needs through helping others. Nonconscious, suppressed self-serving motivation may result in individuals behaving irrationally. They mistake their underlying self-serving intentions for genuine altruistic intention and the point of aiding others is lost.

Analysis and assessment (ADT): Therapists, using a sociogram of the home of patients during their formative years, explores with patients their early recollections. Though initially such an exercise is not about interpretation, presumably this technique can lay the foundation for further work in having patients gain insight through excerptions about issues of suppression, self-autonomy, and self-individuation.

Analysis of resistance and defenses (PAT): Some patients may engage in suppression (censoring distressing thoughts) in order to avoid exploring certain painful issues. Such resistance may manifest itself in particular behaviors (e.g., arriving late to sessions, deflecting questions, silence). Therapists can point out to patients these patterns of behavior and work on developing insight about proclivities to delete and control mentation and discover why they have stored away distressing thoughts.

Analysis of transference (JT): Some patients impose on the therapist characteristics from other people with whom they still have unresolved issues (typically parents or parental figures); this can distort the healing relationship between the therapist and patients. Investigating and breaking down this process by de-associating experiences (de-consilience) can cultivate insight for patients. Several stages are addressed: (1) patients' history of projections onto the therapist; (2) patients differentiate their own "unconscious" (quarantined nonconscious) from the "collective unconscious" (some therapists may choose to reconceptualize this notion into something less mystical, e.g., a collectivity to which patients belong); (3) the therapist's actual relation to patients is differentiated from any superimposed associations; and (4) having recognized issues of transference, insight obtained by patients can be used to enhance self-reflexivity and construct a more authentic relationship with the therapist.

Arbitrary inference (CBT): Occurs when excerption of mental content runs a negative course; to reach conclusions sans evidence or despite evidence to the contrary.

Archetypes (JT): Images representing aspects of the psyche (e.g., anima, animus, persona, shadow, hero, supreme being) informing the structure of one's personality, which are used to view the world. They may concern universal themes of rebirth, one's feminine or masculine side, the need for wholeness, or the search for meaning. According to Jung, these primordial images are inherited from the "collective unconscious." Though the existence of a psychic storehouse with the accumulated experience of humankind is seriously doubted (at least by this writer), these age-old symbols can function as self-individualizing healing elements for the imaginative individual.

Art therapy (PT): Crayons, paper, paints, markers, clay, paste, glitter, glue, scissors, string, stickers, electronic media, etc., may be employed to bring to the mental stage nonconscious material difficult to verbally articulate. Art therapy allows individuals to creatively edit mental contents, allowing them to increase self-awareness and self-objectivity in a non-threatening, highly personal, and self-individuated medium. Evoking and bringing to the surface suppressed material highlights personal uniqueness (self-individuation) and enhances the ability of patients to self-disclose.

Assertiveness and social skills training (BT): Utilized to acquire new skills through modeling and behavioral rehearsal. Patients observe the therapist role-playing. This can be done overtly as well as covertly (on one's mental stage), i.e., an interself interaction between the monitoring self ("I") and the monitored self ("me," i.e., one's less assertive role-self) facilitates the acceptance of a new role-self (more assertive part).

Assertiveness training (FET): Teaching individuals how to effect self-distancing between "I" and "me" (stereotyped sex roles) so they can become more self-authorizing and increase a sense of agency, self-direction, and feelings of self-control over their destiny (self-autonomy). Raising awareness of how to rise above and interrogate socially imposed gender roles can alter deeply internalized negative belief systems so that daily patterns, actions, and interactions can be changed. This reinforces acceptance of other-role diversity.

Assessment of alternatives (CBT): In order to identify alternate ways of behaving other than what they have been doing, individuals require a place where imaginative, hypothetical, and conjectural mentation can be "seen" to transpire (on one's introspectable stage). In this mentalized space, a self-distancing between "I" and "me" can be effected, thereby encouraging a newfound objectivity and listing of alternatives. Patients are then able to brainstorm a menu of options and mentally delete from that list behaviors and thoughts that have been unproductive and mentally select out those that might be adaptive.

Assimilation (GT): Breaking something into component parts and carefully reflecting on one's train of excerptions and examining one's consilience. These elements of mental processing can either be accepted and made part of one's outlook, rejected as irrational, or modified into a positive view of one's life.

Attributing (PAT, PDT): Defense mechanism. One ascribes one's unacceptable desires to others. For this to occur, one must believe that others possess an interiorized mental state similar to one's own, indicating a sophisticated theory of mind.

Authentic mode (EXT): Described by the philosopher Heidegger, a way of being in which one realizes the fragility of one's very existence while accepting personal responsibility for one's own decisions, i.e., self-autonomy and self-authorization.

Automatic thought (CBT): An idea is triggered by particular stimuli (certain excerptions) that lead to an emotional response. Such a habitual chain reaction indicates the pull of nonconscious processes.

Aversion therapy (BT): Patients are simultaneously exposed to a stimulus and exposed to some type of discomfort. The goal is to couple the stimulus with the unpleasant sensations, resulting in the cessation of the undesirable behavior. This can be done covertly on the mental stage of patients, with the objective of introceptually reinforcing the association between the stimulus and negative sensations.

Awfulizing (REBT): Magnifying something usually regarded as inconvenient or obnoxious as awful, horrible, or terrible. An instance of an excerption taking on a life of its own, snowballing into an over-hypotheticalized prospective self-narratization.

Basic mistake (GT): An overarching personal myth about oneself used to organize, give coherency to, and self-narratize one's life. Examples might include overgeneralization of one's faults, a desperate need for security, misperception of life's demands, or denial of one's self-worth.

Behavioral experiments (CBT, REBT): Behavior is covertly interiorized and quasi-perceptually experienced, so that reactions are mentally edited, challenged, and judged to be either helpful or unhelpful for one's change. Patients are asked to "test" their fears or distorted beliefs in a real-life situation.

Behavioral extinction (BT): Rewards for patients are removed to extinguish an undesirable behavior. This technique can be coupled with an introceptual exercise to reinforce its psychotherapeutic impact: patients are instructed to mentally picture themselves (introceive) on their mental stage not receiving a reward while engaging in the targeted activity.

Behavioral observation (BT): Specifying certain behavior and observing it in patients' natural environment. May be utilized within institutional settings such as hospitals, schools, and treatment facilities where clinicians (or parents, teachers, aids, nurses who are trained as observers) can objectively record and analyze activities. Observers, in order to respect patients and develop insight into their motivations, should regard their behavioral patterns as self-autonomously driven and patients in possession of a subject-self ("I") in pursuit of goals.

Being present (ACT): One of ACT's six core therapeutic process. Patients are encouraged to nonjudgmentally experience their surroundings and consciously interiorize events directly. This is achieved by utilizing language as a tool to describe occurrences, rather than to predict and judge them. In this way their reactions are more flexible and consistent with their own values.

Bibliotherapy (CBT, REBT): Relevant books are assigned to patients in order to learn more about the specific issue being addressed. In this way patients self-educate, thereby enhancing self-autonomy.

Bibliotherapy (FET): The therapist empowers individuals by having them read about power differentials between the sexes, gender role stereotypes, gender inequality, patriarchy, the impact of sexism in society, societal obsession with specific types of beauty markers (e.g., thinness). Such self-edification helps individuals make informed choices by encouraging self-control, self-authorization, and self-individuation (self-identity).

Biofeedback (BT): Measures brain waves that can be used as feedback to teach patients self-regulation of brain function. Used to improve blood pressure, heart rate, muscle tension, etc. Such feedback follows a recursive sequence, i.e., one's subject-self monitors one's bodily self: (1) "I" controls bodily processes; (2) bodily processes signal physiological changes to "me"; (3) "me" reflexively transmutes into "I"; (4) "I" controls bodily processes, and then the cycle, reinforced, starts again. Enhances self-autonomy and self-authorization.

Blocks to energy (GT): Forms of resistance can be nonconsciously manifested through bodily tension; posture; keeping one's body tight and closed; shallow breathing; avoiding eye contact; numbing feelings; speaking quietly or in a restricted voice. By having individuals ("I") mindfully observe such physical behaviors (one's bodily self), individuals can become aware of how their physiological reactions, psychological contents, nonconscious processes, and self-presentation interrelate.

Blow-up technique (REBT): Having patients hypothesize in their mentalized space the worst-case scenario of what they fear happening (one's "I" introceives envisioned occurrences). Then, once the feared event is magnified out of proportion, the patient is prodded to find humor in the exaggerated scenario.

Body awareness (GT): Patients are asked to focus on where in the body feelings are experienced when discussing certain issues, and together with the therapist they reflect on inconsistencies between verbalizations and body language. Using breathing techniques, the therapist helps patients become aware of their felt emotions and bodily functions, thereby gaining greater self-awareness of excerption, self-monitoring, and self-autonomy.

Boundary (GT): This has two functions: it connects individuals (interdependence and socio-affiliation) but also separates them (independence; maintains self-autonomy and leads to self-individuation).

Catastrophe scale (REBT): Used to address "awfulizing." Patients are asked to write a scale from 0% to 100% with 10% intervals, then asked to rate whatever the issue they are catastrophizing about and insert it into the scale in the appropriate place. Later, they fill (excerpt) in the other levels with what they believe is applicable to each level. Patients progressively alter items that worry them to fit into the perspective of other items. This exercise in meta-framing expands one's mentalized space and its concomitant range of choices.

Catastrophizing (CBT, REBT): An example of hyper-consciousness. Runaway excerption and consilience exaggerate the consequences of a stressful event.

Chaining (BT): In order to achieve a goal, the links that constitute the chain leading to the desired target behavior are prompted and reinforced, strengthening all the smaller behaviors in the chain. Each link can be understood as mental edits from the train of consciousness that need to be identified.

Checking feelings, thoughts, bodily sensations (GT): Patients are asked to describe what they are physically experiencing or feeling as they discuss an issue, or they may be asked to describe their thoughts while they are experiencing a feeling. This exercise encourages patients to become more aware (mindful) of how their bodily sensations, emotions, and thinking are interconnected, enhancing self-objectivity and self-corrective abilities (self-reflexivity).

Circular questioning (FT): A family member is asked a question about other members. Other members are asked to respond to the same question, going around in a "circular" manner. Various viewpoints are elicited from the different members, providing each member the opportunity to stand back from and have a more self-objective view of the familial unit.

Clay (PT): By forming shapes or just freely manipulating clay somehow (squeezing it through the fingers, smashing it, rolling it into a ball, etc.), individuals can elicit and express their thoughts and emotions by meta-framing and surveying their own self-creations.

Cognitive distortion (CBT, REBT): Pervasive and systematic errors in reasoning caused by hyper-excerption and dysfunctional consilience.

Cognitive reframing (CBT): A type of meta-framing. Changing the way patients conceive things by finding alternative ways of viewing ideas, events, situations, or personal circumstances.

Cognitive rehearsal (CBT): Patients mentally picture a difficult (target) situation and the therapist guides them through the step-by-step process of facing and successfully coping with it. Patients covertly enact and dramatize their "I" by playing an adaptive role.

Cognitive restructuring (CBT): A type of meta-framing. Identifying, challenging, and changing faulty distortions in thinking by applying logical disputation, testing one's belief, and questioning one's nonconsciously held habits of thoughts. In this way alternative explanations can be found that can replace irrational or maladaptive thoughts ("evidence for" and "evidence against").

Cognitive shift (CBT, REBT): A systematic and biased interpretation of life experiences. Therapists might guide patients in cultivating objective self-reflexivity and have them interrogate habitual excerptions.

Committed action (ACT): One of ACT's six core therapeutic processes. Inspired by one's values and "doing what it takes." Moving beyond just *knowing* values and acting in a values-congruent manner. This demands a sharpened sense of selfness (self-reflexivity) and self-individuation. Values-guided action and valued living may give rise to painful and unpleasant feelings, but all experiences make one's life rich, full, and meaningful. One can enrich one's life by learning behavioral interventions (goal setting): exposure; behavioral activation; acquiring new skills; negotiation; time management; assertiveness; problem-solving; self-soothing; crisis coping; and identifying the pitfalls of experiential avoidance.

Compensation (ADT): Human strivings are responses to feelings of inadequacy (inferiority complex). From a positive psychological perspective, "compensatory mechanisms" can make up for the losses caused by a weakness or deficiency. Highlighting one's personal strengths and uniqueness (self-individuation) can facilitate the redressing of imbalances in personal traits.

Compensation (PAT): Defense mechanism. Results from runaway mental editing, i.e., only certain facets of one's self-concept are mentally selected out while others are ignored. Substituting a strength in one area to offset real or imagined personal deficiency or weaknesses in another. This guards against feelings of inferiority and inadequacy.

Compliments (BFT): It is important to validate and reinforce what patients are already doing well. Compliments strengthen a sense of accomplishment and self-autonomy.

Conditional assumption (CBT): An advantage of conscious interiority is an expanded hypotheticality. However, such an imaginary space more easily generates many "if-then" interpretations of events, which can result in mistaken conclusions.

Confluence (GT): One of the five major channels of resistance. It can mean: (1) blurring the boundaries between self and environment (which can threaten self-autonomy); (2) fitting in with others in order to alleviate conflict (another threat to self-autonomy); (3) the assumption that all people feel and think similarly (not appreciating how each person possesses unique self-individualized features); (4) a desire for acceptance and approval (socioaffiliative impulse); (5) never expressing one's own feelings (avoiding self-autonomy). The therapist uses "W" questions (who, what, where, why, when) in order to have patients share and self-disclose issues of resistance.

Confrontation (ADT): Utilized to encourage patients to be self-autonomous. Specific instances might concern taking responsibility for how others respond to one's behavior (one's "I" ruminates on the possible reactions of one's "me's"); presenting existing alternatives during interpersonal conflict (choosing different excerptions); holding oneself accountable for personal change ("I" monitors self-improvements); reflecting on how one should change as one self-narratizes into the future.

Confrontation (RT): Setting specific plans are key to RT. However, if patients do not follow through on their plans, confrontation is unavoidable. In principle, excuses are not accepted in RT, but the therapist continues to be positive and works hard to remain committed to the progress of patients, acknowledging their attempts at self-improvement.

Congruence (CCT): A core condition of client-centered therapy. Involves cultivating a closer agreement between the client's idealized and actual selves (to reduce disparities between ideals and their actions). The therapist acts as a role model, demonstrating attempts toward greater integration and wholeness, encouraging the client's "I" to choose, cultivate, and improve his or her "me's" (better interself dynamics).

Contact (GT): Basic unit of social relationship. It is an experience of the boundary between self and not self. It is the sense that one is linked to the "not me" while maintaining one's self-autonomy.

Contacting the present moment (ACT): One of ACT's core therapeutic processes. Most of us move through the day on autopilot, merely going through the motions. We get caught up in our concerns about the past or future, ignoring here-and-now experiences. Mentally observing the flow of exceptions without focusing on any of them is a good technique to mindfully engage in whatever is happening "at this moment."

Contract (TA): An essential element with patients and group. It establishes the structure of the relationship and of how the patient will be different as a result of work done (especially from the child ego state perspective). The contract is concrete, specific, and measurable.

Control of environment (GT): A form of resistance. It may mean opposing contact (with others, i.e., the "not me") or a violation of one's personal boundaries (one's interdependence or independence is disturbed).

Conversion (PAT, PDT): Defense mechanism. Psychic pain is nonconsciously manifested in some body part or through physical symptoms. Conversion indicates the complex interaction among nonconscious mind, conscious interiority, and physical body.

Coping question (BFT, SOLT): A way of accessing patients' resiliency and level of motivation. Functions to increase self-autonomy and self-individuation by reminding patients that they possess unrecognized and untapped resources, skills, and tools, even when overwhelmed.

Countertransference (PAT, PDT): The therapist's (sometimes nonconscious) reaction to patients and to their transference. Such reactions are based on the therapist's own personal needs and unresolved conflicts. In classical psychoanalysis, countertransference was regarded as an obstacle to the therapist's understanding of patients. However, it is now understood as a source of insight into the patients' impact on others and may be used constructively to advance healing.

Covert conditioning (BT, CBT): Premised on the idea that overt (observable, physical actions) and covert (unobservable, interiorized cognition) behaviors are associated, affect each other, and are learned. Patients mentally picture themselves performing a desired behavior in a problematic real-life situation and reward themselves for mentally engaging in the behavior (one's "I" commends one's "me"). The goal is to obtain an actual change in invisible behavior. Also called covert behavioral reinforcement.

Covert desensitization (BT, CBT): A hierarchy is formulated with a sequence of mental selections ranging from the least to the most anxiety-triggering. Patients then use relaxation techniques while progressively mentally picturing excerptions on the hierarchy until they are able to mentally picture (introceive) the stimulus without feeling anxious. See also **systematic desensitization**.

Covert extinction (BT, CBT): Patients introceptually picture themselves carrying out an unwanted behavior and then introceive themselves failing to be rewarded or to receive positive reinforcement for the behavior. May be used in treating paraphilias.

Covert modeling (BT, CBT): Patients mentally picture a role model, introceive acting as this role model might behave ("I" role-playing a role-self), and then prospectively self-narratize themselves performing specific favorable consequences of the behavior.

Covert negative reinforcement (BT, CBT): Patients first introceive an unwelcome, aversive event and then excerpt scenes in which the adversity and negative associations of the event are reversed.

Covert positive reinforcement (BT, CBT): Patients first introceive performing a desired behavior that is followed by a pleasant, welcome consequence. Repeated interiorized rehearsings can lead to the targeted behavior eventually being adopted.

Covert rehearsal (BT, CBT): Patients use rote repetition (of interiorized, excerpted words or behaviors) in their mentalized space to prepare for actual, overt behavior.

Covert reinforcement (BT, CBT): Informed by behaviorism (operant conditioning: a process in which the frequency of a response is increased by a dependent relationship with a stimulus; classical conditioning: the presentation of an unconditioned stimulus after a conditioned stimulus). "Covert" highlights the psychologically interiorized aspect of this type of reinforcement. More broadly, may also describe "self-talk," i.e., what one's "I" says to one's "me" to affirm or confirm self-identity (may lead to feelings of self-worth or their diminishment). See also **covert negative reinforcement** and **covert positive reinforcement**.

Covert sensitization (BT, CBT): Targets an undesired behavior by linking it with a quasi-perceptual punishment. Patients mentally picture themselves ("I" observes "me") performing the undesired behavior (e.g., overeating) and then imagine an unpleasant consequence (e.g., vomiting). Can be used to discourage paraphilic behavior.

Decatastrophizing (CBT): Patients verbalize their feared consequence of a situation and then, together with the therapist, identify more likely, realistic outcomes. The "what if-ness" of the mind's hypothetical, expansive innerverse, full of potentiality, is put to positive use.

Decentering (CBT): Techniques that challenge patients' overly focused and centered thinking (hyper-concentration), e.g., patients who believe they are the target of the focus of others. Also, patients are taught how to better regulate their concentration and not exclude features of a situation.

Deconstruct the problem (NT): Helping the therapist understand what a presenting problem means to individual patients. Accomplished by elucidating the specifics of the problem and by working together to find solutions. Rising above the quagmire of detailed pieces of information that hinder adaptive and imaginative responses to a problem, one can concentrate on what needs to be addressed and put aside irrelevant mental material.

Defense mechanisms (PAT, PDT): Defense mechanism. Quarantined nonconscious motivations that attempt to protect the ego from anxiety, dissociated thoughts, and unwelcome sentiments.

Deflection (GT): One of the five major channels of resistance. Avoiding contact and awareness by not presenting or accepting feelings or thoughts directly. May be apparent in vague verbalizations, understatement, distraction, overuse of humor, overly abstract generalizations, questioning rather than making clear statements, or verbosity. One may seek to live vicariously through others. Results in diminished emotional experience and a disturbed sense of self-hood, threatening self-authorization.

Defusion (ACT): One of ACT's six core therapeutic processes. People often get pushed around by their thoughts, trying to suppress or confront them as if the thoughts themselves had agency. But if we learn to step back and detach from our thinking (or memories), we can come to understand the less-than-real nature of psychological activity. Cognitive defusion allows us to let thoughts come and go as if they were distant clouds in the sky on a windy day.

Demandingness (REBT): Patients assume that a terrible tragedy will occur if they do not obtain what they want. The result is runaway consciousness, i.e., an overly emotionalized excerption dominates one's interpretation of events.

Denial (PAT): Avoidance of awareness of some painful aspect of reality; refusing to accept reality. The immensity and convoluted connections of the nonconscious, which can be advantageous, in certain situations produces maladaptive self-deception. Also, the hypothetically of the interiorized psyche provides a surplus mentalized space fertile for excuse making, exonerating, and rationalizations.

Dereflection (CNT): Directing one's attention away from one's own self. One's transcendent "I" rises high above one's mental turbulence and acquires a keen awareness of who one really is; individual's self-individuation expands. Dereflection describes recursive self-reflexivity continuing indefinitely: (1) "I" meta-frames above "me"; (2) from "me" emerges "I"; (3) "I" meta-frames above "me"; (4) the process begins again.

Describe (DBT): A mindfulness skill. By verbalizing and labeling one's experiences, the latter are acknowledged but not recognized as inseparable components of one's essential being ("I" stands above and tags what one perceives, conceives, and introceives). One avoids getting entangled in one's fleeting surface mental flotsam (excerptions).

Detriangling (FT): A three-person emotional system presents the possibility of one member being scapegoated or becoming the target of abuse. However, a member of the familial triad can also offer an impartial, meta-framed perspective. Interpersonal strife can be resolved if a third person (therapist) is present who can remain emotionally detached and stand above the fray while relating to the other two family members (who may be a couple). The therapist might have one family member take a position on a contentious issue and maintain that position in the face of opposition from other family members. Such a maneuver counters enmeshment, leading to the differentiation of self-identity from familial entanglements.

Devil's advocate (REBT): A type of role-playing in which the therapist adopts the maladaptive belief of patients and argues for the position. Meanwhile patients attempt to persuade the therapist why their beliefs are irrational, thereby permitting patients to step back from and obtain a more objective view of their thought patterns.

Dialectic (DBT): Characterizes a type of meta-framed reasoning based on the exchange of arguments (theses) and counterarguments (antitheses), resulting in a combination or transcendence of the competing, often contradictory, propositions (synthesis). In the context of DBT, dialectic means a type of dynamic balance, i.e., guiding patients to accept the reality of their problems as well as acquiring the coping skills to change maladaptive behaviors.

Dialogue (EXT, GT): Resonating with the theologian Martin Buber's "I-Thou" relationship, a type of communication between therapist and patients premised on openness, honesty, being fully present, and equality. Requires de-dramatization (dropping affectations and management of self-presentation) and fusing of one's "I" and "me's" (being oneself), i.e., improving one's interself relations.

Dichotomous thinking (CBT, REBT): A type of hyper-excerption in which things, people, or experiences are rigidly categorized as either good or bad, excluding any gray area or middle ground.

Disidentification (CNT): That which constitutes only part of our being (various "me's," i.e., mental content such as thoughts, feelings, etc.) becomes identified with one's complete selfhood (an "it" becomes one's essential being). In order to make a conscious choice and stop automatic associations (unwarranted consilience), one's transcendent "I" can be trained to rise above one's entangling excerptions.

Displacement (PAT): Defense mechanism. An individual redirects their unacceptable feelings (often of anger) toward another person. Results from misguided mental editing.

Distraction (DBT): One of the four crisis survival skills. A distress tolerance skill. Reducing exposure to destabilizing emotional stimuli by relying on wise mind to utilize any number of meta-framing techniques under the acronym of ACCEPTS: activities (something that distracts one such as a hobby); contributing (helping others, volunteer work); comparisons (gain perspective by taking the circumstances of others into consideration); (opposite) emotions (expose oneself to entertainments that portrays the opposite emotion one is experiencing); pushing away (using imaginative metaphors to introceive oneself as escaping from one's problem); thoughts (may range from counting to ten or more involved activities such as watching a movie or journaling); Sensations (using felt perceptions to draw one's attention away from one's introceptions).

Distress tolerance skills (DBT): Coping skills for accepting oneself as well as one's current circumstances, especially when confronted with intense emotions. Rather than being overwhelmed by unsettling situations, one cultivates the skills needed to respond, in a nonevaluative and nonjudgmental manner, to any situation.

Diversion (BT, CBT): Anxious patients are advised to redirect their concentration in the short term toward features of passing strangers, counting windows in buildings, noting car models on the highway, etc. Long-term refocusing targets include sports, physical activities, or hobbies. Strategies for arresting hyper-interiorization (which unnecessarily escalates fear to unwarranted apprehension) are excerpting either: (1) long-term—conceptions and mental material that require planning and mentally time traveling to a different temporal location; or (2) short-term—perceptions that concern one's immediate sensate environment.

Double-standard dispute (REBT): When patients verbalize a demanding "should" belief, they are asked if they would expect someone else (relative, best friend, therapist) to believe the same thing. By adopting the perspective of another, they come to see the double standard. One's "I" detaches from one's "me" and assumes the perspective of another.

Dramaturgical metaphor (PD): Individuals often find it difficult to describe in ordinary terms their problems or how they feel. By borrowing theatrical techniques and framing social interaction and interiorized mental events as scenes in a play, self-expression and self-awareness can be heightened. This is possible because mentalized space functions as a stage on which a "director" ("I") follows a script (perhaps provided by the therapist) and directs a cast of role-selves and imaginary personas standing in for others. Though patients can act as themselves in a given situation ("be oneself," i.e., "I" and "me" fused), they may also role-play someone else (e.g., family member) to adopt a different perspective or rehearse a new behavior ("I" enacts a role-self).

Dream analysis (JT): Dreams are "purposive" and serve a compensatory function by affording the individual access to the unconscious where images reside. Such images, which may be thought of as significant mental edits, offer alternatives to some maladaptive aspect of the ego.

Dream analysis/interpretation (PAT): Dreams are regarded as the pathway to the "unconscious" (quarantined nonconscious) where repressed drives and troubling latent thoughts exist in a tumultuous psychic sea. Exploring dreams helps discover symbol-laden mental content that impacts our current behavior and personal problems.

Dream work (GT): Dreams are believed to be projections containing unresolved business requiring attention. The therapist helps patients bring their dreams to life as if they were occurring in the present. Patients carefully describe their dreams in a detailed manner, noting their emotional tone, then enact parts from their dreams. This allows them to assess and confront their troublesome, contradictory role-selves and initiate a dialogue with different facets of their selfhood ("me's").

Dream work (PAT): Patients obtain insight about a dream's significance by discerning linkages connecting repressed unconscious impulses (quarantined nonconscious); defenses mechanisms; latent symbols with early childhood experiences; attitudes toward family members (especially parents); and current interpersonal issues.

Ecomap (GST): Drawing a diagram with patients to delineate their social environment. This provides the therapist with the types and quality (strong, tenuous, strained, conflicted) of patients' interactions with multiple systems (familial, educational, employment, legal, religious, community, etc.). An ecomap can lead to a fruitful discussion about issues of self-autonomy and self-authorization.

Effectively (DBT): A mindfulness skill. Rise above one's current condition, i.e., allow one's "I" to effortlessly overcome unsettling, as well as welcoming, situations. One should react as skillfully as one can in each situation, meeting the needs that certain circumstances demand. Take each situation as it is. Avoid judging situations (as right versus wrong, fair versus unfair). Letting go of emotions and thoughts (unhelpful excerptions) that do not help one reach personal goals.

Emotion mind (DBT): Strong feelings and sentiments are neither inherently good nor bad. They keep us socioaffiliated and connected to others, color our relationships and experiences, and motivate us to action. But sometimes we lose control of our emotions and they end up influencing our thinking and behavior. Rather than resisting negative feelings, our "I" should step back and merely survey them, letting emotionalized excerptions and overly excited "me's" parade by on the stage of our mind.

Emotion regulation (DBT): Understanding how affective states work and the skills our observing self needs to cope with them. Rather than assuming that our controlling self must manage bodily reactions, our "I" acknowledges and accepts distressing emotions as merely a part of our being or as an aspect of one of our role-selves. Regulating emotions reduces our vulnerability to negative feelings and concomitant maladaptive thoughts. This permits the accrual of positive emotional experiences.

Emotional imagery (CBT): Patients process their negative emotions while in session by utilizing quasi-perceptions; this is made possible, counterintuitively, by distancing from and mentally "observing" one's excerpted feelings.

Empathy (CCT): A core condition of client-centered therapy. Premised on the idea that each person is a self-individuated being, possessed of a rich introcosmos requiring exploration. The therapist endeavors to be open to patients' subjective conscious innerverse and thereby understanding their perspective. Such sensitive, heartfelt engagement is expressed by entering the worldview of patients.

Empty chair (GT, PD): A role-playing technique. Patients address an empty chair as if a person with whom they have an issue were present. They may rehearse conversations or confrontations, or explore facets of their selfhood (i.e. feelings; personified anxiety; a particular personality trait; a future self; various role-selves). Patients may adopt more than one role and may move back and forth between chairs.

Empty chair (TA): Used to represent the various ego states, with patients playing out the various role-selves (parent, adult, and child).

Enantiodromia (JT): From the Greek, "opposite" and "running course"; all things eventually turn into, or are replaced by, their opposite. Describes Jung's "necessary opposition" and "path of individuation" (self-individuation). One incorporates an opposing archetype (e.g., shadow), accepting it in order to achieve psychic completion. More broadly, enantiodromia governs psychic processes, as in the interplay between consciousness and the unconscious. Like DBT's thesis-antithesis-synthesis dynamic, it is a meta-framing process that balances inclinations to achieve adaptation and self-development.

Encounter (GT): A dialogue between two persons. This may occur between two actual persons or with a part role-played by someone else. Or an interself encounter may transpire between two different aspects of oneself (one's "I" communicating with one's "me").

Encouragement (ADT): Persuading patients to become an active participant in their own treatment helps them begin to see themselves as self-directed and capable beings (self-autonomy).

Engaged curiosity (EXT): The therapist elicits information from clients, encouraging them to provide accounts of their personal lives (family relations, work, interests, meaningful experiences). Besides helping the therapist better engage with clients, genuine inquisitiveness also enhances self-individuation and self-reflexivity on the part of the client.

Enmeshed family (FT): Individual family members are overly involved in each other's lives, eroding self-autonomy, self-individuation, and self-authorization.

Evenly suspended attention (PAT, PDT): The therapist adopts an open, attentive, and nonjudgmental listening style so as to not be biased by whatever patients may say. By monitoring one's expectations and preconceptions (excerptions), the therapist is more receptive to whatever transpires during session.

Everything is everything (EXT): Assuming that coincidences do not exist. What occurs in session is not an unusual, one-time event (e.g., arriving late), but reflects a client's way of socially interacting and other habitual behaviors that may be nonconsciously motivated. What happens in session offers topics, themes, and opportunities for exploration.

Exaggerating a behavior (GT): The therapist has patients dramatize certain gestures or movements (their own of those or others). Such role-playing (putting a distance between one's "I" and role-selves) leads to insight by intensifying and clarifying the feelings and thoughts patients have about themselves (interself relations) and others.

Exaggerating feelings (GT): By dramatizing one's inner feelings ("I" directing role-selves), one is able to "see" one's feelings. This allows the client to arrive at a better understanding of previously buried or out-of-reach feelings.

Exception questions (SOLT): Patients are asked to time travel to a period when the presenting problem was not as challenging or when they were able to self-narratize and better handle the problem. Then patients are able to mentally select out the strengths or coping skills they utilized to resolve the problem. This allows patients to gain perspective by noticing that their problems can be successfully confronted.

Existential guilt (EXT): The sentiment a person has of evading personal choices, i.e., not accepting the responsibility and heavy burden of one's self-autonomy.

Existential isolation (EXT): The price self-conscious humans pay for possessing a self-reflexive, self-individuated "I." These two latter FOCI lead to a realization that each of us is inevitably and fundamentally separated from others and the world. Such sentiments may lead to feelings of profound disaffection, and though they can be reduced, they can never be completely eliminated.

Existentialism (EXT): The philosophical movement inspiring existential therapy. It emphasizes the centrality of personal responsibility and self-determination (self-autonomy and self-authorization). It stresses authenticity in human relations, an interrogation of one's own psychological existence (self-reflexivity), the primacy of one's actual existence shorn of self-serving illusions and ideologies, and the use of self-individuated experience in the search for knowledge. Associated with modernity when rapid social change stripped away the comforts of communal connections, existentialism exposes the lone individual to an impersonal, inhospitable, and cold reality unmediated by the assurances of myths and religiosity.

Expand the emotional experience (EFT): In a family therapy setting, when patients make an emotionally charged statement (e.g., "I'm angry!"), the therapist responds by asking him or her to stay with their feelings and to describe and explore them. The therapist then validates what was verbalized and requests that other family members engage and connect with the emotions expressed. The goal is to have socioaffiliative attachment needs met. By mentally selecting out emotional material, feelings and associated thoughts become easier to introceive upon.

Exploring the family constellation (ADT): In order to gain insight about why patients have mentally selected a certain lifestyle, the therapist collects data on birth order, sibling interaction, parent interactions, and patients' sense of their psychological position in their family of origin ("family constellation" designates anyone present in the home during an individual's early formative period). This requires a recounting of key socioaffiliative attachment experiences along an individual's personal timeline.

Exposure therapy (BT, CBT): The therapist has patients confront a feared object or situation in a step-by-step manner by utilizing coping skills such as positive self-talk, breathing exercises, and progressive relaxation. Patients increase their tolerance for discomfort by putting a distance between themselves (subject-self) and their excerptions (emotional–cognitive complexes); they learn that their apprehensions and anxieties are entities that do not necessarily determine their behavior.

Externalization technique (NT): Educating patients to view excerptions related to behaviors or traits that they want to change as being separate from themselves (the "problem is the problem"). Patients might be encouraged to describe their issues with qualifiers that reframe them. Such differentiation affords individuals a sense of control over their challenges.

Family sculpting (FT): The therapist requests that family members position other members (and then themselves) in relation to each other, paying attention to posture, orientations, attitude, etc. These arrangements reflect the arranger's perception of the interaction and issues with family members. More generally, sculpting can be used with any group, which is divided into two subgroups. One subgroup works as "artists" and the other is the "clay." The facilitator then tours the "exhibit" while the artists share their thoughts about their creations. Subgroups can then alternate artist and clay roles. Group dynamics and other interpersonal issues are revealed in a surveying, visual manner that may not be adequately captured with verbalizations.

Fantasy approach (GT): The therapist guides patients through images associated with an anxiety-inducing event and encourages them to verbalize what they emotionally experience in the moment. This introceived imaginary play-out allows patients to more consciously process sentiments (via consilience) related to the event.

Fictional final goal (ADT): Individuals behave as much from their aspirations and ideals as they do from what is readily observed. Much of what a person assumes about their role in the world is nonconscious and they end up acting as if their assumptions are true (the as-if principle), despite the dictates and demands of reality.

Flooding (BT): A form of exposure therapy in which patients directly confront a maximum-intensity anxiety-producing stimulus (real or imagined) minus attempts to lessen negative emotions during the exposure (rather than a controlled, gradual, step-by-step approach). The "fear" (excerption) is diminished or extinguished from the "feared" situation or stimulus. Or individuals confront painful memories with the goal of reintegrating repressed emotions into their current awareness.

Free association (PAT, PDT): Patients verbalize whatever comes to mind, no matter how embarrassing, disjointed, or seemingly irrelevant. With mental editing suspended, inhibited thoughts, repressed emotions, unsettling impulses, fragmented memories of traumatic experiences bubble up from the unconscious which can then be addressed and interpreted. Evidence of resistance may indicate that certain mental manifestations require further probing. Free association is a type of free-flowing consilience, and it may be cathartic for some patients. Some therapists may read a list of words to trigger the free flow of verbalizations.

Fusion (EXT): An attempt to reduce one's sense of isolation by becoming part of another person's life or group, such as a political or religious movement. This can erode one's self-authorization and self-autonomy.

Fusion (FT): Enmeshment. A blurring of boundaries between family members who lose a sense of personal identity, individuality, and selfhood. Impedes self-autonomy.

Future projection (GT): Utilizing a prospective self-narratization, patients introceptually picture themselves and their life sometime in the future; such introception can grant them a healthier perspective.

Gender analysis and intervention (FET): The therapist and patient explore the impact of societal gender role expectations and how these configure personal issues, self-individuation, and self-autonomy.

Genogram (FT): Drawing a family tree (or "map") that includes information about interpersonal dynamics such as marriages, divorces, significant events, quality of relations, conflicts, etc. Such a meta-framing exercise can delineate issues of loyalty, entitlement, indebtedness, and help determine the viewpoint of each family member. It enables hypotheses and insights and can be used to trace recurring patterns over generations. Affords perspective and a snapshot of a kinship system's trajectory through time.

Genuineness (CCT): Related to the core condition of empathy and the honest communication of one's emotions and experiences. Pretense and over-dramatization are dropped ("I" and "me" fused). This allows one to be sensitive to another's subjective conscious world and invites all aspects of one's self into awareness.

Graded task assignment (BT): In order to facilitate activity scheduling that might include complicated tasks, large tasks are broken down into smaller "baby steps." Increasing the number of chained, goal-oriented excerptions affords individuals an enhanced quasi-perceptual view of their tasks, leading to more self-control.

Guided imagery (BT, CBT): In regard to facilitating change, integrating introspectable, quasi-perceptual experiences is more potent than merely verbalizing a problem. Patients set the props of a problematic situation on their mentally spatialized stage. While guided by the therapist, they verbalize feelings and thoughts that emerge and acquire a sense of agency, thereby fortifying resilience and self-confidence. Introceptualized props may reflect the actual physical world or may be symbols of significant issues or events (e.g., trauma).

Guided self-dialogue (CBT): Patients learn to self-dialogue, i.e., their "I" and "me's" (meaning different parts of one's selfhood, i.e., interself relations) engage in a self-reflexive exchange of information. This way, individuals can control intrusive thoughts, feelings, and anxiety.

Hedonic treadmill (PPT): A hindrance to true happiness. Postindustrialization generates an affluence that not only instantly satisfies our basic needs and wants, but causes one to take such satisfaction for granted so that we rapidly adapt to what has been obtained. This raises expectations for the accumulation of more material possessions and accomplishments.

Driven by unquenchable longings that can never be sated, hyper-interiorized anticipation ("desiring desires") results in snowballing consumerism.

Homework (BT, CBT): Reviewing and reinforcing the previous therapy sessions or preparing for the next session is vital for consolidating any progress and cognitive restructuring. One's "I" learns to better monitor excerptions and automatic thoughts. Homework offers opportunities to practice new skills, dispute rational beliefs, test hypotheses, and self-reflect on activating events and emotional responses outside of sessions. Worksheets may be used.

Humor (PAT): Defense mechanism. Uncomfortable feelings and forbidden impulses are freely expressed in a humorous manner. Laughter releases energy normally used to keep negative sentiments quarantined in the nonconsciousness.

Humor (RT): Being spontaneous and happening "here and now," comicality can put people at ease. Therapists can construct an engaging therapeutic working relationship with an individual by laughing at themselves. This encourages patients to do the same, thereby inspiring them to step out of a guarded role-self and see themselves, self-reflexively, in a different light.

Hypothesis testing (BT, CBT): The therapist and patients identify assumptions and questionable beliefs held by the latter and set up an experiment to test them. Exceptions to the hypothesis that nullify the hypothesis are looked for, educating patients about how the mind automatically excerpts and forms linkages (via consilience) that lead to what are often irrational and erroneous thought patterns.

"I" statements: These sound persuasive, expressive, and suggest not so much a solid, impersonal fact but more of an opinion. Such statements make one vulnerable and indicate collaborative teamwork. They can de-escalate a tense situation, leave the door open to negotiation, keep a dialogue going, and allow the other to know that perhaps clarification of what was said is required. From the addressee's perspective, "I" statements de-escalate feelings of being targeted, thereby endorsing their sense of self-autonomy.

Identification (PAT): Defense mechanism. Acting like someone else or incorporating facets of an internal object in order to control anxiety or reduce hostility between oneself and the object. Erodes self-autonomy.

Identification (PDT): Consciously or nonconsciously associating one's self-identity with others, their traits, or views. It concerns developmental life-span issues, self-formation, and self-authorization: infants emotionally grow close to their mothers; children internalize their parents' qualities; adolescents adopt the characteristics of their peers; adults identify with their profession, political movements, etc.

Identification with aggressor (PDT): Defense mechanism. An individual nonconsciously adopts the hostile characteristics of an anxiety-evoking aggressor (or internal object); the individual becomes the aggressor. Often emerges in emotionally extreme situations, e.g., hostage taking. Hinders self-autonomy, self-authorization, and self-individuation.

Imaginal desensitization (BT): Minimizing emotional or physical reactivity to stimuli (perhaps from a traumatic event) by using deconditioning techniques. Requires monitoring excerptions, their associations, and patterns of consilience.

Imaginal exposure (BT, CBT): A type of exposure therapy used for individuals suffering from anxiety disorders, phobias, obsessive-compulsive disorder, and PTSD. Using vivid imagery, the therapist has patients introceive anxiety-evoking stimuli; they learn to mentally edit out the fear, reframing it as just another entity that does not control their behavior.

Imago relationship therapy (FT): Searching for negative sentiments and relationship stresses to find the root cause of dysfunctional communication between partners. Accomplished by exploring nonconscious representations from early socializing experiences—usually of parents—that influence the choice of and attitude toward one's partner ("imago" was originally used by Freud).

Implosion (or implosive) therapy (BT): Similar to flooding. However, the focus is on introceived, imagined stimuli, and the therapist increases anxiety by adding imaginary exposure cues relevant to patients' fears, thereby equipping their psychoscape with more triggers.

Improving the moment (DBT): One of the four crisis survival skills. A set of distress tolerance skills: imagery (mentally traveling to a more positive place in one's psychoscape); meaning (rising above one's situation and discerning some significance); prayer (perhaps relying on one's transcendent "I"); relaxation (calming one's body communicates acceptance to one's psyche); focusing on one thing (one-mindfulness settles the mind); vacation (a break can allow us breathing space to regroup); self-encouragement (role-play by talking to oneself the way someone who cares about us would talk to us).

Individuation (JT): Individuation is the process in which one's elements of personality emerge out of an undifferentiated unconsciousness and are integrated; opposite traits will be balanced with each other in the mature, well-functioning person. The therapist can facilitate this process by making patients consciously aware of elements from their personal unconscious and/or the collective unconscious (some therapists may want to reconceptualize the latter as something less mystical, e.g., an identity-affording group to which the individual belongs). Self-individuation highlights one's uniqueness and self-identity. One's self-discovered personal strengths can then be mobilized to help others. Individuation may be an immediate goal or something that transpires throughout one's life span.

Intellectualization (PAT): Defense mechanism. Thinking rather than feeling. One deals with one's conflicts or emotional problems in an overly abstract manner or conceals them with excessively intellectual analysis.

Intention and/or resistance (PDT): Intention is the drive toward integration, while resistance is the inhibition of this drive. Therapy can focus on either (or both) depending on the presenting problem or the current status of the therapeutic relationship. This is done by the therapist and patient reflecting on the latter's own excerptions. These mental editings might hinder progress or help in obtaining goals.

Internal dialogue exercise (GT): Patients role-play the conflict or issue with which they are struggling, alternating between the passive, controlled "me" (object-self) and the active, controlling "I" (subject-self). This technique involving interself relations enhances hypothetical perspective-taking, allowing one to imagine different versions of oneself. In principle, it can also fortify objective perspective-taking, allowing one to adopt the position of others. Increases role-self diversity.

Internal object (PDT): Representations of a significant other (e.g., a parent) that an individual internalizes as a socioaffiliative "presence." The relations of these psychic structures to each other and to the individual shape their personality. Internal objects may be reconceptualized as mental editing that helps patients clarify their interpersonal issues. See **object relations theory**.

Interoceptive exposure (BT): Purposely having patients experience fear-provoking physical sensations (racing heart, dizziness, breathlessness triggered by panic attacks or phobias) until they are no longer anxiety-inducing. By directly feeling sensate perceptions, patients learn to distance one aspect of their selfhood ("I") from their own unpleasant physiological reactions, associated excerptions, and patterns of consilience, thereby robbing the sensations of their impact.

Interpersonal effectiveness (DBT): This means attending to relationships mindfully; discerning the difference between priorities and demands; balancing "want's and "should's"; clarifying what we desire from an interaction with others; and knowing how to say no. Treating others thoughtfully begins with dealing with our own interself relations in a healthy manner.

Introjection (GT): One of the five major channels of resistance. To passively accept the beliefs of others without self-reflexively accommodating them to make them congruent (i.e., consilience) with one's own processes of self-individuation. To incorporate whatever the external world provides; to uncritically suspend one's self-authorization and self-autonomy.

Introjection (PAT, PDT): Absorbing an idea or image of another so that it becomes part of one's self-identity. It may be a normal part of self-development (e.g., acquiring parental values that shape the superego). However, it may also be used as a defense mechanism and signals a blurring of self-other boundaries, thereby threatening self-autonomy, self-authorization, and self-individuation.

Invariant prescription (FT): Dysfunctional familial patterns are sometimes caused by enmeshment between parents and children. In order to delineate clearer generational boundaries and establish more self-autonomy and self-individuation, parents are advised to spend time with each other, not with their children.

Inversion (PAT, PDT): Defense mechanism. Turning against oneself. The object of one's aggression is switched from another to oneself, i.e., one's "I" targets an aspect of one's selfhood or a role-self. Often apparent in depression.

Invitation to do more of what is working (BFT): Ask patients to self-narratize a period when they utilized a technique or strength that worked. Or encourage them to experiment with something they have considered doing.

I-positions (FT): The therapist relies on messages to differentiate himself or herself from the individual, couple, or family. This instance of self-individuation might illustrate a responsible use of "I" statements (differentiates by defining one's own beliefs and values), as opposed to an irresponsible use (e.g., making unfair and unreasonable demands on others).

Isolation of affect (PDT): A defense mechanism. Nonconsciously detaching thoughts from the feelings originally associated with them (de-consilience). The individual avoids painful feelings by recalling a past traumatic event without experiencing the associated emotions.

Journaling (CBT): Patients keep a record of dysfunctional thoughts, noting situations and emotions that trigger irrational beliefs and learning to counter them with rational responses. Builds a self-narrative of progress.

Journaling (JT): Patients keep track of their thoughts and feelings so they can monitor their progress during therapy. Cultivates self-reflexivity.

Latent content (PAT): Hidden or disguised meanings, desires, wishes, or fantasies operating unconsciously that are often related to early infancy. Such content is symbolically distorted to protect the ego. Dream interpretation decodes such mental material, transmuting it into excerptions.

Letters, definitional ceremonies, reflection (NT): The therapist, family members, and trusted others (and perhaps a support group of some kind) communicate to patients about how they see a new positive storyline emerging in the lives of patients. Such encouragement validates and reaffirms the self-renarratization of the individual.

Looking for exceptions (BFT): Sometimes a previous solution to a problem may be lacking. However, a time may have existed when the presenting problem was less of a challenge. In this case, patients are asked to evaluate their problem from a different angle, to engage in robust hypotheticality, and to consider alternative experiences upon which to build.

Looking for previous solutions (BFT): Given that patients have solved similar problems in the past, questions such as "has this ever been less of a problem?" or "what have you done that has helped?" remind them of their forgotten strengths and that previously they have been successful. Utilizing self-narratization to mentally time travel back to the past to contrast and compare different role-selves can bolster self-autonomy and a sense of self-control.

Magnification (CBT): The significance of an event or experience is mentally selected out and exaggerated. Patients can explore why automatic thoughts and core beliefs blow certain excerptions out of proportion and how to veto irrational thinking patterns.

Making the rounds (GT): In a group setting, patients speak to or make simple requests from each member. This dramatization affords self-confidence in the performance of role-selves (one becomes an audience to oneself), and patients thereby acquire interpersonal skills, learns to feel comfortable taking risks, and become used to freely self-disclosing.

Manifest content (PAT, PDT): The apparent content of a dream is unconsciously processed so that it disguises and conceals its hidden, latent meanings, thereby protecting the ego. More broadly, an issue that is overtly expressed.

Metaphor: A type of meta-framing. A fundamental psychological process; how the mind metabolizes new information, bootstraps itself through time, and adapts to its environment. Therapists can enter the imaginary, personal worldview of patients by paying close attention to the metaphors they use to discuss their problems. In this way clinicians gain a better appreciation of what vexes patients and can tap into their repertoire of images, symbols, and representations.

Mindfulness (ACT, DBT): A type of meta-framing. A core concept in DBT. The typical human reaction when confronted with a problem is to try to explain its circumstances and solve it; we then often become entangled in vexing and worrisome thinking patterns. But by stepping back, allowing sheer experience to wash over us, and merely describing what is occurring, we can "observe" our reactions and experience feelings fully as if from a distance (or as if by another person). Such a nonjudgmental stance of pure awareness (transcendent "I") and living in the moment affords perspective so individuals can cultivate acceptance and tolerate upsetting emotions they may feel when their maladaptive habits are challenged or they are in the midst of a distressing situation.

Minimization (CBT): An event or experience is made far less significant than it actually is. A type of self-deception. Patients can learn to more objectively examine the value they attribute to their excerptions.

Miracle question (BFT): Intended to generate the initial steps of a solution for the short term. It is proposed that a miracle occurs overnight and the problem is resolved. Patients then think about what the initial signs would be that the miracle occurred and what would now be different in their lives. This exercise draws upon the hypothetical generative power of conscious interiority which allows us to self-narratize and envision a future in which the problem is no longer present.

Mirror technique (PD): An auxiliary ego (person acting out a role-self) imitates the affective state and body language of patients to show them how they are perceived by others.

Mirroring: The therapist imitates patients' movements, speech style, and demeanor so that he or she can more readily discern their own behavior. May be used to evoke a sense of empathy and bolster the therapeutic alliance. Or patients may emulate the therapist to acquire new skills, i.e., role-play new skills.

Modeling (BT, CBT): Demonstrating a chain of behaviors for patients and then having them replicate and role-play targeted behaviors. Patients can recognize other alternatives to their behaviors. Stories, books, television, or recorded materials may be utilized by individuals to emulate.

Monodrama (GT, PD): The same patient plays both parts in a scene by alternating between them. Patients simultaneously direct the scene and enact different parts ("I" directs or role-plays different "me's" or role-selves). Such fluid turn-taking educates patients about the flexibility, variability, and changeableness of one's identity, permitting them to see the opportunities and possibilities for growth and self-improvement. This cultivates improved interpersonal and interself relations.

Morita therapy (CNT): Developed by Morita Shoma (1874–1938) to treat anxiety by redirecting an individual's attention away from oneself (a consequence of hyper-interiorized self-focus). After an initial period of strict and isolated bed rest, patients receive occupational therapy and then are reintegrated back into the normal routines of life (familial and occupational). The goal is *arugamama*, or "acceptance of the way things are" (i.e., oneself and one's feelings).

Music (PT): Music invites individuals into an imaginary innerverse where they can find meaning, make connections, and relax. Such experiences generate fruitful discussions with one's therapist about cognitions and emotions and how these relate to one's challenges and current circumstances. Patients might compose their own music.

Musturbation analysis (REBT): Increases self-reflexivity by having patients uncover their patterns of excerptions that unreasonably focus on the litany of "ought's," "should's," and "must's." Bringing awareness and perspective to an individual about their maladaptive cognitions concerning perfectionist goals linked to success or approval.

Mutuality (GT): Contra to a one-way, hierarchical relationship in which the therapist evaluates the client's progress and prescribes treatment, the therapist takes a person-centered approach by empowering the client through a supportive and cooperative co-facilitation. Increases self-autonomy.

Naikan therapy (CNT): Developed by Yoshimoto Ishin (1916–1988) of the Japanese Buddhist Jodo Shinshu sect. Naikan, meaning "introspection," focuses on past relationships in order to increase social and interpersonal contributions. It views the cultivation of character and personal responsibility through intensive self-reflexivity on what patients have received from others; what the patient has given back to others; and how the actions of patients may have harmed others. Patients acquire an appreciation and gratitude of the positive influences in their life.

Narration of a new story (NT): After a problem is identified, solutions are found, and a different and positive storyline is "written" (self-renarratized) that replaces the previous maladaptive storyline.

Nondirective attitude (CCT): Valuing the client's inherent capacity for and right to self-determination. Bolstering a sense of agency is crucial for increasing a feeling of control over one's personal decisions, volitions, and intentions (self-autonomy).

Nonjudgment (DBT): An aspect of mindfulness. Observe the facts but do not evaluate. Rather than discerning whether an event or situation is "good" or "bad," detach one's excerptions from the apparent facts and suspend one's opinion. If one finds oneself judging, do not judge one's judging.

Object relations theory (PDT): A basic human motive is the search for a satisfying internalized object (significant others, especially parents). The personality is composed of internal object representations whose relationships with each other shape one's interpersonal dynamics. Unlike classical PAT, object relations theory views the need to relate to objects as more important to personality organization than libidinal or aggressive drives. See **internal object**.

Observe (DBT): A mindfulness skill. Allowing one's transcendent "I" to experience without becoming part of the experience, whether perceptual, conceptual, or introceptual. Having a "Teflon mind" (feelings and thoughts come into one's mind and slip away); passively watching one's thoughts coming and going, like clouds in the sky; noticing feelings rising and falling, like waves in the ocean; being attentive to what comes through one's senses (eyes, ears, nose, skin) but not clinging to perceptions.

Odd day/even day ritual (FT): The family is given a directive that on odd days one set of rules or routines are to be followed, while on even days another set of rules or actions are adhered to, thereby encouraging more flexible thinking (e.g., on odd days the mother does the parenting, while on even days the father takes over parental duties). Alternating behavioral patterns destabilizes the familial system, allowing members to self-reflexively see their own role-selves, overcome resistance, and ultimately address problematic issues. Used in Milan systemic family therapy.

One mindfully (DBT): A mindfulness skill. Do each thing with the FOCI of concentration so that irrelevant, unrelated mental material is peripheralized—when eating, eat; when walking, walk; when talking, talk; when worrying, worry, etc. If excerptions arise that distract you, let them pass and return to what you were doing.

Overgeneralization (CBT, REBT): Formulating a general rule from isolated anecdotes or unconnected incidents and applying it too broadly. Results when we too readily select out mental representations from our stream of thought and engage in uncontrolled abstraction.

Paradox (RT): In order to lower patients' resistance, the therapist may caution them to not follow through on a plan or encourage them to adopt opposite behaviors. The therapist may recommend that other issues need to be addressed first. Such recommendations, rather than directive guidance, demonstrate to patients the existence of their own self-autonomy.

Paradoxical directive (REBT): The therapist requests that patients do the opposite of what common sense dictates in order to demonstrate the self-defeating and maladaptive nature of their original thinking. They develop a sense of agency and self-control over their own actions. Also called stepping out of character.

Paradoxical intention (CBT, EXT): Patients are asked to magnify a distressing symptom (e.g., anxiety). They are then able to more clearly observe their own behavior, isolate and identify it, and realize that they have more self-control than they assumed; they come to feel capable of ceasing their undesired behavior. Self-reflexive monitoring allows patients to distance themselves from their irrational mental extractions that motivate behaviors. They might also learn that the feared catastrophic consequences associated with their undesired symptoms are not likely to transpire. They may even find humor in their dramatized, exaggerated responses.

Paradoxical intervention (FT): The therapist encourages family members to improve interrelations by engaging in problematic behavior. This generates awareness of how much self-control over their actions they actually possess, as well as opening up prospects for further progress not previously envisioned or self-narratized.

Paradoxical technique (REBT): Patients are told to continue (or even increase) an undesired, maladaptive, behavior. This shows patients that they in fact possess self-control over their actions. Also called paradoxical intervention.

Paraphrasing nonverbals (CCT): A type of facilitated meta-framing. The therapist summarizes patients' verbalizations (presumably based on mental editing); this helps patients self-reflexively consider their own thoughts and feelings.

Parataxic distortion (PDT): A skewed understanding or judgment of others shaped by past encounters. Mental material is not edited impartially in regard to the traits of others, and opinions about them are made to conform to previous experiences in a distorted manner (often nonconsciously motivated). Also called transference distortion.

Participate (DBT): A mindfulness skill. Entering into an experience without any preconceptions (rooted in excerptions that "think for us"). Getting involved in the moment without any expectations (rooted in excerptions that "jump ahead"). Let experience wash over oneself, completely forgetting oneself. Act intuitively from the wise mind. Practice newly acquired skills until they become a part of one so that they can be deployed nonconsciously minus an overly inquisitive hyper-focusing.

Plans of action (RT): To ensure success, patients must be clear on what they want and for what they are taking responsibility. Thus the need for a specific, attainable, and time-limited plan of action. Involves envisioning a personal timeline that extends into the future (self-narratization).

Play the script until the end (CBT): Useful for those suffering from anxiety, this mental time traveling to the future allows patients to conduct a thought experiment in which they mentally extract the outcome of a worst-case scenario. Allowing the hypothetical scenario to play out can help patients realize that even if everything they had feared does come to pass, the outcome is most likely still manageable. This increases a sense of agency.

Playing the projection (GT): Patients act out the role of an individual with whom they are experiencing interpersonal issues. Dialogue, empty chair, or another psychodrama technique may be used. Such dramatization, in which the "I" gains some distance vis-à-vis one's own role-selves for dealing with others, allows patients to drop defenses and observe matters from different angles.

Postponing gratification (REBT): Used with patients who have low frustration tolerance; they are asked to delay gratification (e.g., smoking, eating unhealthy foods, reacting to others inappropriately). This both requires and can enhance self-narratization (i.e., visualizing "seeing" oneself receiving a reward in the future).

Power analysis and power intervention (FET): Assisting patients to discern power differences between the sexes and the baneful effects of sexism and other injustices. Patients come to understand not only how all individuals exercise power, but they also come to appreciate their own power (self-autonomy) and the richness of their own self-individuation.

Prescribing the symptom (ADT): See **paradoxical intention**.

Present and future-focused questions versus past-oriented focus (BFT): Rather than looking toward the past for the origins of a problem, patients are encouraged to maintain a present and future focus so as to stay in the solution, especially if the solution is working. Patients are encouraged to self-narratize prospectively, rather than retrospectively.

Private logic (ADT): A feature of the modern, highly individualistic world due to increasing levels of self-individuation. In contrast to the community's "common sense," which is public and shared, each person contains a personalized introcosmos that informs the basic assumptions they make about how the world works and how they should behave in it. Understanding the private logic of individuals facilitates assessment of their weaknesses and strengths.

Problem identification and assessment (BT): It is crucial to initially develop a clear understanding of the presenting problem, including first occurrence, frequency, and severity. Patients' recountings about prior attempts to address the challenge is important (how they self-narratize the issues), as is a patient's own views of their problem, i.e., how they excerpt relevant mental material.

Problem-solving (CBT): Patients are taught how to cope with life's challenges: (1) problem orientation, or the way one approaches and identifies a problem; (2) defining the problem in clear, concrete, and goal-oriented terms; (3) generating a menu of solutions; (4) decision-making (assessing the consequences of alternative solutions and mentally selecting a course of action that is optimal by considering short- and long-term consequences; this enhances self-authorization); (5) implementing a solution and evaluating its outcome. Effective problem-solving requires robust self-narratizing abilities.

Projection (GT): One of the five major channels of resistance. It may mean disowning facets of one's selfhood by attributing them to the external environment. This leads to trouble distinguishing between the "inside" (one's self-identity) and the "outside world" of others. Or it may signify disowning attributes of one's selfhood that are inconsistent with one's self-definition and assigning them to others. This results in avoiding responsibly for one's feelings and threatens self-identity, thereby eroding self-individuation.

Projection (PAT, PDT): Defense mechanism. Attributing to another person or group one's negative characteristics, impulses, thoughts, feelings, or behaviors, thereby protecting the ego; it indicates a serious erosion of self-autonomy and evasion of personal responsibility. In classical psychoanalytic theory, projection allows individuals to avoid seeing their faults since the attributed trait remains unknown to the self. However, PDT traditions do not require that nonconscious motivations play a role.

Projective identification (PAT, PDT): An interactional form of projection, evident as both a defense mechanism and in normal interpersonal dynamics. Individuals upon whom attributions are made self-conceptualize and self-individuate the projected traits and believe themselves to be characterized by them.

Pros and cons (DBT): One of the four crisis survival skills. A distress tolerance skill. Patients make a list of the advantages and disadvantages of tolerating distress and another list of the advantages and disadvantages of not tolerating the distress. This meta-framing exercise allows patients to focus on long-term goals (i.e., self-narratizing into the future and seeing various, more positive outcomes).

Psychological flexibility (ACT): One of ACT's six core therapeutic processes. The ability to be present (with mindful awareness), to open up to experiences (to fully accept whatever comes our way without hyper-consciously judging), and to do what matters (guided by our values cultivated through self-reflexivity). These abilities, because they allow us to respond more effectively to life's inevitable challenges and problems, improve our quality of life.

Puppetry therapy (PT): By utilizing dolls and other toys, children can re-enact scenes, dramatize role-selves, or play out fantasies. This allows a distancing between their "I" and "me's" so that troublesome or distressing thoughts can be addressed, unsettling emotions articulated, and new behaviors rehearsed having to do with improved communication skills and decision-making (self-authorization). Using puppets can also aid the therapist in diagnosing.

Push button technique (ADT): Patients are asked to visualize a happy event, introceptually experience the concomitant feelings, and then do the same for an unhappy event. Next they are asked to self-narratize themselves back to the happy event and experience the more pleasant feelings. This helps patients appreciate how much self-control they have over their emotions.

Radical acceptance (DBT): This means neither deeming something good nor approving of a distressful situation; rather, it means to acknowledge whatever the situation is (even painful ones) and to tolerate the moment. By dropping confrontations with reality, anger, rage, and resentments lose their potency. A transcendent "I" can discern faulty conceptions more clearly.

Rationalization (PAT, PDT): Defense mechanism. Providing a rationale for painful material that has been nonconsciously quarantined to avoid unsettling or threatening feelings, e.g., guilt, shame, loss of self-respect. Converting an unacceptable outcome into a seemingly logical, reasonable explanation.

Reaction formation (PAT): Defense mechanism. Positioning painful feelings or threatening unconscious impulses as their opposite on the stage of conscious awareness. Converting unacceptable desires into their opposite.

Reasonable mind (DBT): One's "thinking" mind that considers, plans, and evaluates matters logically, meta-framing above one's daily challenges. Reasonable mind is usually beneficial, but negative moods make it difficult to excerpt useful mental content and follow the dictates of such analytical, cool cognition. Also called rational mind.

Reattribution (CBT): A type of meta-framing. Examining automatic thought patterns by questioning unreasonable assumptions and exploring alternative excerptions for an event under consideration.

Recording sessions (REBT): The therapist will have patients record the therapy session and listen to the session at least once before the next session. Listening to the recording is an act of self-reflexivity (self-distancing between "I" and "me") that can cultivate insight, allows a review of what was discussed (reinforces learning), raises one's level of self-awareness, and leads to self-monitoring.

Redefining (CBT): A type of meta-framing. This allows patients to make their problems more specific and concrete and then restating and reconceptualizing them in a more adaptive way. It involves mentally extracting out ideas that can be helpful and rejecting those that are not.

Reflect the feeling (CCT): The therapist moves from the surface content of what patients have stated and attends to underlying or implicit feelings in their verbalizations. The goal of the therapist is to mentally select out key elements from the stream of thought of patients and aid them in identifying emotionalized mental editing. This will aid patients in abstracting out key themes governing (perhaps maladaptively) their habits of thought.

Reframing (CBT, REBT): A type of meta-framing. Seeing the problem(s) from a different perspective. Patients identify and list the positives resulting from a negative occurrence. Reframing can be enhanced by educating individuals on how monitoring the flow of their excerptions can open up new horizons and boost powers of abstraction, thereby potentially offering new solutions.

Reframing (FET): A type of meta-framing. Patients, guided by the therapist, alter their frame of reference for their own behavior, shifting it from an intrapersonal (psychogenic) to an interpersonal (sociogenic) focus, thereby defining issues in a more objective and politically informed perspective. May involve self-renarratization.

Reframing (FT): The therapist, whether convinced of a treatment's efficacy or not, provides a rationale for treatment, so that an individual or family members are more likely to be receptive to treatment. Meta-framing occurs because the therapist stands above and outside of the dynamic psychic interplay within an individual or among family members.

Reframing (FT, GST): A type of meta-framing. A problem is detached from the identified patient and re-excerpted and reconceptualized as a family issue. Now reframed, it becomes the focal point of intervention.

Reframing the problem (EFT): By reframing their cycle of interpersonal dysfunction into a conflict cycle, partners (in couple's therapy) come to see how they are on the same side. They learn to view the problem from their partner's point of view, which helps each partner to understand the other's emotions and needs. Patients come to realize they are no longer victims of the situation.

Regression (PAT): Defense mechanism. Retreating to an earlier psychosexual stage when disturbed by internal conflicts or threatened with interpersonal problems. More generally, a reversion to a prior self or a lower stage of cognitive, emotional, or behavioral development. The therapeutic uses of self-narratizing can help an individual re-evaluate their lack of progress.

Rehearsal exercise (CBT, GT): Patients mentally rehearse new ways of dealing with challenging situations on their introspectable stage; this can occur before patients have to use them in daily living. Patients are encouraged to enact, aided by the therapist, a specific goal-oriented task. Or they may engage in a dialogue not just with the therapist, but with themselves, i.e., their first-person self ("I") and second-person self ("me") hold a discussion in order to extract out mental content that might be useful for self-reflexivity and gaining self-objectivity. Patients may play the role of the director and scriptwriter, interrogating former avatars of their selves or narratizing a more hopeful future.

Relabeling (FET): A type of meta-framing. Patients are asked consider altering their evaluation of or a label attributed to a behavioral characteristic from a negative to a positive; one's "I" self-reflexively monitors assumptions one makes about oneself and inspects excerptions.

Relationship (EXT): How the therapist interacts with patients is key, especially as this interaction relates to what patients are consciously experiencing. The therapist should avoid persuading patients by offering advice on how to overcome a particular problem, cope with stressors, or adapt to a life challenge; such maneuvers deprive them of their agency, self-autonomy, opportunities for self-individuation, and genuine growth. Rather, the therapist should adopt a humble attitude, afford guidance by modeling, and instill confidence while enhancing the sense of self-direction of patients.

Replay (PD, BT, CBT): Patients re-enact a previous scene or episode in their lives. Such role-playing grants individuals ("I") the ability to mentally extract out links in their chain of behavior for examination and evaluation.

Reporting one's earliest recollections (ADT): Patients recount their earliest childhood memories. This focus on their unfolding personal storyline affords insight into patterns or interpretations they have made in developing their general attitudes and lifestyle.

Repression (PAT, PDT): Defense mechanism. Objectionable impulses and painful experiences are kept in the unconscious, thereby guarding the ego against anxiety triggered by unacceptable sexual wishes, hostility, and unsettling memories. In primary repression, instinctual wishes and undesirable thoughts that have never been conscious are blocked and prevented from entering one's mental stage. In secondary repression (or repression proper), the mental material has been consciously interiorized but becomes buried in the unconscious (i.e., forced into the quarantined nonconscious).

Resistance (GT): Individuals attempt to hold on to their habitual psychological functioning; this hinders self-reflexivity.

Resistance (PAT, PDT): Rather than a negative to be overcome, this should be considered as something to be understood as well as an opportunity for positive change. Resistance, after all, is a natural human reaction to ambivalence and the challenge of personal change. Guided self-reflexivity about why one engages in resistance is crucial.

Restatements: Crucial to active listening, this therapeutic skill gives patients the opportunity of "hearing themselves think"; i.e., having their words and thoughts reflected back to them allows them to pay attention to excerptions or patterns of consilience. It also builds the therapeutic alliance since patients begin to feel comfortable with someone who carefully listens to them.

Restraining ("one down" position) (FT): If therapeutic change occurs too rapidly, a family's homeostatic balance may be upset, leading to demoralization. Going slow may be more appropriate, especially if patients claim that they cannot adopt a more adaptive behavior due to anxiety or some other reason. They should be advised not to move too fast and should be validated for any progress they have made by self-narratizing their journey so far.

Restructuring the bond (EFT): Patients and therapist cooperate to identify attachment needs by reviewing relevant excerptions that come to mind when discussing interpersonal relations. Mentally selecting out these identified needs and mentally inspecting them aids in arresting unhealthy patterns of interactions and facilitates positive change.

Retroflection (GT): One of the five major channels of resistance. An impulse or want is made into a one-person event; this may lead to isolation (boundary disturbance). A person (initiator-of-action "I") treats oneself (recipient-of-action "me") in the same way that they desire (aspect of self) to deal with another. Or one ("I") treats oneself ("me") in the same way that one (aspect of self that) wants to be treated. In either case, a facet of one's selfhood is neglected.

Reversal (PDT): Defense mechanism. A form of reaction formation aimed at guarding oneself from painful feelings by mentally selecting out thoughts and their concomitant behavior and replacing them with their opposite.

Reversal technique (GT): The therapist requests that patients do the opposite of their behavior, acting out a counter-scenario. This allows patients to step back (meta-frame) from their usual patterns of activity and survey them to better self-observe and obtain insight and understanding. Hypothetical possibilities for more adaptive behaviors are highlighted on one's mental stage.

Risk-taking (REBT): To challenge their beliefs, patients are requested to engage in a challenging task where the risk of failure or at least not meeting all expectations is high. Accepting such a task that involves possible failure as well as success allows patients to step back and gain perspective on their capacity for self-control.

Rituals (FT): The therapist prescribes a series of actions involving the family to be enacted under specific circumstances, e.g., everyone sitting together daily, each family member getting equal time to speak well of the family, with critical opinions not allowed. Meta-framing family behavioral patterns in this way allows family members to gain insight into their role expectations and covert (often nonconscious) rules that hinder healthy family dynamics.

Role reversal (PD): The protagonist exchanges roles with an auxiliary ego while acting out an interaction. More broadly, adopting the perspective of another to experience alternative cognitive styles, feelings, and behavioral approaches so as to expand one's repertoire of role-selves. A plays B, B plays A, and sometimes, A takes the role of whoever he or she designates B to be (whether present or not), thereby opening the actor's mind to a deeper understanding.

Role-playing (BT, CBT, GT, REBT, PD): Allows patients to try out and experiment with new behaviors while in session. In parallel with overt behavior, patients may covertly enact the desired activity and manipulate imagery on their mental stage. The therapist guides patients through a step-by-step process of successfully coping with the imagined situation. This artificial re-enactment of a situation allows the therapist to observe and better assess any interpersonal issues during the enactment. Patients mentally picture difficult situations to be confronted, envisioning their "I" interacting with edited mental objects (e.g., fears, problems) or imaginary others. Role-playing can also be used to increase role-diversity by increasing perspective-taking, thereby allowing one to imagine different versions of oneself. It may also be used to rehearse for a situation that provokes apprehension.

Role-playing (TA): May be conceived as a "time out" from reality in which actual selves of patients can attempt to draw closer to their idealized self, taking advantage of the immediacy and spontaneity of the here-and-now versus the intellectualized, abstract discussion of what has already occurred or worrisome considerations of what may happen. Role-playing, since it establishes a hypothetical, imaginary space, is also a useful technique to demonstrate how patients' behaviors have created situations in their life; it can assist in teaching them new ways to respond in the future.

Sandplay (JT): Used with figures, symbols, or other miniature objects. Both children and adults freely express themselves and integrate negative as well as positive emotions associated with an individual's experience with complexes, especially maternal and paternal ones (certain excerptions). Jungian sandplay takes advantage of the natural self-correcting and self-healing properties of the psyche.

Sandplay (PT): Children are encouraged to create a "world" or "scene" in a wet or dry sand tray. Various toys, natural objects, dolls, miniature buildings, or other objects are used to express difficult-to-verbalize mental material that may not be readily excerpted by a child. Sand play may or may not be directed.

Scaling questions (BFT, BT, CBT, SOLT): A simple but useful technique for standing back and seeing where patients stand. It assists them in assessing their situation and tracking progress as they move along on their personal timeline. They assign a number, typically on a scale from zero to ten, to help measure abstract concepts like self-esteem, self-confidence, or willingness to change. Also used to gauge motivation, hopefulness, confidence, progress, anxiety, or depression.

Schema therapy (CBT): Integrates behavioral, cognitive, psychodynamic, emotion-focused, and GT techniques. The aim is to change or to reorganize the inner structures (schemata) that individuals have about their self-conceptions, others, and situations that interfere with their functioning. Involves altering excerption, consilience, and self-narratization.

Script analysis (TA): Premised on the notion that an individual's behavior is partly programmed by a "script" that was "written" by early transactions between mother, father, and child. Its examination uncovers the (sometimes quarantined) nonconscious injunctions, decisions, fantasies, attitudes, and games about how life shall be lived. Because they are learned, scripts can be unlearned and rewritten.

Self-as-context (ACT): One of ACT's six core therapeutic processes. The mind has two elements: "thinking self" and "observing self." The former is the part that generates cognitions, beliefs, memories, judgments, plans, etc. Few of us consider the observing self—that aspect of ourselves that is aware of whatever we are thinking, feeling, sensing, or doing. Though we experience bodily, cognitive, emotional, and sociopsychological changes (new role-selves), the transcendent "I" that observes all these adjustments and transformations never changes; it is ceaselessly meta-framing one step ahead of us. The transcendent "I" is pure awareness, i.e., self-as-context. The more we appreciate this type of high-level subjectivity, the more we can thrive as self-autonomous and self-directed beings.

Self-control procedures (BT): Through self-reinforcement, bolstered by biofeedback and progressive relaxation, individuals learn how to maintain a new behavior, so that an individual's sense of agency, self-confidence, and self-autonomy are enhanced. Self-reinforcement transpires when: (1) one's "I" instructs one's "me"; (2) then one's "me," via self-reflexivity, transforms into one's "I"; (3) one's "I" again re-instructs one's "me"; and (4) the cycle repeats, forming a recursive looping system. Used to address anger, impulsivity, insomnia, tension headaches, pain, and stress.

Self-disclosure (FET): Self-disclosure on the part of the therapist to patients helps equalize the therapeutic relationship and provides modeling. If cautiously done, revealing elements of self-individuation can empower and grant confidence to others.

Self-instructional training (BT, CBT): The therapist identifies patients' maladaptive thoughts, models more adaptive behaviors, and suggests constructive self-instructions. Patients rehearse the behavior while verbalizing aloud the instructions or self-statements, which are in fact better described as "statements-to-self" ("I" commands "me"). Self-defeating beliefs are replaced with self-enhancing cognitions.

Self-monitoring (BT): Patients are asked to keep an account of a specific event or reaction and to record their attempts to alter their habits (e.g., dieting). One's "I" observes the behavior of one's "me"; if patients recognize how the two facets of selfhood interact, a sense of "being watched" can instill a sense of encouragement, e.g., frequency, amount of time spent on an activity, form and place of occurrence, concomitant feelings.

Self-monitoring (CBT): "Diary work" used to document the degree and amount of change in targeted thoughts or behaviors occurring between sessions or during a given event or timeframe. Increases self-reflexivity.

Self-regard (CCT): The positive, self-reflexive aspect of selfhood that emerges from the cultivation of respect accorded to one's own person. Related to self-esteem and self-dignity.

Self-soothing (DBT): One of the four crisis-survival skills. A distress-tolerance skill. To distract from an unsettling situation or crisis using one's five senses (vision, hearing, smell, taste, touch). In this way one can shift focus to one's perceptual experiences and thereby arrest unhelpful runaway conscious interiorization.

Self-talk (CBT): One's "I" (active self) attempts to convince one's "me" (receptive self) to objectively examine one's automatic illogical thought patterns. When this is accomplished, altering one's habitual underlying assumptions responsible for maladaptive beliefs and behaviors becomes possible. This can be facilitated through positive self-statements, i.e., auto-communications that authorize our behavior.

Shadow work (JT): Addressing personal qualities that do not fit our self-image. Integrating facets of our selfhood that we try to hide from (anger, hatred, jealousy, greed, lust, shame). It may also address behaviors that are not culturally acceptable, such as aggression. Requires exploration of nonconscious processes that configure self-individuation (self-identity) as well as self-reflexivity.

Shame attacking (REBT): Have patients confront their fear of shame by acting in a way that ostensibly elicits social disapproval (e.g., putting shoes on the wrong feet) while activating coping skills that dispute and reframe one's shame-induced thinking. Patients then discover that the world does not come to end.

Shaping (BT): Behaviors that approximate or move toward the desired behavior are reinforced. Self-narratizing one's progress and focusing on excerpted links in behavioral chains can facilitate shaping.

Skills training (CBT, REBT): Utilizing in vivo demonstration and in-session practice, the therapist educates patients about breathing exercises, progressive relaxation, social skills (how one's role-selves impact others), and guided imagery (introceptually "seeing" oneself).

Socratic dialogue (CBT, REBT): Systematically triggering meta-framing by using questions to point out patients' maladaptive thoughts. Such queries may focus on clarification; probing assumptions or motivations; analyzing viewpoints; scrutinizing outcomes; and employing questions about questions. Enhances self-reflexivity.

Splitting (GT): Individuals split off one of their role-selves, turning it into the polar opposite. They may be unaware of one of the poles. People might vacillate between these opposed facets of selfhood.

Splitting (PDT): Defense mechanism. Objects triggering anxiety are dichotomized into representations of either "all good" or "all bad," becoming "part-objects." An individual mentally edits material about themselves or others with extreme positive or negative qualities. Associated with borderline personality disorder.

Stepping out of character (REBT): See **paradoxical directive.**

Storytelling (PT): Patients create a "show" with the therapist as audience, recounting events, concerns, and issues that led them to treatment. From this dramatized unfolding of a personal timeline, the therapist can acquire information about what patients find vexing. Or the therapist might make use of allegories or symbols to facilitate patients' understanding of issues or instill coping skills.

Stress inoculation (CBT): Combining relaxation skills, systematic desensitization, and other techniques to prepare patients to better cope with stress-triggering events or circumstances ("inoculating" as if against a physical disease). The therapist educates patients about self-talk, guiding their "I" on how to persuade their "me" to think positively, as well as teaching the value of going beyond and surveying one's circumstances (role-playing and rehearsal).

Structural analysis (TA): Conducting first- and second-order analysis by surveying ego states (parent, adult, child), as well as transactions between them as they act and interact with others in the lives of patients.

Subjective reasoning (CBT): Believing that feelings are the same as, or equal to, facts, i.e., the tendency to excerpt the hot/warm affective aspects of cognition while editing out the cold/cool facets of cognition that are associated more with objective observations.

Sublimation (PAT, PDT): Defense mechanism. The rechanneling of unacceptable instinctual energies to objectives that are more socially acceptable to one's ego and superego (i.e., more aligned with one's self-conception).

Substitution (PAT, PDT): Defense mechanism. Substituting one emotion for another, e.g., anger is used to mask one's fear. Such a psychic maneuver is possible due to the ability to dramatize different self-presentations, i.e., one's "I" can mentally select different "me's." In this way the primary affect is not processed or dealt with.

Suppression (PAT, PDT): Defense mechanism. How unacceptable feelings are dealt with. Controlling patterns of excerption by quarantining distracting and distressing thoughts in the nonconscious.

Surplus reality (PD): A key concept in psychodrama that recognizes how imaginary, hypothetical cognition is central to human experience. The spatialization of psyche generates quasi-perceptions, making possible mental time travel and teleportation. Examples include meeting a future imagined partner; a scene of forgiveness or apologizing to others for one's own wrongdoing; a conversation with a relative who has passed; a scene from the future in which one looks back over one's life (prospective-retrospective self-narratization); an encounter with a spiritual entity.

Symptom prescription (FT). What family members consider "uncontrollable" is encouraged by the therapist, who recommends that the problematic behavior not only be allowed but promoted (or a behavior is given a time and space to be acted out). Not only are power and control structures made apparent, but members gain a sense of agency (self-autonomy) and are able to step back from their circumstances and gain perspective.

Systematic desensitization (BT, CBT): Sometimes referred to as exposure therapy. Used to address specific phobias and other anxiety disorders. Initially patients are taught relaxation skills. Then a hierarchy of increasingly anxiety-producing stimuli is agreed upon. Patients begin with the least difficult circumstances and work toward the most anxiety-producing situation, thereby neutralizing their reaction to the stimulus. The objective is to have patients learn to cope with, overcome, and extinguish fear in each step of the hierarchy. Relaxation may be paired with exposure to something patients report as stressful. Patients are taught to relax in response to the anxiety-producing situation, altering the previously paired response. Patients learn to put a distance between their "I" and their problematic excerptions. Systematic desensitization can be done in vitro (imaginal exposure) or in vivo (real-life exposure).

Tap into all systems (GST): Premised on the notion that the therapist–patient relationship is temporary and time-limited, while patients' involvement in other systems (kinship, schools, work, governmental agencies, schools, spiritual communities) is long-lasting and multifaceted. Encouraging patients to take advantage of extra-therapeutic support can be key to long-term recovery; this enhances self-autonomy.

Task setting (ADT): In order to eliminate negative feelings, patients are given tasks that educate them about the significance and value of assuming responsibility for their own lives, thereby increasing social interests as well as self-autonomy.

Thought stopping (BT): Intended to persuade a person from allowing a series of mental extractions to flow in an unproductive direction. The idea is to devise a method of self-communication so one tells one's train of thoughts to "stop!" This way one can retrain and re-direct thinking patterns. This might be accomplished by wearing a rubber band on the wrist and popping it as a method to assist in redirecting thoughts, thereby mentally editing certain cognitions while deleting others.

Time projection (REBT): Patients are asked to introceive a feared or troubling event on their mental stage. Then patients are requested to imagine a temporal line stretching from the stage into the future, while narratizing themselves occupying points on the line representing one week after the event, then one month, six months, one year, etc. Patients are asked to imagine how they feel at each point.

Top dog (GT): The judgmental part of an individual that makes demands based on certain internalized moral standards and societal norms. Such excerpted "should's" and "ought's" produce anxiety and interiorized conflict. See **underdog**.

Transcendence of opposites (JT): Integrating psychic material, such as role-selves, demands a *coniunctio oppositorum* (conjunction of opposites). In an instance of standing above dichotomies, one's "I" excerpts polar opposites, embraces their contradictions, and considers them as a director would on one's mental stage. What emerges is a third, novel, transcendent element that drives forward self-individuation.

Transference (PAT, PDT): Projection by patients of feelings, wishes, and expectations onto the therapist. Such sentiments were originally directed toward significant individuals (typically parents) in a patient's childhood. This process may bring nonconsciously quarantined material to the here-and-now where it can be verbalized, re-experienced, and explored to locate the source of current problems. Working through memories, motives, and emotions can provide patients with new perspectives. In a broader sense, transference applies to any social interaction in which earlier attitudes and behaviors are replicated.

Transference distortion (PDT): See **parataxic distortion**.

Transparency and authenticity (CCT): The therapist displays openness, honesty, and directness vis-à-vis the client. The therapist's own self-autonomy and self-individuation, as well as challenges as a human being, are acknowledged, thereby instilling trust within the client and facilitating the healing endeavor.

Turning the mind (DBT): Orienting one's mind toward acceptance and away from rejecting reality. The first step to acceptance is commitment; this requires an act of self-autonomous choice. This is not a one-and-done act, but demands repeated and deeply consciously interiorized decisions and a bolstering of self-authorizing capabilities.

Two-chair technique (GT): An affective, experiential procedure in which patients dramatize dialogue with another person (or with a different part of the self) as symbolically represented by an empty chair. One's "I" discourses with a hypothetical other or one's role-selves; meanwhile, in the background another "I" directs the exchanges. The client may assume different roles by switching from one chair to the other.

Unconditional positive regard (CCT): A core condition of client-centered therapy. The therapist accepts patients without judgment, affords them dignity and respect, listens actively, and refrains from giving advice. In this way the patients' self-autonomy, self-authorization, and self-individuation are respected.

Underdog (GT): An individual self-justifies why personal moral demands or rules of social conduct are not met. Rationalizations and excuse-making (mental extractions) allay feelings of guilt or shame; this leads to self-sabotage, ensuring that the demands are never met. See **top dog**.

Undoing (PDT): Defense mechanism. Reversing a perceived untoward behavior; canceling out a wrongdoing. The ability to self-narratize convinces one that it is possible to travel back in time and ritualistically perform an act that is the opposite of the original act.

Unique outcomes (NT): By relying on the as-if perspective, patients attempt to recount a life storyline that differs from the negative one that is holding them back.

Values (ACT): One of ACT's six core therapeutic processes. Values are desired qualities of how a person wants to act on an ongoing basis. Clarifying what matters to oneself is a necessary first step in creating a meaningful life; this requires a self-reflexive, self-interrogation of what one really wants from life. "Chosen life directions" guide our ongoing self-narratizing journey through life.

Vicarious learning (BT, CBT): Acquiring behaviors or coping skills through imitating the performance of others. A sequenced, adaptive type of role-playing transpires: (1) "I" observes another; (2) "I" directs one's own "me" to practice new abilities or enact more adaptive role-selves; (3) constructive information is internalized. Also called modeling or observational learning (cf. vicarious conditioning in ethology).

Visualization (CBT, PT): An elementary and fundamental FOCI grounded in the introceptual spatialization of mental events. Allows one to transcend spatiotemporal barriers, i.e., "traveling" to another imaginary place (retrospecting or prospecting one's "me's" along a timeline of personal events; envisioning one's improved, idealized self). Mentally evoking quasi-perceptual qualia permits one to creatively engage hypothetical psychoscapes, thereby "seeing" problems from different angles. One can consider one's choices and reconsider one's strengths.

Vitality (ACT): Premised on developing a sense of meaning and purpose; to engage fully in a value-guided life no matter one's circumstances. Realizing that there is as much living in a moment of sorrow as in a moment of happiness, one's transcendent "I" rises above distracting mental editing, temporary feelings, and embraces the here-and-now.

Will to meaning (EXT): A central theme running through the works of neurologist, psychiatrist, and Holocaust survivor Viktor Frankl (1905–1997). Requires intense self-reflexivity and a keen attention to self-individuation.

Willfulness (DBT): Refusing to make necessary changes. Resisting helpful suggestions. The opposite of adaptive, effective behavior. One comes to believe one's own propaganda that one can solve any problem. The gap between one's "I" and "me" (actual abilities or competent role-selves) is so great that self-objectivity and self-corrective abilities are eroded.

Willingness (DBT): Making necessary changes. Acting effectively. Doing what is called for in each situation. Listening mindfully to one's wise mind. Responding genuinely to one's self-individuated nature.

Wise mind (DBT): The belief that we can control our emotional mind with our reasonable mind is misleading. Accomplished via integration that transcends above one's emotional and reasonable mind, opening up the self-objective aspect of one's being. Wise mind is that facet of each of us that experiences truth and finds balance.

"You" statements: These come off as accusatory, imperative, and demanding. They may sound like an attack and make others defensive. Evokes the "me" mode of emotional experiencing and increases feelings of being targeted in the person addressed; threatens self-autonomy.

References

Ahn, H., & Wampold, B. E. (2001). Where oh where are the specific ingredients? A meta-analysis of component studies in counseling and psychotherapy. *Journal of Counseling Psychology*, 48(3), 251–257.

American Psychiatric Association. (2013). *Diagnostic and statistical manual of mental disorders* (5th ed.). Washington, DC: American Psychiatric Association.

Ancis, J. (2013). Counselors for social justice position statement on DSM-5. Online pdf. Retrieved from: https://www.scribd.com/document/141283235/Counselors-for-Social-Justice-Position-Statement-on-DSM-5

Antony, M. M. (2014). Behavior therapy. In D. Wedding & R. J. Corsini (Eds.), *Current psychotherapies* (10th ed.) (pp. 193–229). Belmont, CA: Brooks/Cole, Cengage Learning.

APA report of the task force on gender identity and gender variance (2008). Washington DC: American Psychiatric Association.

Ariely, D. (2012). *The (honest) truth about dishonesty: How we lie to everyone—especially ourselves*. New York: Perennial Harper.

Arredondo, P., Toporek, R., Brown, S. P., Jones, J., Locke, D. C., Sanchez, J., Stadler, H. (1996). Operationalization of the multicultural counseling competencies. *Journal of Multicultural Counseling and Development*, 24(1), 42–78.

Asnaani, A., & Foa, E. B. (2014). Expanding the lens of evidence-based practice in psychotherapy to include a common factors perspective: Comment on Laska, Gurman, and Wampold. *Psychotherapy*, 51(4), 487–490.

Atkinson, D. R., Morten, G., & Sue, D. W. (1998). *Counseling American minorities* (5th ed.). New York: McGraw-Hill.

Averill, J. R. (2009). Emotional creativity: Toward "spiritualizing the passions." In S. J. Lopez & C. R. Snyder (Eds.), *The Oxford handbook of positive psychology* (pp. 249–257). New York: Oxford University Press.

Baghramian, M., & Nicholson, A. (2013). The puzzle of self-deception. *Philosophy Compass*, 8(11), 1018–1029.

Balint, M. (1948). On the psychoanalytic training system. *International Journal of Psychoanalysis*, 29, 163–173.

Bandura, A. (1997). *Self-efficacy: The exercise of control*. New York: Freeman.

Bargh, J. A. (1997). The automaticity of everyday life. In R. S. Wyer, Jr. (Ed.), *The automaticity of everyday life* (pp. 1–62). Mahwah, NJ: Lawrence Erlbaum Associates.

Barrett, L. F. (2017a). *How emotions are made: The secret life of the brain*. New York: Houghton Mifflin Harcourt.

Barrett, L. F. (2017b). The theory of constructed emotion: An active inference account of interoception and categorization. *Social Cognitive and Affective Neuroscience*, 12(1), 1–23.

Barth, R. P., Lee, B. R., Lindsey, M. A., Collins, K. S., Strieder, F., Chorpita, B. F., Becker, K. D., & Sparks, J. A. (2012). Evidence-based practice at a crossroads: The timely emergence of common elements and common factors. *Research on Social Work Practice*, 22(1), 108–119.

Bateson, G. (1972). *Steps to an ecology of mind*. New York: Ballantine Books.

Batson, C. D., Ahmad, N., & Lishner, D. A. (2009). Empathy and altruism. In S. J. Lopez & C. R. Snyder (Eds.), *The Oxford handbook of positive psychology* (pp. 417–426). New York: Oxford University Press.

Baumeister, R. F., & Sommer, K. L. (1997). Consciousness, free choice, and automaticity. In Robert S. Wyer, Jr. (Ed.), *The automaticity of everyday life* (pp. 75–81). Mahwah, NJ: Lawrence Erlbaum Associates.

Bayne, T., & Fernandez, J. eds. (2008). *Delusion and self-deception: Affective and motivational influences on belief formation.* New York: Taylor and Francis.

Beavan, V. (2011). Towards a definition of "hearing voices": A phenomenological approach. *Psychosis: Psychological, Social and Integrative Approaches*, 3(1), 63–73.

Beck, A. T., & Weishaar, M. E. (2014). Cognitive therapy. In D. Wedding & R. J. Corsini (Eds.), *Current psychotherapies* (10th ed.) (pp. 231-264). Belmont, CA: Brooks/Cole, Cengage Learning.

Beischel, J., Rock, A. J., & Krippner, S. (2011). Reconceptualizing the fields of altered consciousness: A 50-year retrospective. In E. Cardeña & M. Winkelman (Eds.), *Altering consciousness: Multidisciplinary perspectives: History, culture, and the humanities; biological and psychological perspectives* (2 vols.) (pp. 113-135). Santa Barbara, CA: Praeger/ABC-C.

Beutler, L. E. (2014). Welcome to the party, but. . . . *Psychotherapy*, 51(4), 496-499.

Billig, Michael. (1995). *Banal nationalism.* London: Sage.

Bion, W. R. (1963). *Elements of psycho-analysis.* London: Karnac Books.

Boehm, J. K., & Lyubomirsky, S. (2009). The promise of sustainable happiness. In S. J. Lopez & C. R. Snyder (Eds.), *The Oxford handbook of positive psychology* (pp. 667-678). New York: Oxford University Press.

Bohart, A. (2000). The client is the most important common factor. *Journal of Psychotherapy Integration*, 10(2), 127-149.

Bohart, A., & Tallman, K. (1999). *What clients do to make therapy work.* Washington, DC: American Psychological Association.

Boneau, C. A. (1990). Psychological literacy: A first approximation. *American Psychologist*, 45(7), 891-900.

Boniwell, I. (2009). Perspectives on time. In S. J. Lopez & C. R. Snyder (Eds.), *The Oxford handbook of positive psychology* (pp. 295-302). New York: Oxford University Press.

Bordin, E. S. (1979). The generalizability of the psychoanalytic concept of the working alliance. *Psychotherapy: Theory, Research, and Practice*, 16(3), 252–260.

Bortolotti, L., & Mameli, M. (2012). Self-deception, delusion and the boundaries of folk psychology. *Humanamente*, 20, 203-221.

Boscolo, L., Cecchin, G., Hoffman, L., & Penn, P. (1987). *Milan systemic family therapy.* New York: W. W. Norton.

Boszormenyi-Nagy, I., & Framo, J. L. (1985). *Intensive family therapy.* New York: Brunner/ Mazel.

Boszormenyi-Nagy, I., & Spark, G. (1973). *Invisible loyalties.* New York: Harper & Row.

Bowen, M. (1959). Family relationships in schizophrenia. In A. Auerback (Ed.), *Schizophrenia: An integrated approach* (pp. 147–178). New York: Ronald.

Bowen, M. (1976). Toward the differentiation of self in one's own family. In J. L. Framo (Ed.), *Family interaction: A dialogue between family researchers and family therapists* (pp. 111–173). New York: Springer-Verlag.

Bronfenbrenner, U. (1979). *The ecology of human development* (pp. 16–42). Cambridge, MA: Harvard University Press.

Brown, D. (2016). Afterword. In A. Raz & M. Lifshitz (Eds.), *Hypnosis and meditation: Toward an integrative science of conscious planes* (pp. 449-457). Oxford: Oxford University Press.

Brubaker, R. (2002). Ethnicity without groups. *Archives Européennes de Sociologie*, XLIII(2), 163-189.

Brubaker, R., & Cooper, F. (2000). Beyond "identity." *Theory and Society*, 29(1), 1-47.

Buser, S. (2014). *DSM-5 insanely simplified.* Asheville, NC: Chiron Publications.

Bussolari, C. J., & Goodell, J. A. (2009). Chaos theory as a model for life transitions counseling: Nonlinear dynamics and life's changes. *Journal of Counseling & Development*, 87(1), 98-107.

Buzsáki, G. (2006). *Rhythms of the brain*. New York: Oxford University Press.

Byng-Hill, J. (1995). Creating a secure family base: Some implications of attachment theory for family therapy. *Family Process*, 34(1), 45-58.

Cardeña, E. (2014). Hypnosis and psyche: How hypnosis has contributed to the study of consciousness. *Psychology of Consciousness: Theory, Research, and Practice*, 1(2), 123-138.

Cardeña, E. (2016). Toward comprehensive neurophenomenological research in hypnosis and meditation. In A. Raz & M. Lifshitz (Eds.), *Hypnosis and meditation: Towards an integrative science of conscious planes* (pp. 281-302). Oxford: Oxford University Press.

Carver, C. S. (1997). Associations to automaticity. In R. S. Wyer, Jr. (Ed.), *The automaticity of everyday life* (pp. 95-103). Mahwah, NJ: Lawrence Erlbaum Associates.

Carver, C. S., Scheier, M. F., & Segerstrom, S. C. (2010). Optimism. *Clinical Psychology Review*, 30(7), 879-889.

Carver, C. S., Scheier, M. F., Miller, C. J., & Fulford, D. (2009). Optimism. In S. J. Lopez & C. R. Snyder (Eds.), *The Oxford handbook of positive psychology* (pp. 303-312). New York: Oxford University Press.

Cassell, E. J. (2009). Compassion. In C. R. Snyder (Eds.), *The Oxford handbook of positive psychology* (pp. 393-404). New York: Oxford University Press.

Castelnuovo, G., Faccio, E., Molinari, E., Nardone, G., & Salvini, A. (2004). A critical review of empirically supported treatments (ESTs) and common factors perspective in psychotherapy. *Brief Strategic and Systemic Therapy European Review*, 1(27), 208-224.

Charuvastra, A., & Cloitre, M. (2008). Social bonds and posttraumatic stress disorder. *Annual Review of Psychology*, 59, 301-328.

Chin, J., Hayward, M., & Drinna, A. (2008). "Relating" to voices: Exploring the relevance of this concept to people who hear voices. *Psychology and Psychotherapy: Theory, Research and Practice*, 82(1), 1-17.

Chomsky, N. (1957). *Syntactic structures*. The Hague/Paris: Mouton.

Chwalisz, K. (2001). A common factors revolution: Let's not "cut off our discipline's nose to spite its face." *Journal of Counseling Psychology*, 48(3), 262-267.

Clark, A. (2013). Whatever next? Predictive brains, situated agents, and the future of cognitive science. *Behavioral and Brain Sciences*, 36(3), 181-204.

Cohn, M. A., & Fredrickson, B. L. (2009). Positive emotions. In S. J. Lopez & C. R. Snyder (Eds.), *The Oxford handbook of positive psychology* (pp. 13-24). New York: Oxford University Press.

Compton, C., & Hoffman, E. (2013). *Positive psychology: The science of happiness and flourishing*. Belmont, CA: Wadsworth.

Connors, G. J., DiClemente, C. C., Carroll, K. M., Longabaugh, R., & Donovan, D. M. (1997). The therapeutic alliance and its relationship to alcoholism treatment participation and outcome. *Journal of Consulting and Clinical Psychology*, 65(4), 588-598.

Connors, M. H., Barnier, A. J., Langdon, R., Cox, R. E., Polito, V., & Coltheart, M. (2014). Delusions in the hypnosis laboratory: Modeling different pathways to mirrored-self misidentification. *Psychology of Consciousness: Theory, Research, and Practice*, 1(2), 184-198.

Constantino, M. J., & Bernecker, S. L. (2014). Bridging the common factors and empirically supported treatment camps: Comment on Laska, Gurman, and Wampold. *Psychotherapy*, 51(4), 505-509.

Cooper, W. E. (1983). Introduction. In W. E. Cooper (Ed.), *Cognitive aspects of skilled typewriting* (pp. 1-38). New York: Springer-Verlag.

Corey, G. (2009). *Theory and practice of counseling and psychotherapy*. Washington, DC: Cengage Learning.

Corey, G. (2012). *Theory and practice of group counseling* (8th ed.). Belmont, CA: Brooks/Cole.

Corstens, D., Longden, E., & May, R. (2012). Talking with voices: Exploring what is expressed by the voices people hear. *Psychosis*, 4(2), 95–104.

Crits-Christoph, P. (1997). Limitations of the dodo bird verdict and the role of clinical trials in psychotherapy research. *Psychological Bulletin*, 122(3), 216–220.

Cross, W. E. (1995). *The psychology of Nigrescence: Revising the Cross model*. In J. G. Ponterotto, J. M. Casas, L. A. Suzuki, & C. M. Alexander (Eds.), *Handbook of multicultural counseling* (pp. 93–122). New York: Sage Publications.

Cruz, M. R., & Sonn, C. C. (2011). (De)colonizing culture in community psychology: Reflections from critical social science. *American Journal of Community Psychology*, 47(1), 203–214.

Cuijpers, P., Reijnders, M., & Huibers, M. J. H. (2019). The role of common factors in psychotherapy outcomes. *Annual Review of Clinical Psychology*, 15, 207-231.

Davis, G. C, & Nolen-Hoeksema (2009). Making sense of loss, perceiving benefits, and posttraumatic growth. In S. J. Lopez & C. R. Snyder (Eds.), *The Oxford handbook of positive psychology* (pp. 641–650). New York: Oxford University Press.

De Fruyt, F., & De Clercq, B. (2012). Childhood antecedents of personality disorders. In T. A. Widiger (Ed.), *The Oxford handbook of personality disorders* (pp. 166-185). New York: Oxford University Press.

de Shazer, S. (1982). *Patterns of brief family therapy: An ecosystemic approach*. New York: Guilford Press.

Deely, Q. (2016). Transforming experience through the meditation and ritual of chod. In A. Raz & M. Lifshitz (Eds.), *Hypnosis and meditation: Towards an integrative science of conscious planes* (pp. 39-54). Oxford: Oxford University Press.

Dennett, D. (1987). Consciousness. In R. L. Gregory (Ed.). *The Oxford companion to the mind* (pp. 160-164). Oxford, UK: Oxford University Press.

Dennett, D. (1991). *Consciousness explained*. New York: Little, Brown and Company.

Dickerson, S. S., & Zoccola, P. M. (2009). *Toward a biology of social support*. In S. J. Lopez & C. R. Snyder (Eds.), *The Oxford handbook of positive psychology* (pp. 519–526). Oxford: Oxford University Press.

Diener, E. (1984). Subjective well-being. *Psychological Bulletin*, 95(3), 542–575.

Diener, E. (2009). Positive psychology: Past, present, and future. In S. J. Lopez & C. R. Snyder (Eds.), *The Oxford handbook of positive psychology* (pp. 7-12). New York: Oxford University Press.

Diener, E., Oishi, S., & Lucas, R. E. (2009). Subjective well-being: The science of happiness and life satisfaction. In S. J. Lopez & C. R. Snyder (Eds.), *The Oxford handbook of positive psychology* (pp. 187-194). New York: Oxford University Press.

Diener, E., & Suh, E. M. (2000). *Culture and subjective well-being*. Cambridge, MA: MIT Press.

Dienes, Z., Lush, P., Semmens-Wheeler, R., Parkinson, J., Scott, R., & Nais, P. (2016). Hypnosis as self-deception: Meditation as self-insight. In A. Raz & M. Lifshitz (Eds.), *Hypnosis and meditation: Toward an integrative science of conscious planes* (pp. 107-128). Oxford: Oxford University Press.

Dienstbier, R. A., & Pytlik Zillig, L. M. (2009). Toughness. In S. J. Lopez & C. R. Snyder (Eds.), *The Oxford handbook of positive psychology* (pp. 537-548). New York: Oxford University Press.

Dodgson, P. G., & Wood, J. V. (1998). Self-esteem and the cognitive accessibility of strengths and weaknesses after failure. *Journal of Personality and Social Psychology*, 75(1), 178-197.

Doidge, N. (2007). *The brain that changes itself: Stories of personal triumph from the frontiers of brain science*. New York: Penguin.

Dow, J. (1986). Universal aspects of symbolic healing: A theoretical synthesis. *American Anthropologist*, 88(1), 56–69.

Duncan, B., & Miller, S. (2000). *The heroic client*. San Francisco, CA: Jossey-Bass.

Duncan, B. L. (2002a). The legacy of Saul Rosenzweig: The profundity of the dodo bird. *Journal of Psychotherapy Integration*, 12(1), 32–57.

Duncan, B. L. (2002b). The founder of common factors: A conversation with Saul Rosenzweig. *Journal of Psychotherapy Integration*, 12(1), 10–31.

Dunn, D. S., Uswatte, G., & Elliott, T. R. (2009). Happiness, resilience, and positive growth following physical disability: Issues for understanding, research, and therapeutic intervention. In S. J. Lopez & C. R. Snyder (Eds.), *The Oxford handbook of positive psychology* (pp. 651–664). New York: Oxford University Press.

Egan, A. (2008). Imagination, delusion, and self-deception. In B. Tim Bayne & J. Fernandez (Eds.), *Delusion and self-deception: Affective and motivational influences on belief formation* (pp. 263–280). New York: Psychology Press.

Ellenberger, H. F. (1970). *The discovery of the unconscious.* New York: Basic Books.

Emerson, R. W. (2015). *The complete works of Ralph Waldo Emerson: Representative men,* Vol. 4. New York: Andesite Press.

Epston, D. (1994). Extending the conversation. *Family Therapy Networker,* 18(6), 31–37.

Fall, K. A., Holden, J. M., & Marquis, A. (2017). *Theoretical models of counseling and psychotherapy* (3rd ed.). London: Routledge.

Farb, N. A. S. (2016). Self-transformation through hypnosis and mindfulness meditation. In A. Raz & M. Lifshitz (Eds.), *Hypnosis and meditation: Towards an integrative science of conscious planes* (pp. 381–396). Oxford: Oxford University Press.

Fasta, E., & Collin-Vézina, D. (2010). Historical trauma, race-based trauma and resilience of indigenous peoples: A literature review. *First Peoples and Child Review,* 5(1), 126–136.

Fava, G. A. (1999). Well-being therapy: Conceptual and technical issues. *Psychotherapy and Psychosomatics,* 68(4), 171–179.

Fava, G. A., & Ruini, C. (2003). Development and characteristics of a well-being enhancing psychotherapeutic strategy: Well-being therapy. *Journal of Behavior Therapy and Experimental Psychiatry,* 34(1), 45–63.

Ferenczi, S. (1931). Child analysis in the analysis of adults. In S. Ferenczi, M. Balint, & E. Mosbacher (Eds.), *Final contributions to the problems and methods of psychoanalysis* (pp. 126–142). London: Karnac.

Fernandez, J., & Bayne, T. (Eds.). (2008). *Delusions, self-deception and affective influences on belief-formation.* New York: Psychology Press.

Fonagy, P., Gergely, G., Jurist, E. L., & Target, M. (2002). *Affect regulation, mentalization and the development of the self.* New York: Other Books.

Fordyce, M. W. (1977). Development of a program to increase personal happiness. *Journal of Counseling Psychology,* 24(6), 511–521.

Fox, K. C. R., Kang, Y., Lifshitz, M., & Christoff, K. (2016). Increasing cognitive-emotional flexibility with meditation and hypnosis. In A. Raz & M. Lifshitz (Eds.), *Hypnosis and meditation: Towards an integrative science of conscious planes* (pp. 191–219). Oxford: Oxford University Press.

Frank, J. (1974). General psychotherapy: The restoration of morale, vol. 5. In D. Freedman & J. Dyrud (Eds.), *American Handbook of Psychiatry* (2nd ed.) (pp. 117–132). New York: Basic Books.

Frank, J. D., & Frank, J. B. (1991). *Persuasion and healing: A comparative study of psychotherapy.* Baltimore, MD: Johns Hopkins University Press.

Frankl, V. (1959 [1992]). *Man's search for meaning: An introduction to logotherapy.* Boston: Beacon Press.

Fredrickson, B. (2009). *Positivity: Groundbreaking research reveals how to embrace the hidden strength of positive emotions, overcome negativity, and thrive.* New York: Crown Archetype.

French, T. N. (1933). Interrelations between psychoanalysis and the experimental work of Pavlov. *American Journal of Psychiatry,* 89(6), 1165–1203.

Gallagher, S., & Shear, J. (Eds.) (1999). *Models of the self.* Exeter, UK: Imprint Academic.

Gans, H. J. (1979). Symbolic ethnicity: The future of ethnic groups and cultures in America. *Ethnic and Racial Studies,* 2(1), 1-20.

Garfield, S. L. (1995). *Psychotherapy: An eclectic-integrative approach* (2nd ed.). New York: John Wiley & Sons.

Gaston, L., Marmar, C. R., Thompson, L. W., & Gallagher, D. (1991). Alliance prediction of outcome: Beyond in-treatment symptomatic change as psychotherapy progresses. *Psychotherapy Research,* 1(2), 104-112.

Gendlin, E. T. (1962). *Experiencing and the creation of meaning.* New York: Free Press of Glencoe.

Gerrans, P. (2013). Delusional attitudes and default thinking. *Mind and Language,* 28(1), 83-102.

Gibbs, R. (1994). *The poetics of mind: Figurative thought, language, and understanding.* New York: Cambridge University Press.

Gibbs, R. (1999). Taking metaphor out of our heads and putting it into the cultural world. In R. Gibbs & G. Steen (Eds.), *Metaphor in cognitive linguistics* (pp. 145-166). Amsterdam: John Benjamins.

Gibbs, R. (2003). Embodied experience and linguistic meaning. *Brain and Language,* 84(1), 1-15.

Gibbs, R., & Steen, G. eds. (1999). *Metaphor in cognitive linguistics.* Amsterdam: John Benjamins.

Goffman, I. (1959). *The presentation of self in everyday life.* New York: Doubleday.

Goldenberg, I., Goldenberg, H., & Goldenberg Pelavin, E. (2014). Family Therapy. In D. Wedding, D., & R. J. Corsini (Eds.), *Current psychotherapies* (10th ed.) (pp. 373-410). Belmont, CA: Brooks/Cole.

Goldfried, M. R. (1980). Toward the delineation of therapeutic change principles. *American Psychologist,* 35(11), 991-999.

Goldman, R. N., & Greenberg, L. S. (2006). Promoting emotional expression and emotion regulation in couples. In D. K. Snyder, J. Simpson, & J. N. Hughes (Eds.), *Emotion regulation in couples and families: Pathways to dysfunction and health* (pp. 231-248). Washington, DC: American Psychological Association.

Goldstein, A. P., & Stein, N. (1976). *Prescriptive Psychotherapies.* Oxford: Pergamon Press.

Goleman, D. J. (1972). The Buddha on meditation and states of consciousness: Part I. The Teaching. Part II. A typology of meditation techniques. *The Journal of Transpersonal Psychology,* 4(1-2), 1-44, 151-210.

Goleman, D. J. (1985). *Vital lies, simple truths: The psychology of self-deception.* New York: Simon & Schuster.

Goleman, D. J. (1988). *The meditative mind: The varieties of meditative experience.* Los Angeles: UDS Tarcher.

Green, J. P., Laurence, J. R., & Lynn, S. J. (2014). Hypnosis and psychotherapy: From Mesmer to mindfulness. *Psychology of Consciousness: Theory, Research, and Practice,* 1(2), 199-212.

Greenberg, L., & Safran, J. (1987). *Emotion in psychotherapy: Affect, cognition, and the process of change.* New York: Guilford Press.

Greenberg, L. (2004). Emotion-focused therapy. *Clinical Psychology and Psychotherapy,* 11(1), 3-16.

Greenberg, L. S. (2007). Emotion-focused therapy: A video demonstration over six sessions. *PsycCRITIQUES.* Psychotherapy Video Series VII. Washington, DC: American Psychological Association.

Greenberg, L. S., & Johnson, S. M. (1988). *Emotionally focused therapy for couples.* New York: Guilford Press.

Greenberg, L. S., & Paivio, S. C. (1997). *Working with the emotions in psychotherapy.* New York: Guilford Press.

Greenwald, A. (1980). The totalitarian ego. *American Psychologist,* 35(7), 603–618.

Greenwald, A. G., & Banaji, M. R. (1995). Implicit social cognition: Attitudes, self-esteem, and stereotypes. *Psychological Review,* 102(1), 4–27.

Grencavage, L., & Norcross, J. (1990). Where are the commonalities among the therapeutic common factors? *Professional Psychology: Research and Practice,* 21(5), 372–378.

Gross, J. J. (1998). The emerging field of emotion regulation: An integrative review. *Review of General Psychology,* 2(3), 271–299.

Haley, J. (1963). *Strategies of psychotherapy.* New York: Grune & Stratton.

Haley, J. (1971). *Changing families.* New York: Grune & Stratton.

Halligan, P. W., & Oakley, D. A. (2014). Hypnosis and beyond: Exploring the broader domain of suggestion. *Psychology of Consciousness: Theory, Research, and Practice,* 1(2), 105–122.

Halsband, U., Mueller, S., Hinterberger, T., & Strickner, S. (2009). Plasticity changes in the brain in hypnosis and deditation. *Contemporary Hypnosis,* 26(4), 194–215.

Handelsman, M. M., Knapp, S., & Gottlieb, M. C. (2009). Positive ethics: Themes and variations. In S. J. Lopez & C. R. Snyder (Eds.), *The Oxford handbook of positive psychology* (pp. 105–113). New York: Oxford University Press.

Harrington, A. (2016). Thinking about trance over a century. In A. Raz & M. Lifshitz (Eds.), *Hypnosis and meditation: Towards an integrative science of conscious planes* (pp. 19–30). Oxford: Oxford University Press.

Harvey, J. H., & Pauwels, B. G. (2009). Relationship connection: A redux on the role of Minding and the quality of feeling special in the enhancement of closeness. In S. J. Lopez & C. R. Snyder (Eds.), *The Oxford handbook of positive psychology* (pp. 385–392). New York: Oxford University Press.

Havens, R. A., & Walters, C. (2012). *Hypnotherapy scripts: A neo-Erickson approach to persuasive healing.* Hover, East Sussex, UK: Brunner-Routledge.

Hays, P. A. (2008). *Addressing cultural complexities in practice* (2nd ed.). Washington, DC: American Psychological Association.

Hayward, M., Overton, J., Dorey, T., & Denney, J. (2008). Relating therapy for people who hear voices: A case series. *Clinical Psychology and Psychotherapy,* 16(3), 216–227.

Heine, R. W. (1953). A comparison of patients' reports on psychotherapeutic experience with psychoanalytic, nondirective and Adlerian therapists. *American Journal of Psychotherapy,* 7(1), 16–23.

Hendrick, C., & Hendrick, S. S. (2009). Love. In S. J. Lopez & C. R. Snyder (Eds.), *The Oxford handbook of positive psychology* (pp. 447–454). New York: Oxford University Press.

Heppner, P. P., & Lee, D. G. (2009). Problem-solving appraisal and psychological adjustment. In S. J. Lopez & C. R. Snyder (Eds.), *The Oxford handbook of positive psychology* (pp. 345–356). New York: Oxford University Press.

Hewitt, J. P. (2009). The social construction of self-esteem. In S. J. Lopez & C. R. Snyder (Eds.), *The Oxford handbook of positive psychology* (pp. 217–224). New York: Oxford University Press.

Higgins, R. L., & Gallagher, M. W. (2009). Reality negotiation. In S. J. Lopez & C. R. Snyder (Eds.), *The Oxford handbook of positive psychology* (pp. 475–482). New York: Oxford University Press.

Hilgard, E. R. (1977). *Divided consciousness: Multiple controls in human thought and action.* New York: Wiley-Interscience.

Hilgard, E. R. (1992). Dissociation and theories of hypnosis. In E. Fromm and M. Nash (Eds.), *Contemporary hypnosis research* (pp. 69–101). New York: Guilford.

Hill, C. E. (2014). *Helping skills: Facilitating exploration, insight and action* (4th ed.). Washington, DC: American Psychological Association.

Hoch, P. (1955). Aims and limitations of psychotherapy. *American Journal of Psychiatry*, 112(5), 321–327.

Hodgson, S. (1870). *The theory of practice*. London: Longmans Green.

Hoffman, L. (1981). *Foundations of family therapy*. New York: Basic Books.

Hohwy, J. (2012). Attention and conscious perception in the hypothesis testing brain. *Frontiers in Psychology*, 3(96), 1–14. https://doi.org/10.3389/fpsyg.2012.00096

Holroyd, J. (2003). The science of meditation and the state of hypnosis. *American Journal of Clinical Hypnosis*, 4(2), 109–128.

Huang, P. H., & Blumenthal, J. A. (2009). Positive institutions, law, and policy. In S. J. Lopez & C. R. Snyder (Eds.), *The Oxford handbook of positive psychology* (pp. 589–597). New York: Oxford University Press.

Hubble, M. A., Duncan, B. L., & Miller, S. D. (1999). *The heart and soul of change: What works in therapy*. Washington, DC: American Psychological Association.

Huebner, E. S., Gilman, R., Reschly, A. L., & Hall, R. (2009). Positive schools. In S. J. Lopez & C. R. Snyder (Eds.), *The Oxford handbook of positive psychology* (pp. 561–568). New York: Oxford University Press.

Huemer, J., Hall, R. E., & Steiner, H. (2012). Developmental approaches to the diagnosis and treatment of eating disorders. In J. Lock (Ed.), *The Oxford handbook of child and adolescent eating disorders: Developmental perspectives* (pp. 39–55). New York: Oxford University Press.

Huxley, T. H. (1896). On the hypothesis that animals are automata, and its history. In L. Huxley (Ed.), *Methods and Results: Essays* (pp. 199–250). New York: D. Appleton and Company.

Isen, A. M. (2009). A role for neuropsychology in understanding the facilitating influence of positive affect on social behavior and cognitive processes. In S. J. Lopez & C. R. Snyder (Eds.), *The Oxford handbook of positive psychology* (pp. 503–518). New York: Oxford University Press.

Jackson, D. D. (1957). The question of family homeostasis. *Psychiatric Quarterly Supplement*, 31(1), 79–90.

Jacobson, N. S., & Christensen, A. (1996). Studying the effectiveness of psychotherapy: How well can clinical trials do the job? *American Psychologist*, 51(10), 1031–1039.

James, W. (1890). *Principles of Psychology*. New York: Holt.

Jamieson, G. A. (2016). A unified theory of hypnosis and meditation states: The interoceptive predictive coding approach. In A. Raz & M. Lifshitz (Eds.), *Hypnosis and meditation: Towards an integrative science of conscious planes* (pp. 313–342). Oxford: Oxford University Press.

Jaynes, J. (1976). *The origin of consciousness in the breakdown of the bicameral mind*. Boston, MA: Houghton Mifflin.

Jaynes, J. (1982). A two-tiered theory of emotion: Affect and emotions. *Behavioral and Brain Sciences*, 5, 434–435. Reprinted in M. Kuijsten (Ed.) (2012a), *The Julian Jaynes collection: Biography, articles, lectures, interviews, discussion* (pp. 147–151). Henderson, NV: Julian Jaynes Society.

Jaynes, J. (1991). Afterword. *The origin of consciousness in the breakdown of the bicameral mind* (2nd ed.). Boston, MA: Houghton Mifflin.

Jaynes, J. (2012a). Consciousness and the voices of the mind: McMaster-Bauer Symposium discussion. In M. Kuijsten (Ed.), *The Julian Jaynes collection: Biography, articles, lectures, interviews, discussion* (pp. 300–319). Henderson, NV: Julian Jaynes Society.

Jaynes, J. (2012b). Consciousness and the voices of the mind: Tufts University discussion. In M. Kuijsten (Ed.), *The Julian Jaynes collection: Biography, articles, lectures, interviews, discussion* (pp. 288–293). Henderson, NV: Julian Jaynes Society.

Jaynes, J. (2012c). The Consequences of consciousness: Emory University discussion. In M. Kuijsten (Ed.), *The Julian Jaynes collection: Biography, articles, lectures, interviews, discussion* (pp. 345–356). Henderson, NV: Julian Jaynes Society.

Jaynes, J. (2012d). Sensory pain and conscious pain. In M. Kuijsten (Ed.), *The Julian Jaynes collection: Biography, articles, lectures, interviews, discussion* (pp. 168-173). Henderson, NV: Julian Jaynes Society.

Jinpa, T. (2016). Visualization as mental cultivation. In A. Raz & M. Lifshitz (Eds.), *Hypnosis and meditation: Towards an integrative science of conscious planes* (pp. 31-38). Oxford: Oxford University Press.

Johnson, J., Gooding, P. A., Wood, A. M., &Tarrier, N. (2010). Resilience as positive coping appraisals: Testing the schematic appraisals model of suicide (SAMS). *Behavior Research and Therapy*, 48(3), 179-186.

Johnson, S. M. (2011). *Emotionally focused therapy for couples: Key concepts*. Retrieved from: https://www.scribd.com/document/149286423/EFT-Couples-Key-Concepts.

Johnson, S. M., & Greenberg, L. S. (1987). Emotionally focused marital therapy: An overview. *Psychotherapy: Theory, Research, Practice, Training*, 24(3S), 552-560.

Johnson, S., & Bradley, B. (2009). Emotionally focused couple therapy: Creating loving relationships. In J. H. Bray & M. Stanton (Eds.), *Handbook of family psychology* (pp. 402-415). Oxford: Wily-Blackwell.

Johnson, S., Hunsley, J., Greenberg, L., & Schindler, D. (1999). Emotionally focused couples therapy: Status and challenges (A meta-analysis). *Journal of Clinical Psychology: Science and Practice*, 6(1), 67-79.

Jones, E., Fear, N. T., & Wessel, S. (2007). Shell shock and mild traumatic brain injury: A historical review. *American Journal of Psychiatry*, 164(11), 1641-1645.

Jones, M., & Coffey, M. (2012). Voice hearing: A secondary analysis of talk by people who hear voices. *International Journal of Mental Health Nursing*, 21, 50-59.

Jørgensen, C. R. (2004). Active ingredients in individual psychotherapy: Searching for common factors. *Psychoanalytic Psychology*, 21(4), 516-540.

Jourard, S. (1971). *The transparent self*. New York: Van Nostrand Reinhold.

Kahneman, D., Krueger, A. B., Schkade, D., Schwarz, N., Stone, A. A. (2006). Would you be happier if you were richer? A focusing illusion. *Science* 312, 1908-1910.

Kashdan, T. B., & Silvia, P. J. (2009). Curiosity and interest: The benefits of thriving on novelty and challenge. In S. J. Lopez & C. R. Snyder (Eds.), *The Oxford handbook of positive psychology* (pp. 367-374). New York: Oxford University Press.

Kaufman, M. (2007). In memoriam: The idioverse of Saul Rosenzweig (1907-2004). *Journal of Psychotherapy Integration*, 17(4), 363-368.

Keim, J. (1999). Strategic therapy. In F. F. Prevatt & D. M. Lawson (Eds.), *Casebook in family therapy* (pp. 146-168). Pacific Grove, CA: Brooks/Cole.

Kempler, W. (1981). *Experiential psychotherapy within families*. New York: Brunner/Mazel.

Kerr, M. (2003). Multigenerational family systems theory of Bowen and its application. In G. P. Sholevar (Ed.), *Textbook of family and couples therapy: Clinical applications* (pp. 103-126). Arlington, VA: American Psychiatric Publishing.

Keyes, C. L. M. (2002). The mental health continuum: From languishing to flourishing in life. *Journal of Health and Social Behavior*, 43(2), 207-222.

Keyes, C. L. M. (2005). Mental illness and/or mental health? Investigating axioms of the complete state of model of health. *Journal of Consulting and Clinical Psychology*, 73(3), 539-548.

Keyes, C. L. M. (2007). Promoting and protecting mental health as flourishing: A complementary strategy for improving national mental health. *American Psychologist*, 62(2), 95-108.

Keyes, C. L. M. (2009). Toward a science of mental health. In S. J. Lopez & C. R. Snyder (Eds.), *The Oxford handbook of positive psychology* (pp. 89-96). New York: Oxford University Press.

Keyes, C. L. M. (2014). Mental health as a complete state: How the salutogenic perspective completes the picture. In G. F. Bauer & O. Hämmig (Eds.), *Bridging occupational, organizational and public health: A transdisciplinary approach* (pp. 179-192). New York: Springer.

Khilstrom, J. F. (1987). The cognitive unconscious. *Science*, 137, 1445-51.

Kirmayer, L. (1986). Word magic and the rhetoric of common sense: Erickson's metaphors for mind. *International Journal of Clinical and Experimental Hypnosis*, 36(3), 157-182.

Kirschman, K. J. B., Johnson, R. J., Bender, J. A., & Roberts, M. C. (2009). Positive psychology for children and adolescents: Development, prevention, and promotion. In S. J. Lopez & C. R. Snyder (Eds.), *The Oxford handbook of positive psychology* (pp. 133-148). New York: Oxford University Press.

Klein, M. (1946). Notes on some schizoid mechanisms. *International Journal of Psycho-Analysis*, 27, 99-110.

Klein, M., Dittmann, A. T., Parloff, M. B., & Gill, M. M. (1969). Behavior therapy: Observations and reflections. *Journal of Consulting and Clinical Psychology*, 33(3), 259-266.

Kogo, N., & Trengove, C. (2015). Is predictive coding theory articulated enough to be testable? *Frontiers in Computational Neuroscience*, 9(111), 1-4. https://doi.org/10.3389/fncom.2015.00111.

Kornhuber, H. H. (1988). The human brain: From dream and cognition to fantasy, will, conscience, and freedom. In H. J. Markowitsch (Ed.), *Information processing by the brain* (pp. 241-258). Toronto: Hans Huber Publication.

Kövecses, Z. (2000). *Metaphor and emotion: Language, culture, and body in human feeling.* Cambridge and New York: Cambridge University Press.

Kövecses, Z. (2002). *Metaphor: A practical introduction.* Oxford: Oxford University Press.

Kövecses, Z. (2003). Language, figurative thought, and cross-cultural comparison. In F. Boers (Ed.), Special Issue on cross-cultural differences in conceptual metaphor: Applied linguistics perspective. *Metaphor and Symbol*, 18(4), 311-320.

Kövecses, Z. (2004). Introduction: Cultural variation in metaphor. Special issue. *European Journal of English Studies*, 8, 263-274.

Kövecses, Z. (2005). *Metaphor in culture: Universality and variation.* Cambridge: Cambridge University Press.

Krause, T. (2019). *Hypnosis and consciousness: An examination of the relationship between hypnosis and the concept of consciousness.* Master's thesis, Leiden University.

Kross, E., & Ayduk, O. (2017). Self-distancing: Theory, research and current directions. *Advances in Experimental Social Psychology*, 55, 81-136.

Krupnick, J. L., Sotsky, S. M., Simmens, S., Moyher, J., Elkin, I., Watkins, J., & Pilkonis, P. A. (1996). The role of the therapeutic alliance in psychotherapy and pharmacotherapy outcome: Findings in the National Institute of Mental Health treatment of depression collaborative research project. *Journal of Consulting and Clinical Psychology*, 64(3), 532-539.

Kubie, L. (1943). Manual of emergency treatment of acute war neuroses. *War Medicine*, 4, 582-598.

Kuijsten, M. (Ed.). (2006). *Reflections on the dawn of consciousness.* Henderson, NV: Julian Jaynes Society.

Kuijsten, M. (Ed.). (2012a). *The Julian Jaynes collection: Biography, articles, lectures, interviews, discussion.* Henderson, NV: Julian Jaynes Society.

Kuijsten, M. (2012b). Hypnosis as a vestige of the bicameral mind. *Contemporary Hypnosis & Integrative Therapy*, 29(3), 213-224.

Kuijsten, M. (Ed.). (2016). *Gods, visions and the bicameral mind: The theories of Julian Jaynes.* Henderson, NV: Julian Jaynes Society.

Lambert, M. J., & Bergin, A. E. (1994). The effectiveness of psychotherapy. In A. E. Bergin & S. L. Garfield (Eds.), *Handbook of psychotherapy and behavior change* (4th ed.) (pp. 143-189). New York: John Wiley & Sons.

Lambert, M. J. (1992). Implications of outcome research for psychotherapy integration. In J. C. Norcross & M. R. Goldfried (Eds.), *Handbook of psychotherapy integration* (pp. 94-129). New York: Basic Books.

Landau, Mark J. (2017). *Conceptual metaphors in social psychology: The poetics of everyday life.* London: Routledge.

Langer, E. J. (1989). *Mindfulness.* Reading, MA: Perseus.

Langer, E. (2009). Mindfulness versus positive evaluation. In S. J. Lopez & C. R. Snyder (Eds.), *The Oxford handbook of positive psychology* (pp. 279-294). New York: Oxford University Press.

Laska, K. M., & Wampold, B. E. (2014). Ten things to remember about common factor theory. *Psychotherapy,* 51(4), 519-524.

Lazar, A. (1999). Deceiving oneself or self-deceived? On the formation of beliefs under the influence. *Mind,* 108(430), 265-290.

Lazarus, A. (1976). *Multimodal behavior therapy.* New York: Springer.

Lazarus, A. (1981). *The practice of multimodal therapy: Systematic, comprehensive, and effective psychotherapy.* New York: McGraw-Hill.

Lechner, S. C., Tennen, H., & Affleck, G. (2009). Benefit-finding and growth. In S. J. Lopez & C. R. Snyder (Eds.), *The Oxford handbook of positive psychology* (pp. 633-640). New York: Oxford University Press.

Lerner, Richard M. (2009). The positive youth development perspective: Theoretical and empirical bases of a strengths-based approach to adolescent development. In S. J. Lopez & C. R. Snyder (Eds.), *The Oxford handbook of positive psychology* (pp. 149-164). New York: Oxford University Press.

Leary, M. R., & Guadagno, J. (2011). *The sociometer, self-esteem, and the regulation of interpersonal behavior.* In K. D. Vohs & R. F. Baumeister (Eds.), *Handbook of self-regulation: Research, theory, and applications* (pp. 339-354). New York: Guilford Press.

Lester, D. (2015). *On multiple selves.* New Brunswick, NJ: Transaction.

Lethin, Anton. (2002). How do we embody intentionality? *Journal of Consciousness Studies,* 9, 8, 36-44.

Levy, N. (2008). Self-deception without thought experiments. In T. Bayne & J. Fernández (Eds.), *Delusion and self-deception: Affective and motivational influences on belief formation* (pp. 227-242). Washington, DC: Psychology Press.

Lifshitz, M. (2016). Contemplative experience in context. In A. Raz & M. Lifshitz (Eds.), *Hypnosis and meditation: Towards an integrative science of conscious planes* (pp. 3-16). Oxford: Oxford University Press.

Lifshitz, M., & Raz, A. (2012). Hypnosis and meditation: Vehicles of attention and suggestion. *The Journal of Mind-Body Regulation,* 2(1), 3-11.

Linehan, M. M. (1993). *Cognitive-behavioral therapy of borderline personality disorder.* New York: Guilford Press.

Linley, P. A., Joseph, S., Maltby, J., Harrington, S., & Wood, A. M. (2009). Positive psychology applications. In S. J. Lopez & C. R. Snyder (Eds.), *The Oxford handbook of positive psychology* (pp. 35-48). New York: Oxford University Press.

Locke, S. (2007). *Consciousness, self-consciousness, and the science of being human.* Westport, CT: Praeger.

Lopez, F. G. (2009). Adult attachment security: The relational scaffolding of positive psychology. In S. J. Lopez & C. R. Snyder (Eds.), *The Oxford handbook of positive psychology* (pp. 405-416). New York: Oxford University Press.

Lopez, S. J. (2009). The future of positive psychology: Pursuing three big goals. In S. J. Lopez & C. R. Snyder (Eds.), *The Oxford handbook of positive psychology* (pp. 689-694). New York: Oxford University Press.

Lopez, S. J., & Gallagher, M. W. (2009). A case for positive psychology. In S. J. Lopez & C. R. Snyder (Eds.), *The Oxford handbook of positive psychology* (pp. 3-6). New York: Oxford University Press.

Lopez, S. J., & Snyder, C. R. (Eds.). (2009). *The Oxford handbook of positive psychology*. New York: Oxford University Press.

Luthans, F., & Youssef, C. M. (2009). Positive workplaces. In S. J. Lopez & C. R. Snyder (Eds.), *The Oxford handbook of positive psychology* (pp. 579–588). New York: Oxford University Press.

Lutz, A., Greischar, L. L., Rawlings, N. B., Ricard, M., Davidson, R. J. (2004). Long-term meditators self-induce high-amplitude gamma synchrony during mental practice. *Proceedings of the National Academy of Sciences USA*, 101, 16369–16379.

Lutz, A., Slagter, H. A., Dunne, J. D., & Davidson, R. J. (2008). Attention regulation and monitoring in meditation. *Trends in Cognitive Science*, 12(4), 163–69.

Lynch, K. (2013). Self-deception and stubborn belief. *Erkenntnis*, 78(6), 1337–1345.

Lynn, S. J., Green, J. P., Elinoff, V., Baltman, J., & Maxwell, R. (2016). When worlds combine: Synthesizing hypnosis, mindfulness, and acceptance-based approaches to psychotherapy and smoking cessation. In A. Raz & M. Lifshitz (Eds.), *Hypnosis and meditation: Towards an integrative science of conscious plane* (pp. 427–442). Oxford: Oxford University Press.

Lynn, S. J., Rhue, J., & Kirsch, I. (2010). *Handbook of clinical hypnosis* (2nd ed.). Washington, DC: American Psychological Association.

Lynn, S. J., Woody, E. Z., Montgomery, G., & Gaudiano, B. (2014). Hypnosis: Contributions to psychological science and clinical practice (Editorial). *Psychology of Consciousness: Theory, Research, and Practice*, 1(2), 103–104.

Madanes, C. (1981). *Strategic family therapy*. San Francisco, CA: Jossey Bass.

Maddux, J. E. (2009a). Self-efficacy: The power of believing you can. In S. J. Lopez & C. R. Snyder (Eds.), *The Oxford handbook of positive psychology* (pp. 335–344). New York: Oxford University Press.

Maddux, J. E. (2009b). Stopping the "madness": Positive psychology and deconstructing the illness ideology and the DSM. In S. J. Lopez & C. R. Snyder (Eds.), *The Oxford handbook of positive psychology* (pp. 61–70). New York: Oxford University Press.

Mahler, S., Pine, M. M., & Bergman, A. (1973). *The psychological birth of the human infant*. New York: Basic Books.

Maisel, N. C., & Gable, S. L. (2009). For richer ... in good times ... and in health: Positive processes in relationships. In S. J. Lopez & C. R. Snyder (Eds.), *The Oxford handbook of positive psychology* (pp. 455–461). New York: Oxford University Press.

Margison, F. R., Barkham, M., Evans, C., McGrath, G., Clark, J. M., Audin, K., Connell, J. (2000). Measurement and psychotherapy: Evidence-based practice and practice-based medicine. *British Journal of Psychiatry*, 177, 123–130.

Markovic, J., & Thompson, E. (2016). Hypnosis and meditation: A neurophenomenological comparison. In A. Raz & M. Lifshitz (Eds.), *Hypnosis and meditation: Towards an integrative science of conscious planes* (p. 79–106). Oxford: Oxford University Press.

Marmor, J. (1976). Common operational factors in diverse approaches to behavior change. In A. Burton (Ed.), *What makes behavior change possible?* (pp. 3–12). New York: Brunner/Mazel.

Marquis, A. (2009). An integral taxonomy of therapeutic interventions. *Journal of Integral Theory & Practice*, 4(2), 13–42.

Martens, M. P., Martin, J. L., Littlefield, A. K., Murphy, J. G., & Cimini, M. D. (2011). Changes in protective behavioral strategies and alcohol use among college students. *Drug and Alcohol Dependence*, 118(2–3), 504–507.

Maslow, A. H. (1954). *Motivation and personality*. New York: Brandeis University Press.

Masten, A. S., Cutuli, J. J., Herbers, J. E., & Reed, M. G. J. (2009). Resilience in development. In S. J. Lopez & C. R. Snyder (Eds.), *The Oxford handbook of positive psychology* (pp. 117–132). New York: Oxford University Press.

Mayer, R. (2004). Should there be a three-strikes rule against pre discovery learning? *American Psychologist*, **59**(1), 14-19.

Mazzoni, G., Laurence, J. R., & Heap, M. (2014). Hypnosis and memory: Two hundred years of adventures and still going! *Psychology of Consciousness: Theory, Research, and Practice*, 1(2), 153-167.

McCallum, M., & Piper, W. E. (Eds.). (1997). *Psychological mindedness: A contemporary understanding*. Mahwah, NJ: Lawrence Erlbaum Associates.

McCormick, B. P., Funderburk, J. A., Lee, Y., & Hale-Fought, M. (2005). Activity characteristics and emotional experience: Predicting boredom and anxiety in the daily life of community mental health clients. *Journal of Leisure Research*, 37(2), 236-253.

McCraty, R., & Rees, R. A. (2009). The central role of the heart in generating and sustaining positive emotions. In S. J. Lopez & C. R. Snyder (Eds.), *The Oxford handbook of positive psychology* (pp. 527-536). New York: Oxford University Press.

McCullough, M. E., Root, L. M., Tabak, B. A., & van Oyen Witvliet, C. (2009). Forgiveness. In S. J. Lopez & C. R. Snyder (Eds.), *The Oxford handbook of positive psychology* (pp. 427-437). New York: Oxford University Press.

McGeown, W. J. (2016). Hypnosis, hypnotic suggestibility, and meditation: An integrative review of the associated brain regions and networks. In A. Raz & M. Lifshitz (Eds.), *Hypnosis and meditation: Towards an integrative science of conscious planes* (pp. 343-367). Oxford: Oxford University Press.

McGoldrick, M., Carter, B. A., Garcia Petro, N. A. (2011). *Expanded family life cycle: The individual, family, and social perspectives* (4th ed.). New York: Pearson.

McKay, R. T., & Dennett, D. C. (2009). The evolution of misbelief. *Behavioral and brain sciences*, 32(6), 493.

McVeigh, B. J. (1997a). *Spirits, selves, and subjectivity in a Japanese new religion: The cultural psychology of belief in Sûkyô Mahikari*. Lewiston, NY: Edwin Mellen Press.

McVeigh, B. J. (1997b). *Life in a Japanese women's college: Learning to be ladylike*. London: Routledge.

McVeigh, B. J. (1998). *The nature of the Japanese state: Rationality and rituality*. London: Routledge.

McVeigh, B. J. (2000). *Wearing ideology: State, schooling, and self-presentation in Japan*. Oxford: Berg, 2000.

McVeigh, B. J. (2002). *Japanese higher education as myth*. Armonk, NY: M. E. Sharpe.

McVeigh, B. J. (2006a). *The state bearing gifts: Deception and disaffection in Japanese higher education*. Boulder, CO: Lexington Books.

McVeigh, B. J. (2006b). The self as interiorized social relations: Applying a Jaynesian Approach to problems of agency and volition. In M. Kuijsten (Ed.), *Reflections on the dawn of consciousness: Julian Jaynes's bicameral mind theory revisited* (pp. 203-232). Henderson, NV: Julian Jaynes Society.

McVeigh, B. J. (2008). Review of *Consciousness, self-consciousness, and the science of being human* (Simeon Locke). Westport, CT: Praeger, 2007. For Metapsychology Online Reviews.

McVeigh, B. J. (2010). Why did the unconsciousness appear in history when it did? A Jaynesian explanation. *The Jaynesian: Newsletter of the Julian Jaynes Society*. Winter, 4(3), 1-4.

McVeigh, B. J. (2013a). Mental imagery and hallucinations as adaptive behavior: Divine voices and visions as neuropsychological vestiges. *The International Journal of the Image*, 3(1), 25-36.

McVeigh, B. J. (2013b). The emergence of psychotherapies in modern Japan: A Jaynesian interpretation. *Contemporary Hypnosis & Integrative Therapy*, 30(1), 7-23.

McVeigh, B. J. (2014). *Interpreting Japan: Approaches and applications for the classroom*. London: Routledge.

McVeigh, B. J. (2015). *The propertied self: A psychology of economic history*. Hauppauge, NY: Nova.

McVeigh, B. J. (2016a). *How religion evolved: The living dead, talking idols, and mesmerizing monuments*. Edison, NJ: Transaction.

McVeigh, B. J. (Ed.). (2016b). *Discussions with Julian Jaynes: The nature of consciousness and the vagaries of psychology*. Hauppauge, NY: Nova.

McVeigh, B. J. (2016c). *A psychohistory of metaphors: Envisioning time, space, and self through the centuries*. Boulder, CO: Lexington Books.

McVeigh, B. J. (2016d). *The history of Japanese psychology: Global perspectives, 1875–1950*. London: Bloomsbury.

McVeigh, B. J. (2016e). Elephants in the psychology department: Overcoming intellectual barriers to understanding Julian Jaynes's theory. In M. Kuijsten (Ed.), *Gods, voices and the bicameral mind: The theories of Julian Jaynes* (pp. 38–53). Henderson, NV: Julian Jaynes Society.

McVeigh, B. J. (2017). *The "other psychology" of Julian Jaynes: Ancient languages, sacred visions, and forgotten mentalities*. Exeter, UK: Imprint Academic.

McVeigh, B. J. (2020). *The psychology of the Bible: Explaining divine voices and visions*. Exeter, UK: Imprint Academic.

Meichenbaum, D. (1977). *Cognitive-behavior modification*. New York: Plenum.

Mele, A. R. (2006). Self-deception and delusions. *European Journal of Analytic Philosophy*, 2(1), 109–124.

Mele, A. R. (2007). Self-deception and three psychiatric delusions: On Robert Audi's transition from self-deception to delusion. In M. Timmons, J. Greco, & A. R. Mele (Eds.), *Rationality and the good* (pp. 163–175). Oxford: Oxford University Press.

Michel, C., & Newen, A. (2010). Self-deception as pseudo-rational regulation of belief. *Consciousness and Cognition*, 19(3), 731–744.

Miller, S. D., Duncan, B. L., & Hubble, M. A. (1997). *Escape from Babel*. New York: W. W. Norton.

Millon, T. (2004). *Masters of the mind: Exploring the story of mental illness from ancient times to the new millennium*. Hoboken, NJ: John Wiley & Sons.

Millon, T. (with Grossman, S., Meagher, S., Millon, C., & Everly, G.) (1999). *Personality-guided therapy*. New York: John Wiley & Sons.

Minuchin, S. (1974). *Families and family therapy*. Cambridge, MA: Harvard University Press.

Minuchin, S., & Fishman, H. C. (2009). *Family therapy techniques*. Cambridge, MA: Harvard University Press.

Miresco, M. J., & Kirmayer, L. J. (2006). The persistence of mind-brain dualism in psychiatric reasoning about clinical scenarios. *American Journal of Psychiatry*, 163(5), 913–918.

Mittal, D. M., Fortney, J. C., Pyne, J. M., Edlund, M. J., & Wetherel, J. L. (2006). Impact of co-morbid anxiety disorders on health-related quality of life among patients with major depressive disorders. *Psychiatric Services*, 57(12), 1731–1737.

Mooneyham, B. W., & Schooler, J. W. (2016). Mind wandering and meta-awareness in hypnosis and meditation. In A. Raz & M. Lifshitz (Eds.), *Hypnosis and meditation: Towards an integrative science of conscious planes* (pp. 221–240). Oxford: Oxford University Press.

Moreno, J. L. (1959). A survey of psychodramatic techniques. *Group Psychotherapy*, 12(1), 5–14.

Moreno, J. L. (1964). *Psychodrama*, vol. 1 (3rd ed.). Beacon, NJ: Beacon House.

Moreno, J. L. (1987). Psychodrama, role theory, and the concept of the social atom. In J. K. Zeig (Ed.), *The evolution of psychotherapy* (pp. 341–366). New York: Brunner/Mazel.

Nakamura, J., & Csikszentmihalyi, M. (2009). Flow theory and research. In S. J. Lopez & C. R. Snyder (Eds.), *The Oxford handbook of positive psychology* (pp. 195–206). New York: Oxford University Press.

Nash, M. R., & Barnier, A. J. (Eds.). (2008). *The Oxford handbook of hypnosis: Theory, research, and practice*. Oxford: Oxford University Press.

Neff, K. D. (2011). Self-compassion, self-esteem, and well-being. *Social and Personality Psychology Compass*, 5(1), 1-12.

Nesse, R. M. (2019). *Good reasons for bad feelings: Insights from the frontier of evolutionary psychiatry*. New York: Dutton.

Niederhoffer, K. G., & Pennebaker, J. W. (2009). Sharing one's story: On the benefits of writing or talking about emotional experience. In S. J. Lopez & C. R. Snyder (Eds.), *The Oxford handbook of positive psychology* (pp. 621-632). New York: Oxford University Press.

Nobuhara, Y. (2014). Delusion and abnormality in belief evaluation. *Kagaku Tetsugaku*, 47(2), 1-16.

Nongard, R. K. (2012). *Richard Nongard's big book of hypnosis scripts: How to create lasting change using contextual hypnotherapy, mindfulness meditation and hypnotic phenomena*. Tulsa, OK: PeachTree Professional Education.

Norcross, J. C. (2013). *Changeology: Five steps to realizing your goals and resolutions*. New York: Simon & Schuster.

Norcross, J. C., & Beutler, L. E. (2014). Integrative psychotherapies. In D. Wedding & R. J. Corsini (Eds.), *Current psychotherapies* (10th ed.) (pp. 499-532). Belmont, CA: Brooks/Cole, Cengage Learning.

Norcross, J. C., & Goldfried, M. R., eds. (2005). *Handbook of psychotherapy integration* (2nd ed.). New York: Oxford University Press.

Nørretranders, T. (1998). *The User Illusion: Cutting Consciousness Down to Size*. New York: Penguin Books.

North, R. J., & Swann, W. B., Jr. (2009). What's positive about self-verification? In S. J. Lopez & C. R. Snyder (Eds.), *The Oxford handbook of positive psychology* (pp. 465-474). New York: Oxford University Press.

Ogden, T. (1979). On projective identification. *International Journal of Psycho-Analysis*, 60(3), 357-373.

Ogden, T. (1982). *Projective identification and psychotherapeutic technique*. New York: Jason Aronson.

Olatunji, B. O., Cistler, J. M., & Tolin, D. F. (2007). Quality of life in the anxiety disorders: A meta-analytic review. *Clinical Psychology Review*, 27(5), 572-581.

Omer, H., & Alon, N. (1989). Principles of psychotherapeutic strategy. *Psychotherapy: Theory, Research, Practice, Training*, 26(3), 282-289.

Ong, A. D., & Zautra, A. J. (2009). Modeling positive human health: From covariance structures to dynamic systems. In S. J. Lopez & C. R. Snyder (Eds.), *The Oxford handbook of positive psychology* (pp. 97-104). New York: Oxford University Press.

Orlinsky, D. E., Grawe, K., & Parks, B. K. (1994). Process and outcome in psychotherapy--noch einmal. In A. E. Bergin & S. L. Garfield (Eds.), *Handbook of psychotherapy and behavior change* (4th ed.) (pp. 270-378). New York: John Wiley & Sons.

Orne, M. (1959). The nature of hypnosis: Artifact and essence. *Journal of Abnormal and Social Psychology*, 58(3), 277-299.

Ott, U. (2016). Absorption in hypnotic trance and meditation. In A. Raz & M. Lifshitz (Eds.), *Hypnosis and meditation: Towards an integrative science of conscious planes* (pp. 269-278). Oxford: Oxford University Press.

Pacherie, E., Green, M., & Bayne, T. J. (2006). Phenomenology and delusions: Who put the "alien" in alien control? *Consciousness and Cognition*, 15(3), 566-577.

Papero, D. V. (2000). The Bowen theory. In A. M. Horne (Ed.), *Family counseling and therapy* (3rd ed.) (pp. 272-299). Belmont, CA: Thomson.

Pargament, K. I., & Mahoney, A. (2009). Spirituality: The search for the sacred. In S. J. Lopez & C. R. Snyder (Eds.), *The Oxford handbook of positive psychology* (pp. 611-620). New York: Oxford University Press.

Paris, J. (2013). How the history of psychotherapy interferes with integration. *Journal of Psychotherapy Integration*, 23(2), 99–106.

Parloff, M. (1986). Frank's "common elements" in psychotherapy: Nonspecific factors and placebos. *American Journal of Orthopsychiatry*, 56(4), 521–529.

Paul, G. L. (1967). Strategy of outcome research in psychotherapy. *Journal of Consulting Psychology*, 31(2), 109–119.

Pérez-Álvarez, M., Garcia-Montes, J., Perona-Garcelán, S., & Vallina-Fernández, O. (2008). Changing relationships with voices: New therapeutic perspectives for treating hallucinations. *Clinical Psychology and Psychotherapy*, 15(2), 75–85.

Perls, F. S., Hefferline, R. F., & Goodman, P. (1973). *Gestalt therapy: Excitement and growth in human personality*. Harmondsworth, UK: Penguin Books.

Peseschkian, N. (1987). *Positive psychotherapy theory and practice of a new method* (trans. Robert R. Walker). Berlin: Springer-Verlag.

Peterson, C. (2006). The Values in Action (VIA) classification of strengths. In M. Csikszentmihalyi & I. S. Csikszentmihalyi (Eds.), *A life worth living: Contributions to positive psychology* (pp. 29–48). New York: Oxford University Press.

Peterson, C., & Park, N. (2009). Classifying and measuring strengths of character. In S. J. Lopez & C. R. Snyder (Eds.), *The Oxford handbook of positive psychology* (pp. 25–34). New York: Oxford University Press.

Peterson, C., & Steen, T. A. (2009). Optimistic explanatory style. In S. J. Lopez & C. R. Snyder (Eds.), *The Oxford handbook of positive psychology* (pp. 313–322). New York: Oxford University Press.

Phinney, J. (1996). When we talk about American ethnic groups, what do we mean? *American Psychologist*, 51(9), 918–927.

Pipher, M. (2009). *Seeking peace: Chronicles of the worst Buddhist in the world*. New York: Riverhead Books.

Pittman, F. (1994). A buyer's guide to psychotherapy. *Psychology Today*, 27(1), 50.

Polito, V., & Connors, M. H. (2016). Toward a science of internal experience. In A. Raz & M. Lifshitz (Eds.), *Hypnosis and meditation: Towards an integrative science of conscious planes* (pp. 171–187). Oxford: Oxford University Press.

Polkinghorne, D. E. (2000). Narrative therapy. In A. E. Kazdin (Ed.), *Encyclopedia of psychology* (pp. 387–389). Washington, DC: American Psychological Association.

Pope, K. S., & Vasquez, M. J. T. (2011). *Ethics in psychotherapy and counseling: A practical guide* (4th ed.). New York: John Wiley & Sons.

Prochaska, J. O., & DiClemente, C. C. (1984). *The transtheoretical approach: Crossing traditional boundaries of therapy*. Homewood, IL: Dow Jones-Irwin.

Prochaska, J. O., DiClemente, C. C., & Norcross, J. C. (1997). In search of how people change: Applications to addictive behaviors. In G. A. Marlatt & G. R. VandenBos (Eds.), *Addictive behaviors: Readings on etiology, prevention, and treatment* (pp. 671–696). Washington, DC: American Psychological Association.

Prochaska, J. O., & Norcross, J. C. (2013). *Systems of psychotherapy: A transtheoretical analysis* (8th ed.). Pacific Grove, CA: Cengage-Brooks/Cole.

Pury, C. L. S., & Lopez, S. J. (2009). Courage. In S. J. Lopez & C. R. Snyder (Eds.), *The Oxford handbook of positive psychology* (pp. 375–382). New York: Oxford University Press.

Rahula, W. (1974). *What the Buddha taught*. New York: Grove Press.

Rand, K. L., & Cheapens, J. S. (2009). Hope theory. In S. J. Lopez & C. R. Snyder (Eds.), *The Oxford handbook of positive psychology* (pp. 323–334). New York: Oxford University Press.

Rao, R. P. N., & Ballard, D. H. (1999). Predictive coding in the visual cortex: A functional interpretation of some extra-classical receptive-field effects. *Nature Neuroscience*, 2, 79–87.

Rappaport, H., & Rappaport, M. (1981). The integration of scientific and traditional healing: A proposed model. *American Psychologist*, 36(7), 774–781.

Rashid, T., & Seligman, M. (2014). Positive psychotherapy. In D. Wedding & R. J. Corsini (Eds.), *Current psychotherapies* (10th ed.) (pp. 193-229). Belmont, CA: Brooks/Cole, Cengage Learning.

Rashid, T., & Seligman, M. (2018). *Positive psychotherapy: Clinician manual.* Oxford: Oxford University Press.

Raz, A. (2016). Hypnosis and meditation as vehicles to elucidate human consciousness. In A. Raz & M. Lifshitz (Eds.), *Hypnosis and meditation: Towards an integrative science of conscious planes* (pp. 445-448). Oxford: Oxford University Press.

Rogers, C. (1957). The necessary and sufficient conditions of therapeutic personality change. *Journal of Consulting Psychology,* 21(2), 95-103.

Romme, M. A., & Escher, S. (1996). Empowering people who hear voices. In G. Haddock, G., & Slade, P. D. (Eds.), *Cognitive-behavioural interventions with psychotic disorders* (pp. 137-150). London: Routledge.

Romme, M. A., Honig, A., Noorthhoorn, E. O., & Escher, A. D. (1992). Coping with hearing voices: An emancipatory approach. *British Journal of Psychiatry,* 161(1), 99-103.

Rosenzweig, S. (1933). The experimental situation as a psychological problem. *Psychological Review,* 40(4), 337-354.

Rosenzweig, S. (1936). Some implicit common factors in diverse methods of psychotherapy. *American Journal of Orthopsychiatry,* 6(3), 412-415.

Rosenzweig, S. (1937). Schools of psychology: A complementary pattern. *Philosophy of Science,* 4, 96-106.

Rosenzweig, S. (1938). A dynamic interpretation of psychotherapy oriented towards research. *Psychiatry,* 1, 521-526.

Rosenzweig, S. (1940). Areas of agreement in psychotherapy. *American Journal of Orthopsychiatry,* 10(4), 703-704.

Rosenzweig, S. (1949). *Psychodiagnosis: An introduction to the integration of tests in dynamic clinical practice.* New York: Grune & Stratton.

Rosenzweig, S. (1951). *Facets of psychotherapy.* Unpublished manuscript.

Rosenzweig, S. (1954). A transvaluation of psychotherapy: A reply to Hans Eysenck. *Journal of Abnormal and Social Psychology,* 49(2), 298-304.

Rosenzweig, S. (1978). *Aggressive behavior and the Rosenzweig picture-frustration study.* New York: Praeger.

Rosenzweig, S. (1986). *Freud and experimental psychology: The emergence of idiodynamics* (2nd ed.). New York: McGraw-Hill.

Rosenzweig, S. (1987). Sally Beauchamp's career: A psychoarchaeological key to Morton Prince's classic case of multiple personality. *Genetic, Social, & General Psychology Monographs,* 113(1), 5-60.

Rosenzweig, S. (1992). *Freud, Jung, and Hall the king-maker: The expedition to America (1909).* Seattle, WA: Hogrefe & Huber.

Rosenzweig, S. (2002). Some implicit common factors in diverse methods of psychotherapy. *Journal of Psychotherapy Integration,* 12(1), 5-9.

Rosenzweig, S. (2003). Idiodynamics in personality theory and psychoarchaeology. *Journal of Applied Psychoanalytic Studies,* 5(4), 385-394.

Ruini, C., & Fava, G. A. (2004). Clinical applications of well-being therapy. In P. A. Linley & S. Joseph (Eds.), *Positive psychology in practice* (pp. 371-387). Hoboken, NJ: John Wiley & Sons.

Ryff, C. D. (1989). Happiness is everything, or is it? Explorations on the meaning of psychological well-being. *Journal of Personality and Social Psychology,* 57(6), 1069-1081.

Ryff, C. D., & Keyes, C. L. M. (1995). The structure of psychological well-being revisited. *Journal of Personality and Social Psychology,* 69(4), 719-727.

Ryle, A., & Fawkes, L. (2007). Multiplicity of selves and others. *Journal of Clinical Psychology,* 63, 165–174.

Safran, J. D., & Muran, J. C. (1996). The resolution of ruptures in the therapeutic alliance. *Journal of Consulting and Clinical Psychology,* 64(3), 447–458.

Safran, J. D., & Muran, J. C. (2000). *Negotiating the therapeutic alliance: A relational treatment guide.* New York: Guilford Press.

Safran, J. D., & Muran, J. C. (2006). Has the concept of the therapeutic alliance outlived its usefulness? *Psychotherapy: Theory, Research, Practice, Training,* 43(3), 286–291.

Salovey, P., Mayer, J. D., Caruso, D, & Yoo, S. H. (2009). The positive psychology of emotional intelligence. In S. J. Lopez & C. R. Snyder (Eds.), *The Oxford handbook of positive psychology* (pp. 237–248). New York: Oxford University Press.

Sar, V., Akyuz, G., Kugu, N., Ozturk, E., & Ertem-Vehid, H. (2006). Axis I dissociative disorder comorbidity in borderline personality disorder and reports of childhood trauma. *Journal of Clinical Psychiatry,* 67(10), 1583-90.

Satir, V. (1967). *Conjoint family therapy* (2nd ed.). Palo Alto, CA: Science & Behavior Books.

Satir, V. (1972). *People-making.* Palo Alto, CA: Science & Behavior Books.

Satir, V., & Baldwin, M. (1983). *Satir step by step: A guide to creating change in families.* Palo Alto, CA: Science & Behavior Books.

Schechner, R. (1992). Collective reflexivity: Restoration of behavior. In J. Ruby (Ed.), *A crack in the mirror: Reflexive perspectives in anthropology* (pp. 39–82). Philadelphia: University of Pennsylvania Press.

Scheibe, S., Kunzmann, U., & Baltes, P. B. (2009). New territories of positive life-span development: Wisdom and life longings. In S. J. Lopez & C. R. Snyder (Eds.), *The Oxford handbook of positive psychology* (pp. 171–183). New York: Oxford University Press.

Schrank, B., Brownell, T., Jakaite, Z., Larkin, C., Pesola, F., Riches, S. Tylee, A., & Slad, M. (2016). Evaluation of a positive psychotherapy group intervention for people with psychosis: Pilot randomised controlled trial. *Epidemiology and Psychiatric Sciences,* 25(3), 235-246.

Schreiner, L. A., Hulme, E., Hetzel, R., & Lopez, S. J. (2009). Positive psychology on campus. In S. J. Lopez & C. R. Snyder (Eds.), *The Oxford handbook of positive psychology* (pp. 569–578). New York: Oxford University Press.

Scull, A. (2015). *Madness in civilization: A cultural history of insanity from the Bible to Freud, from the madhouse to modern medicine.* Princeton, NJ: Princeton University Press.

Seligman, M. E. P. (2002). *Authentic happiness: Using the new positive psychology to realize your potential for lasting fulfillment.* New York: Free Press.

Seligman, M. E. P. (2011). *Flourish: A visionary new understanding of happiness and well-being.* New York: Free Press.

Seligman, M. E. P., & Csikszentmihalyi, M. (2000). Positive psychology: An introduction. *American Psychologist,* 55(1), 5–14.

Seligman, M. E. P., Rashid, T., & Parks, A. C. (2006). Positive psychotherapy. *American Psychologist,* 61(8), 774-788.

Seth, A. K. (2013). Interoceptive inference, emotion, and the embodied self. *Trends in Cognitive Sciences,* 17(11), 565–573.

Shapiro, D. H., & Astin, J. (1998). *Control therapy: An integrated approach to psychotherapy, health, and healing.* Hoboken, NJ: John Wiley & Sons.

Shapiro, S. L. (2009). Meditation and positive psychology. In S. J. Lopez & C. R. Snyder (Eds.), *The Oxford handbook of positive psychology* (pp. 601–610). New York: Oxford University Press.

Sheridan, S. M., & Burt, J. D. (2009). Family-centered positive psychology. In S. J. Lopez & C. R. Snyder (Eds.), *The Oxford handbook of positive psychology* (pp. 551-560). New York: Oxford University Press.

Simonton, D. K. (2009). Creativity. In S. J. Lopez & C. R. Snyder (Eds.), *The Oxford handbook of positive psychology* (pp. 261-270). New York: Oxford University Press.

Simpkins, C., & Simpkins, A. (2010). *Neuro-hypnosis: Using self-hypnosis to activate the brain for change.* New York: W. W. Norton.

Slade, M. (2010). Mental illness and well-being: The central importance of positive psychology and recovery approaches. *BMC Health Services Research,* 10(26), 1-14.

Slade, M., Oades, L. G., & Jarden, A. (2017). *Wellbeing, recovery and mental health.* Cambridge, UK: Cambridge University Press.

Stanton, A. L., Sullivan, S. J., & Austenfeld, J. L. (2009). Coping through emotional approach: Emerging evidence for the utility of processing and expressing emotions in responding to stressors. In S. J. Lopez & C. R. Snyder (Eds.), *The Oxford handbook of positive psychology* (pp. 225-236). New York: Oxford University Press.

Steger, M. F. (2009). Meaning in life. In S. J. Lopez & C. R. Snyder (Eds.), *The Oxford handbook of positive psychology* (pp. 679-688). New York: Oxford University Press.

Stein, D. J., Harvey. B., Seedat, S., Hollander, E. (2006). Treatment of impulse-control disorders. In E. Hollander & D. Stein D. (Eds.), *Clinical manual of impulse control disorders* (pp. 309-325). Arlington, VA: American Psychiatric Publishing.

Stevens, S. E., Hynan, M. T., & Allen, M. (2000). A meta-analysis of common factor and specific treatment effects across the outcome domains of the phase model of psychotherapy. *Clinical Psychology: Science and Practice,* 7(3), 273-290.

Stone, H., & Stone, S. (1989). *Embracing ourselves: The voice dialogue training manual.* New York: Nataraj.

Strawson, G. (1997). The self. *Journal of Consciousness Studies,* 4, 405-428.

Sue, D. W., Arredondo, P., & McDavis, R. J. (1992). Multicultural counseling competencies and standards: A call to the profession. *Journal of Counseling and Development,* 70(4), 477-486.

Sue, D. W., Bernier, J. E., Durran, A., Feinberg, L., Pedersen, P., Smith E. J., & Vasquez-Nuttall, E. (1982). Position paper: Cross-cultural counseling competencies. *The Counseling Psychology,* 10, 45-52.

Sue, D. W., Capodilupo, C. M., Torino, G. C., Bucceri, J. M., Holder, A. M. B., Nadal, K. L., & Esquilin, M. (2007). Racial microaggressions in everyday life: Implications for clinical practice. *American Psychologist,* 62(4), 271-286.

Super, D. E. (1957). *The psychology of careers.* New York: Harper & Row.

Super, D. E. (1963). Toward making self-concept theory operational. In D. E. Super, R. Starishevski, N. Matlin, & J. P. Jordaan (Eds.), *Career Development: Self-concept theory* (pp. 17-31). New York: College Entrance Examination Board.

Tang, Y. Y., & Posner, M. I. (2016). Influencing conflict in the human brain by changing brain states. In A. Raz & M. Lifshitz (Eds.), *Hypnosis and meditation: Towards an integrative science of conscious planes* (pp. 303-312). Oxford: Oxford University Press.

Tangney, J. P. (2009). Humility. In S. J. Lopez & C. R. Snyder (Eds.), *The Oxford handbook of positive psychology* (pp. 483-490). New York: Oxford University Press.

Tart, C. T. (2016). Meditation: Some kind of (self) hypnosis? In A. Raz & M. Lifshitz (Eds.), *Hypnosis and meditation: Towards an integrative science of conscious planes* (pp. 143-170). Oxford: Oxford University Press.

Teramoto Pedrotti, J., Edwards, L. M., & Lopez, S. J. (2009). Positive psychology within a cultural context. In S. J. Lopez & C. R. Snyder (Eds.), *The Oxford handbook of positive psychology* (pp. 49-57). New York: Oxford University Press.

Thompson, J. M., Waelde, L. C., Tisza, K., & Spiegel, D. (2016). Hypnosis and mindfulness: Experiential and neurophysiological relationships. In A. Raz & M. Lifshitz (Eds.), *Hypnosis and meditation: Towards an integrative science of conscious planes* (pp. 129-142). Oxford: Oxford University Press.

Thompson, S. C. (2009). The role of personal control in adaptive functioning. In S. J. Lopez & C. R. Snyder (Eds.), *The Oxford handbook of positive psychology* (pp. 271-278). New York: Oxford University Press.

Thorne, F. C. (1950). *Principles of personality counseling: An eclectic viewpoint.* Brandon, VT: Journal of Clinical Psychology Press.

Thorne, F. C. (1957). Critique of recent developments in personality counseling theory. *Journal of Clinical Psychology,* 13(3), 234-244.

Thorne, F. C. (1967). The structure of integrative psychology. *Journal of Clinical Psychology,* 23(1), 3-11.

Thorne, F. C., & Pishkin, V. (1968). The ideological survey. *Journal of Clinical Psychology,* 24(3), 263-268.

Tillman, J. G. (2008). A view from Riggs: Treatment resistance and patient authority—IX. Integrative psychodynamic treatment of psychotic disorders. *Journal of American Academy of Psychoanalysis Dynamic Psychiatry,* 36(4), 739-61.

Tinbergen, N. (1963). On the aims and methods of ethology. *Zeitschrift für Tierpsychologie,* 20, 410-433.

Tomm, K. (1984a). One perspective on the Milan approach: Pt. I. *Journal of Marital and Family Therapy,* 10(2), 113-125.

Tomm, K. (1984b). One perspective on the Milan approach: Pt. II. *Journal of Marital and Family Therapy,* 10(2), 253-271.

Toneatto, T., & Courtice, E. (2016). Hypnosis and mindfulness meditation: A psychoanalytic perspective. In A. Raz & M. Lifshitz (Eds.), *Hypnosis and meditation: Towards an integrative science of conscious planes* (pp. 415-426). Oxford: Oxford University Press.

Tov, W., & Diener, E. (2013). Subjective well-being. *Research Collection School of Social Sciences.* Paper 1395.

Tracey, T. J. G., Lichtenberg, J. W., Goodyear, R. K., Claiborn, C. D., & Wampold, B. E. (2003). Concept mapping of therapeutic common factors. *Psychotherapy Research,* 13(4), 401-413.

Trivers, R. (2011). *Deceit and self-deception: Fooling yourself the better to fool others.* London: Allen Lane.

Tryon, W., & Tryon, G. (2011). No ownership of common factors. *American Psychologist,* 66(2), 151-152.

Tuckman, B. W., & Jensen, M. A. (1977). Stages of small-group development revisited. *Group & Organization Studies,* 2(4), 419-427.

Turner, V. (1967). *The forest of symbols: Aspects of Ndembu ritual.* Ithaca, NY: Cornell University Press.

Turner, V. (1969). *The ritual process: Structure and anti-structure.* Piscataway, NJ: Aldine Transaction.

Turner, V. (1974). *Dramas, fields, and metaphors: Symbolic action in human society.* Ithaca, NY: Cornell University Press.

Uliaszek, A. A., Hamdullahpur, K., Chugani, C. D., & Rashid, T. (2016). Mechanisms of change in group therapy for treatment-seeking university students. *Behaviour Research and Therapy,* 109, 10-17. Vaihinger, H. (1935). *The philosophy of "as if": A system of the theoretical, practical and religious fictions of mankind* (translated by C. K. Ogden) (2nd ed.). London: Routledge & Kegan Paul.

Vaitl, D., Birbaumer, N., Gruzelier, J., Jamieson, G. A., Kotchoubey, B., Kübler, A., Lehmann, D., Miltner, W. H., Ott, U., Pütz, P., Sammer, G., Strauch, I., Strehl, U., Wackermann, J., & Weiss, T. (2005). Psychobiology of altered states of consciousness. *Psychological Bulletin,* 31(1), 98-127.

Van Gennep, A. (1977) [1909]. *The rites of passage (Les rites de passage)* (trans. and eds. M. B. Vizedom & G. L. Caffe). London: Routledge and Kegan Paul.

Van Leeuwen, N. (2007). The product of self-deception. *Erkenntnis,* 67(3), 419-437.

Van Leeuwen, N. (2013). Review of Robert Trivers' *The folly of fools: The logic of deceit and self-deception in human life*. *Cognitive Neuropsychiatry*, 18(1-2), 146-151.

Veissière S. (2016). Varieties of tulpa experiences. In A. Raz & M. Lifshitz (Eds.), *Hypnosis and meditation: Towards an integrative science of conscious planes* (pp. 55-75). Oxford: Oxford University Press.

Vera, A. H., & Simon, H. A. (1993). Situated action: A symbolic interpretation. *Cognitive Science*, 17, 7-48.

Vervaeke, J., & Ferraro, L. (2016). Reformulating the mindfulness construct. In A. Raz & M. Lifshitz (Eds.), *Hypnosis and meditation: Towards an integrative science of conscious planes* (pp. 241-268). Oxford: Oxford University Press.

Vignoles, V. L. (2009). The motive for distinctiveness: A universal, but flexible human need. In S. J. Lopez & C. R. Snyder (Eds.), *The Oxford handbook of positive psychology* (pp. 491-499). New York: Oxford University Press.

Von Hartmann, E. (1884). *Philosophy of the unconscious*. London: Trübner.

Wampold, B. E. (2001). *The great psychotherapy debate: Models, methods, and findings*. Mahwah, NJ: Lawrence Erlbaum Associates.

Wampold, B. E. (2015a). How important are the common factors in psychotherapy? An update. *World Psychiatry*, 14(3), 270-277.

Wampold, B. E. (2015b). *Great psychotherapy debate: The evidence for what makes psychotherapy work*. New York: Routledge.

Wang, S., & Kim, B. S. K. (2010). Therapist multicultural competence, Asian American participants' cultural values, and counseling process. *Journal of Counseling Psychology*, 57(4), 394-401.

Warner, R. (1963). *The Confessions of St. Augustine* (trans. Rex Warner). New York: Mentor.

Watkins, P. C., Van Gelder, M., & Frias, A. (2009). Furthering the science of gratitude. In S. J. Lopez & C. R. Snyder (Eds.), *The Oxford handbook of positive psychology* (pp. 437-446). New York: Oxford University Press.

Watson, D., & Naragon, K. (2009). Positive affectivity: The disposition to experience positive emotional states. In S. J. Lopez & C. R. Snyder (Eds.), *The Oxford handbook of positive psychology* (pp. 207-216). New York: Oxford University Press.

Watson, G., Adler, A., Allen, F. H., Bertine, E., Chassell, J. O., Durkin, H., Rogers, C. R., Rosenzweig, S., & Waelder, R. (1940). Areas of agreement in psychotherapy: Section meeting, 1940. *American Journal of Orthopsychiatry*, 10(4), 698-709.

Watzlawick, P., Weakland, J., & Fisch, R. (1974). *Change: Principles of problem formation and problem resolution*. New York: W. W. Norton.

Weakland, J. H. (1977). Family somatics: A neglected edge. *Family Process*, 16(3), 263-272.

Wedding, D., & Corsini, R. J. (Eds.). (2014). *Current psychotherapies* (10th ed.). Belmont, CA: Brooks/Cole Cengage Learning.

Wehmeyer, M. L., Little, T. D., & Sergeant, J. (2009). Self-determination. In S. J. Lopez & C. R. Snyder (Eds.), *The Oxford handbook of positive psychology* (pp. 357-366). New York: Oxford University Press.

What is emotion focused therapy? (2009). *International Society for Emotion Focused Therapy*. Retrieved from http://www.iseft.org/What-is-EFT.

Whitaker, C. A. (1975). Psychotherapy of the absurd: With a special emphasis on the psychotherapy of aggression. *Family Process*, 14(1), 1-16.

Whitaker, C. A. (1976). The hindrance of theory in clinical work. In P. J. Guerin (Ed.), *Family therapy: Theory and practice* (pp. 154-164). New York: Gardner Press.

Whitaker, C. A., & Keith, D. V. (1981). Symbolic-experiential family therapy. In A. S. Gurman & D. P. Kniskern (Eds.), *Handbook of family therapy* (pp. 187-225). New York: Brunner/Mazel.

Whitcomb, S. A., and Merrell, K. W. (2013). Foundations of assessment. In *Behavior, social, and emotional assessments of children and adolescents* (pp. 3-31). New York: Routledge.

White, M. (2000). *Reflections on narrative practice: Essays and interviews*. Adelaide, Australia: Dulwich Centre Publications.

White, M. (2007). *Maps of narrative practice*. New York: W. W. Norton.

White, R. E., Kuehn, M. M., Duckworth, A. L., Kross, E., & Ayduk, Ö. (2018). Focusing on the future from afar: Self-distancing from future stressors facilitates adaptive coping. *Emotion*, **19**(5), 903–916.

Williamson, G. M., & Christie, J. (2009). Aging well in the 21st century: Challenges and opportunities. In S. J. Lopez & C. R. Snyder (Eds.), *The Oxford handbook of positive psychology* (pp. 165–170). New York: Oxford University Press.

Wilson, T. (2004). *Strangers to ourselves: Discovering the adaptive unconscious*. Cambridge, MA: Belknap/Harvard University Press.

Winnicott, D. W. (1971). *Playing and reality*. London: Tavistock Press.

Wohl, M., DeShea, J. A., Wahkinney, L. R. (2008). Looking within: Measuring state self-forgiveness and its relationship to psychological well-being. *Canadian Journal of Behavioural Science/Revue canadienne des sciences du comportement*, **40**(1), 1–10.

Wolpert, Lewis. (2008). *Six impossible things before breakfast: The evolutionary origins of belief*. New York: W. W. Norton.

Wright, B. A., & Lopez, S. J. (2009). Widening the diagnostic focus: A case for including human strengths and environmental resources. In S. J. Lopez & C. R. Snyder (Eds.), *The Oxford handbook of positive psychology* (pp. 71–88). New York: Oxford University Press.

Yalom, I. D. (1980). *Existential psychotherapy*. New York: Basic Books.

Yalom, I. D. (1995). *The theory and practice of on group psychotherapy*. New York: Basic Books.

Yalom, V. (2011). Sue Johnson on emotionally focused therapy. *Psychotherapy.net*. Retrieved from https://www.psychotherapy.net/interview/couples/sue-johnson-interview

Yapko, M. D. (2011). *Mindfulness and hypnosis: The power of suggestion to transform experience*. New York: W. W. Norton.

Yapko, M. D. (2012). *Trancework: An introduction to the practice of clinical hypnosis*. London: Routledge.

Yapko, M. D. (2016). Suggesting mindfulness: Reflections on the uneasy relationship between mindfulness and hypnosis. In A. Raz & M. Lifshitz (Eds.), *Hypnosis and meditation: Towards an integrative science of conscious planes* (pp. 371–379). Oxford: Oxford University Press.

Yeh, V. M., Schnur, J. B., & Montgomery, G. H. (2014). Disseminating hypnosis to health care settings: Applying the RE-AIM framework. *Psychology of Consciousness: Theory, Research, and Practice*, **1**(2), 213–228.

Young, F. (2015). Dialogical disputation of negative self-statements conversations with God. Unpublished article available at www.solutionorientedcounselling.ca.

Zeidan, F., & Grant, J. (2016). Meditative and hypnotic analgesia. In A. Raz & M. Lifshitz (Eds.), *Hypnosis and meditation: Towards an integrative science of conscious planes* (pp. 397–414). Oxford: Oxford University Press.

Zilboorg, G., & Henry, G. W. (1941). *A history of medical psychology*. New York: W. W. Norton.

Zimmerman, M., Morgan, T. A., & Stanton, K. (2018). The severity of psychiatric disorders. *World Psychiatry*, **17**(3), 258–275.

Zimring, F. M. (2000). Empathetic understanding grows the person. *Person-Centered Journal*, **7**(2), 101–113.

About the Author

Brian J. McVeigh received his MA (anthropology) and MS (counseling) from the University at Albany, State University of New York, and his PhD in anthropology from Princeton University. He works as a licensed mental health counselor and is also a scholar of Japan and China where he lived and taught for sixteen years. For ten years he taught in the Department of East Asian Studies at the University of Arizona. The author of fifteen books, he has an interest in how humans adapt, both through history and therapeutically. His current projects include *The Psychology of Ancient Egypt: Reconstructing a Lost Mentality* and *Global Anthropology: Person, Politics, Property*.

Index

For the benefit of digital users, indexed terms that span two pages (e.g., 52–53) may, on occasion, appear on only one of those pages.

Tables and figures are indicated by *t* and *f* following the page number